Liberation
Diaries

First published by Jacana Media (Pty) Ltd in 2024

10 Orange Street
Sunnyside
Auckland Park 2092
South Africa
+2711 628 3200
www.jacana.co.za

ISBN 978-1-4314-3454-1

Cover design by Aimèe Armstrong and Maggie Davey
Editing by Megan Mance
Proofreading by Sean Fraser
Set in Sabon LT Std 10/14.5pt
Printed by Inside Data
Job no. 004170

See a complete list of Jacana titles at www.jacana.co.za

Liberation Diaries
Reflections on 30 years of democracy
Vol. 2

Busani Ngcaweni

This book is dedicated to all patriotic South Africans whose hopes, aspirations, resilience, resistance, disappointments, critique and protests have helped shape the country we have today. Through them we know that, tragedies of inequality and poor governance notwithstanding, the trajectory of South Africa is that of progress. To those for whom the democratic dividend has trickled, they should remember that democracies thrive when prosperity is shared.

Contents

About the editor

Busani Ngcaweni is Visiting Adjunct Professor at Wits School of Governance, Visiting Professor at Fudan University (2024) in Shanghai and Senior Research Associate at the University of Johannesburg. His day job is at the National School of Government (NSG) where he has been Director-General since March 2020. He joined the NSG after spending a decade and a half in the Presidency where he occupied different positions, including managing offices of four deputy presidents and being senior policy analyst. His monograph *Statecraft and National Development: Critical Insights from South Africa and Beyond* will be published by Jacana Media in the last quarter of 2024. With Africa World Press he has published *Nelson R. Mandela: Decolonial Ethics of Liberation and Servant Leadership* (2018), coedited with Sabelo Ndlovu-Gatsheni. Other publications include *The Contested Idea of South Africa* (Routledge, 2022) coedited with Sabelo Ndlovu-Gatsheni, *We Are No Longer at Ease: The Struggle for #FeesMustFall* (Jacana Media, 2018) coedited with Wandile M. Ngcaweni, and *Youth Development in South Africa: Harnessing the Demographic Dividend – Diverse Perspectives on Creating a Fairer Society* (Emerald Publishing, 2023) coedited with Botshabelo Maja.

List of contributors

Amos Hadebe is a senior corporate affairs executive working in the banking sector. He has worked for both multinational and JSE-listed companies, and writes in his personal capacity. He holds BSc, Master of Management (Wits) and MSc (LSE) degrees. He completed the Private Markets Investment Programme at Saïd Business School, University of Oxford.

Bongani Mayimele is Director for International Relations and Partnerships at the National School of Government, South Africa. His interests are in international relations, governance and development. He is a graduate of the University of Limpopo. He has completed executive education on innovation with INSEAD and is currently doing his master's in business management at the University of Chinese Academy of Social Sciences, specialising in innovation management and corporate.

David Matheakuena Mohale holds a doctor of literature and philosophy degree focusing on the developmental state and local government. He is currently employed as Director: Special Projects in the Office of the Vice-Chancellor and Principal at the Durban University of Technology. He also serves as chairperson of the Free State Development Corporation and Deputy Chairperson of the Municipal Demarcation Board.

Gilbert Motsaathebe, PhD, is a full professor at the North-West University. An NRF-rated academic, Motsaathebe is also an author and global speaker with a long history in academia, government and media practice, having previously worked for broadcasters such as Bop-TV and e-TV and taught at academic institutions such as the University of Johannesburg, the United Arab Emirates University in the UAE, the Cape Peninsula University of Technology and several institutions in Nagasaki, Japan, before working in the Chief Directorate of Communication, North West Office of the Premier. He was a SEPHIS Fellow at the Centre for the Study of Culture and Society in India.

Gugu Ndima is a writer and activist who contributes to political and current affairs commentary in publications such as the *Mail & Guardian*. She has contributed chapters to various publications and continues to expand her footprint in the public discourse. She is author of a self-published book titled *All in a Galz Life*.

Helena van Urk is a postgraduate English scholar and researcher focusing on postcolonial and South African literature, with a particular interest in the intersection of postcolonial and medieval vernacular philosophy. She graduated with a BA and BA(Hons) from the University of the Witwatersrand, and is currently completing her MPhil in English studies at the University of Cambridge.

Izimangaliso Malatjie, PhD, is a research associate in the School of Public Management, Governance and Public Policy (SPMGPP), College of Business and Economics (CBE) at the University of Johannesburg (UJ) and is also employed by the National School of Government (NSG) where she heads the Cadet and Foundation Management faculty.

Karabo Mohapanele holds a PhD in sociology from NWU. She previously received the Erasmus+ scholarship for a PhD exchange programme in 2019, which she undertook at JLU Giessen, in Germany. She has published individually and co-authored in a book and in various journals. She worked as a researcher at the HSRC and is currently working as a sociology lecturer at the University of Fort Hare (Alice campus).

Khaya S. Sithole is a chartered accountant, academic, activist, radio broadcaster and financial writer. He currently serves as a board member at various advocacy and civil society organisations, listed and private companies in South Africa. He is the founding director of Corusca Consulting, which focuses on academic and financial consulting. Sithole has accounting and finance qualifications from the universities of KwaZulu-Natal, Oxford and Queen Mary University of London. He was also awarded the Atlantic Fellowship for Racial Equity by Columbia University and the Nelson Mandela Foundation in 2020.

Matshepo Faith Seedat is a government communicator and former spokesperson for a former deputy president. She has written extensively about gender-based violence. She is currently a master's candidate in Industrial Sociology at the University of Johannesburg, studying discriminatory relationships between women in national government.

Mbongiseni Buthelezi is Executive Director of the Public Affairs Research Institute (PARI) and an associate professor of anthropology and development studies at the University of Johannesburg. His research focuses on studying land, governance and the state in South Africa. He holds a PhD in English and comparative literature from Columbia University in New York. His most recent co-edited publication with Peter Vale is *State Capture in South Africa: How and Why it Happened* (Wits University Press, 2023).

Mongi Henda is an independent researcher and consultant currently based in Hamburg, Germany. Mongi's research interests lie in conflict resolution, public policy, political risk in Sub-Saharan Africa and collective emotions as a form of politics. Mongi has previously worked at the Institute for Security Studies, PricewaterhouseCoopers, and most recently within the International Relations Department of the City of Cape Town. Mongi holds an MA degree in international studies from Stellenbosch University.

Nkululeko Shabalala is a qualitative facilitator at the Centre for Community-based Research at the Human Sciences Research Council. He holds an honours degree in public policy from the University of

KwaZulu-Natal. He is currently pursuing his master's degree at the University of KwaZulu-Natal. His research areas of interest vary from education to indigenous knowledge systems agriculture and, more recently, public health. He was appointed as a junior researcher for a special report on youth climate advocacy by the South African Institute of International Affairs in 2020.

Nompumelelo Zungu holds a doctorate in psychology from the University of Cape Town. She is a strategic lead/deputy executive director in the Public Health, Societies and Belonging Research Division of the Human Sciences Research Council, where she leads a sub-division called Identity and Belonging. She has been a PI, co-PI, and a chief of party on several national population-based surveys and research projects. She is also a senior honorary lecturer at the University of KwaZulu-Natal, Department of Public Health and the current Editor in Chief of the SAHARA Journal. During her career spanning over 27 years, she has co-authored over 70 peer-reviewed journal articles, 18 books, 15 book chapters and 15 research reports.

Nomthandazo Mbandazayo has extensive experience in research and research management. Mbandazayo has managed large-scale and multi-country research projects across Eastern and Southern Africa in education, gender and sexual reproductive health rights. She has worked in civil society space, international and national development organisations, and academic institutions.

Nozipho Tshabalala is CEO of The Conversation Strategists. She is the go-to moderator for presidential and executive panels around the world. Her academic background is in development economics, development finance, political sciences and diplomacy. Her practice background includes serving in the office of the deputy president of South Africa, as a communications specialist for the Tata Group in Africa and as an award-winning anchor in the field of financial broadcasting.

Ntobeko Magubane is currently an executive office support at the National School of Government (NSG). Since Joining the NSG in 2020, his research projects advanced towards the field of good governance and issues of public administration at large. He has been engaged with continuous research projects, chapters, papers and book contributions. He is currently pursuing a PhD in governance studies at the Wits School of Governance. He holds a master's degree in economics and a graduate degree in commerce studies, all from the University of KwaZulu-Natal. As a young South African, he is interested in large organisations that focus on good governance, competitive growth and sustainability, the economy, international development and equality in the South African labour market.

Oscar van Heerden is a scholar of international relations (IR), where he focuses on international political economy, with an emphasis on Africa and SADC in particular. He completed his PhD and master's studies at the University of Cambridge from 2006 to 2010. He lectured IR at the University of the Witwatersrand (part-time) and was also a post-doctoral fellow at the University of Johannesburg under the NRF chair for International Relations and African Diplomacy. His work experience over the last two decades has been in strategic support at the ANC headquarters in the late 1990s, the South African Qualifications Authority in 2000 and since then as an independent management consultant at his own company, Kelello Consulting, working mostly but not exclusively with various government departments, in particular the security cluster. He was Director Operations: Mapungubwe Institute for Strategic Reflections (MISTRA). Here he was responsible for overseeing the implementation of all priority key performance areas within the organisation, including its financial sustainability. He was associated with various universities: UJ, Stellenbosch and Fort Hare. He was a trustee for the Kgalema Motlanthe Foundation. He is a council member of the University of Venda.

Samantha Herbst is a Johannesburg-based podcaster and journalist who writes about parenting, sexual and reproductive health, mental health, literature and entertainment. Her work has been published across several News24 channels, as well as in *The Citizen*, *Engineering News*, *Mining Weekly* and *Polity*, among others. Herbst is currently pursuing a master's degree in creative writing at the University of the Witwatersrand.

Sandile Nogxina holds a PhD from the University of the Witwatersrand with a focus on mining law and policy. He served as Director-General of the erstwhile Department of Minerals and Energy for more than 10 years before becoming South Africa's Ambassador to Mexico. His last position in the South African government was as Special Advisor to the Minister of Mineral Resources and Energy. He currently works as a consultant on mining law and energy policy.

Sihle Booi is young African woman who is passionate about human rights advocacy with a special interest in the substantive realisation of the right to equality for vulnerable and marginalised groups. She is also strongly passionate about emphasising equitable protection of minorities within minorities and/or vulnerable groups within vulnerable groups. She holds a Bachelor of Arts in Philosophy and History from the University of Fort Hare; an LLB; a PG-Dip. in Law; an LLM; and a PGCE from the University of the Witwatersrand. She is a PhD candidate at the Wits School of Law and currently works as a research advisor at the South African Human Rights Commission.

Siyabonga Hadebe is a seasoned government official with extensive experience in South Africa's labour, economic and diplomatic sectors. Currently, he serves as South Africa's Labour Attaché in Geneva, Switzerland, fostering strong ties with the International Labour Organization (ILO) and ensuring his country's adherence to international labour and human rights standards. His academic background, encompassing degrees from institutions in the US, Italy and South Africa, complements his ongoing PhD in international economic law and human rights at Maastricht University in The Netherlands. Besides the ILO, Hadebe also represents South Africa in international forums like the G20, OECD, BRICS and the African Union. His voice extends beyond his official role, with frequent contributions to public discourse concerning critical issues facing South Africa, Africa and the developing world.

Tawanda Makusha is an NRF-rated researcher employed by the Human Sciences Research Council as a chief research specialist. He specialises in applied social and public health. Dr Makusha's work particularly focuses on men, masculinities, fatherhood, and male involvement in maternal and child health – particularly early child development in the first 1 000 days and the impact of poverty and HIV and AIDS on children and families.

Tebogo Gumede is a social science researcher, specialising in qualitative methodologies, based at the Human Sciences Research Council. She holds a doctorate in language practice. Her recent work includes investigating the impact of the Choice on Termination of Pregnancy Act, cost-coping strategies of households with an HIV/AIDS-positive member, and investigating the implementation of African languages in public service technologies for different government departments. Her doctorate explored the use of these technologies by isiXhosa and Northern Sotho visually impaired participants.

Tshepo Madlingozi is a full-time commissioner of the South African Human Rights Commission. Madlingozi studied law and sociology in South Africa, Cameroon, and the United Kingdom. He is a visiting professor at the International Institute of Social Studies of Erasmus University Rotterdam and a faculty member of the Vienna Master of Arts in Applied Human Rights. He is a co-editor of the *South African Journal on Human Rights*. He is a co-editor of *Symbol or Substance: Socio-economic Rights in South Africa* (Cambridge University Press) and a co-editor of *Introduction to Law and Legal Skills in South Africa, 2nd Edition* (Oxford University Press, South Africa). He has consulted for government departments, inter-governmental organisations and NGOs.

Wandile Sihlobo is Chief Economist of the Agricultural Business Chamber of South Africa (Agbiz) and the author of two books, *A Country of Two Agricultures: The Disparities, the Challenges, the Solutions* (2023) and *Finding Common Ground: Land, Equity, and Agriculture* (2020). He is a senior lecturer extraordinary at the Department of Agricultural Economics at Stellenbosch University and a visiting research fellow at the Wits School of Governance, University of the Witwatersrand.

Wonderboy Peters provides communications support in the public service. He has previously taught languages, literature and media studies at Wits, SOAS and NEMISA. He is passionate about documentary film-making and an activist who fights stigma against mental ill-health.

Ylva Rodny-Gumede is Head of Division for Global Engagement and a professor in the School of Communication at the University of Johannesburg. She holds a PhD from the School of Oriental and African Studies (SOAS), London University, as well as an MA degree in politics from the University of the Witwatersrand in South Africa and an MA in journalism from Cardiff University in the United Kingdom.

Zukiswa Mqolomba is a national commissioner and deputy chairperson of the Public Service Commission. She is a PhD candidate at the University of Cape Town, doing her PhD on the professionalisation of the public service using SAPS as a case study. She has two master's degrees from the University of Cape Town in South Africa and University of Sussex in the United Kingdom. She loves to read biographies of legendary leaders with global impact. She is also a born-again Christian and deeply loves the Lord!

With a background in economics, development studies and social policy, **Zukiswa Nzo** developed a passion for social justice following a life-changing injury that resulted in an impairment. This personal experience ignited her passion for fairness and equality. She has since held diverse roles in civil society, the private sector, the public sector, and academia, all promoting diversity, inclusion and equity. She is studying at Waseda University in Japan and is part of the National Council of and for Persons with Disabilities in South Africa.

Foreword

South Africa is a nation with several complex dynamics that pose various contradictions or paradoxes. Over the last 30 years of our democracy, the stark contradictions prevalent within our nation have increasingly come into full view. It is these contradictions that have shaped this country into the remarkable nation it has become.

Our nation bears the scars of apartheid woven together with the healing and uniting power of reconciliation. Our nation is endowed with the natural beauty of its landscapes intertwined with the horrific pain inflicted by poverty, unemployment and inequality. Our nation boasts diverse cultures, languages and traditions representing a rich tapestry of heritage but spotlighting the historical divisions and struggles between the various ethnic groups.

As said by the then Deputy State President, Thabo Mbeki, during the debate in the National Assembly in May 1998, South Africa is a country of two nations. The first part of our nation is prosperous and urban, and the second part is poor and living in rural and underdeveloped parts of our country. Over the last 30 years of our democracy, we have made progress to eradicate the legacy of apartheid, but there is far more that remains to be done to give full meaning to the aspirations our people had in 1994.

One of the pleasing sides of the cultures amongst most of the people of South Africa is our ability to cast aside our differences and unite when the occasion requires. This we witnessed in 2010 during the Rugby World Cup when the nation united to support our national rugby team, the

Springboks. Countries such as China, Singapore and South Korea were faced with similar development challenges as South Africa. National unity, discipline and determination coupled with putting their national interest first ahead of narrow economic interests have resulted in them achieving shared prosperity marked by a high GDP per capita. Similarly, South Africa has, over the last 30 years, laid the foundation to foster unity and what we need is virtuous leadership in all spheres of our society to work towards equality and the common good.

There is no benefit one can derive from being pessimistic. Harping on mistakes of the past committed since the advent of democracy is not going to improve our material conditions. Going forward, we must continue with the project of nation building, learning from the good and adverse experiences and never losing hope that we will achieve a better life for all. Our forebears laid the foundation by striving for a democracy; it must now be our mission to strive for the development of all our people and the country.

Liberation Diaries Vol. 2 is one of the important building blocks towards the future we desire. It presents well considered scholarly material that we can draw from as we shape our policies, strategies and programmes to develop our nation. Each one of us has a great responsibility to do all that we can always to contribute towards building a non-racial and democratic society in which all its citizens can achieve their full potential.

Malose Kekana
Former CEO of Umsobomvu Youth Fund
Chief Executive Officer – Pareto Limited

Acknowledgements

First, I would like to acknowledge the peer reviewers and readers who critiqued the chapters in this book. Their feedback contributed immensely to the current product, with the editor taking full responsibility for any content limitations and snags in the volume. Second, I wish to thank Jacana Media for agreeing to run with this project, taking it through rigorous review and copyediting processes. They have once again delivered a superior product. Without the support of Mr Malose Kekana from Pareto Limited, this project would have taken longer to materialise. His stepping in to endow the project as part of his commitment to the writing of history is greatly appreciated. To each of the authors, your trust is acknowledged. You could have published your work elsewhere, but you chose this project, believing in its value and significance.

Busani Ngcaweni
April 2024

Acronyms and abbreviations

AAMP	Agriculture and Agro-processing Master Plan
ANC	African National Congress
APP	Annual Performance Plan
APRM	African Peer Review Mechanism
ARD	Alliance for Rural Democracy
ASGISA	Accelerated and Shared Growth Initiative for South Africa
AU	African Union
BEE	Black Economic Empowerment
CASAC	Council for the Advancement of the South African Constitution
CIAG	Cape Independence Advocacy Group
CIP	Cape Independence Party
Cope	Congress of the People
DA	Democratic Alliance
DALRRD	Department of Agriculture, Land Reform and Rural Development
DBE	Department of Basic Education
DDG	Deputy Director-General
DHET	Department of Higher Education and Training
DME	Department of Minerals and Energy
DPME	Department of Performance Monitoring and Evaluation
EDB	Economic Development Board (Singapore)
EDC	Early Childhood Development

FOSAD	Forum of South African Director-Generals
GBVF	gender-based violence and femicide
GEAR	Growth, Employment and Redistribution
HDSA	Historically Disadvantaged South Africans
HSRC	Human Sciences Research Council
ICASA	Independent Communications Authority of South Africa
IJR	Institute for Justice and Reconciliation
ILC	Independent Living Centre
IMF	International Monetary Fund
LEAF	Leadership Education and Advancement Foundation
LGE	local government election
MDG	Millennium Development Goal
MERG	Macroeconomic Research Group
MITI	Ministry of International Trade and Industry
MK	uMkhonto we Sizwe
MPRDA	Mineral and Petroleum Resources Development Act
NCPD	National Council for Persons with Disabilities
NDP	National Development Plan
NGC	National General Council
NGO	non-governmental organisation
NGP	New Growth Path
NP	National Party
NPC	National Planning Commission
NPO	non-profit organisation
NSP	National Strategic Plan
OAU	Organisation of African Unity
OECD	Organisation for Economic Co-operation and Development
PAP	People's Action Party (Singapore)
PC	Portfolio Committee
PCAS	Policy Coordination and Advisory Services
PSC	Peace and Security Council
PSC	Public Service Committee
PSET	Post-School Education and Training
RDP	Reconstruction and Development Programme
RWAR	Rural Women's Action Research Programme
SADC	Southern African Development Community

SADTU	South African Democratic Teachers' Union
SAHRC	South African Human Rights Commission
SANDF	South African National Defence Force
SARB	South African Reserve Bank
SASL	South African Sign Language
SHiNE	Social Harmony Through National Effort
SOE	state-owned enterprise
SONA	State of the Nation Address
SRC	Student Representative Council
TRC	Truth and Reconciliation Commission
TUGSA	Transport User's Group of Persons with Disabilities in South Africa
UNSC	United Nations Security Council
WPRPD	White Paper on the Rights of Persons with Disabilities
YCM	Young Christian Movement
ZANU-PF	Zimbabwean African National Union – Patriotic Front

Introduction

In the first volume of *Liberation Diaries* (*Reflections on 20 Years of Democracy*, 2014), I put forward a thesis that the success of project democracy in South Africa should be assessed against and within the context of the main democratic promise: building a non-racial, non-sexist, democratic, united and prosperous South Africa. This analytic framework was put forward as a foundational instrument to measure progress in society – both as an aspiration of what we want to be and as the antithesis of what came before 27 April 1994. Such an approach allowed contributors to the first volume and society in general to discourse about the future we chose without being hindered by academic mystifications and zero-sum-game analysis that sometimes characterise our public debates.

In the main, the numbers in 2019 suggested that, challenges notwithstanding, the democratic polity was evolving in a positive direction. That is, evidence pointed towards a more non-racial, non-sexist, democratic and prosperous society. If we use the governing party's motto, a better life for all was being created. The biggest challenge, however, as the World Bank report concluded, was addressing inequality which falls under the prosperity indicator. This was, as is the case a decade later, as a consequence of the confluence of a few factors, more especially, poor returns on education (the country spends more and gets less due to quality, throughput rates, etc.), rising unemployment and the reversal in universal access to quality basic services. Setbacks in the distribution of assets and resources that may result in breaking generational inequality and poverty were recorded. Prosperity, in basic terms, means access to assets such as land, housing and forms of capital that individuals and households may monetise into tangible and sustainable resources.

More recently, Statistics South Africa (StatsSA), the country's official statistics agency, presented more data to showcase the country's progress in a positive trajectory. We will not repeat those here, save to say that, compared to 1994, millions of people now work, go to school, drink potable water, have subsidised transport to school where fees and meals are subsidised, are free to exercise their democratic rights to choose public representations, have houses and electricity, have freedom of movement, have access to a free press, can attend any university and college they qualify for, and can marry anybody without the fear of such racist laws as the Immorality Act. As already stated, what muddies the post-apartheid prosperity story is the weakening of delivery capacity especially at local government level, access to services interrupted as a result of poor maintenance of municipal infrastructure, mismanagement of contracts, rampant rent-seeking and political indifference. A two-year-old report by the Department of Planning, Monitoring and Evaluation highlighted a trust deficit as being the biggest challenge facing society, especially as the people look away from government because of perceptions of rampant corruption and incompetence. This distrust in institutions and the erosion of the legitimacy of the state were forewarned in the 10-, 15- and 20-year review reports of the Presidency. Again in the 30-year review this issue is raised, somewhat dampening an otherwise illustrious contribution to national development by the successive democratic administrations. We will not repeat these findings as the reports concerned speak for themselves. For his part, at the 2024 State of the Nation Address, President Cyril Ramaphosa introduced the idea of Tintswalo as a metaphor for the changes that have occurred in the lives of many individuals and households in society.

Between success and challenges

A little over a year ago, Professor Eddie Maloka wrote a widely read article in which he theorised what South Africa should do to make a leap into a more thriving democracy where the majority of citizens have access to basic necessities and jobs whilst sustaining a vibrant democratic arrangement. Maloka argued that South Africa should actively pursue the idea of the Second Republic. For him the First Republic was founded in 1994 following the democratic breakthrough that saw the country replace the tyranny of apartheid with democracy. Maloka argued that the democratic arrangement arrived at in 1994 might have reached its sell-by date, requiring a revival through a major overhaul of institutions, including the electoral system to redetermine how people choose those who represent them in Parliament. This proposition gained significant attention in both public opinion and in intellectual spaces. Academic projects like conferences and edited books were commissioned by institutions like the University of Johannesburg. In the main, there is consensus that a reimagination of what was conceived in 1994 needs review, as much as 30-year-olds do when they make full entry into adulthood, now confronted by different realities of adulting such as taking responsibility for oneself, planning for the medium to long term, foregoing all the innocence of formative stages in life and competing head on with peers and counterparts. At this stage of life, as we witness how some in the world now regard South Africa (as an established democracy that must take responsibility for itself), there is less sympathy for mistakes in the management of economy and society.

Whilst I take no issue with the Maloka proposition of the Second Republic, I pointed out to him that democratic South Africa is in fact the Third Republic or the Third New South Africa. Let me briefly explain what I meant by this idea then and now.

The First New South Africa was born in 1910 when the Union of South Africa was created out of four republics (colonies) that were ruled by the Dutch (read Afrikaners) and the English. After fighting two wars over the control of the territories and the economy, the English won and the parliament of the empire settled by forming this Union – a union of the descendants of the settlers, excluding the natives. The name South Africa effectively now became formal as it soon appeared in statutes. All the laws passed since that time referred to the country as South Africa. This was followed by successive institutions and parastatals that bore the name South Africa. This geographic and political entity called South Africa was founded on two pillars: racial segregation and colonial violence.

The Second New South Africa was created in 1962 after the

Afrikaner nationalist government took over in 1948 and consolidated racial segregation as official state policy. By declaring the Republic, the Afrikaner nationalists were technically ending indirect British political control of the country. They were consolidating their power as a political block with a distinct national identity. Of course, the English remained in charge of the economy. The two groups would again converge as a capitalist class with common interests in the 1970s and 1980s. Scholars like Nattrass and Ardington write about this in the book *The Political Economy of South Africa*. The interests ranged from consolidating racial oppression and consolidating economic dominance. There was no disagreement on the exclusion of the black majority from the national body-politic. In *The Making of the Racist State*, Bernard Magubane studiously chronicles this evolution of racial oppression and how the two groups pursued the common purpose of dividing the country and accumulating wealth. In the seminal book *The History of Inequality in South Africa*, Sampie Terreblanche details how dispossession since 1652 up to the end of apartheid planted the seeds of the human tragedy that would be bequeathed to the democratic policy in 1994.

The Third New South Africa was born in 1994 following the democratic breakthrough that ended apartheid in favour of majority rule and equal representation. This was meant to be an antithesis of the earlier Republics characterised as colonialism of a special type that were racist, sexist, undemocratic and divided, with the black majority condemned to social and economic bondages. The so-called growth of the 1960s and 1970s was not equitably shared across the colour line.

The Third New South Africa, or Republic, was to reverse all this. It was to remove racial oppression by building a non-racial society. It was to liberate women by making laws and implementing programmes that end sexism in all its manifestation – from access to healthcare to the labour market. It was to be democratic in form and content, where citizens enjoy all civil liberties regardless of the colour of their skin, geographic and economic status. Building national unity was a major task of the new democratic government which, guided by the new Constitution, took an oath to unite the people by, among other things, addressing the imbalances of the past. This unity in diversity was not to be automatic, but a product of direct government intervention. Finally, the Third New South Africa (Republic) was to redistribute wealth, end poverty, create jobs, reduce inequality and improve human capital – all in pursuit of the goal of prosperity for all. It is given that effective governance of public affairs was to be the main propeller of these endeavours.

Nested between the contested stories of successes and challenges of 30 years of democracy are human stories of triumph and progress, dreams deferred, mainstreaming women into the social and economic life of the country, alongside rampant gender-based violence; occasional flare-ups of racism, although the non-racialism is the permeating zeitgeist; access to water and sanitation, and their interruptions; access to housing and shelter, although there are quality and quantum concerns; access to education and training, regardless of their outcomes and impact; ability to choose public representatives, their propensity to disappoint notwithstanding. A more nuanced assessment of the success of the democratic project is necessary, in order not to subject it to a zero-sum game. After all, societies, like human beings and institutions, go through circles and curves, booms and bursts. That is the story of civilisations and empires alike.

Navigating the adolescence of democracy

Whilst it might sound repetitive, let us close the Introduction to this volume by exploring this growing-up story, as a further nuance advancing our understanding of why the idea of South Africa's democracy being a success is contested – many chapters in this book contend with this theme of success and failure.

In this instance I am using the "cradle to adulthood" motif. The growing-up metaphor aims to help the reader view the 30-year-old country the same way they witness ordinary people going through the stages from birth up to age 30. This is no excuse for missed opportunities, but a relatable frame of reference. Using the metaphor of growing up or paralleling the growth stages of a country to human life provides a lens for understanding the complexities and achievements of this era.

The first decade: Childhood innocence and foundational growth

The initial decade of democracy can be likened to the childhood of a person, a time marked by innocence, foundational growth and significant external support. For South Africa, this period was about laying down the new rules of a free society, establishing institutions that embody democratic principles, and embracing the international community's support. Like a child whose needs are met with joy and support by their parents, South Africa, in its infancy of democracy, experienced a global goodwill and assistance in constructing a post-apartheid identity. This era was characterised by the hopeful and optimistic spirit of the Rainbow Nation, where the dreams of equality and justice took root.

The second decade: Adolescence and self-discovery

Transitioning into the second decade, South Africa, much like an adolescent, started facing the realities and challenges of identity, growth and the complexities of its society. This phase involved grappling with the legacies of apartheid, addressing inequalities and striving for economic and social stability. This period was one of self-awareness and confrontation with external realities. The nation had to navigate the delicate balance of preserving its democratic ideals while addressing the practicalities of governance, economic disparities and social cohesion. This stage was marked by significant growth pains as the nation struggled with excesses such as corruption, unemployment and the resurfacing of racial tensions. Think of what teenagers do as they navigate life into adulthood, trying to define their identities, choosing careers, experimenting with substances and alcohol, and confronting the realities of life that were somewhat shielded to children.

The third decade: Adulthood and striving for independence

Entering the third decade, South Africa found itself in a stage comparable to early adulthood, where the quest for independence and self-sufficiency becomes paramount. This period was about taking full responsibility for our destiny, competing on the global stage and addressing our national challenges as honestly as we could – of course, this last decade is a mixture of both denial and coming to terms with our blemishes. We started to question whether we are the fledgling democracy that we are renowned for. We tried, recording both failures and successes, to actively seek solutions to exogenous and man-made challenges. Staring in our wide-open eyes is stunted results of the economic reforms, rising inequality, runaway corruption and the hollowing out of state institutions. The very idea of the Rainbow Nation is in question. The integrity of the political establishment is in question. Yet, as we have seen in many cases, this third decade has also been a period of consolidation, resilience and striving for a mature, inclusive society that can navigate the complexities of the twenty-first century.

Conclusion

As this introduction explored the growing-up motif, examining the developmental stages and the inherent challenges and triumphs each stage (broken into three decades) represents, many would wonder, given what we know of South Africa today, is there hope for the future. That is a vexing enquiry, yet not necessarily a black swan. What will become of South Africa in the next decades is a function of three variables: the total experience of the three decades of democracy (together with all the legacies preceding them), the behaviour and performance of the state in delivering services and governing the economy effectively, as well as agency of non-state actors who will hold government accountable and contribute their resources (capital, ideas and labour) to national development. Of course there are geopolitical factors as well that may impact on the growth trajectory. But such factors can be navigated by a government that masters statecraft to perform all its functions – from security and the social and economic interests of citizens to building effective institutions and navigating geopolitical dynamics.

The 30-year-old South Africa has learned. It has come of age. It has made its mark in the global community – from sport, arts, music, science and innovation to politics, trade and other human endeavours. It has competed for its rightful place under the sun. It has been accommodated and nurtured. It has been rejected and failed. It has taken care of many of its children, whilst some feel neglected. It is evident, however, as most chapters in this book argue, that those who are disappointed feel so understanding what it is possible to achieve. They appreciate the potential of the country; they have witnessed and experienced the changes, and their reversal. Authors have tried to be objective, although that is a difficult ask when addressing a subject as intimate as how one feels about the country. Neither can readers be expected to be emotionally unattached from such a subject, hence we expect and accept all the criticism that will come our way. This is not a hagiography of South Africa. It is critical reflection by young and experienced writers and commentators. They own their views. Even those who lament failures are as patriotic as those who are critical. After all, being critical is a revolutionary and patriotic duty.

Join me and let us enjoy these diverse liberation diaries as part of the future we chose whilst using them to prospect the inclusive prosperous future we choose.

On State Formation
and Performance

1

Asikhulume! Conversations for the next 30 years of South Africa's democracy

Nozipho Tshabalala

Democracy is more than a system of government. It is an ongoing courageous conversation between the governors and the governed. Conversation sits at the heart of a democratic society. In a truly democratic society, citizens are engaged in a continuous dialogue, with multiple everyday opportunities to express their opinions, preferences and concerns. In this chapter, I will offer why conversation must be centred in the democratic experience. I will share a reflection on the democratic conversation that South Africa has had in its three decades of a democratic society. Finally, I will offer a framework for how we might have conversations that lead to better democratic outcomes in the coming decade and beyond.

I am a conversation strategist. My work involves journeying with organisations, institutions and enterprises whose decisions and actions impact how societies function. In the decade that I've dedicated myself to this work, I have observed that organisations, institutions and enterprises that use conversations as a catalyst for change and a tool to drive strategic outcomes have more visible impact on the sectors of society they seek to shape. In this chapter, I attempt to apply these observations to the democratic project in South Africa to unpack the quality and impact of our national conversation today. The question I pose is: What might need to be true for us as a citizenry to have better conversations that meet our democratic ideals and aspirations?

Let's start with agreeing that democracy is the culmination of many threads of conversations taking place all at once. Public discourse is probably the most visible of these conversations where citizens actively participate with the intent to influence government policy and their own lived experience in a democratic society. This often takes the form of dialogue on various platforms from public meetings to social media.

Elections, while a less frequent form of public discourse, are high-visibility moments when the democratic conversation takes centre stage. This is a conversation where the dialogue is loud between the candidates of political parties and the electorate. The elected representatives become intermediaries in the national conversation, representing the views of their constituents, and carrying the voices of those communities in the legislative actions of debates, discussions and voting for and against policy stances.

The process of policymaking itself is a continuum of discussion, debate and negotiation between stakeholders, reverberating as an important part of the national conversation that reveals what a society has chosen as the best possible way to address its societal issues and challenges.

Democracy also calls for the involvement of civil society organisations, advocacy groups and ordinary citizens to lift their voices on issues that impact them. The very act of protesting is itself a conversation that takes place between those demanding change and those intent on protecting the status quo. This broader conversation can enrich the national conversation provided that the diverse voices are heard.

Thirty years since the dawn of democracy in South Africa, there is much to reflect on the impact of the national conversation. Our divided history demanded that the national conversation be a way of finding our way to each other, finding the words and exchanges that would allow us to address and reconcile our differences. The democratic transition in 1994 marked the end of institutionalised racial segregation, and since then we have been in a continuous conversation to build a more inclusive and just society. And just like any authentic conversation, we have struggled. Challenges and tensions to the inclusive and just society dream have been plenty.

As we struggled towards some form of reconciliation the conversation of the Truth and Reconciliation Commission (TRC) played a critical role in creating the space for pain and forgiveness to live side by side, making visible the path towards healing for all of us. The conversation of social justice is ongoing as policymakers formulate and refine policy to reduce economic, social and spatial inequalities to someday arrive at an equitable society. Our inheritance of cultural diversity has demanded a conversation to keep expanding the space for different communities to express their identities, practise their cultural rights, speak in their native languages and have their traditions recognised. Democracy in South Africa is a tapestry of ongoing threads of conversation, each contributing to strengthening or weakening the social fabric as we make progress and at times regress. What is indisputable is that despite the moments of regress, South Africa would not be the society it is today in the absence of a deep and meaningful conversation.

What conversations do we need to have in the next decade to deepen democracy in our society? The list could be as long as all the requirements for a perfect society. And because the perfect society does not exist, I offer here 10 conversations that hold the promise of deepening democracy in South Africa in the next decade and many more to come.

1. Social inequality and economic transformation

South Africa's economic and social inequity remains a stark reminder of the incomplete project of freedom for most of the black population. We need a conversation that allows us to reflect honestly on our historical inequalities whilst building forward with economic policies rooted in equality and equity. We need to find new ways of empowering marginalised communities through education and job opportunities. These conversations will call on our collective courage to address the concentration of wealth in the hands of a few and to act decisively to accelerate inclusive economic growth.

2. Land redistribution and ownership

One of the most difficult conversations has been that of land redistribution and ownership. Nothing short of a transformative conversation that will guide the country towards fair and just land distribution that benefits both rural and urban populations will be enough. This conversation will not be easy, as anything transformative rarely is; we will need to strike a balance between the need for land reform and the protection of property rights.

3. Education and skills development

Whilst as a society we appear to value education, as evidenced by our push for universal access to education, the conversation that will catapult our educational outcomes beyond just access to quality outcomes that allow us to hold our own in a competitive global market will need to be far more robust than it has been. This conversation calls on our imagination to equip our people with the mindset and skills required in a fast-changing world of work largely powered by technology. The nature of our institutions will need a shake-up as they reconfigure themselves to be fit-for-purpose in this new world. Curricula will have to be increasingly fluid and responsive to the pace of change in every sector. We will need to release ourselves from unhelpful beliefs about the value of vocational training and build the attraction of this form of skill attainment for the millions of young people looking to enter the labour market.

4. Social justice and human rights

Our Constitution reflects our highest and most noble dreams for our society. It is a reference point for many constitutional architects the world over. However, if we want to live up to these dreams, we must do the work and have the conversations that will safeguard human rights and deliver social justice and equality. We need to become fluent in speaking to gender equality issues, uplifting and protecting LGBTQ+ rights, and the rights of minority groups broadly. Tolerance calls on us to let go of our own closely held beliefs about what it means to be human, and thus we must find ways to ensure that diverse communities have full, happy and healthy experiences as equal and full citizens.

5. Corruption and good governance

Corruption and the absence of good governance have been corrosive on our society, eating away at our institutions and reducing the impact of our hard work to progress society meaningfully. This condition will continue unless we turn to open, transparent and accountability-inducing conversations that help us identify systemic solutions to rid the rot of corruption. We need to encourage civic participation and watchdog initiatives to hold ourselves and others accountable across sectors.

6. Reconciliation and nation building

The concept of the Rainbow Nation has long lost its lustre and has been archived as a branding gimmick of the past. If we are to ever reach reconciliation and build the nation that we say we aspire to, our conversations must give us the capacity to reflect on the past so that we are able to build a better future. We must promote a national identity that transcends racial and ethnic divisions, and we must support initiatives that build bridges towards different communities.

7. Environmental sustainability

The impact of climate change on vulnerable communities cannot be left to the conversations at COP or any other global platform. We need to bring these conversations closer towards the realities of the poor and rural in the country who are feeling the brunt of a changing environment on which they are dependent for their livelihoods. Our climate conversations must challenge consumption behaviour and encourage responsible resource management and conservation efforts.

8. Youth engagement and participation

Societies that have been successful in their democratic aspirations have often found a way to foster dialogue with the younger generation and create platforms for young people to share their perspectives and concerns. Leaders the world over are learning the hard way that when young people are eclipsed out of the political conversation, they can claim their space in socially disruptive ways. The South African conversation must be intentional about encouraging youth participation in politics and in decision-making processes that impact them as a constituency. Young people must have a voice on how we address youth unemployment and access to funding for their entrepreneurial ventures, and other opportunities that an evolving economy presents.

9. Media and information literacy

The blast-off of information communications technology and artificial intelligence are making media and information literacy increasingly important. At a baseline, promoting media literacy will ensure a well-informed citizenry that can participate in the national conversation on both traditional and evolving technological platforms. In tandem with this, we must encourage, incentivise and reward responsible journalism and the protection of press freedom, to keep sacred the truthfulness of the broadcast and print conversation.

10. Healthcare access and social welfare

Finally, we must not lose sight of the things that keep driving a wedge between those who have and those who do not have in a society. Amplifying both the conversation and the action on public delivery will keep the tone of the conversation positive and constructive. Key amongst the service delivery opportunities will be the policy implementation conversation and the extent to which it is able to improve access to healthcare, quality education and housing as just a few examples. The difficult conversation of ensuring an adequate safety net, including the required taxation to finance it, will all be critical.

It should go without saying that these conversations should be inclusive, integrating voices from various backgrounds, ideologies and perspectives. These conversations must lead to concrete action and a change towards what we collectively uphold as a good and functioning society. Our conversation of the new decade must deepen the democratic project in South Africa rather than derail it. Ultimately, creating a vibrant and effective democracy in South Africa requires a courageous conversation that leads to the empowerment of citizens and the narrowing of the conversation between the governed and the governors.

It is all well for us to have a compass that points us to the conversations we need to have, but we must all have the ability and know-how to drive and participate in these conversations. The framework I offer here speaks to the environment required for a conversation to take place and to the factors that make the conversations consequential; in other words, leading to tangible actions and outcomes. The framework is as simple as it is powerful: (1) understanding the atmosphere of the country within which the conversation takes place; (2) consciously building the muscle to listen broadly and deeply; and (3) remaining committed to conversations that are consequential, that lead to action and tangible outcomes. If we can better understand and work with the atmosphere in the country, be able to better listen and remain committed to consequential conversations, we would be able to have and make progress in all of the conversations that our democratic projects demand of us.

Atmosphere

In the context of the national conversation, the national atmosphere is infused by the socio-political and cultural climate. It is made up of the prevailing attitudes, values and sentiment of the population. Atmosphere is also determined by the political events and social movements that have the attention of the nation. We therefore must be mindful that any new conversation we wish to start as a country will be subject to public perception. Public perception is the filter through which those engaged in the conversation will interpret and engage with the conversation. The national atmosphere also sets the agenda of the conversations to be had. For example, in times of economic crisis, the conversation will be radically different from that in times of economic boom. In societies with deep polarisation, the atmosphere will lend itself to a conversation that is likely to be more adversarial and the work of finding common ground is that much harder. All this is not to say that the atmosphere is all powerful. No. In fact, the relationship between the national atmosphere and the national conversation is dynamic and reciprocal. While the national atmosphere can shape conversations, public discourse also has the power to shift the national atmosphere over time.

Active listening

In the national conversation active listening looks like a collective and engaged effort by citizens, policymakers, the media and other stakeholders to understand, respect and respond to different perspectives and issues. A country shows that it is listening through the platforms it creates to hear. Platforms can take the form of community meetings, commonly referred to as 'imbizo' in South Africa, local radio stations, forums, televised debates and conferences. In the context of media, a country that listens will likely have a media landscape that reflects a diverse range of opinions and issues, and media outlets that are able to offer balanced views that represent a variety of perspectives. The media also includes social media, which gives the minutiae of individual perspectives and opinion. Active listening also means creating the space for disagreement, which can often be a catalyst for the exploration of alternative solutions and an opportunity for continuous learning and to reassess perspectives. Active listening in the national conversation is about creating an environment where diverse voices are heard, respected and considered. It is the basis upon which a culture of dialogue, empathy and shared ownership and responsibility to engage with the country's challenges and opportunities are built.

Consequence

Conversations at a national level are often criticised for being talk-shops, especially when they take the form of conferences and forums. The national conversation must be consequential. Consequential conversations are distinct in that they have significant impact, influence decisions and relationships, and have a bearing on policymaking and policy outcomes. The national conversation offers input and cues to policymakers as they formulate and implement policy. The issues raised in the national conversation should influence the government's agenda, its priorities and decision-making processes. At the core of a national consequential conversation is the ability to hold government and government officials accountable. At its best the national conversation can influence and shape cultural and moral values within a society. Discussions on ethics, morality and cultural identity form the threads of a tapestry of shared norms and values. The consequential conversation breaks beyond national borders, influencing the country's global image and its standing on the international stage. The national conversation reflects the ongoing discourse within a country that ultimately defines the character and direction of a society.

Where to start?

South Africa has the ingredients to improve the national conversation. Our respect for freedom of expression means that we already have a tolerance for diverse views for a robust national conversation. Our Constitution protects this right, creating the first building block for a real national conversation. We have work to do in driving inclusivity in how we have the national conversation. We need to create mechanisms to reach a broader range of voices from different demographics, communities and social groups. Access to information determines who is empowered to engage in the conversation and who is not. A well-informed citizenry pushes for greater transparency in government actions and policies for a more informed conversation. We have a diverse and pluralistic media landscape, and we need to remain vigilant to avoid the concentration of media ownership that can lead to undue influence. Our approach to civic engagement must go beyond door-to-door campaigns in the election season. Town hall meetings, public forms and other platforms must be part of the everyday engagement of citizens to create feedback loops between the different voices in the national conversation. The contact opportunities ensure that leaders and institutions are responsive, taking public input on board and communicating government decisions effectively. Lastly, we need leaders who understand that conversation is a strategic tool that is as powerful as any other in their leadership toolbox and an empowered citizenry ready to engage through the platforms available to build the democratic society we want and deserve.

If we hold bold and frank conversations about ourselves, as a people and a country, we are bound to have many more breakthroughs. As the late radio personality and journalist, Xolani Gwala, used to call on us: "Asikhulume!" For the next 30 years of democracy to be more meaningful, let's have a conversation.

2

As the leader of society, has the ANC fulfilled its historical mission of creating a better life for all?

Oscar van Heerden

When, on Sunday, 26 June 1955, about 3 000 ANC delegates of all colours and backgrounds gathered in an open veld outside Johannesburg in what the historian Saul Dubow, in his account of the event, has described as a "carnival-like show of popular strength"[1] to draft the Freedom Charter, they had in mind not ideology, but the dreams and aspirations of millions of people. Among their aspirations were the rights to share the country's wealth; to enjoy human rights and equality before the law; and to secure equal access to education, housing and medical care. These aspirations, recalled Rusty Bernstein in his memoir, *Memory and Forgetting*, were written by thousands of people on pieces of paper, scraps of cardboard and toilet paper. They were, wrote Dubow, relatively uncontroversial. "Rather more problematic were two ambiguous provisions: the statement that 'South Africa belongs to all who live in it, black and white', and the provisions to transfer into common ownership the country's mineral wealth, banks and monopoly industries."[2]

What the Freedom Charter proclaimed was a post-apartheid state that would rely on interventions to deliver the people's democratic aspirations. It strongly advocated socio-economic rights and state intervention in securing such rights. These aspirations, writes Dubow, were consistent with the development of an interventionist state based on the social rights of citizenship, capable of ensuring that economic arrangements would create full employment and giving effect to post-war social policies for a national health service, free comprehensive education and a non-stigmatising system of social security.

The state's repressive response to the upsurge of popular resistance that followed the Defiance Campaign in the early 1950s and the adoption of the Freedom Charter led to the banning of the ANC in 1960, which lasted until 1990. This period meant that the anti-apartheid struggle for universal suffrage overshadowed discussions of post-apartheid socio-economic policies.

With the unbanning of anti-apartheid organisations in 1990, there revived in the ANC a dynamic debate on post-apartheid socio-economic policy. And so, almost forty years after the adoption of the Freedom Charter, the "Ready to Govern"[3] policy document focused much of its content on the ANC's plan "to create a strong, dynamic and balanced economy". Interspersed with democratic aspirations was the language of a "mixed economy", in which the democratic state would consider increasing or reducing the public sector. The document advocated state involvement in economic activity to strengthen the ability of the government to respond to the massive inequalities in the country. And it envisioned an activist post-apartheid state with policy measures directed at "ensuring employment creation, industrial restructuring, the elimination of poverty, responding to the basic needs of the population, achieving sustainable growth and curbing monopolies".[4]

One must try to understand the ANC's performance as a governing party against its policy goals since 1994 in order to answer the question: Has the ANC fulfilled its historical aspirations? If I can track its historical performance since 1994, then perhaps the party's successes and failures – its attempts, in other words, to adjust its policies and practical interventions to changing conditions since 1994 – will become clearer; so, too, will its relevance – or irrelevance as the case may be – to the very pressing challenges of the day and its prospects in 2024 and beyond.

My overall approach is to map the evolution of the ANC's policies and their outcomes since 1994 against the party's actual performance. I make no claim to being an economist, and my approach is not an economic dissection or analysis of the country's macro and fiscal policies, nor is it an analysis thereof. Instead, it is a broad account of policy choices and outcomes set against electoral outcomes since 1994.

The policy evolution since 1994

Outlines of the 1994 settlement

When, in the early 1990s, the ANC and National Party engaged in talks about the terms of a settlement, some of what the ANC argued for differed significantly from the founding principles in the Freedom Charter. This meant that the constitutional settlement, enshrined in the Interim Constitution of 1993, circumscribed the role the state could ideally play in radically transforming the economy. Ultimately, the agreement rested on a system of universal suffrage, a separation of powers, multiparty elections and a Bill of Rights.

The Interim Constitution, writes Hein Marais,[5] had to comply with a set of 33 binding constitutional principles that crystallised important compromises agreed to in the final stages of the negotiations. Altering these principles required a two-thirds majority in Parliament. They required, for instance, that:

- The diversity of language and culture be protected;
- Collective rights of self-determination in forming, joining and maintaining organs of civil society be recognised and protected;
- The rights of ownership of private property be protected;
- Exclusive and concurrent powers and functions be delegated to provincial governments;
- National government be prevented from exercising its powers in ways that encroached upon the geographical, functional or institutional integrity of the principles;
- Minority parties be enabled to participate in the legislative process;
- The independence and impartiality of the Reserve Bank be protected.[6]

What these principles effectively meant was that the terms of the settlement, despite far-right bombing campaigns around that time, would "reflect the influence of forces outside the multiparty negotiations specifically"[7] – large corporate entities, for example, which would allow business to fashion a great deal of the kind of socio-economic reforms needed to drive growth and development.

Despite these limitations, the settlement represented a political milestone which, justifiably, won the admiration of the international community. A peaceful transition to the 1994 elections occurred, with historical foes agreeing to negotiate the economic transition through a series of mutually agreeable trade-offs in the national interest.

The question is whether those trade-offs represented fundamental departures from the ANC's historical mission. Here it is important to understand that the ANC always had in mind a redistribution of wealth, the eradication of racial inequality and the construction of a non-racial, non-sexist and prosperous South Africa in which all citizens, black and white, would live in harmony. The task assumed by the ANC in 1994, however, meant that some of the radical breaks with apartheid envisaged in its policies had to be postponed. But, to bring clarity to that moment, the goal remained a post-apartheid "transition", rather than rupture, that would allow divergent interests to "pass through a gateway of concessions and compromises in order to avert disaster for their respective agendas".[8] This amounted to an attempt to forge a new basis for a social contract – "an essential basis of any bid to restructure South African society", as Marais observes.[9]

Whether the terms of that social contract were along unequal or egalitarian lines is a matter of historical record. That the ANC entered the post-1994 era without dismantling the country's "two nation" character through a radical redistribution of resources, opting instead for a gradual dismantling of its institutional architecture, is now widely accepted. But that does not mean abandonment of its mission.

What matters for this analysis is whether the outcomes of a series of gradual policy adjustments since 1994 have benefitted those historically excluded from political and economic life. Broadly speaking, understanding the historical record means understanding the policy evolution since 1994, to which I now turn.

Recasting the terrain: From "Ready to Govern" to the RDP

The economic views of the ANC significantly changed from, in essence, concurring with the economic views and policy prescriptions of the left in the tripartite alliance until the early 1990s, to fully embracing mainstream economic and policy prescripts within two years after the 1994 settlement. This was not an inconsequential change. It shaped the post-apartheid government's role in the economy, its economic policy choices for and constraints on the country's growth and development outcomes over the last 26 and more years.

What must be borne in mind is that, notwithstanding the rose-tinted lens through which the drafters of the "Ready to Govern" document imagined post-apartheid South Africa, the document did not consider the removal of imperfections, frictions and market rigidities as a way to achieve full employment to meet the people's basic needs or to restructure South African trade and industry. Moreover, it did not view government expenditure as something that would crowd out the private sector, and thus did not consider the dependence of South Africa's future economic growth on foreign direct investment flows. In the "Ready to Govern" document, therefore, "the ANC's intent, strategy and specific economic policy ideas continued to mainly reflect a heterodox view of the South African economy".[10]

After the ANC's national conference in June 1992, which adopted the "Ready to Govern" document, the party leadership gradually gravitated towards mainstream views and policies. Initially, the ANC supported, and led, work on the Reconstruction and Development Programme (RDP) and Macroeconomic Research Group (MERG) initiatives, both of which were guided by redistributive policies on the country's future growth and development path beyond apartheid. Concurrently, the ANC leadership was engaged in economic policy issues with advocates of mainstream views and policies, such as the National Party, representatives of organised domestic capital, and international financial agencies like the International Monetary Fund (IMF).

By the end of 1993, the ANC leadership had already decided to fully distance itself from the MERG analysis and policy recommendations, and became a signatory to an IMF mainstream medium-term economic policy package, referred to as the "Statement of Policies", that accompanied an US$800-million loan agreement in 1993. Even though the ANC by this time had adopted the RDP as an integral element of its manifesto for the first democratic election in 1994, the party started to distance itself from the RDP policy framework soon after the 1994 election. In the

RDP White Paper, released in September 1994, six principles were subtly infused with mainstream economic views.

However, the changes to the original RDP policy framework were significant. In the original formulation the RDP followed a "growth through redistribution" policy that rested on both export promotion and inward industrialisation aimed at significantly expanding domestic demand and social infrastructure. In the RDP White Paper, the goal of redistribution was dropped as the main objective, and the government's role in the economy was reduced to the task of managing the transformation agenda. Fiscal policy would be driven by emerging concerns not to sacrifice fiscal discipline. Thus, monetary policy was set to be independent in its policymaking with no specific measures to allow for government interference.

Such thinking quickly came up against left-wing criticism, but it was, in economist Nicoli Nattrass's view, a route chosen in the specific context of the negotiations towards a constitutional settlement in the early 1990s that "served the political purpose of uniting various constituencies within the ANC" – implying, as Marais argues, "a certain degree of expediency and awareness that the policy had a short shelf life".[11]

By 1995–6, the ANC government had already moulded the RDP into a mainstream economic policy document, the analysis and policy framework of which sat closer to the IMF's 1993 "Statement of Policies" than the original RDP document. The groundwork had been laid for a decisive policy shift.

Neoliberalising development: The adoption of GEAR

When, in 1996, Thabo Mbeki, an economist by training, began convincing former ideological foes in the ANC's labour alliance of the real state of the economy and the challenges that lay ahead, he had in mind an economy reeling from debt and desperately in need of foreign investment and growth in order to drive the ANC's redistribution agenda. Mbeki's reasoning was twofold. First, he argued that when the ANC was unbanned in 1990, it had no economic policy. Its 1988 Constitutional Guidelines and "Ready to Govern" document, as I have argued, had committed it to a mixed economy, but this was largely based on vague references to the Freedom Charter that "the people shall govern"; "the national wealth of the country, the heritage of all South Africans shall be restored to the people"; and "the mineral wealth beneath the soil, the banks and monopoly industry shall be transferred to the ownership of the people as a whole".

The ANC's first attempt to fill the policy gap was its 1990 "Discussion Document on Economic Policy", which stressed the planned initial restructuring of industry and the financial sector, along with the redirection of domestic savings into productive activity and infrastructure development. But Mbeki saw that the distance between those aspirations and economic reality was too vast to bridge with the lofty goals of the RDP. His concern by 1995 was that a growth through redistribution approach would overheat the economy and worsen its debt position. South Africa, to be sure, entered the transition with an economy reeling from a growth rate that had plunged to –1.1 per cent in the early 1990s.[12] The following key indicators, articulated by Marais, demonstrated the gravity of the crisis:

- Declining rates of gross fixed investment (which plunged as low as –18.6 per cent in 1986, and stayed negative from 1990 to 1993), and high rates of capital flight;
- Low rates of private investment, which led to the under-utilisation of manufacturing plant capacity (dropping from 90 per cent in 1981 to 78 per cent in 1993) and declining levels of competitiveness;
- Plummeting levels of personal savings, which, as a proportion of disposable income, dropped from 11 per cent in 1975 to 3 per cent in 1987;
- Very high unemployment, and the economy's inability to create enough new jobs to absorb even a fraction of new entrants into the labour market, a trend exacerbated by under-investment in labour-intensive services;
- Chronic balance of payments difficulties.[13]

In broad terms, this meant that the ANC had inherited an economy in a structural crisis, dependent on raw materials (mainly minerals), prone to exchange-rate fluctuations, and reliant on imported capital goods and services, leading to balance of payments problems. The result was low investment rates, capital flight, a shortage of skilled labour and a surplus of unskilled, unemployed black labour – and, of course, unmanageable debt to GDP ratios. A number of economic scenarios presented at conferences during the political negotiations in the early 1990s had demonstrated the scale of the crisis and the limitations of various policy choices. Mbeki was all the while aware that work on the RDP tended to downplay the crisis and the growth imperative.

Convinced that redistribution would have to occur on a gradual, differential basis over a relatively longer timescale, Mbeki engineered a push towards the second policy adjustment to the post-1994 reality. In 1996, the government adopted an export-oriented growth path, dispensing with the RDP's inward-looking industrialisation strategy geared to servicing domestic redistributive needs in the first instance. In short, the "growth through redistribution" strategy was deemed unsustainable, with the "Mont Fleur scenario" likening it to the fateful flight of Icarus, warning: "After a year or two the programme runs into budgetary, monetary and balance of payments constraints. The budget deficit well exceeds 10 per cent. Depreciations, inflation, economic uncertainty and collapse follow. The country experiences an economic crisis of hitherto unknown proportions which results in social collapse and political chaos."[14] The primary concern of Mbeki by this time was that South Africa simply lacked the advantages of East Asian economies like Malaysia and China to pursue state-led policies. The result was the Growth, Employment and Redistribution (GEAR) strategy, which leaned heavily towards supply-side measures to boost industrial performance, enhance the country's competitiveness and restructure industry.

Among the factors that produced these setbacks, several tend to be overlooked. The left mistakenly assumed it had achieved sufficient weight within the ANC-led tripartite alliance. It also disregarded the extent to which the parameters of the RDP in practice would be drawn on the basis of setbacks suffered outside the political negotiations. Most obvious was the abandonment, first, of the growth through redistribution formula and, later, of the substitute formula of growth and redistribution. Instead, the left sought solace in the predictable rhetoric of the ANC government, which, for obvious reasons, continued to pay lip service to the transformative elements of the RDP, which, in practice, had been superseded.[15]

By mid-1997, elements within the government had begun an attempt to graft a developmental framework (based on RDP principles) on to

GEAR – "a futile bid", writes Hein Marais, "since a social development programme could not be appended to (let alone be integrated with) a macroeconomic strategy characterised by privatisation, deregulation, fiscal austerity and the predominance of the financial sector over production and commerce".[16] Not only the programme's sweep but "its very character and logic had been overwritten by the regressions that were consummated in the GEAR strategy".[17] Indeed, as Marais has written, "the actual utility of the RDP as a government programme had changed dramatically".[18]

To be clear, GEAR hinged on a promise of increasing annual growth by an average 4.2 per cent, creating 1.35 million new jobs by the year 2000, boosting exports by an average 8.4 per cent per annum through an array of supply-side measures, and improving social infrastructure. The methods chosen to achieve those targets included:

- Slashing state expenditure to drive the budget deficit down to 3 per cent of GDP by 2000;
- Keeping inflation in single digits;
- Reducing corporate taxes and providing tax holidays for certain investments;
- Gradually phasing out exchange control regulations;
- Encouraging wage restraint by organised workers;
- A more flexible labour market, possibly by regenerating certain categories of unskilled work and exempting small businesses from aspects of the new labour regime; and
- Speeding up privatisation.[19]

GEAR's growth projections – from 3.5 per cent in 1996 to 6.1 per cent in 2000 – hinged on investment driven by the private sector. That was the crux of the policy. The fiscal deficit, it was argued, "crowded out private investment, drove up interest rates and reduced investor confidence".[20] Thus, fiscal restraint was needed to attract investment. The free market was viewed as the ideal way to achieve efficiency and maximise social welfare. A small government was advocated with a minimal role for the state. Deregulation was to be promoted because labour, capital and other regulations were regarded as hindrances to the otherwise full employment tendency of the market.

The shift to state intervention: ASGISA

In his May 1998 speech on nation-building, President Thabo Mbeki famously declared South Africa was a country of two nations. "One of these nations is white, relatively prosperous, regardless of gender or geographic dispersal... The second and larger nation ... is black and poor."[21]

Six years later, in his May 2004 State of the Nation address, Mbeki embroidered on the notion of two nations. Embedded in the two-economies thesis was the concept of a developmental state acting by way of strategic interventions to address the concerns of both the first and second economies in an interconnected way through growing attention to microeconomic reform, transfer payments to the vulnerable and skills development initiatives.[22] To put that in perspective, GEAR advanced trickle-down economics, where the proceeds of growth were, at least notionally, expected to address socio-economic development challenges. By eliminating "dissavings", it was envisaged that more resources for public and private investment would be released.[23] By this economic logic, high investment would in turn lead to a higher national income and employment. Thus, GEAR saw prudent fiscal policy as a means towards development and the reduction of poverty and inequality.[24]

The government claimed that GEAR's "integrated approach" would create an average of 400 000 jobs annually, achieve an annual growth rate of 6 per cent by 2000, boost exports by an average 8.4 per cent per annum and drastically improve social infrastructure. Accordingly, it was believed that redistribution would emerge from a trickling down of jobs and more focused public expenditure.[25]

Conversely, there were no specific measures and instruments to guarantee the private sector's assigned duty of productive investment. Nor for that matter was there any focus on developing skills to meet the human capabilities and employment challenges of industrial growth. To be sure, between 1995 and 2002, about 1.6 million net new jobs were created in the South African labour market – an average growth rate of about 2.1 per cent per annum. However, more than half a million jobs were lost as a result of the introduction of labour-saving technologies by business, increased outsourcing, and a determined shift towards casual and contract labour.[26]

By the early 2000s, the drift back to earlier theorisations of the developmental state thus "crystallised as a wide-ranging discussion in government on the expansion of services by a state capable of taking forward a far-reaching agenda of national economic development, whilst at the same time placing people and their involvement at the centre of this process".[27] Discussions of a pro-poor, interventionist (or developmental) programme prompted the state to introduce the Accelerated and Shared Growth Initiative of South Africa (ASGISA).

Thus the government's developmental interventions from the early 2000s were part of a broader approach to reduce poverty and increase unemployment.[28] Indeed, as Salim Akoojee and Simon McGrath argued in 2005, many of the interventions in education and training for the first economy could "only make sense in the context of a virtuous cycle of educational and economic development progressing together".[29] In this approach, poverty reduction in the second economy was to be addressed through an expansion of transfer payments and through an extension of services by the state, often in partnership with NGOs.

The drift to a developmental state: The NDP

By the time new political leadership under President Jacob Zuma took office in 2009, the ANC's election manifesto tended towards more decisive economic interventions in the national interest: "One of the defining features of a developmental state is the state's intervention in the economy in favour of the needs of society as a whole. A key instrument for state intervention will be a state-led industrial policy programme that will guide key aspects of economic transformation, supported by an appropriate and sustainable macroeconomic policy stance, as well as trade and labour market policies."[30] Specifically, the manifesto flagged as an urgent issue and a blueprint for economic development the state's capacity to intervene through the implementation of massive industrial programmes, and stressed "the centrality of coordinating state-guided strategies towards engaging key stakeholders in an inclusive process towards the implementation of key aspects of economic transformation grounded in a sustainable macroeconomic and labour market policy".[31]

In his political report to the ANC's 2010 National General Council (NGC), President Zuma indicated that "the new growth path must start with the recognition that, on the one hand, we have had economic growth for a sustained period since the advent of democracy, with particularly high growth since the early 2000s and net job creation. On the other hand, poverty remains high; inequalities have remained the same and even grown worse, while some of the jobs created often brought low wages and poor conditions."[32]

The New Growth Path (NGP) was the result. It too was concerned that some of the jobs created were low-wage forms of employment. The nucleus of the NGP, then, was a developmental state that would enhance the labour-absorption capacity of the economy and find ways to connect knowledge and innovation to the challenge of growth and new jobs. It stressed as priority areas the knowledge economy, the green economy, the manufacturing sector, the social economy and cooperatives.[33]

At least partially in response to the challenge, Zuma in 2009 appointed the National Planning Commission (NPC), comprising a team who shared the vision and principles of the democratic movement, to develop a diagnostic report. Drawing on the findings of its Diagnostic Report, released in June 2010, the NPC identified as priority interventions the following nine challenges:

1. Too few people work;
2. The standard of education for most black learners is of poor quality;
3. Infrastructure is poorly located, under-maintained and insufficient to foster higher growth;
4. Spatial patterns exclude the poor from the fruits of development;
5. The economy is overly and unsustainably resource-intensive;
6. A widespread disease burden is compounded by a failing health system;
7. Public services are uneven and often of poor quality;
8. Corruption is widespread; and
9. South Africa remains a divided society.[34]

Four more pressing challenges were subsequently added: social protection, the rural economy, citizens' safety and South Africa in relation to the southern African region and to the world.

South Africa, in the NPC's diagnosis, was in need of "a long-term perspective, focus and determination to realise our vision".[35] Rather than relying on macroeconomic levers to achieve growth targets, the

NPC focused on deeper structural impediments to inclusive growth. The most significant, and perhaps radical, formulation was a reorientation of strategic priorities linked to the state's ability to play a catalytic, facilitating role in the commanding heights of the economy that would lead to development and a more equitable distribution of resources. In this regard, the ANC saw the developmental state agenda as one that would enable South Africa to play a role in the global market through increased foreign trade and foreign investment. All this would allow the state to focus on building the international competitiveness of the economy through multinational corporations formed and managed by South Africans.

Subsequent to these processes, ideas were crystallised in November 2011 in the form of the National Development Plan's Vision 2030, a long-term strategic framework within which more detailed planning could take place towards the achievement of a range of overarching strategic goals by 2030. The guiding philosophy of the NDP can be summarised as a "virtuous cycle" of expanding opportunities, growth, employment and development. Indeed, in this reasoning, many of the interventions in the first economy could "only make sense in the context of a virtuous cycle of social and economic development progressing together".[36] In this approach, growth was to be accompanied by poverty alleviation interventions through an expansion of transfer payments and an extension of services by the state.

The success of the NDP has therefore depended on sustainable outcomes. The object has been to ensure particular policies and activities of priority sectors were aligned to the NDP. Unfortunately, much of the statist approach in the NDP exposed implementation weaknesses that were exploited by the state capture agenda, which entailed the looting of state resources by Zuma and a network of senior government officials.

The post-Zuma era: Ramaphosa's reforms

In 2019, National Treasury published a strategy document that also heavily used the growth diagnostic approach for its analysis and policy recommendations. However, contrary to the earlier plans, the document did not claim that the implementation of its recommendations would lead to high rates of economic growth and employment. In fact, the document's quantification section showed that the plan was likely to add only an estimated 2.3 percentage points to the baseline growth of 1.5 per cent and create one million jobs over a 10-year period, which is far short of the 10 million jobs needed.[37]

Two years later, a joint National Treasury, World Bank and IMF estimate of the impact of the National Treasury's recommendations showed that the average annual economic growth, including the baseline growth, would be 1.5 per cent between 2022 and 2026, with the unemployment rate gradually increasing to 38.3 per cent by 2026.[38] In their 2021 report for the Treasury, a team of international economists confirmed the constraints identified in the National Treasury 2019 document and basically made similar recommendations without predicting that their implementation would produce accelerated economic growth and employment.[39] On the contrary, the report included a grim outlook for the economy.

Thus, the government's long-standing conviction that the removal of binding constraints would lead to medium- to long-term accelerated economic growth and employment has, since 2019, given way to the current understanding that even with all identified constraints removed, the economy would still be stuck in low growth and high unemployment. This shift in the government's macroeconomic outlook represents a major contradiction between its earlier promise of achieving an average annual growth rate of more than 5 per cent, reducing the unemployment rate to 6 per cent and eradicating poverty by 2030, and its current expectations of low economic growth and the worsening of an already high unemployment rate over the next five years.[40]

To a large extent, the ANC government is standing at a historically important crossroads. It needs to decide whether to continue the economic views and policies of the post-2007 growth path, which the party now knows will not deliver the levels of economic growth and employment needed, or to learn from other countries that have used heterodox economic views and policies over the past 50 years to influence the working of market economies and achieved much better outcomes.

Ramaphosa, for his part, seems to have taken steps to reorientate the economic policy agenda to the pre-2007 period. His 2022 State of the Nation speech concentrated on investment and growth, the top priority being revenue to fund social grants. By 2023 there were 18 million people on social grants in South Africa. The original emphasis on BEE had essentially drawn some black professionals into wealth and propped up a small black middle class, but the distributive effects of growth had so far been unequal.

Neither fiscal nor monetary authorities have presented any evidence that the current suite of supply-side measures will improve economic and developmental outcomes. In fact, as stated earlier, the government seems to pursue the current economic policy path, knowing that on the current trajectory growth is projected to linger at 1.5 per cent and less during the 2022–2026 period and the unemployment rate is expected to rise to 38.3 per cent by 2026. Furthermore, National Treasury's projections show that policies that have been advanced to increase savings and investment, reduce government dissavings and improve the debt to GDP ratio are once again expected to disappoint.

A balance sheet of progress and challenges

Since GEAR, the government's fiscal policy strategy has pursued at least two aims: to avoid permanent increases in the overall tax burden and to use medium-term deficit targets to eliminate government dissaving. In practice, these aims have constrained the government's ability to raise taxes or borrow as part of financing the expected post-apartheid socio-economic transformation.

Fiscal policy data from the last 25 years show the implementation of this framework has been successful. According to the economist Asghar Adelzadeh, "between 1996 and 2019 the government's total annual revenue was on average equal to 24 percent of GDP, and the annual deficit to GDP ratio was on average 3 percent. That meant the size of the government's annual expenditure was on average equivalent to 27 percent of GDP." The overwhelming emphasis has been on bringing down the fiscal deficit to address low economic growth and rising unemployment, poverty and inequality.[41]

At the same time, the mainstream fiscal strategy has, in essence, been different from that proposed in the "Ready to Govern" policy document, which stated that in a democratic South Africa "the budget fits into an overall development plan".[42] Consequently, relative to OECD (Organisation for Economic Co-operation and Development) countries, the South African government has spent less on delivering public goods and services and providing social protection over the past few decades. This is contrary to the myth that South Africa had become a nanny state. It has also had a negative impact on government's ability to counterbalance the country's uneven development, poverty, and income and wealth inequality. This implies that if the government's main concern has been to eliminate government debt, it came at the cost of its ability to raise revenue. And that has significantly benefitted the country's well-off classes. In reality, this policy has been at the expense of the majority of South Africans, who have had to endure its direct negative impact.

The common argument for this policy stance has been that the greater the economy's savings, the greater its investment level. Therefore, measures that help raise savings will automatically help private investment. But the tool used to curb expenditure has been high real interest rates. Unfortunately, this monetary tool has inversely impacted on private investment and, according to some analysts, has limited investment and therefore growth.

According to official data from Statistics SA, the South African economy grew at an average annual rate of 2.8 per cent between 1996, when GEAR was introduced, and 2019, the year before the Covid-19 pandemic. During these years, the economy went through at least four periods: the GEAR extended period of 1996–2003, the ASGISA period of 2004–2007, the international financial crisis period of 2008–2009, and the NDP period of 2010–2019.

In terms of actual outcomes, the government succeeded in institutionalising restrictive fiscal and monetary policies, but the policies did not produce the promised outcomes in terms of economic growth, employment and exports. South Africa's economic growth outcome did not improve much until the ASGISA period, when the average annual real GDP growth almost doubled, from 2.8 per cent during the GEAR period (1996–2000) to 5.2 per cent between 2004 and 2007. What helped this improved outcome were significant increases in public and private expenditures. This included substantial growth in public investment, especially investment by public corporations.[43]

GEAR, to be sure, served its purpose as a stabilisation measure. It was not necessarily a redistribution strategy, but rather an emergency programme to bring the country's debt down to acceptable levels. The global economic recession of the late 2000s was a game-changer in South Africa, and led to the collapse of South Africa's non-gold real exports from a high average annual growth rate of 8.8 per cent during ASGISA to 7.3 per cent during 2008–2009.[44]

What is important to note is that, during this period, real public investment continued to grow, especially investment by public enterprises, leading once again to a strategy of fiscal restraint. As a result, during the 10-year period after the international financial crisis, the average rate of economic growth dropped to 1.7 per cent as expenditure overtook investment.

Unemployment consequently rose from 16.4 per cent in 1995 to 28.7 per cent by 2019. According to the Quarterly Labour Force Survey (QLFS), the official unemployment rate reached 35.3 per cent during the fourth quarter of 2021.[45] The largest casualty was manufacturing, which saw a drop in the total share of employment from 15.6 per cent in 1996 to 10.8 per cent in 2019.[46]

Since 2019, the South African government has embarked on a more austere version of its post-1996 macroeconomic policies. This means that the growth of the government's planned total expenditure should be below the expected rate, to cushion the blow in poverty and inequality.

So, has the ANC fulfilled its historical mission?

Cyril Ramaphosa won the ANC presidency in 2017 on a "reform, rebuild and reunite" ticket. In government, he has reformed and rebuilt – not fast enough, not nearly decisively enough, but steadily. There has been some solid progress, especially in terms of restoring the institutional independence of key agencies of the state, such as the National Prosecuting Authority and the South African Revenue Service.

Progress on economic recovery has been weak, partly as a result of externalities such as the Covid-19 pandemic and geopolitical insecurity, but also partly because of Ramaphosa's lack of strategic vision and a weak cabinet. But how much of his term can be judged by the yardstick of the ANC's rapid decline since Zuma took office in 2009? Understanding the ANC's decline has to be measured against its history, principles, traditions and vision. But it also has to be measured against the sort of adjustments that have had to be made along the party's journey towards its vision.

The present moment is one of profound crisis in the party and economy. At the ANC's 55th national conference in Nasrec in December 2022, talk of policy and ideology was conspicuously absent. The ANC is, instead, consumed by power and patronage, and the contest between those who are corrupt and those who want to do something about corruption. There has been little space for anything else.

If Ramaphosa is willing to seize the moment and sustain the momentum since he bounced back from the brink of political disaster, then he could escape the drag factor of his own party. And here we must keep in mind that his rise in 2018, in the context of the party's decline and economic ruin, was in one sense a last-ditch effort to save the party from terminal decline. In that sense his presidency has always been inseparable from the declining fortunes of the party. His successes and failings will be measured by his ability to resolve the massive economic crisis in the country and the scourge of factionalism and corruption in his party.

The final question that must be asked is whether the ANC has negotiated the transition since 1994 with the interests of historically deprived black people in mind. That is not easy to answer given the contradictions it has had to navigate. And here we need to see the party's long walk through various phases. The very establishment of the ANC was important in giving voice to the black majority in South Africa after the white-dominated Union was formed in 1910. Beyond 1994, the task was to resolve some of the pressing economic challenges inherited from the apartheid government, principally the country's massive debt.

Whether the party has managed to balance the need for investment and growth against its redistribution priorities is an evolving narrative. I want to suggest that the party's historical mission is thus a journey rather than a destination. Along the way there have been successes and failures. But, overall, the party has succeeded in creating greater inclusion. The mere fact that we can speak of a black middle class is testimony to this. I have argued earlier that the ANC's mission was always to occupy the middle ground against the radical inclinations of the left and the right-wing tendencies of those who would prefer to return the country to its racially exclusive past.

For reasons already stated, much of the policy evolution since 1994 has set the boundaries of permissible change. These changes and constraints have had unintended consequences, however. They have recast the terrain of social alliances as a basis for unity in the ANC. Meeting these challenges of dealing with the policy and political dilemmas that confront the ANC has had electoral consequences for the party and its ability to mobilise its support base.

References

Adelzadeh, A. 2022. 'Why is the South African economy stuck in chronic crises?' Applied Development Research Solutions Working Paper, May.

African National Congress. 1992. 'Ready to govern: ANC policy guideline for a democratic South Africa'. http://www.anc.org.

Dubow, S. 2000. *The African National Congress*. Johannesburg: Jonathan Ball Publishers.

Gelb, S. 2006. 'The RDP, GEAR and all that: Reflections ten years later'. *Transformation*, 62.

Jeffery, A. 2010. *Chasing the Rainbow: South Africa's Move from Mandela to Zuma*. Johannesburg: South African Institute of Race Relations.

Marais, H. 1998. *South Africa: Limits to Change – The Political Economy of Transition*. Cape Town: University of Cape Town Press.

Mbeki, T. 1998. 'Statement at opening of debate in National Assembly on "Reconciliation and Nation-Building"', Republic of South Africa.

Monyae, D. 2011. 'The liberation movement's conception of the pre-1994 South African state'. Paper presented at Mapungubwe Institute for Strategic Reflection (MISTRA), Woodmead, Johannesburg.

Mthethwa, R.M. 2011. 'New growth path and the transformations of the ANC government policy'. *New Agenda, South African Journal of Social and Economic Policy*, 43 (Third Quarter).

National Planning Commission. 2012. National Development Plan, launch speech by Trevor Manuel, 15 August.

Nattrass, N. 2011. 'The new growth path: Game changing vision or cop-out?' School of Economics, University of Cape Town.

The Presidency. 2009. Green Paper: National Strategic Planning. Pretoria: South Africa.

3

Thirty years of attempting to dismantle racism and build a society based on human rights

Sihle Booi with Tshepo Madlingozi

Having been born and raised in Ngangelizwe township, one of the most dangerous areas in Mthatha, I do not need academic research to explain the irony in the means employed by people in spatial dumps to achieve a minimum semblance of decent human living. I grew up with a brother who was thug, a gangster. Sizwe, my brother, believed that the only way to protect and provide for his family was through Darwin's law of the jungle; meaning that it's either you ate or got eaten. In a notebook letter he wrote to our mother, he emphasised the "inevitable poverty-stricken future of our family", that we could never rise above the destiny the white men designed for us unless we became criminals according to "umthetho wabelunu".

According to my big brother, our world would remain the same, the law would always be a weapon against the poor and black, and those born poor would grow old in the squalor. Sizwe was the perfect social paradox in that he was a savagely kind man. People loved and feared him, but I only loved him and hated his perspective of a hopeless static world.

So I spent most of my life trying to prove my brother wrong and show my family that we could rise above the fate that apartheid fashioned for us, and that 1994 was a testament that we, the people, could change the status quo.

To mention a few black-student-relevant struggles I faced at the University of the Witwatersrand (Wits), I spent half of 2016 sleeping in libraries and study rooms, would go a day without a meal, and could hardly make to it to class. Eight years after Sizwe's death, I found myself living his philosophy that says that "the system will never let us be better unless we make it fear us". So, I gave myself to the Fees Must Fall (FMF) cause.

I was one of only four jail support team members. Our job was to ensure that every FMF detainee was known and provided with legal representation. This job was traumatising. Me and the other female student had to endure sexual harassment from the police when we were just trying to get basic details of FMF-related detainees.

It seemed the post-1994 police have not changed. I remember one incident very well when it seemed to me that those police officers were ready to pull the "He fell from the ninth floor" stance, as so viscerally captured in Christ van Wyk's 1980s protest poem 'In Detention'.

I remember how one day we found Khanya Cekeshe at the Hillbrow Police Station. We had just got a window to show a parent to their detained child when Cekeshe saw me walking past the holding cells through a cell window and shouted out my name. The police had denied that there were still FMF activists without representation in their precinct, yet Khanya had been there for more than three days, being denied his rights, including making a single phone call. Khanya is an FMF activist who was arrested (for FMF protest-related activities) in 2017 and sentenced to eight years in prison, three of which were suspended. He was released on parole in 2019; the only FMF activist who was arrested and sentenced to imprisonment for over a year. We had got acquainted during the Wits FMF protest disruptions, and we later realised that we actually grew up in the same church. This whole FMF ordeal reminded me of my brother's view of the country's governance, that it only sought to exalt those already in power and suppress those without power until they resorted to crime.

As I let go of my dignity and gave in to sexual harassment, from the police who are meant to protect me, in order to obtain the basic details of fellow FMF detainees, I was reminded that the police worked to defend and protect the government against the governed. I reconciled that the current justice system, from the courts to law enforcement, is informed by the predecessor regime, thus its sought outcome is inevitably to win against black bodies.

In summary, it became clear that the system was not designed for a Ngangelizwe-born and -bred youth. A strong motivation to pursue studies in law was to avenge my brother's brutal death. He had been shot dead; the killer was known, but the case just disappeared, and the killer walked free. I wanted to personally see the case reopened and the killer arrested. I also wanted to use the law to prosecute crimes committed against neglected communities such as Ngangelizwe. However, the FMF experience; watching the law being sophisticatedly interpreted to protect institutions against vulnerable human beings; and reading media headlines exaggerating and overstating the number of white students who were against the FMF protest while the black students were branded as hooligans for making use of the only resort (protesting) they had to be heard, significantly changed my motivation. I had realised that transitional justice had failed in its accountability and restoration project, and I became fixated on changing the laws themselves because how could I be comfortable with ambiguous laws that could – with some money, ignorant arrogance and a twang – be interpreted as weapons to silence, violate and destroy the very people it purports to protect.

I believe in connecting the legal and social consciousness to shape the law into a vessel of true peace and harmony, not an illusion of reconciliation or an agent of tolerance without respect. I do not wish for more FMF protests, but for a legal regime that eradicates injustice from its root so we may begin to see a real change of the status quo, where Sizwe is fortunately proven wrong; the police identify as members of communities; the law is used for and not against the people; Ngangelizwe is not an isolated squalor but a recognised and dignified community with dignified homes and families; and dignity is not only afforded to the beneficiary-communities of previously racist regimes.

We, the oppressed and the privileged races, need to address oppressions of the oppressed and marginalised, and the marginalised within marginalised races through open and positive dialoguing as encouraged by the Social Harmony Through National Effort (SHiNE). I believe that the police, correctional services and the general republic would find understanding and harmony through SHiNE and facilitate a series of open and positive conversations about the relations between the law and the people who ought to be the beneficiaries of the law and law enforcement. Until the law is changed to reflect the voices and protect the true needs of its society as echoed by its diverse communities, and until racism is treated as the pandemic that endures today instead of some shadow of the past, we will continue to be a racially divided country dancing to the old school tunes of apartheid in contemporary sneakers that grasp firm to the foundations of colonisation.

In 1994, this historical settler colony went through an internationally acclaimed process of transition to democracy and adopted an interim constitution that guaranteed civil and political rights as well as socio-economic rights to all. These processes were followed by the establishment of the Truth and Reconciliation Commission (TRC) in 1996. However, as this article will show, these processes and mechanisms were not decolonising acts and processes, and thus did not go to the root causes of historical atrocities.

This paper argues that though the current legal system needs some reform, the project of eradicating racism and its consequences requires a social reform too. While the laws can modify overt conduct, it does not always change attitudes and/or covert behaviours. This article identifies the South African Human Rights Commission's Social Harmony Through National Effort (SHiNE) initiative as a measure through which the nation can pierce through the legally fostered hardware of our moral fiber, and into the software of innate humanity. These assertions will be substantiated by a brief discussion of the preservation of racism, the contemporary state of racial injustice in South Africa (SA), the failure of the transitional justice process, and the recommendations that transcend reliance on deterrence through fear of the punishing law.

The preservation of racism

The notion and socially accepted pretence that racism was only a legal system that can be resolved by amending and repealing apartheid laws is one of the major preservers of racism. This diverts attention from interpersonal racism and the fact that people did not experience racism from the papers on which the laws were written but from the people who implemented the laws that were written by other people in the first place.[1] Systems are created by people, thus it is imperative to pierce through the "structure, system, or regime" veil to reach the human architectures and sustainers of racism.

Treating the pervasive internalised oppressive view of self by the dispossessed as a superfluous appendage to "the system" is an impediment to substantive anti-racism projects.[2] This results in only dealing with the overt racism and not the internalised racism perspectives. Moreover, it ignores the need to create spaces for both victims and perpetrators to honestly speak about their views on and experiences of racism.[3]

The elites' inability, or more accurately unwillingness, to deal with the afterlives of colonialism makes SA an effective preserver of racism and its atrocities.[4] The failure to recognise that the root cause of the recurrence of racially charged crimes and racial discrimination against Black Africans is the unfinished business of colonialism and colonisation means the people in positions to reform the country have only been scratching the surface of the problem.[5] Racism, ethnic discrimination and other inequality crimes that were accentuated by apartheid were the logical consequences of this original sin.

It follows, therefore, that to uproot racism and thus the other inequality and discrimination conducts that flow therefrom, there is a need to propose solutions that dismantle the totality of the colonising structure. After all, as Patrick Wolfe, the Australian scholar of settler colonialism, reminds us: "invasion is a structure and not an event".[6]

The law has always been a crucial tool in enforcing, protecting and maintaining racist societies since the advent of colonisation; therefore, the law can also be crucial in dismantling racism.[7] However, SA's democratic legal system suffers the fatal flaw of being conceived from the very legal regime it sought to eradicate.[8] South Africa still has several statutes that are amendments of the old regime and still carry parts of the anti-Black people spirit and implications. This is also seen in the lack of emphasis on the principles of Ubuntu, as understood by the Black community, in the Constitution of the country.[9]

This article proposes that in the case of SA and other historical settler colonies, the main recommendation to effectively dissolve the racial tensions and mitigate the brewing risk of the recurrence of atrocity crimes is a comprehensive and intentional programme of decolonisation, including what can be referred to as the three Rs of decolonisation: restitution-reparation-redress.

Racism in contemporary SA

The indoctrination of inferiority and superiority complexes remains today.[10] Though the victims of legally entrenched racism knew the racist treatment they suffered was unjust, they were accustomed to the stratifications. The people felt superior and inferior according to the racial stratification that defined the social, economic and political design of the society.[11] Today, there are no laws that overtly create such a hierarchy, but people experience it and know it exists.

The social and political racism that exists today is a result of taught and learnt attitudes, whether deliberately or subconsciously.[12] In its *Information Sheet on Hate Speech*, the South African Human Rights Commission (SAHRC) reported complaints of racist hate speech to have constituted the highest number of overall complaints received in 2016–2017 and Black people are often at the receiving end of racial slurs because all the other races believe themselves to be above the Black race.

Though the democratic South African laws continue to codify provisions that prohibit racism, people, especially white South Africans, continue to harbour racist beliefs and they find ways to covertly exclude non-white people from their spaces through, for example, "access reserved" policies in establishments they own or making Afrikaans the medium of instruction in schools, thereby substantively excluding Black children from accessing education in their schools.

In a study composed by *The Journal of Southern African Studies,* one finding demonstrated how "from 1994 to 2014, the proportion of Black workers occupied in positions considered 'skilled' rose by 3%, a rise which appears paltry compared to the 19% increase in the proportion of white workers in skilled positions".[13]

Income distribution is still mediated by gender and race. In 2015, the average annual income of male-headed households was double that of female-headed households.[14] In 2015, 'the annual median expenditure for whites was more than ten times higher than that of Black Africans'.[15] A recent Human Rights Watch[16] study found that "87 percent of Black

African, 81 percent of coloured, and 58 percent of Indian/Asian older people received means-tested social security entitlements in 2020, compared to only 30 percent of white older people."

Chatterjee, Czajka, and Gethin[17] conclude that "despite having a progressive constitution and policy mandate, post-apartheid democratic society seems to have reproduced inequality along the same [racial] lines". A study by the state-funded Human Science Research Council (HSRC) effectively concluded that the lives of many (nominally) South African citizens, "remain constituted as bare life, disempowered and … 'marginal' to society…".[18]

A *Geographical Review* journal article found that "some 80% of children in Cape Town continue to attend schools intended for their race group under apartheid … most such schools have poor resources and have enjoyed little improvement in their facilities since the end of apartheid".[19] Here, the detrimental legacy of the apartheid era persists. Quality of education and inadequate access to educational facilities and resources disproportionately affect Black communities throughout the nation.

These inequities, alongside poor access to quality healthcare benefits, perpetuate the cycle of poverty and further exacerbate the detriments of SA's socio-economic discrepancies. The legacy of forced removals is obvious. All races predominantly remain in the areas in which previous racist systems placed them.[20]

Black people, without ownership of and economic means to afford to purchase land in economically conducive areas, remain in inner-city informal settlements and township squalor when not confined in economically barren rural areas.[21] These areas are often characterised by, *inter alia*, poverty, lack of public and private investment, environmental racism, and social stress.[22] These residents' protest of the structural violence of their surroundings is met with physical violence by the police force and private security.

Abahlali baseMjondolo/the Shack Dwellers Movement of South Africa, the largest social movement of impoverished people, do not recognise "Democratic SA", rather they view it as a state of Unfreedom, and they explain it as follows:

Twenty years after apartheid we live like pigs in the mud, our children die of diarrhoea, we are forced into transit camps at gunpoint, the police beat and shoot us in the streets and the assassins kill us with impunity. If we stand up and demand that our humanity is recognised, we are removed from the housing list and placed on the death list.[23]

They view black political leaders [black colonialists] as the political leaders who have internalised their historical oppressors' mode of thinking and governance.[24]

The internalised racial inferiority is a significant contributor to the constant xenophobic attacks against Black and other non-white non-nationals. In 2022, three UN Special Rapporteurs released a joint statement raising alarm about increasing xenophobic sentiments in SA. These xenophobic sentiments and sometimes physical xenophobic attacks are often perpetrated by Black South Africans. The UN Special Rapporteurs warned that xenophobic sentiments had reached fever proportions with self-styled vigilante groups openly conducting raids against "illegal migrants".[25]

It is important to point out the racial element to xenophobia as SA's xenophobic sentiments and attacks are mostly reserved for black non-nationals. It is also worth noting that Black South Africans have sometimes been victims of xenophobia because their skin is "too dark"; in the words of Michael Neocosmos,[26] they are treated like "native foreigners". It is on this basis that some commentators choose to refer to this form of discrimination as Afrophobia or a "new racism".[27]

In July 2021, social unrest broke out in two of the nine provinces of SA and resulted in deaths of more than 350 people and thousands injured. While there were many factors fuelling the unrest, the racial tension was apparent in the racially charged Phoenix massacre when war broke out between Indian people and Black people.

Persisting racial injustice and the failure to address historical injustices have an obvious impact on the state of race relations. Mutual mistrust, fear, and in some instances, antipathy continue. A 2021 annual Reconciliation Barometer carried out by the Institute for Justice Reconciliation (IJR) found that 72 per cent of respondents said that SA is still in need of reconciliation.[28]

The irony of the South African transitional justice process

This section analyses the impact of SA's transitional justice through the Truth and Reconciliation Commission (TRC). It highlights a few ironies, such as the further reconfirmation of white privilege as the white perpetrators benefitted the most out of the process while some victims were retraumatised.

The recourse availed to the fortunate few was not enough. It seems the process achieved its shallow reconciliation at the expense of victims and, as a result, the dissatisfaction of the victims looms over the young democracy as feelings of betrayal by their own government threaten to shatter the thin glass of forced social reconciliation. The following subsections highlight a few aspects in which the process did not provide substantive justice for the victims of racism.

- **Satisfaction**: Some victims felt better because they received official recognition and public acknowledgment after years of denial of their victimisation. However, because the focus was really on the stability and reconciliation of elites (and thus a perpetrator-centric process), many felt that their tears and testimonies served to legitimise the elite compromise. The victims' wounds were opened without any balm being put to soothe them. While perpetrators got amnesty immediately, victims had to wait for many, many years for financial restitution. Furthermore, there were only a handful of cases of victim-perpetrator reconciliation. This is in addition to the more significant fact that because of its focus on individual harms, the TRC did not enable social reconciliation.[29]
- **Rehabilitation**: More than ten years after the end of the TRC hearings, Khulumani members reported that they still had bullets in their bodies, they continued to need wheelchairs and prosthetic equipment, and their psychosocial needs remained unmet.[30]
- **Guarantee of non-repetition**: The culture of impunity continues because perpetrators who did not go to the TRC have not been held to account or prosecuted.
- **Restitution**: Only 8 per cent of the land has been redistributed; poverty is still endemic and black; and SA is the most unequal country in the world.
- **Compensation**: Only a once-off pay-out of R30 000 was given to

victims of human rights abuses. This was only made to those victims fortunate enough to be determined to have been victims by the TRC. The state still operates based on this "closed list" in making decisions about which victims to help. This means that victims and survivors who did not go to the TRC are excluded. The TRC recommended a programme of community reparations for the worst affected communities; this has not been done to date.

What is to be done?

A comprehensive and multi-layered decolonisation programme would have addressed the afterlives of conquest and colonisation, including ongoing land dispossession, white supremacy and institutionalised racism, internalised racism, and cultural subjugation and epistemicide.

This view has been supported by several contemporary resistance movements, such as the #RhodesMustFall and #FeesMustFall that emphasised the need to decolonise universities, and eventually society. As Gillespie and Naidoo[31] put it: "Black students' protest was against their own alienation inside the white institution, but also against their assimilation as the new elites into a society that remains stuck in white institutional time." Students thus understood that in SA racial capitalism was still the primary mode of oppression. This meant that the struggle to decolonise universities and society had to confront both white supremacy and socio-economic marginalisation.[32]

There is no closed list of measures that can effectively contribute to building a true national cohesion and social harmony; however, this paper will highlight two. One is the scary consideration of amending the "best" democratic constitution in the world and the other is focus and investment in programmes that bridge the gap between the legal system that mostly fosters tolerance and the real attitudes that govern the realities of social communities.

Amendment of the Constitution

- Amend the preamble of the Constitution to make it explicit that the Constitution responds to and seeks to dismantle the legacies of colonialism and apartheid. This will become the guiding spirit for interpreting the Constitution.

- As it currently stands the Constitution does not mention colonialism, conquest or apartheid at all. The Constitution only talks about "conflict of the past", thereby minimising the odious legacy of the monstrous colonialism and the perverse apartheid.
- Amend the property clause to make it explicitly clear that the state can expropriate land without compensation.
- The current clause is not clear on this issue and has thus been interpreted in the spirit of "willing buyer-willing seller". This has hamstrung land restitution and land redistribution.
- Introduce Ubuntu as a fundamental value of the Constitution.
- A constitution is a mirror of society. The majority of South Africans – Black people – don't see themselves when they look at the Constitution, an overwhelmingly EuroAmerican liberal document. Introducing Ubuntu will go a long way to countering ongoing epistemicide.

An amendment of the Constitution would enable a safe space to effectively consider other measures such as, *inter alia*, wealth tax levied in respect of beneficiaries of apartheid and colonisation (white people) as a start of reparative justice to dismantling white privilege and a way of demonstrating penance; Africanisation of formal education curricular; prosecution of perpetrators who did not seek or obtain amnesty from the TRC; means for substantive acknowledge of and reparations for victims and survivors of apartheid; and reform of the rest of the legal system to ensure substantive and equitable access to justice.

Endorse and resource of the SAHRC's social harmony through national effort

- The TRC did not move the country towards social reconciliation. Studies show that racial groups and various ethnic groups continue to grapple with mistrust and sometimes antipathy. The state needs to emphasise the value of initiatives that seek to create and promote a culture of social cohesion through the lens of human rights. The SAHRC SHiNE initiative, which seeks to use positive dialoguing to foster harmony in our diversity, is one such initiative. Integral to SHiNE is the overarching principle of Ubuntu as the initiatives seeks to remind everybody, including, among others, law makers, implementers of the law, those governed by the law and those who carry out the mandate of the Constitution in their respective public institutions, that we are because of others and the success of one is not mutually exclusive from that of another.

- SHiNE is foregrounded on the following principles:
- **Self-reflection** – SHiNE encourages people to engage in self-reflection practices to realise their own contributions to the state of disharmony in their surroundings, and take independent responsibility to play an active role in building national harmony.
- **The creation/maintenance of healthy families** – SHiNE recognises the role played by families in the creation or maintenance of healthy societies and therefore promotes that care is taken to promote healthy family life through regular hosting of family meetings. This fosters healthy family relations and conflict resolutions to avoid domestic ills such as, among others, gender-based violence.
- **Sharing stories** – sharing stories is a form of positive dialogue that invokes empathy, understanding, respect instead of tolerance, and love for one another. It fosters a culture of respect for inherent human dignity, acknowledging, understanding and appreciating the diverse backgrounds that shape the human being. It encourages the recognition of synergies within our diversities instead of highlighting what sets us apart.
- It is a fundamental instrument in creating, in addition to legal obedience, a culture of internalised respect and appreciation for human rights. It finds relevance in all social environments such as schools, churches, workplaces, special homes such as centres for older person, etc. It can be translated in, among other codification instruments, policies, formal education curricula, social context training materials and pedagogies. It seeks to change attitudes so that the sought outcome isn't a compromise of coexistence but the desire to live together in harmony.

Conclusion

The case of SA makes it clear that recommendations focused on the achievement and maintenance of liberal peace, a transitional justice process whose overwhelming focus is individual harms and repair, and whose constitutional rearrangements and framework do not seek to dismantle coloniality of power, coloniality of knowledge, and coloniality of being are not enough to address the racism and the threat of recurrence of crimes against humanity it poses.

Moreover, while enforcement of tolerance is crucial for the protection of vulnerable groups, people often commit crimes in fits of rage or when they do not think anyone is watching. This makes a simultaneous and equal focus on both the legal reform and the human reform imperative. The ultimate goal should not just be progressive laws, but also a society whose moral fibre generates, within its people, an organic respect for humanity. As discussed in this article, people create the systems. The desired change in people will translate in the desired change of the system.

References

Abahlali baseMjondolo. 2006, April 27. 'Unfreedom Day! No freedom for the poor! Why we mourn on April 27th'. http://abahlali.org/node/123/.

Adams, M., Bell, L.A. and Griffin, P. 1997. *Teaching for diversity and social justice: A sourcebook*. New York: Routledge.

Addae, D. and Quan-Baffour, K.P. 2022. 'Afrophobia, "black on black" violence and the new racism in South Africa: The nexus between adult education and mutual co-existence.' *Cogent Social Sciences*, 8(1):1–13.

Barolsky, Vanessa. 2012. '"A better life for all", social cohesion and the governance of life in post-apartheid South Africa'. *Social Dynamics*, 38(1)"134–151.

Bou Zeineddine, F. and Leach, C.W. 2021. 'Feeling and thought in collective action on social issues: Toward a systems perspective'. *Social and Personality Psychology Compass*, 15(7), Article e12622. https://doi.org/10.1111/spc3.12622

Byrne, C. 2010. *All that was lost: Apartheid violence – Thirty TRC participants speak*. Benoni: Sheron Printers.

Chatterjee, A., Czajka, L. and Gethin, A. 2020, April. *Estimating the Distribution of Household Wealth in South Africa*. Wits University. https://www.wits.ac.za/media/wits-university/faculties-and-schools/

commerce-law-and-management/research-entities/scis/documents/Estimating%20the%20Distribution%20of%20Household%20Wealth%20in%20South%20Africa.pdf

Department of Human Settlements, *Annual Report* 2019/2020.

Gillespie, K. and Naidoo, L. 2019. 'Between the Cold War and the fire: The student movement, anti-assimilation, and the question of the future in South Africa'. *South Atlantic Quarterly,* 118(1):226–239.

Institute for Justice and Reconciliation. 2021. South African Reconciliation Barometer Survey: 2021 Report. https://www.ijr.org.za/home/wp-content/uploads/2021/12/IJR_SA-Reconciliation-Barometer-2021.pdf

Jeske, C. 2018. 'Why work? Do we understand what motivates work-related decisions in South Africa?' *Journal of Southern African Studies*, 44(1).

Leach, C.W. 2021. 'Sentiments of the dispossessed: Emotions of resilience and resistance'. Routledge Handbook of Prejudice, *Stereotyping & Discrimination*.

Lemon, A. and Battersby-Lennard, J. 2009. 'Overcoming the Apartheid Legacy in Cape Town Schools', *Geographical Review*, 9(4):520–521.

Madlingozi, T. 2007. 'Good victims, bad victims: Apartheid beneficiaries, victims and the struggle for social justice'. In *Law, Memory & Apartheid: Ten Years after Azapo v President of South Africa*, edited by Wessel Le Roux and Karin van Marle. Pretoria: PULP.

Mamdani, M. 2002. 'Amnesty or impunity? A preliminary critique of the report of the truth and reconciliation commission of South Africa (TRC)', *Diacritics*, 32(3/4).

Mdlalose, B. 2012. 'Marikana shows that we are living in a democratic prison', 22 September 2012. http://abahlali.org/node/9061/

Neocosmos, Michael. 2006. *From 'Foreign Natives' to 'Native Foreigners': Explaining Xenophobia in Post-apartheid South Africa*. Senegal: CODESRIA.

Nkosi, T. and Mahlako, N. 2020. 'Are courts going out of their way to accommodate racists? A critique of South African Revenue Service v Commission for Conciliation, Mediation and Arbitration and Others'. *Law, Democracy and Development*, 24:338–363. https://dx.doi.org/10.17159/2077-4907/2020/ldd.v24.14

Oelofsen, Rianna. 2015. 'Decolonisation of the African mind and intellectual landscape'. *Phronimon*, 16(2):130–146.

Socio-Economic Rights Institute of South Africa (SERI). 2018. 'Informal settlements and human rights in South Africa submission to the United Nations Special Rapporteur on adequate housing as a component of the right to an adequate standard of living', *OHCHR*.

Statistics South Africa. 2019. 'Inequality trends in South Africa: A multidimensional diagnostic of inequality.' http://www.Stats SA.gov. za/publications/Report-03-10-19/Report-03-10-192017.pdf

Stuurman, S. 2017. 'Student activism in a time of a crisis in South Africa: The quest for "black power"'. *South African Journal of Education*, 38(4):1–8.

Toivonen, A. and Seremani, T. 2021. 'The enemy within: The legitimating role of local managerial elites in the global managerial colonization of the Global South'. *Organization*, 28(5):798–816.

Wijeyesinghe, Charmaine L., Griffin, Pat and Love, Barbara. 1997. 'Racism-Curriculum Design', in *Teaching for Diversity and Social Justice*, edited by Maurianne Adams, Lee Anne Bell and Pat Griffin. New York and London: Routledge.

Wolfe P. 2006. 'Settler Colonialism and the Elimination of the Native', *Journal of Genocide Research*, 8(4): 387–409.

4

Thirty years on, what will it take for South Africa to be a truly developmental state?

Gilbert Motsaathebe

The concept of a developmental state has gained currency in South Africa – a country that is constantly being referred to as a developmental state by politicians. As a concept, the developmental state has a long history, dating back to the protectionist measures of Germany and other now-developed countries, orchestrated to promote infant industries with the potential ultimately to compete with British manufacturing supremacy. Japan and Latin American countries have also had their version of developmentalism in which they used commercial state-owned entities to pursue the objectives of the developmental state. President Jacob Zuma set the tone in endorsing South Africa as a developmental state in his 2008 (8 January) speech in which he said, "South Africa as a developmental state should maintain its strategic role in shaping the key sectors of the economy."[1]

Zuma's pronouncement was important in hegemonising the idea of a developmental state as a key agenda for the nation. Hegemony is about gaining some level of consent through ideological manipulation. According to Gramsci's Theory of Hegemony, to remain unchallenged, the ideas of the dominant have to be seen as a norm. In that sense, then, the pronouncement by the state president is an important part of an ideological hegemony to desensitise others. The concept has since become a common slogan in many strategic documents, including the National Development Plan (NDP). Mkandawire[2] concurs in highlighting that "the elite must be able to establish an ideological hegemony so that its developmental project becomes, in a Gramscian sense, a hegemonic project to which key actors in the nation adhere voluntarily".

For a long time, it was clear that the South African government was unwavering in its conviction that South Africa would achieve its developmental goals. This sort of commitment forms key indices that dovetail with Mkandawire's[3] assertion that "a developmental state is essentially one whose ideological underpinning is developmentalist in that it conceives its mission as that of ensuring economic development, usually interpreted to mean high rates of accumulation and industrialisation". However, there have been other attenuating factors that greatly obliterated the country's grand developmental agenda.

Recent contributors to the literature on the developmental state in the South African context include scholars such as Bond,[4] Ukwandu,[5] Hendrickse,[6] Mhone[7] and Mkandawire.[8] However, these studies do not detail what must be done for the country to be a truly developmental state. By studying the notion of a developmental state from a South African perspective exactly three decades after South Africa's democratic dispensation, the study contributes to the knowledge about how South Africa is fearing in its quest to deal with past inequalities and the economic deprivation of the black majority and put the country on a firm developmental trajectory. The next section clarifies the concept of a developmental state together with the notion of developmentalism to provide a compressible theoretical framework for the study. The literature review will also be embedded in this section. The methodology will then be outlined before focusing on the discussions and the findings.

Developmental state defined

Typically, a developmental state is one that deliberately uses the country's resources profitably to uplift the living conditions of its people. Such a state is characterised by progressive policies geared towards capacitating state enterprises not only to grow the economy but also to capacitate its citizens economically. Following the double tragedy of colonialism and apartheid that economically disposed the black majority, South Africa tried a variety of measures to level the playing field and improve the lives of all South Africans. This view is in line with a developmental agenda as obtained in the following assertion:

> A developmental state plays an active role in guiding economic development and using the resources of the country to meet the needs of the people. A developmental state tries to balance economic growth and social development. It uses state resources and state influence to attack poverty and expand economic opportunities.[9]

From its National Development Plan, South Africa wanted to restructure the economy to ensure that all South Africans benefit in a meaningful way. However, all the policies that the country put in place ever since its democratic dispensation appear to have benefitted only a few people who have become the elite. This failure has been widely acknowledged by political leaders. In his speech marking the fifth anniversary of the adoption of the National Development Plan in 2017, former president Jacob Zuma said that the country's efforts have "not fundamentally transformed the structure and ownership patterns of the economy. Too many people who need jobs to support themselves and their families are still unemployed. The fruits of the economic growth that we have experienced since the advent of our freedom in 1994 have tended to be enjoyed by a few."[10] This means the country is still struggling to bring about inclusive economic growth. The country wanted to provide direction for economic development to meet the country's drive to ensure that the yields are distributed for the benefit of all South Africans. Capable state-owned enterprises (SOEs) were earmarked for this purpose. This is again supported by the assertion that "a developmental state must be able to direct and support economic development through building a strong public service, creating an investor-friendly environment, supporting small business development, using state-owned enterprises effectively and driving strategic investment initiatives".[11]

The role of parastatals in South Africa

The role of parastatals in developing countries has been widely recognised.[12] There is no doubt that once fully realised, the country's drive to become a developmental state will provide opportunities for economic growth and expansion for business and investment for organisations operating within the current context of rapid economic development. In an ideal set-up, this should enable companies, particularly SOEs, to become efficient and contribute to the state's developmental goals. This would enable the country to ultimately address the triple challenges of poverty, unemployment and inequality. However, South Africa's attempt to follow the Asian Tiger example by using parastatals to build a strong economy has not been successful. According to the Presidency Annual Report of 2021, many of the country's parastatals suffered underperformance or total loss-making as they had no "sound internal control environments and effective governance structures and processes in place".[13]

To succeed, the country needs robust and efficient SOEs which should help the country to turn the situation around. However, currently, state-owned enterprises experience problems and have typically become a liability to the state. As a result, the state has not succeeded in translating its programmes into tangible projects to address the country's triple challenges due to multiple factors that include corruption, poor leadership within parastatals and various spheres of government. As the Education Training Unit explains:

> The developmental state's technical capacity is its ability to translate broad objectives into programmes and projects and to ensure their implementation. Economic growth and development need high-quality and reliable government services – ranging from water and sewage to electricity generation, to transport and spatial planning.

Because the country is very distinct in terms of its political, cultural and economic orientation, SOEs operating in that context would need efficient leadership who share the views of the state to successfully establish and nurture bankable organisations that directly support the country's developmental agenda. It is argued in this study that an understanding of the agility critical for fostering SOEs' success in this specific context will put the country in good stead for its pursuit of socio-economic transformation as part of its developmental requirements.[14]

Using insights derived from developmentalism, this chapter attempts to imagine what it would take for the country to become a truly developmental state focusing on its ailing SOEs that should help the country create jobs and contribute to the economy.

Developmentalism

Developmentalism is seen as crucial because it provides a compressible context for the issues raised in this study and therefore needs to be discussed from the onset to keep issues raised in the study in a more comprehensible context. Mhone[15] sees developmentalism as a "proactive role of the State in pursuing and defining a developmental vision to be attained in the long-term, in coordinating economic activities and steering them toward desired outcomes, mobilising and synergising class and social forces in support of the developmental agenda". The concept of a developmental state is especially critical in understanding social, political and economic intricacies within which organisations operate, and which ultimately have a bearing on the success of an organisation. It contributes to our understanding of ensuring sound financial management and the application of good corporate governance principles that are both progressive in terms of the bottom line and political peremptoriness.

Typically, the developmentalism process starts with a country undergoing economic reforms. During this period the country invests in building new and sustaining existing industrial production capabilities as in the case of South Africa. Naturally, as more new industrial production capacity is built, new national knowledge and intellectual property (IP) are created, bringing with it new innovative, often technology-based know-how. During this period human capital is developed and with time it becomes sophisticated. At the same time, the lives of ordinary people are improved in terms of access to basic services like water, electricity and health, for example. All these developments are some of the hallmarks of South Africa's developmental agendas as the country has been hard at work to prioritise these as part of its service delivery.

The industrialisation process will continue until a certain point of maturity is achieved and the process of industrialisation slows down.

At this maturity point, the country will have built enough industrial production capacity to sustain future capacity requirements, as in the case of the so-called Asian Tigers, namely Hong Kong, Taiwan, Singapore and South Korea, regarded as some of the world's most advanced economies.

In addition to political pronouncements, as highlighted elsewhere in this study, I rely also on the Human Development Index to characterise South Africa as a developmental state. According to the HD Index as used by the United Nations in ranking countries, South Africa does not fall under the developed countries. Although South Africa has been a leading country in Africa both economically and politically for a considerable number of years,[16] it is still seen as having a mixed economy and, for this reason, it is sometimes labelled as an emerging country as it is assumed to fall somewhere between developing and developed countries, hence the developmental state.

Linked to the foregoing, therefore, this study ultimately hopes to propose a distinct model of developmentalism that can anchor the socio-economic transformation in South Africa. From the above summation, one can safely posit the following as major constituents of a developmental state:

- Strong political will
- Ideological hegemony – clear ideological stance
- Tacit developmental planning
- Industrialisation
- Human capital development.

It is posited that a combination of skilful leadership and a good business model is critical for the success of entrepreneurial ventures in an emerging market. Teece's assertion[17] that "a good business model yields value propositions that are compelling to customers, achieves advantageous cost and risk structures, and enables significant value capture by the business that generates and delivers products and services" supports the study's contention as highlighted above.

Methodological framework

This qualitative study makes use of specific cases like the South African Broadcasting Corporation (SABC), the South African Airways (SAA) and the country's power utility the Electricity Supply Commission (Eskom). All these organisations have a history of dismal performance and have had to be bailed out by the government time and again. These companies are regarded as critical case studies in this research because of their relevance to the problem investigated in this study. As Flyvbjerg[18] asserts, "[a] critical case is defined as having strategic importance to the general problem". Thus, the case studies are also expected to offer insights into managing SOEs successfully for them to contribute to the country's developmental agenda.

Data used

The various methods used to gather data for this chapter include literature reviews of published materials, including public protectors' reports, annual financial results, auditors' reports, government policies, journals and newspaper articles. The key interest in perusing such material is to discern from the material evidence of the selected companies' efficiency that contributes to their veracity to assist or negate the state's efforts towards a developmental state. The data will be critically examined and thematised to paint a clear picture emerging from the data. As such, for its empirical base, the study focuses on the three parastatals in South Africa that have been rocked by problems of leadership and a depressed bottom line in South Africa.

A cursory review of the performances of the selected cases and issues they grapple with

The first company, the South African Broadcasting Corporation (SABC) is the country's public broadcaster. The corporation is often in the headlines due to its habitual problems. These problems include a flurry of leadership crises characterised by resignations and firing of top management at the corporation. For instance, the broadcaster's former Group CEO, Lulama Mokhobo, resigned early in 2014 just two years into her five-year term after being appointed by former communications minister Dina Pule.[19] Then there was a report that revealed that the broadcaster's Acting Group Chief Operating Officer Hlaudi Motsoeneng did not have a matric. Motsoeneng was also marred by allegations of improper conduct and maladministration (Public Protector's Report, 2014). The Public Protector found him guilty of misrepresentation of his qualifications, abuse of power and improper conduct in the appointments and salary increments of various employees.

The corporation's management was required to present a turnaround strategy that was ultimately approved by Parliament's Portfolio Committee on Communications. Among the issues of concern at the SABC at the time were the company's handling of financial irregularities exposed by both the Auditor-General and the Special Investigative Unit and the concerns about unfilled top management positions, including the vacant positions of the GCEO, the Chief Operations Officer and the Chief Financial Officer. The chairperson of SAA, Dudu Myeni, was also implicated in controversial leadership decisions.

Apart from these acute problems, the organisation habitually struggles to generate a healthy bottom line. For example, in its 2022/2023 annual report, the corporation recorded a net loss of R1.13 billion. The cash reserves consequently decreased by R709 million, which marked a whopping 60 per cent increase compared to the R300 million recorded in the previous year.

The second company is state-owned national carrier, South African Airways (SAA). It has equally been marred by troubles, which includes an operating loss of over R12 billion in capital over the past few years, failure to pay bonuses to employees, an unqualified audit opinion for the 2011/12 financial year, irregular expenditure, and fruitless and wasteful expenditure amounting to millions of rands. As a result, the government had to approve a loan of R5 billion (US$600 million) to the cash-strapped carrier in 2012, to enable it to continue operations. The company was also required to develop a turnaround strategy to be approved by the Minister of Public Enterprises in agreement with the Minister of Finance.

The company was also badly managed and relinquished some of its lucrative international routes due to what has been described as political interference related to state capture.[20] Tough competition from well-managed private airlines also presented a big challenge for the state-owned airline. The business model of some of these airlines meant that they could offer cheaper flights in what is often referred to as budget airlines, completely outshining SAA, which was still expensive compared to these new airlines.

As a result, the past few years saw the company recording significant losses. It accumulated over R9 billion in debts. By 2020, the financial situation was out of control. As Wasserman[21] wrote at the time, "SAA is on its knees – it doesn't have enough cash to pay staff or keep its planes in the air for much longer, and government is currently scrambling to borrow R2 billion to keep it going." The company was ultimately put under business rescue. According to Ensor in 2023, from 2019 to 2022 the airline made losses in each year totalling a combined R23.5 billion. According to this source, the airline's 2022/23 annual financial statements were still being audited by the Auditor-General and only expected later in 2024.

The third company, Eskom (the Electricity Supply Commission of South Africa) has equally been marred by troubles and is often blamed for the sluggish economic growth in the country. Its problems include failure to deliver much-needed electricity as it is constantly characterised by power outages and failure to stabilise senior management positions. Despite being the largest supplier of electricity in Africa, it has been unable to reliably provide electricity to South Africans, ultimately making it difficult for businesses and investors that the country needs.

The utility is failing dismally to provide adequate electricity to the country. Some of the major problems at Eskom are mounting debt, falling availability of generation capacity, an increase in load-shedding, and rising prices for power. Like other SOEs mentioned above, Eskom has also been rocked by a leadership/management crisis.

The power utility has a record list of CEOs such as Jabu Mabuza, Phakamani Hadebe who resigned after just 18 months, Jacob Maroga and Mpho Makwana who took over temporarily after Maroga resigned. He was succeeded by Brian Dames who resigned in 2013 and was succeeded by Collin Matjila in an acting capacity, who was succeeded by Tshediso Matona who also resigned and was followed by Brian Molefe, who is often credited for managing load-shedding successfully at Eskom.[22] He was followed by Matshela Koko, John Dladla and Sean Maritz before the appointment of André de Ruyter, who resigned after three years in what the media referred to as "a tumultuous three years in office".[23] The spate of such resignations was aptly captured by journalist Omarjee[24] in the caption of an article dubbed "Eskom's revolving door: 10 CEOs in 10 years". This source noted that at the time De Ruyter was appointed government also announced R150 billion (US$8 billion) in bailouts, planned over 10 years, including a front-loaded injection of R59 billion (US$3.2 billion) between 2019 and 2021.

The financial picture is also not looking good. It recorded a loss in operational and financial performance in its 2022/2023 Annual Results. Its operating profit significantly declined to R5.6 billion from R20.9 billion. It also reported an arrear of municipal debt totalling R58.5 billion.

Eskom's failures in providing electricity have been so epic that the country was forced to create a new ministerial portfolio focusing on electricity. As a result, President Cyril Ramaphosa appointed Kgosientsho Ramokgopa as the new Minister in the Presidency for Electricity. The president said Ramokgopa's primary goal was to "drive government's programme of significantly reducing the severity and frequency of load shedding as a matter of urgency and to expedite government's work to ensure the full implementation of the Energy Action Plan".[25] It was hoped that this would give the government direct responsibility, authority and control over all critical aspects of the Energy Action Plan. As the president puts it in his State of the Nation Address 2023, "The Minister of Electricity will be focused day in and day out only on addressing the load shedding crisis, working together with the management of Eskom and the board." However, many months after the appointment the utility is still battling to provide electricity and load-shedding continues unabated.

After a cursory critical review of the preceding selected cases, I now present the findings before presenting prescriptive and instrumental implications.

Key issues

From the brief excursion above, I thematise key issues debilitating these organisations and demonstrate how they support the study's overarching argument that South Africa's desire to be a truly developmental state has been compromised by ailing SOEs that fail to support the country's developmental agenda in a meaningful way. The key issues emerging from these are poor financial performance, corporate governance failures, management/leadership problems and competition from the private sector.

Loss-making/poor financial performance

From the preceding, it is evident the reviewed parastatals habitually suffered loss-making and struggled to generate healthy profits to sustain themselves. This places a heavy weight on the government to bail them out. This poor performance contributes to their failure to meet their mandate. This has implications for how these companies are managed and on the skills they attract.

Acute leadership crisis

The state-owned companies reviewed are marred by constant leadership crises and have a record number of resignations and dismissals at the executive management level. Across the three companies, it is clear that leadership is quite a challenge as they are often faced with a flurry of resignations from senior management. The latest CEO to resign from Eskom, André de Ruyter, who resigned at the end of 2022, left unceremoniously and was not even allowed to serve the balance of his notice period. Such constant resignations breed instability in those companies. This finding has implications for poor performance in those organisations.

Tacit plan of action, systems and capacity

It is clear from the findings that the state does not have proper systems in place to enable it to monitor the implementation of its developmental plans and initiatives. The workforce appears to lack a highly developed sense of commitment and shared vision. Thus, the state, committed to a developable agenda, requires a capable workforce with sophisticated skills, abilities, shared vision and developed sense of commitment, an attribute that is often evident in many Asian countries such as Japan, South Korea and Taiwan. Linked to this, a developmental state requires a hands-on approach and proper systems to be able to direct its programmes to meet and exceed set targets. This finding resonates with much of the research literature, particularly the assertion that the developmental state's technical capacity lies in its ability to translate broad objectives into programmes and projects and to ensure their implementation.[26]

Stiff competition from the private sector

In some instances, stiff competition from private companies contributes to some of the failures of state-owned companies. For instance, SAA was completely unprepared for the competition mounted by private airlines after the government decided to open the domestic market, which for many years had been monopolised by SAA, to private airlines. This particular finding has implications for how the state ought to regulate the industries in which state-owned enterprises operate.

Implications

This study's findings paint a bleak picture of South Africa's ambition of being a true developmental state. However, it suggests that the situation could be turned around with a series of measures that have been proffered towards the end of the chapter as part of the recommendations. The study that informs the chapter has implications for state policies. The study highlights the need for well-functioning parastatals as a key driver of economic development in the country. Prior studies have demonstrated that the parastatals are characterised by corruption, lack of visionary leadership, maladministration and mismanagement.[27] The role of the state in providing direction is equally crucial, hence this study proposes that there should be some form of bureaucracy that will give the state the authority to enforce developmental initiatives. From the study's findings, there is a need for properly qualified and experienced managers with the right attributes required in those organisations. As May[28] finds, mapping leadership attributes helps you identify and understand the specific leadership behaviour entailed in each organisational competency. It is hoped that these would give executives a competitive advantage and help them excel in propelling their companies into the future.

Limitations and future research

This study used a minimal sample consisting of only three parastatals. Future studies could broaden this sample. Nonetheless, the results are still generalisable as the picture that emerges is the same in other contexts beyond the three cases studied.

Conclusion

The chapter provides insights into the notion of a developmental state as it pertains to South Africa. It highlights the strategic role that could be played by SOEs in enabling the country to become a viable developmental state. A key finding of the study is that most SOEs are struggling to generate a healthy bottom line. Their systems are debilitated, and they must consistently be bailed out by the government instead of the other way around. It is also hoped that this study will inform policies and strategic direction of public enterprises. In conclusion, the following recommendations are made:

Firstly, the government must consider regulating the market in which parastatals operate to give state-owned enterprises a competitive edge. It is a course of action intended to empower society, foster economic growth and distribute the wealth of the nation in a meaningful way. In this way, state-owned companies such as SAA could easily be brought back to profitability. The reason SAA was profitable was that it had a large share of the domestic market and faced no unfair competition. Secondly, care must be taken to appoint highly qualified and experienced managers. The appointment of employees must be based on meritocracy; thus, appointments must be based on merits and not so much on cadre deployment as is sometimes the case. This recommendation resonates with Ukwandu's observation[29] that "the ANC's policy of cadre deployment, irrespective of skills, competence and know-how, to government departments, will not help the country at all or even allow the concept of the development state to take off". Strict meritocracy is therefore the answer.

Thirdly, the government must put systems in place to uproot corruption in parastatals. In the past, Eskom and SAA were often accused of being infiltrated by state capture. The appointment of Dudu Myeni and how SAA lost its lucrative Johannesburg–Mumbai route are often attributed to this phenomenon. Fourth, there is a need for periodical skills audits in all parastatals to ensure that employees are highly skilled and efficient. Fifth, the government must resort to some levels of bureaucracy that will give it the authority to effectively enforce the developmental agenda. From the example of the Asian Tigers, which have been very successful as developmental models, one notices that bureaucracy was a central feature of their massive success. Until this happens, a developmental state will just remain a dream.

References

Amsden, Alice H. 1985. 'The state and Taiwan's economic development'. In *Bringing the State Back In*, edited by Theda Skocpol, Peter B. Evans, and Dietrich Rueschemeyer. Cambridge: Cambridge University Press, pp 78–106.

Bond, P. 2008. 'South Africa's "developmental state" distraction'. *Mediations*, 24(1):8–27.

Chu, Yw. 2016. 'The Asian developmental state: Ideas and debates'. In *The Asian Developmental State*, edited by Yw Chu. New York: Palgrave Macmillan. https://doi.org/10.1057/9781137476128_1

Dr Kgosientsho Ramokgopa appointed Minister of Electricity in the Presidency (March 6, 2023). https://www.sanews.gov.za/south-africa/dr-kgosientsho-ramokgopa-appointed-minister-electricity-presidency

Education Training Unit. 2014. Community Organisers Toolbox. http://etu.org.za/toolbox/index.html (accessed 31 October 2022).

eNCA. 14 December 2022. 'Eskom's CEO André de Ruyter resigns'. https://www.enca.com/news/eskom-ceo-andre-de-ruyter-resigns

Eskom 2022/2023 Annual Results. https://www.google.com/search?q=eskom+2022%2F2023+financial+report&rlz=1C1CHZN_enZA994ZA994&oq=eskom+2022%2F2023+financial+report&gs_lcrp=EgZjaHJvbWUyBggAEEUYOdIBCTExMDU2ajBqNKgCALACAA&sourceid=chrome&ie=UTF-8

Eskom Holdings Limited. 2010. Integrated Report. https://ungc-production.s3.us-west.amazonaws.com/attachments/5768/original/Eskom_Reporting_on_Progress_UN_GlobalCompact_22_July_2010_Final_.pdf?1279814809 (accessed 31 October 2024).

Eskom Holdings Limited. 2011. The Eskom Factor. https://www.eskom.co.za/wp-content/uploads/2021/02/eskom-factor-2014.pdf (accessed 31 October 2022).

Flyvbjerg, B. 2006. 'Five misunderstandings about case-study research'. *Qualitative Inquiry*, 12(2):219–245.

Gramsci, A. 1971. *Selections from the Prison Notebook*. New York: International Publishers.

Hendrickse, R. 2022. 'Towards a South African developmental state: The Electricity Supply Commission (Eskom) – victor or villain in this endeavour?' *International Journal of Research in Business and Social Science (2147–4478)*, 11(9):289–299. https://doi.org/10.20525/ijrbs.v11i9.2208

Johnson, C. 1999. 'The development state: Odyssey of a concep'. In *The Developmental State*, edited by M. Woo-Cumings. Ithaca: Crnell University Press.

Gumede, V. 2011. 'Policy making in South Africa'. In *South African Government and Politics*, 4th Edition, edited by C. Landsberg and A. Venter. Pretoria: Van Schaik.

Ensor, L 2023. 'Some outstanding SAA annual reports finally tabled.' *Business Day*. 14 December 2023. https://www.businesslive.co.za/bd/national/2023-12-14-some-outstanding-saa-annual-reports-finally-tabled/

May, R. 2014. 'Implementing a leadership development program for your business'. *Journal of the Knowledge Economyi*, IX:137–146.

McLeod, D. 3 February 2014. 'SABC CEO Mokhobo resigns'. *Mail & Guardian.* https://mg.co.za/article/2014-02-03-head-of-sabc-resigns/

McCorriston, S. and MacLaren, D. 2016. 'Parastatals as instruments of government policy: The Food Corporation of India'. *Food Policy*, 65:53–62. https://doi.org/10.1016/j.foodpol.2016.10.005

Mhone, G. 2004. 'Organizational and institutional implications of a developmental state'. Human Social Research Council. Pretoria: HSRC.

Mkandawire, T. 2001. 'Thinking about developmental states in Africa'. *Cambridge Journal of Economics*, 25(3):289–313.

Motsaathebe, G. 2011. 'Journalism education and practice in South Africa and the discourse of the African Renaissance'. *Communicatio: Journal of Communication Theory and Research*, 37(3):381–397.

Motsaathebe, G. and Rena, R. 2022. 'Towards an aggressive economic growth: Promoting entrepreneurship as a catalyst for development in the Global South with special reference to South Africa', a conference paper presented at a BRICS-SA conference held in Durban, South Africa, 3–6 April 2022.

Omarjee, L. 2 August 2019. 'Eskom's revolving door: 10 CEOs in 10 years'. Fin24. https://www.news24.com/fin24/eskoms-revolving-door-10-ceos-in-10-years-20190802-2

The Presidency Annual Report 2020–2021. https://www.thepresidency.gov.za/sites/default/files/The%20Presidency%20Annual%20Report%202020-2021.pdf

Presidential Review Committee (PRC) report. 2010. South Africa.

Public Protector's report. 2014. Report of the Public Protector in terms of Section 182(1)(B) of the Constitution of the Republic of South Africa, 1996 And Section 8(1) of the Public Protector Act, 1994. https://static.pmg.org.za/140827sabc_final_report_17_february_2014.pdf

SABC 2022/23 Annual Report. https://www.sabc.co.za/sabc/annual-reports/

SA Government News Agency. 6 March 2023. 'Dr Kgosientsho Ramokgopa appointed Minister of Electricity in the Presidency'. https://www.sanews.gov.za/south-africa/dr-kgosientsho-ramokgopa-appointed-minister-electricity-presidency

SONA 2023. https://www.stateofthenation.gov.za/

Teece, D.J. 2010. 'Business Models, Business Strategy and Innovation.' *Long Range Planning*, 43:172–194.

Ukwandu. 2019. 'South Africa as a Developmental State: Is it a Viable Idea?' *African Journal of Public Affairs,* 11(2):41–62.

United Nations. *Economic Commission for Africa; United Nations.* Economic Commission for Africa (2021-08). 'Governance of state-owned enterprises in South Africa: Enhancing performance, efficiency and service delivery.' Addis Ababa: https://hdl.handle.net/10855/45908

Wasserman, H. 2020. 'EXPLAINER: How SAA landed in such a mess', News24. https://www.news24.com/news24/bi-archive/what-happened-at-saa-2020-1

Zuma, J. 2017. Address by His Excellency President Jacob Zuma on the occasion of the 5th anniversary of the adoption of the National Development Plan, Cape Town, on 12 September 2017.

Zuma, J. 2008. Statement of the National Executive Committee of the African National Congress read on the occasion of the 98th Anniversary of the ANC, 8 January 2008. http://www.anc.org.za/show.php?id=50

5

Is South Africa's developmental state model working? Retrospective musings

Amos Hadebe

As we reflect on 30 years of democracy in South Africa, the governing party, the African National Congress (ANC), adopted at its 2007 conference a Strategy and Tactics document that called for South Africa to become a developmental state, which highlights people-centred change and restructuring of the economy for social inclusion.[1] This became the South African government's overarching economic growth model, stated in the opening paragraph of Chapter Thirteen of the National Development Plan (NDP), which asserts that no social or economic transformation is possible without a capable and developmental state.[2]

I argue that South Africa's developmental state model is not working and must be reviewed. It is not achieving its main objectives, stated in the National Development Plan, which are to eliminate poverty, and reduce inequality and unemployment by 2030.[3] The fundamental problem with implementing South Africa's developmental state model is the lack of a common vision of an overarching macroeconomic policy framework for the country by the past post-apartheid presidents, including the incumbent; lack of public policy coordination in government; and poor policy implementation due to the disbanding of the former Policy Coordination and Advisory Services (PCAS), also known as the Policy Unit. The National Development Plan is good at stating "what" must be achieved by "when" but does not explain "how" to go about implementing those policy objectives.

I suggest that the Singapore Model of economic development could be a viable alternative for South Africa to consider as it enters the fourth decade of democracy. In a way, this essay is more about the next 30 years than it is about the past. In that connection, amongst the things South Africa needs going forward is to establish an effective Policy Unit in the Presidency, led by astute technocrats with solid academic background, strong policy research skills, socio-political and economic awareness, and must be given long-term employment contracts post the end of terms of elected government officials for consistency and continuity in public policy coordination.

Non-expert thoughts on the theory and practice of the developmental state

The origin of the term "developmental state" is attributed to Chalmers Johnson,[4] who first used it in his study of the role of the Japanese state in achieving rapid growth and industrialisation between 1925 and 1975. In his book, *MITI and the Japanese Miracle*, Johnson distinguishes between the concept of a developmental state and normal government intervention by focusing on why and how state intervention happens.

Johnson defines a developmental state as an economic development model where the state plays a leading role in macroeconomic planning in driving economic growth, and improving socio-economic development of its citizens. Government uses state resources such as public procurement as a lever to guide economic growth.

Initially, the developmental state model was synonymous with authoritarian states and was thought not possible to be implemented in democratic conditions.[5] However, the most cited developmental state model is that of Singapore, Japan, Taiwan and South Korea – commonly referred to as the "Four Asian Tigers" or "Asian Dragons", which have achieved high levels of economic growth since the 1960s.[6]

The definition of a developmental state used in this chapter is the one given by Guy Mhone,[7] considered one of the leading African development economists, who defined a developmental state as a "proactive role of the state in pursuing and defining a developmental vision to be attained in the long-term, in coordinating economic activities and steering them toward desired outcomes, mobilising and synergising class and social forces in support of the developmental agenda".

South Africa's macroeconomic policy framework trajectory

South Africa's post-democracy macroeconomic policy framework trajectory has had varying successes and failures as follows:

The Reconstruction and Development Programme: 1994–1996

South Africa's first democratically elected president, Nelson Mandela, and the ANC came up with the Reconstruction and Development Programme (RDP) in 1994, aimed at addressing socio-economic challenges brought about by apartheid. Specifically, the RDP sought to alleviate poverty and provide social services such as water, electricity and housing to the majority previously disadvantaged communities.

RDP committed to firm monetary and fiscal discipline, including affirming independence of the South African Reserve Bank (SARB), but fell short of mentioning nationalisation as envisaged in the ANC's Freedom Charter. Some of the RDP successes were establishment of social security; up to five million free meals were provided to school children; 500 clinics were built; free healthcare was provided to pregnant women; and more that two million houses were connected to electricity, resulting in 63 per cent of the population having access to electricity. However, RDP was abandoned two years later due to lack of policy coordination and inadequate economic growth to finance it.[8]

Growth, Employment and Redistribution (GEAR) policy: 1996–2006

In 1996, when Thabo Mbeki was still the country's deputy president, and de-facto leader of government businesses, he unveiled the Growth,

Employment and Redistribution (GEAR) policy. It was an ambitious blueprint aimed at stimulating South Africa's economy to 6 per cent, as well as creating 400 000 jobs per annum by 2000. GEAR also targeted budget deficit at 3 per cent by 1999, down from 4.9 per cent in 1994. It also called for trade liberalisation to be accompanied by greater flexibility in the labour market and focused on inflation targeting and relaxation in exchange controls.

According to Habib,[9] GEAR's review was mixed. It strengthened South Africa's financial position, lowered interest rates, and brought inflation under control. However, Tripartite Alliance's COSATU and SACP were critical of GEAR, and labelled it neo-liberal and anti-labour as it came at a huge social cost. Inequality as measured by the Gini coefficient increased from 0.672 in 1993 to 0.685 in 1999.

A growth rate of 6 per cent per annum was promised by GEAR. However, the growth rate never exceeded 5 per cent and it was accompanied by well above 30 per cent unemployment.[10] GEAR was replaced in 1996 by the Accelerated and Shared Growth Initiative of South Africa (ASGISA).[11]

Accelerated and Shared Growth Initiative for South Africa (ASGISA): 1996–2010

In 1996, the then deputy president, Phumzile Mlambo-Ngcuka, during Mbeki's administration, unveiled the Accelerated and Shared Growth Initiative for South Africa (ASGISA), which aimed to halve poverty and unemployment by 2014 in line with the Millennium Development Goals (MDGs). Furthermore, government sought to promote a growth rate of 4.5 per cent from 2005 to 2009, and then by 6 per cent from 2010 to 2014 with the hope that the trickle-down effect will bridge the gap between the first economy and the second economy.[12]

According to Hirsh,[13] ASGISA's performance was mixed. On one hand, the infrastructure programme in public spending increased from 4.6 per cent of GDP in 2006 and 2007 to 9.6 per cent. However, poverty and unemployment remained high or worse.

New Growth Plan (NGP): 2010–2012

Then President Jacob Zuma unveiled another macroeconomic policy framework, the New Growth Plan (NGP), during his State of the Nation Address (SONA) in 2010. NGP had ambitious targets of creating five million jobs and reducing unemployment by 10 per cent in 2020 and reducing South Africa's inequality. It prioritised infrastructure spending.[14] The NGP was short-lived and replaced by the National Development Plan (NDP) in 2012.

National Development Plan (NDP): 2012–2030

In 2012 the then Chairperson of the National Planning Commission (NPC), Trevor Manuel, unveiled the National Development Plan (NDP) during the presidency of Jacob Zuma, which is South Africa's current macroeconomic policy framework. It is an 18-year plan, and its main priorities are the reduction of unemployment, poverty and inequality by 2030.[15]

According to the NDP, unemployment was targeted to fall from 27 per cent in 2011 to 14 per cent by 2020, and to 6 per cent by 2030. Total employment was targeted to rise from 13 million to 24 million by 2030. The NDP envisages a reduction in the proportion of people living below the lower bound poverty line from 39 per cent of the population to zero, and there would be reduction in inequality measured by the Gini coefficient from 0.69 to 0.60.

Critically important, NDP envisages a corruption-free society with strong adherence to ethical conduct of government and society, and a government that is accountable to its people.

10-point economy recovery plan: 2018–

In his maiden State of the Nation Address (SONA) in 2018, President Cyril Ramaphosa announced the appointment of a Presidential Economic Advisory Council to ensure implementation of economic policy, and unveiled a 10-point economy recovery plan for South Africa, which includes (1) a Job Summit to help address youth unemployment; (2) an Investment Conference, targeting both domestic and international investors; (3) reviving the manufacturing sector through the strategic use of incentives, and localisation programmes for textiles, furniture and water meters to be locally procured; (4) supporting black industrialists and investing in small businesses in townships; (5) a Youth Employment

Service Initiative to place unemployed youth in paid internships in companies; (6) establishment of Youth Working Group to advance the interest of young people; (7) infrastructure investment to be set up to speed up the implementation of new projects for water infrastructure, road maintenance and health facilities; (8) small business development support by setting aside 30 per cent of public procurement to small and medium enterprises, as well as township and rural enterprises; (9) grow the tourism sector; and (10) setting up Digital Industrial Revolution Commission to seize opportunities in the digital industrial revolutions.

NDP 10-year review: 2012–2022

A 10-year review of the National Development Plan, 2012–2022, by the National Planning Commission paints a disturbing picture of how the overarching challenges of inequality, unemployment and poverty remain, and in some instances have got worse.

(i)   Employment

This is the one element of the NDP target in which South Africa is performing disturbingly poorly. According to the National Planning Commission, the NDP sets a target of reducing unemployment from 25.4 per cent in 2010 to 6 per cent in 2030, with interim targets of 20 per cent by 2015 and 14 per cent by 2020. The unemployment rate, which increased from 25.4 per cent to 27.7 per cent from 2012 to 2018, increased substantially over the 2018–2022 period to 33.9 per cent in the second quarter of 2022, which is one of the highest in the world. This means 11.6 million unemployed and about 3.6 million discouraged people.

The National Planning Commission further breaks down the unemployment rate in terms of race as follows: the unemployment rate among the black African population group remains higher than the national average and other population groups at 37.8 per cent. It was 8.6 per cent for the white population group, 15.5 per cent for the Indian population group, and 27.4 per cent for the coloured population group during the same period.

(ii)   Inequality

The NDP sets a target of a reduction in inequality measured by the Gini coefficient from 0.69 to 0.60 by 2030. However, according to World Bank research, South Africa remains the most unequal country in the world with incomes that are highly polarised. The top decile of the South African population is estimated to own between 71 per cent and 95 per cent of the nation's wealth, compared to a global average of 55 per cent to 65.3 per cent.

(iii) Poverty

According to the National Planning Commission, income poverty in South Africa has been rising and affected 40 per cent of the population by 2016.

Approximately 13.3 million people were living below the food poverty line in 2015, with this number increasing to 19.4 million in 2020. This means that almost 32.6 per cent of the population could not afford the minimum required for their daily energy intake.

The National Planning Commission further divides income poverty according to race as follows: Between 2006 and 2015, poverty rates for black Africans fell from 60 per cent to 47 per cent, for coloureds from 36 per cent to 23 per cent, for Indians from 5 per cent to 1.2 per cent, and for whites from 0.6 per cent to 0.4 per cent. The rate of change varied dramatically as well, with black African and coloured poverty rates falling by 21 per cent and 32 per cent, respectively. In 2015, 49 per cent of black African women lived in poverty compared to 45 per cent of black African men.

Lack of public policy coordination in government

In a constitutional democracy like South Africa, the Presidency, which is led by the president, should take charge of decision-making, policy coordination, monitoring and evaluation, and long-term planning. The election manifestos of the governing party play an important role in influencing government's policies. Policy formulation and coordination in government entails bringing together all actors and government departments impacted by public policy early in the development of the policy and ensuring that they work together in a seamless way to implement the policies.

During the first five years of Nelson Mandela's administration, the focus was largely on policy, legislative and institutional reforms, and not much on state capacity of policymaking, coordination, monitoring and evaluation, and long-term planning.

Towards the end of 1997, the highly respected Policy Coordination and Advisory Services (PCAS), also known as the Policy Unit or the "engine room", was established in the Office of the then deputy Thabo Mbeki. The Policy Unit coordinated all policies and reforms, monitoring and evaluation, and long-term planning in government.[16] As Gumede puts it, "The Policy Unit was the main clearing-house in the policy making processes in South Africa." It led policy development and policy analysis, policy coordination and policy advice function. The Policy Unit was a "one stop shop" that also conducted medium- to long-term planning, and government-wide monitoring and evaluation.

The Policy Unit had six main policy sectors: (i) crime prevention and security; (ii) economic; (iii) social justice; (iv) governance; (v) administration; and (vi) international relations. There were four additional sub-units/special programmes, including the Office of the Status of Women (OSW), the Office on the Rights of Children (ORC), the Office on the Status of Disabled Persons (OSDP) and the Youth Desk.[17]

The Policy Unit worked very closely with the Forum of South African Director-Generals (FOSAD) clusters and served as a link between cabinet and policy coordination to ensure policy coordination and implementation across government departments. The Policy Unit sectors mirrored the five forums of FOSAD and cabinet committees, except the economic sector. There was also regular interaction between the senior leadership of the Policy Unit and the ANC to ensure policy coordination between the governing party and government.[18]

A planning framework guided interface between various policy-making structures and ensured that specific activities took place at specific mutually predetermined dates at national, provincial and local government levels to ensure policy coordination across all spheres of government.

During Mbeki's presidency, the government had the *Izimbizo* public consultation initiative where the president, deputy president, ministers, advisors, senior government officials and Policy Unit management would visit and engage various communities at large gatherings to understand their challenges, the impact of government policies on the communities, and come up with new government interventions to improve their lives.[19]

The critical mistake of Zuma's administration, which contributed to lack of public policy coordination in South Africa, was the disbanding of the Policy Unit in 2010. A new Department of Performance Monitoring and Evaluation (DPME) was established, and government-wide policy monitoring and evaluation was moved to the DPME. The National Planning Commission and the Ministry of Planning in the Presidency were also established in 2010. Policy planning was centralised within the Policy Planning Ministry and the National Planning Commission.[20]

Another new government Department of Women, Children and People with Disabilities was established, which coordinated policy related to gender and children's rights. Initially it was a stand-alone independent national department, and later was moved to the Presidency in 2014, and renamed the Department of Women in the Presidency. A Deputy Minister for Youth Affairs and Development was appointed. A portfolio of people with disability was moved to the National Department of Social Development.[21]

Due to the policy coordination vacuum created by the disbanding of the Policy Unit, government departments in the Presidency and across government at national and provincial levels formulated and implemented their own policies, which took away the focus from the National Development Plan. There was no longer formal or informal interaction between FOSAD, cabinet and the ANC on policy coordination and implementation. The Policy Unit had been the glue that kept all government structures and the ruling party together.

The same trend of creating additional government departments continued during Ramaphosa's administration, such as the knee-jerk reaction to the electricity crisis in the country by unilaterally creating a post for and appointing the new Minister of Electricity to deal with the electricity crisis in the country, which is against the resolution of the ANC's Policy Conference that was adopted by the ANC's 55th National Conference in 2022. This caused energy policy confusion and lack of coordination between the Department of Public Enterprises, which has oversight over the power utility Eskom, and the Department of Minerals and Energy (DPME), which drives South Africa's energy policy.

As Gumede[22] puts it, "disbanding of the Policy Unit has left a lacuna in coordination in the presidential, ruling party and government policy making processes".

South Africa's development state a dream deferred?

It is the main argument of this chapter that South Africa's developmental state model is not working and not achieving the set National Development Plan objectives of reducing unemployment, eliminating poverty and reducing inequality by 2030. The main reason, as demonstrated in the preceding section, is that all previous government leaders in a post-democratic South Africa, including the incumbent, had their own visions and macroeconomic policy frameworks instead of a common developmental framework towards achieving developmental state objectives, and there is lack of policy coordination in government due to the disbandment of the erstwhile Policy Unit.

An NDP review by the National Planning Commission has established that South Africa had underperformed on key targets in the NDP overall. Among contributing factors was lack of coherence in executing the NDP and poor implementation, challenges of leadership across society, the deterioration of the policy environment, and a turbulent regional and global environment such as the Covid-19 pandemic.

In summary, according to the National Planning Commission, the implementation of the NDP was not achieved as follows:

- Economic growth had been stagnant and was in recession terrain.
- Poverty was on an upward trend, and inequality was persistent and remained unchanged over time.
- Unemployment had been on the rise, amid the economy's weak performance, and the highest burden is borne by women and youth.
- The record of service delivery had worsened, and coupled with the economy's labour market difficulties, negatively affected the delivery of the social wage to the poorest households.
- Spatial inequality challenges persist.
- South Africa's energy challenges are well known.
- Both freight and commuter rail had been in decline over the 2018–2022 period. In terms of passenger rail, Stats SA's National Household Travel Survey estimates a decline of 80 per cent in 2020.

For the country to achieve the overarching goals of the NDP of eradicating poverty and reducing inequality and unemployment by 2030, it needed to grow its economy by 5.4 per cent per annum over 20 years and create about 11 million new jobs. This is very much unlikely, given the slow pace of economic growth.

The NDP articulates a vision of a developmental state capable of driving the country's development and free of corruption. However, the Zondo Commission Report on State Capture and the Auditor-General findings for the period 2021/2022 show that state-owned entities (SOEs), which are meant to drive the developmental agenda, are a source of corruption and malfeasance, particularly Eskom, South African Airways, Denel and Alexkor. Only two of 20 SOEs received clean audits.

Of the 257 municipalities, only 38 received a clean audit, 104 have credible financial statements, 78 received a qualified audit, six received adverse findings, 15 have disclaimers and 16 have outstanding audit outcomes due to late submission of financial statements, with the overall standard of financial management having regressed in the past five years.

Is the Singapore model of economic development an alternative for South Africa?

It is a recommendation of this chapter that South Africa should do away with the current developmental welfare state model as it is not achieving the desired results and should consider adopting the Singapore model of economic development.

It is common knowledge that Singapore transformed within one generation from being poor at independence from Britain in 1965 to a highly developed economy. At independence Singapore had no significant industries, no mineral resources, and imported its energy, food and water. In 1965, Singapore's nominal GDP per capita was US$500. In 2015, which was 50 years later, the country had caught up with industrial powers; the country's GDP per capita had risen to US$56 000, which was a similar level to Germany.[23] In 2022, Singapore's GDP per capita had increased to US$82 807; GDP growth rate was 3.6 per cent; the unemployment rate was 1.9 per cent; and the Gini coefficient after taxes amounted to 0.36, after a high of 0.41 in 2012.[24]

How did Singapore achieve this feat? Singapore's economic development model centred around five pillars, namely a strong clear vision; strong and decisive leadership when dealing with corruption; private sector-led and export-oriented industrialisation; education and technical skills development; and entrepreneurship.[25]

1 A strong and clear vision

In 1954, Lee Kuan Yew, the Cambridge-educated lawyer, considered the founding father of modern state Singapore, co-founded the People's Action Party (PAP) which campaigned for an end to British colonialism and a merger with Malaya. In 1957, Malaya was granted independence, and the next year the British Parliament elevated the status of Singapore from colony to state and provided for new local elections. The PAP won the elections held in May 1959, and Lee Kuan Yew was installed as the first prime minister until 1990.[26]

On 9 August 1965, Singapore was expelled from Malaysia due to ethnic and racial conflict that engulfed Malaysia and became an independent sovereign nation. Faced with this daunting challenge, Lee Kuan Yew had a strong, clear vision of building Singapore's economy from a third-world country to a first-world country and turn Singapore into a metropolis within one generation. This vision transcended the entire society and all government officials, which is what is missing in South Africa.

2 Strong and decisive leadership in dealing with corruption

When the PAP started as a liberation movement opposing colonialism, it was a broad church bringing together different ideological groups from the left, centre and to the right. It had trade unions, religious leaders and the conservatives. When it came into power and became government, PAP, under the leadership of Lee Kuan Yew, repositioned itself as a pragmatic developmental party.

Singaporean government and the PAP decisively implemented business-friendly policies that focused on manufacturing for export, entrepreneurship, gave equal power to business and labour, appointed skilled officials in government and fired incompetent, corrupt officials with struggle credentials.[27]

Senior PAP government officials involved in corruption and malfeasance were fired and prosecuted to set an example, such as Education Minister Chew Swee Kee who was forced to resign, and Phey Yew Kok, the powerful leader of the National Trade Union Council, who was sent to jail for corruption. Government clamped down on gangsterism and criminals to create a safe environment for everyone.[28]

When the communists in the PAP broad-church objected to the new direction that the party, and therefore Lee Kuan Yew's government, was taking, and the ensuing ideological and leadership differences with the central democratic wing, Lee Kuan Yew demonstrated strong and decisive leadership by forcing the communists out of the PAP instead of wasting time and energy trying to build unity in the PAP. The communists ended up forming the Barisan Socialist Party.[29]

3 Export-led industrialisation

To alleviate the problem of unemployment, Singapore promoted industrialisation in four phases. Phase 1 was through an import substitution strategy. To attract foreign investors to manufacture locally, Singapore established the Economic Development Board (EDB), which drove industrialisation policies, and offered tax incentives and tax holidays for firms investing in the country. Petrochemicals was the first sector to benefit under this scheme and Shell was the pioneer company. Tariffs were raised and import quota were imposed on various products to protect local firms from foreign competition. Laws were enacted that limited firms from producing certain goods to prevent competition.[30]

Phase 2 of the industrialisation strategy was export promotion, which was a move away from import substitution. Import restrictions were removed and tariffs came down. EDB actively sought foreign companies to manufacture locally in a low-wage country with a strategic location in Asia. Further incentives were introduced, like lower corporate taxes on companies manufacturing for export. This led to rapid expansion of the electronics, petroleum refining, ship repair and textiles sectors, which helped to absorb much of the unemployed labour force. This was labour-intensive and created many jobs.[31]

Phase 3 was industrial restructuring, which was a move from labour-intensive industrialisation to technology catch-up. This led to policies that would encourage investments in technology-intensive sectors, such as computers, electronics, machinery and pharmaceuticals to generate more value added from the same amount of labour.[32]

Phase 4, which is the current one, is an economic diversification strategy where EDB began to offer a wide range of incentives to encourage locally owned and partially locally owned firms to establish operations abroad in low-wage countries while retaining their headquarters in Singapore. As a result Singapore, together with Indonesia and Malaysia, established the Johor-Batam-Singapore growth triangle in 1989.[33]

4 Education and technical skills development

Alongside import substitution and industrialisation strategy, the Singaporean government realised the importance of education and skills development of the workforce, and developed a five-year education plan focusing on mathematics, science and technology. This strategy extended to primary and secondary schools, which saw an enrolment of 33 per cent and 94 per cent respectively in 1965. There was a 70 per cent increase in university enrolment with the establishment of technical and vocational institutions. A skilled workforce was brought in from the private sector and employed by government to implement strategic projects. For example, a banker, Lim Kim San, was brought in to manage the rollout of a critical social housing project, which he did successfully.[34]

5 Entrepreneurship

Under Lee Kuan Yew's leadership, Singapore fostered a countrywide entrepreneurship spirit by including entrepreneurship in school curricula and encouraged local companies to become international. The state itself became entrepreneurial and appointed people from outside the PAP with entrepreneurial minds in key government positions.[35]

Conclusion

This chapter sought to argue that South Africa's developmental state model is not working to address the triple challenges of unemployment, poverty and inequality envisaged in the National Development Plan due to lack of coherent development vision and lack of policy coordination in government. It highlighted South Africa's macroeconomic policies trajectory under different government leaders and the poor results achieved as shown in the NDP 10-year review from 2012 to 2022. It highlighted a lack of policy coordination in South Africa due to the disbandment of the former Policy Unit.

I am suggesting that the Singapore model of economic development is a viable alternative for South Africa to adapt, which is hinged on five pillars, namely: (i) having a strong clear vision; (ii) strong and decisive leadership when dealing with corruption; (iii) private sector-led and export-oriented industrialisation; (iv) education and technical skills development; and (v) entrepreneurship.

I must state that I might not be an expert in this subject. But as a professional living in free South Africa, I have made some observations about why the pace of progress has slowed down, and proceeded to make recommendations for what could help change our fortunes in the next 30 years. These include re-establishing the Policy Unit in the Presidency, led by astute technocrats with solid academic backgrounds, strong policy research skills, socio-political and economic awareness; and they must be given long-term employment contracts post the end of terms of elected government officials for consistency in public policy coordination and continuity. In many other chapters of this book, authors offer perspectives of why things have slowed down, and make recommendations. My submission should be read in context, and not just as a stand-alone silver bullet proposal.

References

African National Congress. 2007. 'Adopted Strategy and Tactics of the ANC.' Accessed 25 October 2023, https://www.anc1912.org.za/adopted-strategy-and-tactics-of-the-anc/

Bercuson, K. 1995. 'Singapore: A case study in rapid development'. International Monetary Fund. Accessed 31 October 2023, https://www.elibrary.imf.org/display/book/9781557754639/ch003.xml

Department of Finance. 1996. 'Growth, employment, and redistribution strategy. 1996.' Accessed 26 October 2023, http://www.treasury.gov.za/publications/other/gear/chapters.pdf.

DPME. 2017. 'The developmental state: An exploration of South Africa's National Development Plan, 2nd Draft'. Department of Planning, Monitoring and Evaluation: Research Unit.

Gevisser, M. 2009. *Thabo Mbeki: The dream deferred*. Cape Town: Jonathan Ball Publishers.

Gumede, V. 2008. 'Public policy making in a post-apartheid South Africa: A preliminary perspective'. *Africanus: Journal of Development Studies*, 38(2):7–23.

Gumede, V. 2011. 'Policy Making in South Africa'. In *South African Government and Politics*, edited by C. Landsberg and A. Venter, 4th ed. Pretoria: Van Schaik, pp 61–80.

Gumede, W. 2022. 'What can the ANC learn from Singapore's People Action Party in remaking itself into an effective Developmental Party?' Occasional Paper – Inclusive Society Institute, Cape Town.

Habib, A. 2013. *South Africa's Suspended Revolution: Hopes and prospects*. Johannesburg: Wits University Press.

Hirsh, A. 2009. 'Global economic crisis hinders AsgiSA efforts'. Accessed 30 October 2023, https://www.sanews.gov.za/south-africa/global-economic-crisis-hinders-asgisa-efforts

Jeffery, A. 2010. *Chasing the Rainbow: South Africa's move from Mandela to Zuma*. Johannesburg: South African Institute of Race Relations.

Johnson, Chalmers. 1982. *MITI and the Japanese Miracle: The growth of industrial policy, 1925–1975*. Stanford: Stanford University Press.

Mhone, G. 2004. 'Organisational and Institutional Implications of a developmental state'. Human Social Research Council paper. Pretoria. HSRC.

Mosala, S.J. and Venter, J.C.M. 2017. 'South Africa's economic transformation since 1994: What influence has the National Democratic Revolution (NDR) had?' *The Review of the Black Political Economy*, 44:327–340.

National Planning Commission. 2012. 'National Development Plan 2030: Our future – Make it work.' Pretoria.

Rice Jones, G. 2013. 'A Beginner's Guide to the Developmental State.' Accessed 26 October 2023, http://www.romeconomics.com/beginners-guide-developmental-state/

Sanith, S. and Saravanakumar, A.J.R. 2020. 'The economic development of Singapore: A historical perspective'. *Aut Aut Research Journal*, XI(VII):441–459.

Statista. 2023. 'Gini coefficient after taxes in Singapore from 2013 to 2022.' https://www.statista.com/statistics/951976/singapore-gini-coefficient-after-tax/

Trade Economic. 2023. Singapore unemployment rate. https://tradingeconomics.com/singapore/unemployment-rate

African National Congress. 1994. *The Reconstruction and Development Programme*. Johannesburg: Umanyano Publications.

Wade, R. 1990. *Governing the Market: Economic Theory and the Role of Government in East Asian Industrialisation.* Princeton, New Jersey: Princeton University Press.

White, G. ed. 1988. *Developmental States in East Asia.* Johannesburg: Macmillan.

World Bank Group. 2018. 'An incomplete transition: Overcoming the legacy of exclusion in South Africa'. World Bank, Washington, DC.

World Bank. 2022. Singapore GDP per capita. Accessed 30 October 2023, https://data.worldbank.org/indicator/NY.GDP.PCAP.CD?locations =SG&most_recent_value_desc=true

Zondo, R.M.M. 2022. Judicial Commission of Inquiry into allegations of State Capture, Corruption and Fraud in the Public Sector including Organs of State, Part 1, 2, 3, 4, Pretoria.

6

Sakubona sakubeletha: A backward and forward account of the professionalisation of the South African civil service

Zukiswa N. Mqolomba

I am a public sector leader who serves as the National Commissioner and Deputy Chairperson of the Public Service Commission. I have worked for more than fourteen years in senior management in the public service, both at the national and local levels, where I have observed and formed part of critical discussions on why and how to professionalise the public service in an effort to understand how best government can build an ethical, capable and developmental state. I have worked for the Presidency (Department of Planning, Monitoring and Evaluation) where I provided research and technical support to the National Planning Commission. I am also doing my PhD with the University of Cape Town on the professionalisation of the public service, and have made observations of the South African Police Service, which I use as a case study and lens to understand the challenges of state incapacity and professionalism in South Africa. Mine is a scholastic contribution to this volume, and represents my own research and observations, both backward and forward, of the professionalisation of the public service. Whilst my chapter may appear as a thesis, it contributes to the volume by providing an academic or scientific lens to the performance of the democratic state when it comes to public-sector transformation. It looks at the challenges of professionalism in the public service, with a focus on the police service in South Africa, as well as reflects on how the democratic government has acted to provide solutions to these challenges. It is, in essence, a research paper, which also offers scholastic insights and personal reflections of professionalisation of the public sector under the leadership of the ruling party at the helm of the democratic state the past 30 years.

Here is my account of what I have observed in my life in government, which I can summarise through a Nguni saying: Sakubona sakubeletha! Loosely translated, we have seen flames.

South Africa's aspirations of building a professional public service

The Constitution's Chapter 10 requires public servants to demonstrate professionalism, responsibility and a development-oriented mindset. The National Development Plan (NDP), which is South Africa's most current development policy, renders a persuasive argument for the establishment of a capable state. It states that for South Africa to become recognised as a capable state, it must have effective state institutions and public employees who are dedicated to serving the public interest and who possess the abilities to continuously provide high-quality services with a focus on people and the advancement of the country as a whole. It will only be at that juncture that South Africa can truly claim to be a capable state. The South African government, however, acknowledges that it has failed to professionalise the public service and (re)build state capacity, according to the National Planning Commission, 2020. Corruption, inadequate training, a lack of professionalism, unequal compensation, personal and patronage-based appointments, and a high labour turnover rate among DGs are among the problems associated with public service. Additionally, there are wide variations in the quality of public services, which are often sub-par. The chapter contends, however, that South Africa's prospects for public service are promising given the new professionalisation framework that cabinet adopted in October 2023.

Challenges of state incapability and professionalism in South Africa

The disparity in capacity, which leads to disparities in performance at the local, provincial and national levels of government, is the primary challenge that South Africa's public service has been facing, as stated in Chapter 13 of the National Development Plan 2030, which focuses on building a capable and developmental state. This is as a result of a confluence of factors, including disagreements at the point where politics and administration meet, the inconsistency of administrative leadership, a dearth of necessary skills, the abdication of responsibility and authority, an ineffective organisational design, and a lackluster morale among workers. The capacity and performance gaps are more severe in historically disadvantaged areas, which are also the places in which engagement from the state is most important to improve the population's quality of life. There have been several attempts to address the challenges, but there is an inclination to jump from one quick fix or policy trend to the next.

This tendency has led to a number of failures. Because of these frequent changes, organisational structures and policy approaches have become unstable, further draining the few resources that are available. The search for a rapid solution has caused the emphasis to shift away from issues that are more fundamental. A lack of professionalism and expertise has an adverse effect on every facet of the public service. At high levels, reporting and recruitment systems have allowed for an excessive amount of political influence in the selection and administration of top employees. The unnecessary instability in high positions that has resulted as a direct consequence of this has had the effect of lowering both the morale of public officials and the faith that people have in their government. In the junior levels, not nearly enough attention has been put on the creation of interesting career trajectories that ensure the duplication of abilities and generate a sense of professional shared purpose. The state has to have a crystal-clear picture of where the next generation of public servants will come from and how they can replicate their specific professional abilities in order to do their jobs effectively.

The settlement of these issues is made more difficult by insufficient administrative competence and a lack of leadership at the various spheres of society, with the exception of some pockets of excellence.

In South Africa, the local, provincial and national administrations have had a difficult time cultivating constructive partnerships with one another. Tension and instability have been exacerbated across all three levels of government as a result of a lack of clarity on the distribution of responsibilities and a reluctance to manage the system. There is no consensus on how this matter will be handled, and there is a lack of leadership in choosing the most effective way to go with addressing the problem. These coordination issues aren't unique to South Africa by any means. The issue is with the way that they are managed. Often, recent initiatives have been carried out on an ad hoc basis, with remedies to specific problems being implemented without giving enough regard to the cumulative effect. This has led to an increase in the amount of documentation that public officials must complete. While trying to prevent unethical behaviour, people often focus their efforts on narrowing their discretion, but this has the unintended consequence of stifling their creative potential. To make it possible for workers to carry out their responsibilities, reforms need to be implemented to improve workers' abilities and morale, define responsibility lines and cultivate a culture of public service.

When it comes to the South African Police Service, according to the White Paper on Policing, 2016, SAPS continues to face a number of issues within its own internal functioning. These issues are connected to a lack of discipline, criminality and corruption in the system. According to this White Paper, the process by which police employees are recruited, selected and appointed continues to be a barrier to effective efforts to professionalise the police service, and to combat crime and provide services to the public. The South African Police Service is currently not professionalised if one looks closely at the multifaceted process of professionalisation that leans closely to accountability and earning the trust of the public. This can be further argued by the NDP 2030:[1] "[the] police will earn public respect if they are efficient and effective and display a professional approach to combating crime." This, however, remains a pipedream since the lack of trust in the police service remains an unresolved issue and crime rates spike every day. Reports of police misconduct and inadequate service continue to be widespread, which continues to erode public faith in the police and makes life more difficult for officials who may have a more balanced perspective of the role they play in society. The end result of this is that members of the SAPS are still seen with mistrust and terror in many different situations. According to data from the Corruption Perceptions Index (CPI), 2022, of Corruption Watch that is available, an increasing number of individuals feel that the majority of law enforcement professionals are corrupt. In August 2019, Corruption Watch rated the South African police as the most corrupt public servants. These views are confirmed by the StatsSA Victims of Crime Survey 2020/2021, which confirms that public perception of law enforcement is generally very low. According to Faull and Rose[2] "abusive language used by police can be a powerful barrier to healthy police-community relations if it is deemed unnecessary by civilians; the use of force elicited similar barriers". This therefore forms part of the limitations on the successes community policing would have achieved.

The SAPS continues to be unprofessional and due to the following reasons. In my observation, supported by extensive research in the area, the SAPS has been characterised by:

- patronage-based and non-meritocratic appointments (i.e., irregular and covert appointment of unqualified persons to positions of authority within the SAPS);
- political meddling or political capture;
- corruption and corrosive attitudes and behaviours;
- abuse of force;
- inadequate training;
- low professional ethics and values;
- little advanced formal education;
- lack of high-level skills and competencies (particularly to occupy higher roles);
- lack of professional bodies;
- leadership volatility;
- poor service quality, poor service availability and poor service levels;
- lack of discipline or consequence management for ill behaviour;
- ineffectiveness and inefficiencies in delivering positive service outcomes; and
- other undemocratic and unprofessional practices.

There are challenges and causes of state incapacity and non-professionalism. State incapacity, or the inability of government institutions to effectively fulfil their functions and deliver public services, can stem from a variety of interconnected causes. State incapacity and non-professionalism in South Africa can be attributed to various factors, including:[3]

- historical legacy of apartheid;
- structural challenges;
- socioeconomic factors;
- weak governance and institutional failures;
- political instability and leadership challenges;
- skills shortages and human resource constraints;
- economic inequality and poverty;
- corruption and state capture;
- fragmentation and inefficiencies in service delivery;
- complexity of social and economic challenges;
- resource constraints and fiscal pressures; and
- lack of citizen engagement and participation.

South Africa's understanding of professionalisation of the public service and the police

The National Development Plan 2030 (NDP) recommends in Chapter 12 that the South African Police Service (SAPS) demilitarise and recruit personnel who will be impartial and professional. In order to achieve this, the National Planning Commission, 2020, suggests that the South African Police Service (SAPS) develop a set of indicators that can be used to assess individual and organisational behaviour. It also suggests that officers whose actions are judged to be abusive or unprofessional face clear consequences in terms of discipline and future career opportunities. According to the National Planning Commission, 2020, there should be a professional and well-resourced police force. It should also be staffed by highly skilled police officers who value what they do, serve the community, safeguard people's rights to equality and justice, and protect people's lives and property without discrimination.

According to the National School of Government (NSG, 2021), the NSG developed a National Implementation Framework titled "A National Implementation Framework Towards the Professionalisation of the Public service", which is aimed at professionalising the public service. This document renders an important distinction between professionalism and professionalisation, with professionalism being defined as an individual's practices, conduct, behaviour and values regardless of their training, qualifications or level of education. In this context, professionalisation is therefore concerned with altering people's attitudes, behaviours and performance when it comes to serving the public.

The NSG defines professionalisation as adhering to the Public Service Charter, the Batho Pele principles, and the supreme law of the land while also observing and serving others with empathy. According to the NSG, professionalisation also entails having individuals who are knowledgeable, qualified and well equipped to carry out their duties with diligence. This implies that ongoing training is necessary in order to improve public servants' "know-how" and abilities, making them more competitive. An approach that is nonpartisan in nature is one of the most critical pillars of professionalising the public service, as stated by the NSG. The NSG emphasises the necessity of depoliticising the public service and insulating government departments from politics and/or undue political party influence for it to make this a reality.

To put it succinctly, based on the aforementioned, I define professionalisation as the processes that the government has put in place to reform a specific occupation or branch of the public service. It ought to be viewed as specialists operating within a highly trained occupational group to protect public safety, similar to Mr Beukman (Chairperson of the Parliamentary Committee on Police). It includes the processes by which the government intends to build a professional who is ethical, values driven, meritocratic, educated, well trained and competent, who is also efficient and effective and who possesses the right behaviour, conduct and attitude in the service of society.

Transforming the police service from being racist and authoritarian to being inclusive, democratic and caring

South Africa's new police force was supposed to uphold the law with professionalism, compassion and respect for all South Africans, in contrast to its previous policies of repression and racial prejudice. The nation's police force was once well known for its racist policies and oppressive practices. It was hoped that South Africa's police force would move past its history of authoritarian and racially discriminatory means of enforcing the law and instead treat every citizen with professionalism, compassion and dignity. Consequently, it was necessary to reorganise and elevate the South African Police Service to the status of a professional service. Some 30 years ago, in 1994, the country's first democratically elected government started the process of reorganising the South African Police Service and this was the first SAPS reorganisation. At the time, the vast majority of South Africans thought that the police force was experiencing a serious crisis of legitimacy due to decades of policies that had been employed to impose apartheid in a violent and discriminatory manner. The apartheid government abused and exploited non-white police officers as a sort of cheap labour, and the police force itself was a reflection of the racist mentality of the political masters in control of it.[4] With the rise of democracy came the beginning of one of the most comprehensive and extensive efforts to reform the police force that had ever been attempted. Efforts were made to transform the SAPS from a violent and racist institution that defended the interests of a minority white elite into a democratic institution that represented the demographic diversity of the nation and protected the interests of all South Africans. Historically, the SAPS was known for its defence of the interests of a minority white elite.

George Fivaz, the first national commissioner of the SAPS, distinguished three components forming the three stages of the police reform process: "rationalization, amalgamation, and transformation."[5] "Rationalization" refers to the administrative process of restructuring the SAPS to enable it to operate within the new institutions of both the federal and provincial governments. "Amalgamation" was the term used to describe the process of uniting several distinct police agencies that had been founded during apartheid to form a unified national police force. The SAPS was supposed to be changed into a "professional, representative, efficient and effective, impartial, transparent, and responsible service" in accordance with the dictionary meaning of "transformation".[6] Van Kessel claims that even though there were multiple policy documents that addressed the importance of representativeness, very little forward movement occurred in the first five years. After Jackie Selebi was appointed national commissioner of the SAPS in 1999, the movement to ensure improved racial representation and equity gained popular traction. This was a watershed moment for the newly elected ANC-led government and the broader democratic movement in South Africa at the time.

Batho Pele "people first" initiative launched

In a democratic South Africa, the new administration inherited a public service that remained unchanged and possessed the skills and attitudes needed to meet the enormous development challenges confronting the country, according to the Department of Monitoring and Evaluation DME, 2020. The new government held the view that the public service lacked professionalism both in general and in its ability to serve the majority of South Africans, not only the white minority. "Batho Pele", which means "people first" in Sesotho, was an idea that the new government used to launch its initial attempt to professionalise the state. Batho Pele, which was initiated in 1997, had as its primary objective the transformation of the public service from the lowest level employee to the highest levels. This objective was accomplished by attempting to change the "old culture" and ensuring that all public service staff would dedicate themselves fully to their vocations and handle state resources with care and respect.

It has been concluded that modernising the police department is necessary for it to become a more professional and service-oriented government agency. The Police Act (South African Police Service Act 68 of 1995), the Police Code of Conduct, Chapters 10 and 11 of the South African Constitution, and Chapters 12, 13 and 14 of the National Development Plan 2030 for 2012 all mandate the essential changes to the SAPS.

The South African Police Force, or SAP as it is commonly called, was founded on 1 April 1913. The military forces often requested aid from the SAP in repressing the armed wing of the ANC, or uMkhonto we Sizwe, across the nation in the years that followed, up to the regime's overthrow in the early 1990s. This police force was especially crucial in maintaining apartheid and an oppressive status quo during the period of apartheid, when South Africa was generally considered to be a police state.[7] Having been viewed as an "enemy of the state" for a considerable period of time, the ANC took control of South Africa in April 1994. The SAP participated directly in the apartheid era, which is why reforming the country's policing system has focused a lot of attention on the present government. The organisational transformation that occurred inside the South African Police thus necessitated a significant reorganisation and restructuring of management, administration and service delivery. A significant reorganisation of the new SAPS occurred after 1994. Since then, there have been a few restructuring processes that were introduced to transform and professionalise the police force, which also included constitutional reforms.

Code of Conduct published

In 1997, the SAPS published a Code of Conduct. This document outlines precise guidelines and expectations for professional policing in a democratic society. The Code of Conduct mandates that the police must "exercise the powers entrusted to us in a responsible and controlled manner; actively work to prevent any form of corruption and bring its perpetrators to justice; and act impartially, courteously, honestly, respectfully, transparently, and in an accountable manner". This Code of Conduct was developed as a preventative measure against unethical activities and misdeeds that occurred during the period of apartheid to serve as a deterrent against such actions. Through the development of this code, the SAPS has not only gained the public's trust and confidence but also spread the ideas of professionalism and responsiveness to the needs of the community.

On the other hand, these codes have been subject to criticism for a very long time because they are unreliable. Such critics include civil society organisations such as Corruption Watch. The following have been dissected to be amongst the challenges of non-professionalism of the SAPS, just to mention but a few: a problem of organisational incapacity, a problem of low morals and ethics, a problem of corruption, a problem of poor coordination, accountability and oversight and other structural inadequacies, a need for structural reforms, poor resourcing of police, i.e., inadequate equipment and facilities, police brutality, poor relations within the community, ineffective recruiting procedures, dearth of effective training and police skills acquisition programmes, a hostile working atmosphere, uncompetitive salaries (when compared to private security personnel), as well as insufficient retirement payout for retirees, poor administration, favouritism, bias, nepotism, political interference, poor community relations, "remilitarisation" of the police, a serial management crisis, and a lack of capacity and skills, amongst others.

Measuring SAPS performance

The South African government recognises, according to the National Planning Commission (2020), that it has not been successful in (re)building state capacity and professionalising the public sector, including the SAPS. The state has been characterised by personal and patronage-based appointments, corruption, inadequate training, low professional ethics, unequal compensation and excessive labour turnover. The quality of public services varies widely, and they are generally of a poor standard. Whilst the public confidence in the police is currently at 26 per cent, the percentage of corrupt employees in public service still remains relatively high. This may seem contradictory. Perhaps police visibility has improved over the years. Yet still, according to the Corruption Perceptions Index (CPI) of Transparency International of 2022, which is a respected leading global indicator of public sector corruption, and which scores and ranks 180 countries and territories across the globe, South Africa has a CPI of 44/100.

According to Gallup's 2019 global Law and Order Index, South Africa scored fifth lowest out of 142 countries. Only Liberia, Gabon, Venezuela and Afghanistan fared worse. Poor service delivery outcomes have been the combined result of the lack of a professional public service, the absence of career paths for officials working within the service, the absence of competency determinants and the prevalence of political assignments at local government administrative levels (NPC, 2020). This, however, may not necessarily be true for the SAPS. There are career paths for SAPS members, as well as competency requirements. Whereas there are government departments where it is absent, there are government departments where it is present. This is true for the SAPS.

According to Bello,[8] Bouckaert et al. established many critical metrics for measuring SAPS performance, including service quality, service availability and service level. This was done in terms of SAPS micro-performance. When residents have the impression that state institutions, like the police, are paying attention and can respond appropriately to instances of criminal activity, we say that the state has behaved well.[9] On the other hand, at the macro level, the success of the police is judged by measures such as the crime rate, the fear of crime, the level of insecurity and the degree to which there is disorder in the area.[10] Both on the micro level, where the public has low to no faith in the police, and on the macro level, where they are failing to cope with the high crime rate numbers, the SAPS have done poorly and that is why the public has little to no trust in the police.[11] These views are confirmed by the StatsSA Victims of Crime Survey 2020/2021, which confirms that public perception of law enforcement is generally very low. Also, in recent years, there has been a growing number of disputes about the use of excessive force and other forms of physical intimidation by members of the SAPS. According to Media24 reports, law enforcement officials have previously instituted a "shoot-to-kill" strategy.

So why have they been unsuccessful?

The question then is why have the efforts of the government to render this part of the state more professional and service-oriented not been successful? What are the challenges of (re)building a professional state in the post-colonial setting of contemporary South Africa?

The Public Service Commission's[12] State of the Public Service Report highlights the Public Service's Capacity and Capability. The lack of implementation skill, not the absence of effective ideas, is accountable for poor outcomes in many nations. It is hypothesised that the success of nations depends on the capacity to implement policy plans successfully and a public sector that can optimally align resources for policy execution. In addition, the formulation of "implementable" strategies and the necessary capability for their implementation are essential for service delivery. Emerging evidence from South Africa's National Planning Commission reveals that poor policy implementation is responsible for poor service delivery outcomes, even though several of the policies have gained critical acclaim. A strategy that does not consider the implementation environment is not a good plan, though. Considering the sluggish execution of the National Development Plan 2030, the state's competence and capability to deliver have become even more crucial. Therefore, it is still unclear why, to attain these desired service-delivery outcomes, the government has not yet rebuilt state capacity or professionalised the public service. There is a lack of an evidence-based determination to what extent government interventions are making a difference in (re)building institutional capability and professionalising the public service, and the SAPS to be specific.

A watershed moment: Adoption of the National Framework for Professionalisation of the Public Sector

The National Framework for Professionalisation of the Public Sector represents a momentous moment in the life of the public service under the democratic government. It was developed by the National School of Government, working together with the Public Service Commission and the Department of Public Service and Administration, and other critical stakeholders. It was adopted by cabinet in October 2022. This, in my opinion, is the most recent and significant accomplishment of the democratic government towards the transformation of the public service – the establishment of the National Professionalisation Framework. Minister Thulas Nxesi, who was acting as the Minister of Public Service and Administration at the time, oversaw publishing the National Framework for Professionalisation of the Public Sector on 19 October 2022. This publication was allowed by the cabinet. The publication of a draft National Implementation Framework for the professionalisation of the public sector had been first approved by cabinet, and the document was made available for public comment in December of 2020. In February 2021, a public consultation process was initiated with the primary stakeholders, which included representatives from a wide variety of organisations, institutions and professional bodies. The framework was officially adopted by cabinet in October 2022. The NSG, the PSC and the DPSA are now working on an Implementation Plan to give full effect to the professionalisation framework.

The framework proposes five critical pillars of professionalisation of the public service. These pillars will be essential to the development of the professionalisation initiative. The five pillars include: pre-entry recruitment and selection within the public service; induction and onboarding; planning and performance management; continuing learning and professional development; and career progression and career incidents.[13] The intention of the Professionalisation Framework in South Africa is to enhance the quality, effectiveness and efficiency of the public service by establishing standards, guidelines and mechanisms for recruiting, developing and managing public-sector employees. The framework aims to professionalise the public service by promoting:

- merit-based recruitment;
- performance management; and
- career progression based on competency and skills.

Specifically, the Professionalisation Framework seeks to achieve the following objectives:

- promote merit-based recruitment;
- strengthen capacity and skills development;
- establish standards and guidelines;
- enhance performance management;
- foster a culture of professionalism and integrity;
- promote transparency and accountability in public sector operations;
- improve service delivery and governance; and
- build public trust and confidence in the public sector.

Overall, the professionalisation framework in South Africa is intended to transform the public service into a more efficient, effective and accountable institution that can meet the needs and expectations of citizens and supporting the country's development objectives. By establishing clear standards, promoting merit-based recruitment and investing in skills development and performance management, the framework aims to build a professional public service that can deliver high-quality services, promote good governance and contribute to sustainable development.[14]

Conclusion

South Africa faces a number of serious challenges when related to state capacity and professionalism of the public service, and in particular of the police service. Whilst the structural challenges seem immense and insurmountable, the democratic government has, over the past 30 years, and as recently as 2023, shown immense leadership in trying to find solutions to these challenges.

The creation of the National Implementation Framework is regarded as being of the highest significance in terms of the process of professionalising the public service. The current administration, under the leadership of President Cyril Ramaphosa, has therefore made a considerable commitment to concentrating efforts toward the construction of a competent, ethical and progressive state as part of the Medium-Term Strategic Framework (2019–2024).

Indeed, looking forward, the future of public service looks bright! With all the ups and downs, I do not regret being here.

References

Bello P.O. 2021. 'Do people still repose confidence in the police? Assessing the effects of public experience of police corruption in South Africa'. *African Identities*, 19(2):141–159, DOI: 10.1080/14725843.2020.1792827

Beukman, F. 2017. National Development Plan recommendations for Policing: SAPS, Civilian Secretariat for Police & Civil Society briefing. https://pmg.org.za/committee-meeting/24985/

Boateng, F.D. 2015. 'Trust in the police: An analysis of urban cities in Ghana'. Doctoral dissertation. USA: Washington State University.

Brewer, J.D. 1994. *Black and Blue: Policing in South Africa*. Oxford: Clarendon Press.

COGTA. 2023. 'Enhancing State Capacity and Capabilities to Accelerate Basic Service Provision, Infrastructure Development and Maintenance'. https://www.cogta.gov.za/index.php/2023/05/31/enhancing-state-capacity-and-capabilities-to-accelerate-basic-service-provision-infrastructure-development-and-maintenance/ (accessed 21 February 2024).

Di Maro, V., Evans, D.K., Khemani, S. and Scot, T. 2021. 'Building State Capacity: What Is the Impact of Development Projects?' https://www.cgdev.org/sites/default/files/building-state-capacity-what-impact-development-projects.pdf (accessed 10 February 2024).

Edigheji, O. 2005. 'A Democratic Developmental State in Africa. A concept paper'. Johannesburg: Center for Development Studies.

Faull, A. and Rose, R., 2012. 'Professionalism and the South African Police Service: What is it and how can it help build safer communities?' *ISS Africa*. https://issafrica.org/research/papers/professionalism-and-the-south-african-police-service-what-is-it-and-how-can-it-help-build-safer-communities (accessed 28 February 2023).

Green, T. and Gates, A. 2014. 'Understanding the process of professionalisation in the police organisation'. *The Police Journal*, 87(2):75–91.

Government of South Africa: Department of Monitoring and Evaluation. 2020. Medium Term Strategic Framework 2019–2024. Pretoria: Government Printing Press.

Mgweba, T. 2023. Framework Towards Professionalisation of the Public Sector: NSG, PSC & DPSA briefing. https://pmg.org.za/committee-meeting/36958/ (accessed 17 February 2024).

Public Servant, The. 2023. 'Minister Kiviet outlines the goals of professionalisation of the public service'. https://www.dpsa.gov.za/thepublicservant/2023/07/17/minister-kiviet-outlines-the-goals-of-professionalisation-of-the-public-service/ (accessed 20 February 2024).

National School of Government. n.d. 'Professionalising the public service', http://www.agsa.co.za/Portals/0/Reports/PFMA/202021/NSG%20-%20Professionalising%20the%20public%20service%20-%20FINAL.pdf

NDP. Chapter 13. https://www.nationalplanningcommission.org.za/assets/Documents/NDP_Chapters/NDP%202030-CH1Building%20a%20capable%20and%20developmental%20state.pdf (accessed: 21 February 2024).

Ndlovu, S. 2016. 'State Fragility as State Incapacity: The Case of Post-apartheid South Africa'. In *State Fragility and State Building in Africa: Cases from Eastern and Southern Africa* edited by D. Olowu and P. Chanies. Germany: Springer, pp:61–87. https://www.researchgate.net/publication/300334510_State_Fragility_as_State_Incapacity_The_Case_of_Post-apartheid_South_Africa (accessed 20 February 2024).

Newham G., Masuku T. and Dlamini J. 2006. 'Diversity and Transformation in the South African Police Service: A study of police perspectives on race, gender and the community in the Johannesburg policing area'. Criminal Justice Programme March 2006.

Nkomo, M.O. 1986. 'A comparative study of Zambia and Mozambique: Africanization, professionalisation, and bureaucracy in the African postcolonial state'. *Journal of Black Studies*, 16(3):319–342.

NSG. 2023. 'A national framework towards the professionalisation of the public sector'. https://www.thensg.gov.za/wp-content/uploads/2022/10/NATIONAL-FRAMEWORK-BOOKLET.pdf (accessed 17 February 2024).

Staatskoerant, 2020. 'A National Implementation Framework towards the Professionalisation of the Public Service'. *Government Gazette*. www.gpwonline.co.za.

Presidency – Republic of South Africa. 2012. National Development Plan 2030. Pretoria: The Presidency.

Public Service Commission. 2016. 'Building a Capable, Career-Oriented and Professional Public Service to Underpin a Capable and Developmental Sate in South Africa', Discussion document, May 2016. Pretoria.

Van Kessel, I. 2001. 'Transforming the South African Police Service (SAPS): The changing meaning of change'. Paper delivered at the South African Sociological Association congress, 1–4 July 2001.

7

Strenue

Samantha Herbst

We were headed to school today and you had that serious look about you, pensive under your ever-present knitted brow. You nodded out towards the window and said, "Look at that man in the black shirt, Mom. He's picking up litter."

I stole a glance across the double-laned avenue and there, rounding a corner on one of the side streets off Louis Botha, was a homeless man with a white plastic packet. He was, as you said, picking up litter. I didn't share my assumption that the man was more than likely a type of waste picker looking for scraps to recycle. In your mind, he was just a do-gooder out in the world. Maybe that's exactly what he was.

"He's picking up litter and he lives by himself," you commented, sad.

I asked you how you knew he lived by himself, and you replied, "It's so early in the morning, and there's no family around him."

We'd woken up with the sun, the four of us piled around each other in one big bed of limbs. Then, as we do every school morning, we got up (mostly grumpy), to haphazardly make our way through to the day.

Thinking about it now, I realise that, to you, this is a lucky way of being, because you're a little person in a bigger family. Because you have people who don't mind waking up with your limbs in their face, and because those people would do early-morning litter runs with you, the way your brother thinks it's fun to hold the bag while you pick up the dog poo in the garden. Lucky.

In the car, when the light turned green, I turned up the radio, edging forward at the wheel. The music was my choice that day, and next on the playlist was Tallest Man on Earth and a song about the autumn of life, and a certain love: "old but heavy". You weren't sold on it yet, but I persisted, the way I made you a Swiftie through doggedness, determination and sheer force of exposure.

"Sometimes sad songs can be the most true," I told you. And that's when you started listening with intent.

You were looking out the window as I yielded, 10 cars deep, at the back of the next intersection – the part of the suburb where load-shedding had taken over that morning. You asked me to turn down the music, which you always do when you want to say something important. When I obliged, you said, "Mom, sharks don't actually hate people, right? Because sometimes they're just hungry."

Your old play group used to be 10 minutes from home. It was across from the Greek school, the one founded by Advocate George Bizos, in one of the east's more affluent neighbourhoods. The school (not yours, the Greek one, but same-same) famously promotes Hellenism based on the notion that incorporating the Greek language, and the study of civilisation and culture, will instil in young people an understanding of independent and critical thinking against the backdrop of democracy. Bizos's vision was to "produce worthy citizens who [would] enrich South African society at large".

I looked into it once, when I considered whether the school would be a good fit for you. But, if your dad and I had applied for you to attend that school, the yearly fees would've cost a tenth of the value of our house. The Hellenic vision is a noble one, but expensive. Not just for us, though, I like to remind your dad (and myself). It's unaffordable for most people in our country. Ninety-eight to 99 per cent, I'd guess.

But I digress.

When you were still a toddler, not yet at big school, you'd play all day at the Reggio Emelia-inspired playgroup across from the Hellenics, and I'd spend my time not veering far from a five-square-kilometre radius around the Hellenics bubble. There's a coffee shop nearby that I'd write in until pick-up time, and I'd enjoy the WhatsApp group updates from your teacher while I judged overconfident suits at an adjacent table.

You know the ones, they beat the dead horses of on- versus offshore investment and say things like, "It's important to have an evaluation method in place." I'd shamelessly listen in on a table of mommy gossipers from the nearby girls' school, taking note how the conversation shifted when one woman in the group left for the loo. I'd bank those details, thinking how one day they would be characters in a story I write about ladies who lunch.

But this year, things changed somewhat, as did my radius, as did our route, as did we. I'd predicted that our world would be different, but only because of your school's location, and not because of everything that came with it.

You are now the same age I was when South Africa – the South Africa you've inherited – came of age. It was hardly worth acknowledging at the time, but the start of my "big school" career dovetailed with South Africa's first year of racial integration. I was six, sheltered from the chaos of the world, so the impact of the new dispensation was largely lost on me. Nevertheless, it feels like kismet that such a personal transition, the commencement of my formal education, lined up with this much larger historical milestone. And my child facing the same transition a neat three decades later? Even more so.

Your new school is the only public school in a triad of traditional monastic establishments that have been around for more than 120 years. Together, the schools are nestled in what can only be described as a geographical Schrödinger's Cat – a bizarre paradox of potential that exists in this particular Johannesburg real estate.

Imagine dropping a location pin at your new school, your back to the rest of Africa. Look right and you smile at Mandela's Houghton, but leer left, and you cast a shade on the outskirts of an underserved inner city. It feels ugly, and dangerous, and no one talks about it. I don't think anyone even likes to think about that darker side of the city.

Steeped in history, your school takes pride in its old boys, and in tradition. But it's also well aware of its location, and what that means against the backdrop of its own history. King Edward VII was, after all, a figurehead of British colonial rule. And so, for those who look for it, the very name of the establishment echoes a history of oppression rather than a school rooted in strength, vigour and trying. Strenue.

To its credit, for a school so steeped in history, it's committed to community, and not just the one on its more palatable right, as rich in colour and extravagance as the popularised Madiba shirts.

I've noted how your school refuses to shy away from the underserved, turning its chin to the dark side of Schrödinger's box, looking for potential and a way to help, through outreach, scholarship programmes and feeding schemes. There are boys in class with you who are fully funded by the school – though you won't know who they are. Boys who walk to class in the mornings from what are often perceived to be the more nefarious lairs of Joburg's inner city and surrounds. Boys who live in one-bedroom flats in Yeoville or Hillbrow; boys who live with other families so they can be close to school while their parents work on the other side of the city; boys with parents who depend on scholar transport to get their children safely from home to school and back again; boys with single moms who pray that this institution is as safe as they need it to be for their boy.

While I coax "two more bites" of sugary OTees into your mouth before we leave for the day, some of your peers go quietly to the aftercare centre in the early hours to get a school-issued breakfast and some lunch. It's important work, but something we don't talk about, because difference and privilege aren't drilled into you like it was me. I wonder if we should be talking about it, to normalise it… Or will that label your classmates as "other" or "lesser than" because you arrive at school with a belly full of OTees and a packed lunch, but they don't.

I've noticed the same handful of boys in your class who are absent when it rains. Your teacher explains that some of those boys are the ones who walk to school, and I wonder how many parents would be happy to chip in for school-issued transport to get those boys to class, or if some would be willing to divert their morning commute to pick up a boy on the way. Would it help to single out the boys who need a lift? Would it mean that we operate more as a team, or a family, rather than siloed individuals stuck in a self-serving frenzy? Or would it disturb the unique dynamic you've fostered with your classmates?

You and your peers are only five and six, and it seems to be enough that you've assimilated into a motley pack of little wolves who doff their caps with Cheshire cat smiles and walk proudly with hands clasped behind your backs – "Because that's how gentlemen walk, Mom."

In a way I'm not accustomed to, your motley pack of wolves acknowledges and accepts differences that don't put any one of you on the rungs of a hierarchical ladder. Your group knows and accepts that some among you don't have fathers, while others live with their grandmothers in the week. Some get a school-issued lunch, which you sometimes envy, and others use scholar transport to get to school, which you don't.

Difference is a part of your group's culture – neither good nor bad – and I wonder how long it will stay this way, because it feels almost lucky that you don't know the burden of having to believe that we are all cut from the same multicultural cloth. A "rainbow nation" who all bleed the same shade of red.

There was one encounter this year that taught you – with a saddened, earth-grounding punch to the gut – that not everyone gets a turn at the same trough, even if they're six, like you. While there are some boys who are fully funded by the school, others are not as fortunate, and they don't go to school at all. Sometimes, these boys wait for the last school bell to ring so they can intercept parents at pick-up to ask for food or money. The boys are normally about your age, or sometimes two to three years older, and you always wonder out loud where their parents are, or why they're not in school. Is it something we should all be wondering out loud?

On the day of the gut-punch encounter, we were walking to the car from your classroom, hands full with phones and keys and fingers intertwined, backs burdened with end-of-day schoolbags and errant artwork, when one of the school-less boys approached us for some food or money. I tried to ignore him, then told him we had nothing to give. I was hyperaware of the phone in my hand, my handbag vulnerably slipped over my shoulder, and his younger, quicker legs.

But you pulled back, insistent that you had some leftovers in your lunchbox. I obliged, and you gave the boy what food you could. Together we watched as he ran off – on younger, quicker legs – and divided the spoils among friends and brothers who were waiting around the corner. You asked me why I'd lied about having something to give, and I said nothing.

Like your school, the name of the main road we take to get to Schrödinger's Cat in the mornings recalls a pioneer of our country's oppression. Louis

Botha was a Boer war veteran who became the first prime minister of the Union of South Africa, in office during King Edward VII's rein. It was around this time too that renowned and celebrated English architect James Alfred Cope-Christie lived in Johannesburg, and when he designed and constructed three legacy homes that have since become heritage sites in the city.

House Hains in Yeoville was Cope-Christie's first project in Johannesburg. The house's plans date back to 1903 and, interestingly, out of the three provincial heritage sites (the others, House Page in Waverley and Dolobran House in Parktown), House Hains reflects "all the signs of Yeoville decay and neglect", according to writer and activist Kathy Munro.

"What more should be done to save this small gem?" pleads the Heritage Association of South Africa chairperson in a piece on The Heritage Portal. She laments that House Hains doesn't yet have a blue plaque, even though it was awarded Provincial Heritage status in 1994.

Munro describes Yeoville as "a bellwether for social changes and new demographic mixes". She highlights the former leafy suburb as one of the first to open up to racial integration – "far earlier than the other suburbs" – giving it "an early reputation for being alternative".

Alternative, or neglected? When the integration happened, did we all turn our collective chins west, towards Mandela's Houghton, allowing for House Page, in Waverley, and the Dolobran mansion, in Parktown, to stand tall and proud and without decay, while House Hains and the rest of the "alternative" suburb fell below the radar, underserved? I'm not placing blame, because town planning and municipal investment are not my forte. But how this particular Schrödinger's Cat came to be fascinates me as I zigzag between the new money of Johannesburg east and the established affluence of Upper Houghton, only feeling the need to close my eyes in prayer and fear as we cross the double lane over Louis Botha, and back to safe suburbia within the minute.

You didn't know I was doing it, but when we first started our morning commutes to your new school, I preferred to take the more scenic drive via Norwood. I found that taking the long route through Joburg's leafier suburbs, getting you to school via Madiba's Houghton, was much more palatable than driving the straight route down Louis Botha Avenue which still feels lawless, dangerous, decaying.

It's a drive pockmarked with poverty, potential, crime and hope – sometimes won, sometimes lost. I can see that those who live and work on the drive are trying (strenue) but still, on the days we had time, I opted to commute via Norwood and Houghton, up Munro Pass, which looms over our City of Gold. And every time we'd get to the top I'd remind you that we could see the whole of Johannesburg from there, and you'd look with me as we circled round the bend, and together we'd be proud.

Did you know that Munro Pass, one of only a handful in our country that are shorter than a kilometre, dates back to the gold rush days of early pioneer Johannesburg? It was named after John Munro, a former director of mining giant JCI, which was offered as a Black Economic Empowerment vehicle in 1995. The company divided and grew roots in the new South Africa under different names, but the name Munro stuck as it pertained to that particular pass. As did King Edward VII. As did Louis Botha.

Together with Sylvia's Pass and Stewart's Drive, Munro Pass was built to connect Upper Houghton and Houghton, giving Johannesburg residents of yore access to new, liveable places in the south. Cutting through Yeoville and Observatory, the rocky ridges of these passes serve as a natural barrier between the north and south of the city.

Conveniently for me, I found that the passes also served to divert your attention from the misspelt billboards advertising evangelical churches on "Loius Botha" Avenue. My ability to use Munro Pass gave me permission to evade your inevitable questions about the faded chalk signage outside low-priced crèches. It helped steer our family Mazda away from the homeless bodies cocooned in blankets on the early-morning sidewalk, away from the people lined outside the betting establishment before seven in the morning, away from the sun-bleached and peeling posters of celebrities, pasted years ago above the musty doorways of hair salons and barber shops.

Munro Pass gave me leave to turn my chin away from the unkempt, unruly integration of poverty and need, to the manicured lawns of Upper Houghton, which are always nicer to look at.

When I was younger, and somewhat more removed from the socio-political economy, driving down a road like Louis Botha would have thrilled me. Like the pre-gentrified Bo-Kaap, the supposedly "less-scenic" route down Louis Botha would colour Africa in for me. It showcased a culture so rich and buoyant and fat with life that it made me proud to be in such close proximity to promise, to a "liberated Africa". In close proximity, but conveniently removed from the thick of it, I could appreciate the richness of Louis Botha's fat-with-life culture from the safety of my suburban stoep, which lay within a five-kilometre radius of everything I needed. I could watch, without getting my hands dirty.

This remained conveniently true for me until I had to think of you. Until I had to think of your future, immediate and distant. Until I had to leave you, my baby, with other people during the day while I worked. People who would initially be strangers, at a place that would, at first, be foreign and scary for you and for me.

Until I became a mother, I would have revelled in the faded chalk drawings of Disney characters lining the walls of someone-else's-kid's crèche. Until I became a mother, seeing *You* magazine-like cut-outs of Will Smith and Beyoncé pasted so incongruously above a local barber, or seeing children as young as you are now stopping at a spaza shop on their way to school, would have delighted me. But when I became a mother, the peeling faces started to make me sad. The thought of my baby having to walk to school without holding my hand, or letting anyone other than the best-trained staff at one of the most prestigious crèches in the city look after you, made my blood run cold.

Until I became a mother, I saw Johannesburg differently.

There are some days when I catch glimpses of the city as I saw it before, especially now that I've grown used to the new school route. On my way to fetch you in the afternoon, when I'm alone in the car with nothing but my tangled thoughts, I take note of dressy young execs crossing the busy street – arms hooked, lunchboxes crooked, braids swaying in the warm autumn breeze. I spot the lady across the Pick n Pay parking lot shucking mealies over a makeshift box braai, or I peak into those musty barber shops and see a story: two or three newly shaven gents, a combination of barber and customer, cackling at one joke or another between fist bumps and phone scrolls, leaving me wondering what the joke is.

Every day, as I drive past the Super Sconto, I consider the bougier Melvillians sipping foamy cappuccinos at our-side-of-town's authentic Italian coffee shop, picking up their weekly supply of genuine Italian prosciutto crudo. And then there's the Radium Beerhall, which is still standing and, rumour has it, quite the establishment.

Like its family-friendly counterpart The Doll House roadhouse, which was shuttered in 2017, Radium is an institution, a remnant of Old Johannesburg. It claims to be the city's oldest surviving bar, which first opened its doors in 1929. Back then it was renowned for selling alcohol to black customers from a secret shebeen, which was illegal in a district designated for whites. Now it's better known for its wood-fired pizza and still-good beer. And we drive past it every day, twice a day. Lucky.

I think about this, and about the little old lady who sweeps the pavement outside Samaz Butchery & Braai Lounge at 7:15 am every day. I think about the young mom, bundled in her doek and pilling-grey nightgown, who chats with the little old lady at Samaz Butchery & Braai while she waits with her son for his transport to arrive in the mornings. I've noticed other moms too, some in doeks and pilling-grey nightgowns, others dressed smartly for the rush-hour commute, lugging the dead weight of their tired children, big and small. Children who, I notice, have started wilting earlier and earlier in the day as the months of the year wear on.

There's a certain time here in Gauteng that feels like a pressure cooker. It happens before the rain each November, when the welcome chill of a fresh spring morning – short-lived – gives way to Summer Proper. When a barrier of heat hits the Highveld by eight in the morning, and temperatures keep rising to an almost-unbearable max at midday.

If you pay attention to the children, you know when the wall has hit its peak in the year. Johannesburg's young people sense this pressure-cooker period before we do. Their teachers complain about their restlessness in the classroom, and their little bodies, which need to be carried everywhere, fall asleep on the home-time commute. It's like the collective burnout and fatigue of parents seep into the pores of Johannesburg children, like osmosis. We can carry the weight, but it's too much for them, and it's not theirs to bear.

I'm probably doing it now, burdening you with my fatigue, your teacher wondering why you haven't felt yourself this week, why you can't sit up straight at carpet time and why you refuse even the simplest tasks. But, as you've said to me, it all feels a little overwhelming right now, and sometimes you just need to lie down.

This week, my boy, we'll take the scenic route again. Together we can turn our chins to the more palatable side of town and close our eyes in fear and prayer as we cross the double drive into the safety of suburbia, not only because it's time to take brief leave of our burden, but also because we can.

Next week we'll retrieve the load because it doesn't feel right when we don't. And we'll turn our chins both ways, because you're a gentleman among your gentlemen peers, and because I'm a South African and now you are too.

Strenue.

References

Munro, K. 2021. 'Iconic heritage home survives Yeoville,' *The Heritage Portal*, 30 September 2021. https://www.theheritageportal.co.za/article/iconic-heritage-home-survives-yeoville (accessed 16 December 2023).

8

On epidemics, epigraphs and Roshila Nair's "Fanon's land"

Helena van Urk

As a child of the new millennium, I can't recall too much about the HIV/AIDS crisis that rendered a newly independent South Africa infamous on the world stage as the country where over 600 men and women, usually in the prime of their lives, would die of the disease in a single day. The virus that Mandela pronounced our "new struggle" at his son Makgatho's funeral,[1] much like all other viruses, is not really something one can explain to a toddler – and besides, I was from a nice, white suburban Johannesburg home, the sort of place where "those things don't really happen". However, as the epidemic and Mbeki's AIDS denialism continued to define the landscape of an independent South Africa, it nonetheless started leaching into the horizons of my life ever so slightly.

I was taught to never, ever touch someone else's blood or open wounds before starting kindergarten – we kept surgical gloves in the house long before it would become fashionable about two decades later – and whined once or twice that I wanted to wear a beadwork pin with a red AIDS ribbon crowned by the South African flag to school, just like my mother sometimes did. I enjoyed spending my Saturday mornings helping to pack food parcels at the church hall, eager to be helping children who were "just like me" – only they no longer had a mummy and daddy, and lived in a place called Alexandra. I learnt to pronounce the name of outreach committee members who sometimes gathered at our home as best as I could, and always made sure to hug my father when he came home and told my mother that another colleague had been sent home on bereavement leave.

When I was gifted Alexander Parker's *50 People Who Stuffed Up South Africa* as a preteen, and the names Manto Tshabalala-Msimang, Zackie Achmat and the Treatment Action Campaign (TAC) acquired some flesh and blood, righteous anger welled up at the fact that it seemed, in the words of Pieter-Dirk Uys, that we "had one government that killed people, now we have one that lets them die".[2] Or, if one prefers slightly more Fanonian, less sanctimonious parlance, "the unpreparedness of the elite, the lack of practical ties between them and the masses, their apathy, and yes, their cowardice at the crucial moment in the struggle, are the cause of tragic trials and tribulations."[3]

When the Covid-19 pandemic began in earnest for South Africa in March 2020 I was an awkward twenty-something with a bad haircut who had just started my second year at university. The long sunny lull of the December holidays had been not quite punctured, but rather rocked slightly, by the news of a new respiratory virus having reared its head in the Chinese city of Wuhan. I had paid it little mind. After all, new zoonotic diseases inevitably emerge now and then, and the last time I could remember such international hysteria about a looming pandemic, in 2009, I did end up catching swine flu – and turned out just fine.

It was on a Sunday afternoon, after weeks of joking about hoping to find easier seating in restaurants and panicked runs on disinfectant and garlic pills in the nearby Dischem, that things were finally brought home. First the announcement came from the faculty that the next day's exam, which I had been diligently putting off studying for, was postponed. A flurry of other emails from the university then began hinting at a reduction, or even temporary cessation, of its academic activities. In hindsight, the fact that, a week or so previously, a meeting on campus about the Palestinian crisis had devolved into panicking students voicing questions about their health and safety after the plane from Italy was confirmed to have brought the virus into the country, should have been a warning sign. Then something truly extraordinary happened: it was announced that the president would address the nation that night. Exactly how severe would he look, and would he start the broadcast with a grave "My fellow South Africans…", just like in the movies? Everyone knows more or less how the story goes from here: a week spent preparing feverishly for Stage 5 lockdown, the eerie quietness of deserted city streets across the world as smog lifted and dolphins returned to the canals of Venice, a seemingly endless series of hobbies and culinary experiments ranging from the everyman's sourdough starters and banana bread to elaborate three-layered chocolate cheesecakes. I, at long last, managed to finish Milton's *Paradise Lost*.

Staying at home became a bit more stifling as it became clear we "were all in this together" for a longer run than first expected. Walks around the block, sometimes punctuated by strange bits of happiness like a take-as-you-need box of lemons left on a park bench, became tenuous threads tethering our collective sanity as images of refrigerated trucks filling with corpses in New York, and the elderly in Italy refusing ventilators in the hopes of saving a younger life, circulated around the world. Jokes about wearing pyjama pants to work, lectures and job interviews quickly became stale, and episodes of crying in the closet or the shower more frequent. For two and a half years, iterations of this were our reality, as the exact nuances of different levels of lockdown revealed itself to us. Groceries were sprayed down after being brought into the house and the country's ICU capacity and the comparative value of cloth and N-95 facemasks were discussed breathlessly.

Though spray-painted slogans like "PayTheGrants" sometimes showed up on walls near our local park, and the recent graduates in the family ended up moving back home to save money on rent, the second once-in-a-lifetime economic collapse that the world was enduring in less than twenty years remained far outside our suburban frame of reference for the most part – except for the odd charming story of a hardworking husband and wife who rolled up their sleeves when they lost their jobs, transforming their home into the most delightful little deli in a recently gentrified neighbourhood nearby. (I hear the chicken pies are to go *crazy* for.)

And then, almost like mist melting away before the sun, life started returning to normal all at once; the masks were thrown away, we congratulated ourselves on having risen to and conquered the biggest challenge our young democracy had yet faced, and carefully deferred questions of the full impact of the pandemic to the back of our collective minds. Considering the unquestionable intensity of it, we are mostly content to wait and see, or roughly estimate, just exactly how many people have and will continue to die of Covid-19 and its complications, precisely how many the world over were left broke and homeless, and what artistic genius this unique upheaval will have awakened in some of our world's most brilliant minds.

One of the first things I read when I finally stepped foot on campus once again, now a postgraduate with some light teaching responsibilities of my own, was a poem dug up by a lecturer coordinating a tutoring session on comparative poetics: Roshila Nair's "Fanon's land". As I started skimming through it, I at first could not believe that it was almost three decades old. If it were not for the epigram, which reads: "In honour of the late Gugu Dlamini, Zackie Achmat and other members of the Treatment Action Campaign, and all AIDS activists in Africa and elsewhere – the brave people who dare to remind us that freedom is a never-ending journey,"[4] I would have remained convinced that the virus being described so graphically as maligning and choking the life out of our body politic was Covid-19.

In the 1960s, the feminist critic and philosopher Julia Kristeva coined the term "intertextuality" to refer broadly to any relationship between different texts: just as it was understood that no man can truly be an island, no text can be said to exist but in relation to the texts that came before it, and the texts that come after it will inevitably have some relationship to the text in hand as well.[5] In fact, not only can a text only be a text through other texts, intertextuality itself is a factor that appreciably shapes and determines how we as readers perceive or receive the text; what we ultimately end up making of a piece of literature. Great theorists of the twentieth century, including Barthes and Derrida, heartily approved of this claim,[6] and the literary scholar Gérard Genette set out to build on Kristeva's work further, utilising the umbrella-term "paratext" to refer to any production, literary, verbal or visual, that accompanies and surrounds the main text – anything, that is, that may be said to "mediate the (work)[7] to the reader".[8] While we can debate whether some forms of what Genette called paratext may be classified as belonging strictly to the main text (when it is defined as a finite collection of words that produces meaning/s), the fact remains that a book's cover, illustrations and the publicity surrounding it are part and parcel of what presents a work of literature to a reader, in the literal sense of making it more, or most, *present*.[9] The addressee of paratextual elements is also a contentious matter, extending both beyond the reader in some cases, and limiting itself to a smaller circle than "the general public" in others. At any rate, Genette stresses that "the definition of paratext involves the necessity that someone should always be responsible for it" – in other words, that it is used deliberately by either the author, the editor or those otherwise surrounding the work to influence, often greatly, how the reader receives, perceives and ultimately accepts it.[10] While a paratextual element such as an epigram is thus always subordinate to its text and can only seek to exist in relation to it,[11] such an epigram may be taken as a pure statement of authorial intent, an instruction to readers as to how the work "should" be read.

"Fanon's land" and the epigram that accompanies it, denoting it for all time as originating from the early 2000s, when the HIV/AIDS epidemic was in full swing and Mbeki and Tshabalala-Msimang's AIDS denialism was being fiercely resisted by the TAC, was first published in 2004 in an anthology titled *Nobody Ever Said AIDS: Poems and Stories from Southern Africa*. Whilst the epidemic had been raging for years at this point, the anthology's editors were concerned by the lack of English-language literature about experiencing the disease, and the almost non-existent literary voice of its sufferers.[12] They sought to create a space where literature (still generally believed to be the key to some magical gateway to empathy in spite of warranted cynicism in recent times) could potentially pave a way forward for a broader national dialogue on the epidemic and its devastation.

The stigma that surrounded, and in some cases continues to surround, the disease today was after all notorious: it led directly to the killing of Gugu Dlamini, an activist from Kwamashu who was stoned and beaten to death by community members in 1998 after revealing her HIV-positive status on a radio broadcast. The case generated outrage, with the international media sagely lamenting the difficulty of combatting AIDS at its epicentre when sufferers could expect such barbarous reprisals.[13] To return to the anthology, it emerged from a national competition organised by its future editors and judged by the famed poets Ingrid de Kok and Njabulo Ndebele in the hopes of eliciting a sizeable number of contributions. In the year of its publication, it is reported, only 85 000 HIV/AIDS sufferers out of over five million were being treated with the antiretroviral medications (ARVs) that the Mbeki government had fought tooth and nail not to provide them with.[14]

"Fanon's land" is written in free verse and consists of four stanzas and 25 lines. Slightly devoid of punctuation, it reads almost as a continuous stream of consciousness. Thoughts seem to spill out and over onto the page in a mad rush, with cries of "the land! the land" repeated almost as if in anguish and the twisting and blurring together of "the old world the new world/the new world the old world" confronting the reader. These cries seem to be demanding an answer to the nagging question of how much of a qualitative difference can be seen in the "new world" of post-apartheid South Africa in the face of so much death and misery – suggesting that, "if you stared just long enough", the answer may not be a particularly comforting one, and the temporal break we have all established in our collective consciousness "before and after" 1994 may disappear entirely.[15]

This "new/old" world of Nair's poem exists collectively (the majority of the pronouns to be found in the poem are second- and third-person), as an almost uncomfortably physical representative of the nation as a single unitary body. The epidemic/s that ravaged us did not attack us as individual bodies, Nair's speaker suggests, but has as a whole body politic seen us "wrung dry of the fight/on laundry day". This simple simile is not merely comparing the diseased, emaciated and generally impoverished body to a piece of washing, but also suggests abuse, misuse and, above all, a different kind of poverty with the application of a verb with such harsh connotations as "wrung".[16] It is suggested that the economic, developmental and human potential of a nation is being dried up as the epidemic(s) rage and the death toll rises; its lifeblood and all means of continuing on is faltering and being drained away, like a national neck being wrung. The bedsheet in question, the very land of the country, is also noteworthy for being "old", imbued not only with blood-soaked history but drawing attention to the fact that in the "post-colonial hour",[17] this same bedsheet is being put through even more trauma of a history-defining nature: the people are tired, worn out and seem to have little fight left in them.

While such imagery is certainly an apt one for the HIV/AIDS epidemic on both an individual and collective scale, I was shocked by the poem's overall, emotive invocation of the context of the Covid-19 pandemic. Even the most bodily descriptions of the disease ravaging the nation and its people seemed eerily familiar. "Threadbare in the blood", for example, could imply an oxygen deficiency in the blood as much as a compromised immune response, whilst "bloody in the tongue" could denote not merely Kaposi sarcoma, but severe respiratory tract distress resulting in the coughing up of blood. Any sufferer of Covid who battled to get up the stairs after being infected, or has to live with damaged lungs and weakened lung capacity for the rest of their lives, would certainly experience being "wrung dry of the fight" just as physically.[18] The "grand things" that have "curled around us" that Nair references may seem familiar or comforting at first, but when considered in conjunction with the use of the word "wrung" in line 6 becomes distinctly more ominous and is suggestive of a hand or something more sinister wrapped around a throat, depriving sufferers and the nation of oxygen and choking the life out of us all. Though the poem was written in 2004, this particular bit of imagery seems almost tailor-made to describe the Covid pandemic, or any deadly respiratory virus. Likewise, the lines "god's creatures/vainly trying to transport us to paradise" that follow immediately after have an aura of menace about them, especially considering that "god" is not capitalised and the "heavenly creatures" in question are deliberately not referred to as angels, but rather have something almost bestial implied in them – being transported to paradise (again, not capitalised) is therefore not portrayed as something good or desirable, but something forbidding to be resisted.

"[T]he politics of viruses/and neo-liberal economic policies" should be intimately familiar to all of us who had to buy cigarettes on the black market or stayed up at night anxiously wondering how South Africa could afford to buy enough vaccinations for its population – knowing that unforgiving intellectual property laws in the field of life-saving medicine is currently a severe and urgent symptom of the inequitable realities of our neo-colonial world.[19]

Interestingly, the poem has only two capitalised words: the first being "threadbare" – possibly to emphasise the inherent physicality of any epidemic, or due to grammatical convention – and, of course, the titular "Fanon". An inspiration for liberation movements that range from the Black Panther Party to the Boycott, Divestment and Sanctions effort,[20] the Martinican-born physician-philosopher Frantz Fanon wrote some of the most influential anti-colonial Marxist tracts of the twentieth century, much of it focused on his own experiences in the Algerian war for independence. While his work mostly concerns the psychopathology of colonisation and the manifestation of violence in the colonial context, Fanon has special relevance to the AIDS epidemic. His influential essay "Medicine and colonialism" examines the relationship and complicities between western medicine and colonialism and claims, correctly, that no interaction between the (neo)colonised subject and western medicine can be free of the historical baggage inherent in it.[21] One of the great tragedies of this paradigm, Fanon argues, is the fact that even if western medicine or medical practices would be advantageous for (neo)colonised subjects to take or adopt, s/he will be more likely to reject it or view it with suspicion, as just another manifestation of colonial paternalism or arrogance.[22] The Mbeki government would go on to do just that, with plenty of arrogance of its own, using Fanon's writings on the subject to compile the paper "Castro Hlongwane, Caravans, Cat, Geese, Foot & Mouth and Statistics: HIV/AIDS and the Struggle for the Humanisation of the African" – the core text of the Mbeki government's AIDS denialism.[23] Bearing this history in mind, some critics have questioned the wisdom of Nair's choice of title, considering the subject matter.[24] However, Fanon's assignation to the name of the South African "no-man's land" is entirely justified on account of his blisteringly insightful notions of what happens in a neo-colonial, post-liberation (or apartheid) state.

Theorising that the leaders who take power after a colonised state gains full independence will, more often than not, face disjunction and therefore discontent between themselves and the people, Fanon foretells bleak things for the "postcolonial hour".[25] The new elites' desire to appropriate for themselves the wealth and prestige that defined their coloniser-forebears' position will surely prove irresistible,[26] Fanon writes, and in pursuit of this self-enrichment they will inevitably bring the status of a neo-colonial state down upon their country: still slavishly dependent on the colonial powers at the centre of world affairs in all but name.[27] While this happens, the new government will often neglect its bureaucratic and civic duties towards its citizens, leading to corruption becoming endemic and an increase in xenophobia and/or religious violence.[28] To put the cherry on top of this "insult and … outrage",[29] the leaders of this "no-man's",[30] effectively leaderless land, will frequently extoll the nation's epic history of liberation in order to quiet discontent, instructing the people to be grateful for "the immense distance they have covered" – a distance the ordinary person on the street will not be able to see, appreciate or even accept as factually correct, seeing as their reality of poverty and neglect will have changed little.[31] Proof of success of any liberation movement, Fanon writes, lies in whether or not the social fabric of a society has been turned inside out and upside down – not in demanding, therefore, that the same old bedsheet carries on as usual, accepting abuse from, and being wrung dry of fight by, slightly different hands.[32] If a newly independent nation that has managed to throw off the shackles of oppression wishes to succeed, it must learn from, but also reject, the models of European/colonial nationbuilding and lifestyle that came before and chart its own course:[33] learning "how to make everything/out of nothing again," in a nutshell.[34] Anything less will lead only to a feeling of helpless socio-political paralysis, which Kierkegaard termed "the anguish of liberty".[35]

While some might question the validity of rereading Fanon at this juncture, considering the fact that he got so many things "wrong" – I am personally no fan of the way women are portrayed in his works, for one – his prescience in defining the nature of the problems of the "postcolonial hour" must be given due credit, and certainly warrants Nair's assignation of South Africa to his name. In writing about Fanon's continued relevance in struggles for freedom across the world, Richard Philcox, his most recent translator, has suggested that one thing that keeps drawing in readers is Fanon's anger, which indeed sometimes seems to seep out from the pages, acerbic and acidic in its sarcasm. If I may speak for a generation, I will say that we do indeed have a lot of it to spare today.

The pre-eminent historian, political scientist and public intellectual Achille Mbembe wrote on the fiftieth anniversary of Fanon's death in 2011 that his work's most valuable contribution not merely to the academic sphere but indeed to the world, is its unwavering belief that the human spirit is indominable. His work, what it inspired and continues to inspire (and if we are to take Kristeva and Genette seriously, "Fanon's land" is just that in the most literal of senses), is a continuous, echoing clarion call for those who "yesterday confronted colonialism and today who strive to herald the dawn".[36] As we think back over 30 years of democracy and look to the future, it remains to be seen what this new dawn will bring and whether hope deferred may still be called "hope" any more – and if it could blossom into something new and beautiful.

References

Fanon, Frantz. 2021. *Black Skin, White Masks*. London: Penguin Books.

Fanon, Frantz. 1967. 'Medicine and Colonialism'. In *A Dying Colonialism*, translated by Haakon Chevalier, 121–145. New York City: Grove Press.

Fanon, Frantz. 2021. *The Wretched of the Earth*. New York: Grove Press.

Genette, Gérard and Maclean, Marie. 1991. 'Introduction to the Paratext.' *New Literary History*, 22(2):261–272.

Mbembe, Achille. 2013. 'Frantz Fanon's *Ouvres*: A metamorphic thought.' *Nka: Journal of Contemporary African Art*, 32:8–17.

McNeil, Donald G. Jnr. 1998. 'Neighbors Kill an H.I.V.-Positive AIDS Activist in South Africa.' *The New York Times*, 28 December 1998, https://www.nytimes.com/1998/12/28/world/neighbors-kill-an-hiv-positive-aids-activist-in-south-africa.html (accessed 18 August 2023)

Mirenayat, Sayyed and Soofastaei, Elaheh. 'Gérard Genette and the Categorisation of Textual Transcendence.' *Mediterranean Journal of Social Sciences*, 6(5):533–537.

Nair, Roshila. 2004. 'Fanon's land.' In *Nobody Ever Said AIDS: Poems and Stories from Southern Africa*, edited by Nobantu Rasebotsa, Meg Samuelson and Kyle Thomas, 179. Cape Town: Kwela Books.

Parker, Alexander. 2012. *50 People Who Stuffed Up South Africa*. Cape Town: Burnet Media.

Ross, Elliot. 2013. '"Fanon's no man's land": The difficult inheritance of anti-apartheid struggle in South Africa's HIV/AIDS literature.' *Scrutiny2: Issues in English Studies in Southern Africa* 18(2):36–45.

Thompson, Ginger. 2003. 'THE SATURDAY PROFILE: In Grip of AIDS, South African Cries for Equity.' *The New York Times*, 10 May 2003, https://www.nytimes.com/2003/05/10/world/the-saturday-profile-in-grip-of-aids-south-african-cries-for-equity.html (accessed 23 August 2023).

9

Umsinsi Wokuzimilela: A conversation on identity in post-apartheid South Africa[*]

Wonderboy Peters (WP) in conversation with Busani Ngcaweni (BN)

Thank you, Wonderboy Peters, for making time for this interview. This is not just an ordinary conversation because, as agreed, some of what will emerge is influenced by our reading of literature, and to an extent, history. We will allow the reader to meander through this journey of identity, being and becoming in South Africa which marks 30 years of democracy this year.

BN: Some people are surprised that you speak isiZulu so fluently. Should they be?

WP: Their surprise is fully understandable. It no longer surprises me. I'm no longer shocked or bothered by it. When I was still young that used to worry me a lot because I had this sense that I had to somehow constantly explain myself, especially to people who were interacting with me for the first time.

Politics of racial identity have shaped much of our engagements and

---

[*] Some names have been changed to protect the identities of certain individuals.

expectations of one another as South Africans. The bemusement from people derives from the fact that being biracial, I look very much like a coloured person. Although I have met a few coloured people who can converse in African languages, it is still a novel experience. It's the same as when you hear a white farmer speaking in Sesotho, isiXhosa or isiZulu. While it is a heartening experience, people still find it somehow odd because our experience has been that it is normal for African people to speak English or Afrikaans, but not for whites, coloureds or Indians to be fluent in our languages. This is the South Africa you and I grew up in, and many of our past behaviours are still with us to this day.

Around 1996, during an HIV and AIDS awareness campaign in Soweto, Chief Mangosuthu Buthelezi heard me conversing in isiZulu with one of the speakers, Professor Nhlanhla Maake. He was pleasantly surprised and he roared in laughter, "Hey, Dr Maake, *lomfana ukhuluma isiZulu. Hey, ukhuluma isiZulu esihle.*" We exchanged pleasantries with the [then] Minister of Home Affairs and it was the first time in my life to have a business card of a cabinet minister. As we parted ways, he insisted, "Wonderboy, *ungayeki ukukhuluma isiZulu uyezwa. Ubongibhalela uyezwa?*"

BN: Wonderboy, you don't just speak isiZulu, but you speak it even much better than many African people…

WP: Well, I have a friend, uMapholoba from eMlazi, who sometimes teases when I say *"kibo"* instead of *"kubo"* and says, "No, Mkholwa, now you are speaking the isiZulu from eMlomo (Ermelo) … that's Siswati, Mkholwa. No, my friend. That's Siswati." I usually laugh while I manage my disenchantment because most people from my home town of Ermelo believe they speak isiZulu, not Siswati.

I did isiZulu all my school life right up to university. The exception was when I did Standard Two [Grade 4], I moved with my grandmother who had resigned from living at the nearby farms around Ermelo to Dundonald, at the former Kangwane homeland. As you know, isiZulu and Siswati are part of Nguni languages, but I recall I struggled in the beginning with the Siswati spelling and pronunciation, although I could fully grasp what was taught.

I eventually mastered the differences, especially the orthography. Although I did well and later in my life I could even review Swati literature manuscripts based on my one year of classroom training in

Siswati, I never thought of Siswati as my "mother tongue".

I returned to the township at Ermelo for my Standard Three [Grade 5], and I had to quickly unlearn Siswati pronunciation and orthography. Our teachers insisted on proper pronunciation and you could be mocked by your classmates if you didn't talk, write or pronounce "proper" isiZulu.

The isiZulu teachers were dedicated, proud and enthusiastic teachers of the language. You were respected if you did well in the language, and I remember that the old Radio Zulu used to even announce the top learner in isiZulu national matric exams. That's the kind of success and recognition many of us aspired to from our primary-school days.

I had an excellent, committed teacher in my first two years of school at Topernite Bantu School. We knew her as Mam'Nxumalo and her husband was a respected induna at Spitzkop Colliery Mine where we lived with my mother and stepfather. It didn't take long for me in my first year to master reading what we called *isipele*. I recall when I had just mastered the alphabet and how to form words, I ran home and waited for my mother to return from work. I read the entire isiZulu reader which had pictures and I could read properly the different clicks.

When we moved to the township and I did my Standard One, my teachers were impressed with my reading ability. In Standard Five, I wrote the best essay for our exams, and I was taught by Mr Khumalo – a great isiZulu teacher and I knew the idioms, metaphors and narrative techniques.

Although it felt so good to be recognised, I always had the sense that it was still looking a bit strange for some of my peers that this light-skinned boy could do that. It was just drawing too much attention to the light-complexioned boy of the school and township, and making the younger learners ask all kinds of questions about my origins.

Even during athletic competitions, I felt exposed and vulnerable, especially when we were competing with other schools. I was a 100-metre sprinter and quite good at it. While I would be focused on the finishing line, the 100 metres could sometimes look like a marathon … I could pick up from the spectators the cheers for the white boy … *uyahamb'umlungu madoda … uyavay' umlungu* [there goes the white kid], they would say.

Sometimes such comments would break into fights when kids from my school stood up for me saying, "He's not a white person, he has a name. He's not white, *ngumuntu*." Umuntu here was not just a reference to a human being. It meant he is black … black like the rest of us. That's what my school mates and friends meant. The protesters, of course, would stand their ground saying, "*Akusiye umuntu, ngumlungu*" (He is not a black person, he's a white person). Certainly, in these instances *umlungu* was not an apolitical label. It was meant to hurt you, humiliate you and mark you as a strange existence in the sea of African people.

BN: Growing up must have been hell.

WP: Not necessarily. There were moments and experiences that were dumbfounding, hurtful and absurd. But, overwhelmingly, I had a normal, joyous childhood. I was loved and adored by my family. In my family, it never occurred to me that I was different from my siblings and other children. I only have one recollection when my difference was mentioned by an aunt to her friend, but other than that incident, I fully belonged in my family and extended family. My aunts, uncles, cousins nourished me with love, and my complexion was never an issue. I was not mocked.

I was very close to my grandmother, Khwayiza Mavuso. She was a strict disciplinarian and was known for her yelling and fighting if she did not agree with something. She was known for rising early in the morning and that she abhorred a dirty place.

I was also close to my grandfather, Mpiyakhe Mavuso. He treated me like one of his children. When he left the farms, he came and worked as a tractor driver at Spitzkop Colliery Mines. He collected dirt with a group of men who could not speak (*izimumu*). That was the year I had started school. One day, he got me a dog and my brother named it Zimba. We were normally an item with my dog. With Zimba by my side, I was unafraid to go to the forest and the veld to hunt. I recall days when I spent hours lying with my dog either in the veld or in the forest just watching time pass by.

My grandfather also got me my first bicycle. I rode on a train for the first time in my life with him to town where he used his hard-earned cash to buy me Barker shoes, which were in fashion and expensive by our family standards. He used to play a guitar and was a fantastic storyteller.

When I look back, my grandfather and grandmother had a soft spot for me. Although my grandmother was known for her short temper and beating up naughty children, I think she turned a blind eye to many of my misdemeanours.

When I lived with her at Dundonald, she would take me to town [Ermelo] at the end of every month. She would be visiting my uncles who lived in the township and was there to get money from them before they would waste it on gambling, women and booze. She would make me wear a hat, saying she does not want the township kids to make fun of me and mock me that I was a white child.

She suffered from asthma and persistent tuberculosis (TB). She would say she got her TB in 1973, during the year of my birth. She narrated how she had to run from one farm to the next in the cold trying to hide me from white farmers and police who were curious how it is that our family had a white child. She would often warn me not to be "useless" like a number of my uncles, encouraging me to be responsible. She was a pensioner who managed her home very well. I lived with her children, my siblings, grandpa Mpiyakhe's kids – and she would wake up in the morning to cook *uphuthu* (pap) which we ate with *amankanyiso* (saturated fat). It was a delicacy. I adored my grandmother and had a desire to build her a proper home when I started earning. I used to watch her rebuilding her mud house each time there were heavy rains and I would say, "One day you will live like a queen and I will make it my duty that you are spoiled."

I became closer to my mother after the death of my grandmother in 1984. My mother was just a brilliant woman who treated me and my siblings with the same love. She thought I was tricky and nicknamed me Chakijane. I hated the nickname because I could not contemplate boiling grannies in hot water as the trickster Chakijane does in one of the folktales. My mother never praised easily, but when she did, you knew it came from the depth of her being. She was very close to her uncle, grandpa Mavuso, and she was a generous and kind person. She loved family. I recall her telling me that I should always know and appreciate my family. She used to travel me with me and introduce me to many relatives I didn't know. She was always patient to explain our family bonds and relations.

After leaving the farms, most of my uncles were migrant labourers at Spitzkop and Ermelo mines. They were reckless though, but my mother taught me never to be ashamed of them.

I recall her saying, "My boy, if you are with your school friends and you meet one of your uncles, even if he is a lunatic, you must never be embarrassed to tell your friends that he is your blood, that he is family."

She could tell I was more cautious in life and handled myself better than my elder brother, Elvis. I recall her saying that when I was old enough, I must concern myself that my brother is not wearing torn shoes. I bought my brother a pair of Salvatore shoes with my first job after matric.

BN: You say growing up was also absurd. Please explain.

WP: Let me give you an example. One day when I was in Standard One at Pieter Mabuza Primary School in the township, school inspectors showed up and interrupted our class with Mam Nkosi. They were there to take ethnic statistics. They said, "Can Zulu children stand up!"

As more than half the class stood up, my mind was racing whether I was Zulu or not. The question of our family tribe was never discussed at home. It was never an issue, and nobody had informed me what my tribe or that of my family was. You could tell from the glare of my classmates that they were curious which tribe I would claim as mine. My mind raced while they were counting the "Zulu" children.

I recalled a story I had heard from an aunt who was married to one of my uncles. My aunt was from Swaziland. She used to tell me there were many children who looked like me in Swaziland. She would say I would feel so welcome and so much at home in Swaziland. This never made sense and I never probed her what she meant. I was still too young to comprehend how Swaziland was different from my country. On this occasion, I decided to stand up with Swazi children. The inspector asked if there were Xhosa kids, Shangaans [Vatsonga], and when he said, can Swazi children stand up, I stood up with the handful of Swazi children. All eyes were on me. There were whispers and I could sense disapproval, not only from my classmates, but also from the inspectors who had come to cause this scene.

Here is another one. Again, in the same year, in the evening at a communal tap, Dlozi, whom I went to school with, mocks me as *umlungu*. One punch just below the diaphragm, Dlozi was down, eyes white and not breathing. I was so scared he was dying and I prayed to God to bring him back to life. Luckily, after a while, he regained consciousness and I was so terrified I could have turned into a murderer at such a tender age.

I also used to be suspicious of jokes. In Grade 4, a classmate was in the habit of keeping the class entertained by cracking jokes when our class was left unattended by a teacher. We were organising a party for our class. He stands: "At the party, Jeaneth, you will bring us tripe." The class roars in laughter because Jeaneth's father was selling tripe in the township. And then, "You, Phindile, you will bring us the elephants from your house to decorate." At Mabilisa Street, where Phindile Buthelezi lived, their house had two elephant statues. Sgero wasn't done. "And you, Wonder, you must bring us the *Boesmans* from your family to clean up after the party." In a split second, I was throwing a thunder of fists to the taller Sgero. He never had a chance to hit me back, because we were soon separated by our friends who saw our class teacher approaching our class.

I hated being called *Boesman*. I had no qualms when my grandmother Khwayiza would once in a while tease me, *Boesman la Phindile* (Phindile's Boesman). You could count people who were called *Boesmans* at Ermelo. The few actually worked mainly as domestic workers or were known as alcoholics at the local beerhall. They certainly had no roots in Ermelo… These few came from places like Middelburg or Standerton, and they didn't live in the township. You could sense that *Boesman* was meant to insult or degrade.

I took martial arts as a young boy. Bruce Lee was my idol. From the Zulu literature my brother Elvis gave me from a young age, Shaka Zulu was my hero. I fought many battles in the streets and at various schools.

But the fights never stopped the voices of young innocent children shouting, "*Nang'umlungu, nangu umlungu.*" I began appreciating that some of these children did not call me *umlungu* as a way of scorning me, but they were honestly amazed to see me in the township. Sometimes they would say, "*Mlungu umuhle ufana no no spopi*" [White person, you are cute like a doll].

White people rarely came to the township although our homes were close to town. We used to walk to town, where I got strange looks from white people. Many could not look me straight in the eye … it was like my existence drew attention to them; as if I brought shame or scandal to them.

BN: You may be uncomfortable being seen as a white person, but surely your looks must have opened some doors for you.

WP: Possibly, and if that did occur, it was never because I went out of my way to claim any allegiance to my white side or my coloured look.

I suspect, apart from good manners, a number of my girlfriends were fascinated with my looks and wanted to try something they thought might be different. I would sometimes hear a girl bragging to her friends that she has her *mlungu* not *izinkwishinga* or *abomnyamane* like them. In Grade 4, a stunning girl at my school, out of nowhere, handed me a note saying, "I love you like a chicken in the oven." She had actually taken time to even draw a full chicken inside an oven. I lost respect for her because I found her figure of speech unsettling and foolish. I never followed her advances.

In 1987 or 1988, we went on a school trip to Central High School in Soshanguve. When I got out of the bus, all the girls were screaming, "Ricardo, Ricardo, u-Ricardo." Ricardo was a young coloured singer who became an instant celebrity with his hit song, "I love you, daddy … you are my superstar." I had also heard from friends in my township who had seen Ricardo on TV that we looked alike. I got the hottest girl from Central High – Trudy. I knew I was the envy of my friends that evening. We exchanged addresses, wrote to one another and exchanged photographs in our love letters.

You should recall that I grew up at a time when white images were actively promoted in the media. I had aunts who were buying bleaching detergents to lighten their dark pigmentation.

At Wits University, I began to notice that a certain girl might be interested in me. We would start conversing in English, and the moment I code-switched to isiZulu and she realised I was actually not a "proper" coloured, she would immediately lose interest.

I had a lot of friends who would deliberately take me out to meet girls, hoping to score because the girls think they have a white or coloured friend. In my later life, I no longer mind being called *mlungu* or coloured since it sounds more like a well-meant joke these days.

My wife still brags that her choice was the best in me. She celebrates that we have beautiful children. She claims that growing up in Alexandra township, and later in the United States, she wasn't interested in dark-skinned guys. I love her to bits and adore my children, but it never occurred to me that my looks had anything to make her listen to my rumblings when I met her.

The looks didn't work wonders all the time. At St Luke's, my advances were turned down by one gorgeous Tebogo. Out of this rejection, I wrote my first poem in isiZulu. It criticised materialism, conspicuous consumption and had a nationalistic tone. In it, I asserted I had come to the school to find the weapon that would liberate Africa, that is, I did not come there for her. Titled, "*Ngikomunye Umhlaba*", it opened with the line, *Lapha ngisekuqeqeshweni/Laph' eyam' ingqondo/Iqeqeshelwa esenkululeko ye-Afrika isikhali/Emaqaphelweni ngibe ngigqokiswe imvula*. Matters of the heart, my brother – Yeah, they can make you discover there is a poet in you.

When I was teaching at Wits, I was invited to deliver a keynote address on the legacy of Zulu scholar, novelist and poet B.W. Vilakazi at Mariannhill. Just before I spoke, a young poet stole the stage and performed an emotive, powerful poem in isiZulu. I knew it would be an anti-climax if I went straight to my talk after such a dramatic performance by this young man. I began by performing my St Luke's poem, which had been inspired by my rejection by Tebogo. I had a standing ovation, the crowd of Zulu writers and scholars were taken aback that this Peters had mastered their language. When I finished my talk in isiZulu, I had another standing ovation. My wife and Professor Mzilikazi Khumalo, who was my linguistics lecturer at Wits, were proud of my performance on the day.

Politics of ethnicity remain prevalent in South Africa. I often pick up that many coloured communities or families I meet are actually proud of whatever modest achievements I have. They see my success as one of their own and I have no problem with lifting the spirits of my fellow coloured community or friends. I only have a challenge when one racial or ethnic group starts thinking it is better than another one. I once met a Chantel when I lived in Hillbrow and I tried my luck with her. We were in her mother's flat and there was noise from one of the flats, and I heard her screaming, "Stop making noise. This is not Soweto." When I left that day, I never looked back.

Yes, I have benefitted from my looks. One evening, driving with a friend Sipho, we entered the road on the wrong side of one of Joburg's street. In an instant, the metro police officers stopped us. Sipho was the first to get out to explain and he was taking cash out to bribe a black metro officer. I was politely apologising. He would have none of that and was threatening to arrest us. Another metro police vehicle stopped, and a coloured man who was a senior to the fellow who was about to arrest us intervened. He asked where I worked and what I did and where we were heading to. I informed him and telling him I was going straight home. I think he was impressed by the job I was doing at Ochre Media and he told me to drive straight home. Sipho and I were convinced that the coloured officer showed mercy on us because he thought he would be bringing trouble to one of his own.

It can be risky to look like that at times. One afternoon in Joburg, I was driving with Sipho again. The windows of the car were open and we were caught at a busy intersection as the traffic light went red. Two men came to my side and took out the ignition key. They demanded that we give them our cellphones. Without hesitation, I handed mine – a new but cheap phone which didn't even cost me R200. Meanwhile, my dear friend Sipho was struggling to hide his expensive smartphone. I said, "Sipho, *mfowethu, bagaye i*-phone. *Gaya Labantu.*" This was some *Tsotsitaal* (streetwise parlance), basically telling my friend to give the thugs the phone. The thugs looked at me in bemusement. They gave me back my key and my phone. One of them said, "Aah mfethu!, kanti *uwu-darkie. Thina sithi uyingamla. Sithi uwumlungu.* Sorry, *asgangangeli abodarkie.* (Oh, my brother, we didn't realise you are a black person. We thought you are white person. We don't steal from black people.) Off the pair went. The incident didn't even last a minute. My skin complexion had betrayed me, but speaking in their language secured me and my rascal friend Sipho.

BN: Tell me more about the aunt in the family who once talked about your identity.

WP: Oh! Aunt Ntombini. I lived in the township renting a room with my mother and stepfather. My uncle Totombane Mabizela lived with his family and my brother not far from where we stayed. I went to see my brother. Aunt Ntombini was there. I overheard her telling her friend, "Hey, Sdudla, do you remember Phindile's child? Hey, Phindile had guts to sleep with a white man. Look at his white child. He's an *amper-baas.*"

I left as soon as I heard her; running to my mother. I never used to mention to my mother people's remarks on my looks, and this was the first time I ran to tell her what I had heard my aunt saying about her sleeping with a white person. My mother didn't utter a word. She held me by the hand and we went back to my uncle's house. As soon as she saw my aunt, she was all over her, punching her and using her head to knock her face. She was screaming, "I'm sick and tired of you, Ntombini, going around insulting me. Were you with me when I was sleeping with a white man?"

I recall my mother wrestling with my aunt on the floor, her dress got lifted up, and her bums and underwear got exposed. I felt really embarrassed to see her looking like that. After the fight, as we walked back home, I vowed in my heart I would never report any scolding or insults to her. And I never did.

BN: You said your friend calls you Mkholwa. Why?

WP: Oh, that's my mother's clan name. Her last name is Mabizela, and in their clan praises they say, "*Mkholwa onsundu oma ngezinyawo zakhe*" [Mkholwa, son of the soil/black one/the self-reliant one]. My friend is a Ngcobo, hence Mapholoba or Fuze. We met at National Electronic Media Institute of South Africa, where we were colleagues. I was fond of addressing him by his clan name, and one day he told me he wished he could return the gesture, but he had no clue about the clan praises of Peters. Because there was none, I shared my mother's, and when he calls me Mkholwa, I know he is talking to me.

BN: If I may ask, who is Peters?

WP: Peters is me.

BN: Peters is you…

WP: Yes. We were five children in my family and I am the last born. The last name of my siblings is Zulu. As a young girl living at the farms around Ermelo, my mother bore three girls and one boy. The father of her children was a man called Gesi Zulu. They were never married, and one day, they went their separate ways. The children were brought up by my grandfather, Mpiyakhe Mavuso, and grandmother, Khwayiza Roseline Mavuso.

My earliest childhood memories were at my grandfather Mpiyakhe's place at White City, a farm just outside Ermelo. As his grandchild living in his house, I was a Mavuso – like all the children in his house. When I lived with my grandmother at the homeland, I used Hlongwane because at that time she was married to my grandfather Kenneth Hlongwane. I remember that there was a time I was a Mabizela, because I lived in my uncle's house who was a Mabizela. In my baptismal certificate, I was registered as Sithole because my mother was in a relationship with one Whitey Sithole at the time of my birth.

Just before I started school, my mother was in a relationship with Sizo Peter. He was a Xhosa migrant labourer working at Spitzkop Mine. He married my mother, took her with all her five children. I became a Peter.

He is the father figure I knew in my life. He had a major influence in my upbringing.

My mother raised us to respect and honour him for bringing us up even though we were not his blood. We lived with him at the Spitzkop Mine family house. One day he fought with my mother, chased her outside, and neighbours heard and saw it all. He was reported to the Mine Manager and subsequently fired. We lost the house. I had to complete my Grade 2 living with my uncle Mbola who also had a house at the mine. He was married to Aunt Tholakele, my wonderful aunt who told me about children who looked like me in Swaziland.

Later on, we lived by renting rooms at the Ermelo township with my father and mother. He later quit drinking and smoking, and became a born-again Christian. As children, we joined him at his church with my mother.

He was a king in our lives because we valued that he took care of us and our mother, who was a domestic worker. One day, he quit his job at the coal mine. Without bidding goodbye, he vanished. He wrote to my mother that he had a calling to go minister the gospel in Johannesburg.

Life became tough for my mother, who was earning R50 a month. My mother later decided to join her previous employers, Mr and Mrs Coetzee, who had left Ermelo earlier for Krugersdorp. My mother was very close to the madam, Mrs Sophie Coetzee. When they were at Ermelo, they used to give her food and clothes. I grew up wearing Henk's clothes, and the suits Mr Coetzee gave my mother, she gave them to her beloved uncle, grandpa Mpiyakhe Mavuso. When she joined the Coetzees in Krugersdorp, my brother had started working and was paying rent for the four-roomed house we were renting at Kunene Street.

My mother reunited with my father in Krugersdorp and they both shared her domestic quarters. In 1989, my mother had a heart attack, and she died at Leratong Hospital. Her body was returned to Ermelo and we buried her. I was 16 years old. My father, without us pressuring him to do so, had committed he would be with us. There were many plans we were discussing how we would all move on, but two months after my mother's death, he wrote to us telling us he was cutting himself from us. He was planning to get married, and did not want anything to do with my three sisters and my brother, except me. He was asking that I be given to him as the youngest child so that he could take care of me. He wrote in the letter that my mother had given me to him as his child, and he wanted to focus on me.

I could not fathom him wanting to take me away from my siblings and my extended family. I was a part of them and I did not want to be treated differently from them. After much deliberations with my siblings, I came to my own conclusion that, "Baba, thanks but no thanks. If you wish to help me, you are not going to alienate me from my brother Elvis, my sisters, uncles…"

In 1989 I had to get an identity document (ID). The following year I was going to a boarding school, St Luke's Senior College. I had obtained a scholarship for my last two years of high school. I was using his surname and needed him to assist me to get this all-important document. I was very clear I would not use Zulu, Mavuso or Mabizela as my last name. Peter had proved more neutral and acceptable. I had been through hell when I used an African last name because, each time I used it, people would say, "No, that can't be your surname. It may be your mother's surname, but your father is certainly not a black person." My father had disappeared without assisting me to obtain an ID.

My brother had a friend who worked at Home Affairs. We used to call it *Kwandabazabantu*. I approached a local pastor – got a baptismal certificate that said my last name was Peter. I added an "s" on this new baptismal certificate. I approached my brother's friend with the certificate, a copy of my mother's marriage certificate to Sizo Peter, and my mother's death certificate. I told him he also had to add "s" to Peter because the "Peter in the marriage certificate" sounded too much like a name. He was reluctant to help, advising I take my mother's last name. I could not explain a lot of things to him, so I just left him.

I met the fellow by accident in the township and he said I should visit him again with my documents. He filled in the forms, and by Christmas of 1989, I had my ID with Peters as my last name. My new last name was actually a small act of rebellion against my stepfather who was not there when I needed him the most. I bought my brother's friend a litre of Old Buck Dry Gin for the excellent work he had done to beat the system and bring some resolution to this last-name matter. With Peters, people accept and they don't ask me questions I do not have answers to nor time for. Peters does not provoke unnecessary attention to how I look.

BN: Is a last name critical for a person's identity?

WP: A last name can be everything to a person. People can fight and discriminate against each other because of a last name. Initially my grandmother was married to a grandfather I never met, Daniel Mabizela. I hear he was stabbed to death in Germiston while he was gambling. They had six children together. After his death, my granny married Kenneth Hlongwane, a migrant labourer at Spitzkop Mines. They had three children. When my grandmother left the farms and settled at the Kangwane homeland, two homes were built. The house of Mabizela and the house of Hlongwane. I recall my uncles and aunts from the two houses – both children of my grandmother quarrelling and insulting each other. The Hlongwanes would tell the Mabizelas, "This is our house. Hlongwane rules here. Mabizelas must do as they please at their house, not here." Strange enough, it used to be my aunts, more than my uncles, who would brag about their status and last names. I was sensitive to such and detested such conversations. Although I was a child, these conversations annoyed me. It was simply embarrassing to see adults being so petty about their last names and entitlements.

I somehow took a conscious decision very early in my life not to be bothered about who my biological father was or what my "real" surname was. I didn't want to be miserable like grandpa Mpiyakhe's last born.

My grandfather had two wives. His younger wife once left him and lived with another man whose last name was Khuzwayo. They made peace with my grandfather because when I was born, they had reconciled. This wife from the junior house gave birth to a son, a year or two before my birth. We grew up together, played together, fought with one another and rode bicycles together. This uncle of mine – I have never addressed him as uncle because we were the same age – was nicknamed "Khuzwayo" by the elder aunts and uncles. There was this persistent rumour that he was Khuzwayo's son, not Mavuso's son. The scorning was terrible, and it bothered this last born of my grandfather. At times he would withdraw and break down in tears.

He adored my grandfather and my grandfather loved him dearly. He had a soft spot for him. Never in my life did I ever hear my grandfather suggesting his last born was not his son. But the talks were always there. The nickname "Khuzwayo" stuck with him. As we grew up and I saw how my grandfather's son suffered alone because of the insults that his mother conceived him when she was with Khuzwayo, I started asking myself if I would ever know what my last name was. I realised I may not know because no one had ever said anything about it. I resolved I didn't want my life to be dictated by a surname. If I recall, I took the decision when I was in Grade 1 or 2. On my own, I came to the conclusion that my happiness was not going to depend on things I do not have an answer on. As I said, the issue of my father was never raised in family circles when I was growing up.

I was luckier than this uncle in the family – I was overwhelmed with love and had this assurance that my uncles or my brother could go to war if they detected I was being insulted or marginalised because of how I looked.

One day during break time, when I was doing Grade 3 (Standard One) at Pieter Mabuza Primary School, I was conversing with Uncle Mlindwa who was with his wheelbarrow full of wood and a huge, shiny axe. Some children from a nearby house started calling each other to come see this white child. My uncle heard them and he charged at them with his big axe. I ran after him, saying, "Uncle Mlindwa, Uncle Mlindwa, please forgive them. They are only children. They don't understand what they are saying." He listened, but called them by their mother's private parts. My school mates used to tease me about this incident, repeating how I pleaded for mercy for these children from Uncle Mlindwa.

In the same year, my uncle Totombane sent me to buy him a litre of Coca-Cola at the Thembisa Store Complex. I normally avoided these stores because they were always busy. Men used to gamble next to the beer hall and once or twice I had heard people saying, "There is a white child." Whenever I left Mabuza Street where we lived with my mother to Uncle Totombane's house, I used to walk, and when I was near the shopping complex, I would pretend I am in a rush. I would run from the stores towards my uncle's house for fear that I would attract attention and insults.

Begrudgingly, I took the money and went towards the stores to buy the cold drink. When I came out, I heard a voice from the men who were gambling near the beer hall. "Hey, white boy, what are you doing in the location? White boy, who is your father?" I didn't look in the direction of the slandering voice. I pretended I had not heard it. Suddenly, I heard, "Wonder, Wonder, come to me, *bafo*." That's how my brother Elvis used to call me. *Bafo*. My brother! He took the bottle of cold drink from me and went straight to the man. The man my brother was approaching was a well-known martial artist. He ran a gymnasium and was feared in the whole township. I was so scared and felt guilty that my trip to the store would be a source of my brother's harm. My mother was always nervous that my brother was a bit reckless and that if he was not careful with his gambling life and fights, he would be stabbed to death like grandpa Daniel Mabizela, her father. She used to say that I must pay attention to her son, and do what I could to warn him to stay away from danger.

My brother went straight to Eric, held him by the collar of his sweater. "*Ye wena msunu kanyoko, uyamazi umlungu? Wake wambona umlungu elokshini? Umlungu lo?* Doesn't he have a name? [You piece of shit, my boy has a name. Hey, your mother's cunt, do you know a white person? Have you ever seen a white person among us in the township? Is this a white person?]

He went on, "If you don't apologise immediately, I will crack your skull with this bottle. I will show you your mother's pussy." "*Awubazi abantu ubezwa ngendaba. Ngiyizinyane likaZulu mina angibhenywa. Ngelusa. Ngiyayishaya induku.*" I couldn't believe my eyes. The much-feared Eric was shivering. He said, "Sorry, Presley. I didn't know this is your boy." Many of my brother's peers called him Presley. He was a skilled fighter and many had lost their teeth during his fights with them. Some had scars from his Okapi knife. This crowd of thugs and gamblers knew him too well. Although he was quiet and peaceful, they feared him. The crowd of onlookers said, "Hardy Presley", which was a way of saying sorry Presley. He said, "Fuck you all, *msunu yenu...* Why didn't you stand up for my boy when this lunatic, ugly, pitch-black Shangaan was insulting him?" He put me on his shoulders and off we went back to my uncle's house. From that day, I had no trouble going to these stores. I would often meet men and they would say, "*Hey ntwana ka* Presley, how are you? (Presley's boy, how are you?). Where's your brother?"

As I grew up, I understood that many of the children were innocently startled by my presence. It was the voices of adult males calling me a white person that baffled me. Never on a single day did I tell my mother, my brother or uncles about these voices of disapproval.

BN: So, *ntwana ka* Presely, is there also a story behind your name, Wonderboy?

WP: My brother Elvis taught me very early in life that a person could call himself whatever he was happy with. In his youth, he was called "Pipi". When he was born, everybody, especially the women and my grandmothers, were fascinated by his big penis, and they called him "Pipi". One day, when he was doing Standard Five at Spitzkop, he told the family that no one would ever call him "Pipi". He said his new name was Elvis. I remember I used to run up and down telling many of our relatives and his friends not to dare use that name. "Pipi" was now Elvis. Period.

Okay – to return to my name. The way it came to be written as Wonderboy, my brother Elvis had something to do with it. As I said, we were five at home. The first born, Delisile Zulu, a girl, she was born in 1964. The second born, my brother, Elvis Zulu, was born in 1965. My sister, Phumlaphi, in 1966. Then my sister that I was very closed to, Ntombifuthi, was born in 1969. Ntombifuthi's Christian name was Tryphine, named after her paternal aunt. She didn't like her name Tryphine, saying it was a name of grannies. Following in my brother's name-giving revolution, she changed Tryphine to Treasure, and that's what she had in her ID. When Ntombifuthi was born, my grandmother had hoped for a boy, hence the name Ntombifuthi, meaning, another girl. When I was born in 1973, my grandmother Khwayiza was thrilled, saying, "*Banda abafana ba Phindile*" (Phindile's sons have multiplied/ increased). So I was *Wandamfana* or *Wandaboy*. My brother somehow thought my illiterate grandparents didn't know how to spell my name, and decided it must be spelled Wonderboy. So each time a person says Wonderboy, I hear two meanings, Wonder for Smanga, and Wanda for more.

My Christian name is Doctor. It was given to me by my mother in recognition of doctors who conducted a successful, but complicated caesarean section when I was born at the African section of the Ermelo Hospital – *esibhedlela sabantu*. She says she almost died during labour, but by the grace of God and the miracle of doctors, her life was saved. At all the schools I attended at Ermelo, I was known as Doctor by my teachers and school mates. I was surprised the other day when I was at Ermelo and an old classmate addressed me as Doctor. My ex-teachers still know me as Doctor, although I hardly use the name these days.

BN: I see. So *Wandamfana*, are you coloured?

WP: Hey, Busani, that's not an easy, straightforward question. It's a tough one, my brother. Very much complicated by my childhood experiences.

At the Ermelo farms when I began making sense of life, there was no coloured community. At Spitzkop Mine where I began school, there was no coloured child. At Dundonald and Glenmore where grandfather Mavuso and her sister eventually settled, there were no coloured people. At Ermelo in the different townships that formed Wesselton township, there were no coloured people that lived with us. I had no experience of what it meant to be coloured.

There was a boy, Parayi, and Nomvula, who were from different families in the township. They were labelled as Indians because they were apparently fathered by Indian men. They were never called coloured during my time. Kids generally called them in the derogatory word "*amakula*" or "coolies". I was never teased to be a "coolie". I have no idea how the gorgeous Nomvula and the lonely Parayi battled it out because we were never friends and never spoke about our experiences.

I heard the word coloured for the first time in my life from my stepfather, Sizo Peter. My father was unfortunate not to have had a child with my mother. There was a child born after me, but he died a few days after birth at hospital. If I recall, there were also twins who also died at infancy. My father still does not have a child he has a claim on, except me.

When he was married to my mother, my siblings and I used his last name, Peter. He was extremely disappointed when the time for my brother to take his ID came. My brother decided to use his biological father's name, Zulu. Although their father had not contributed a penny to their upbringing, my mother could not stand in his way when he wanted to register as Zulu. My father was hurt. The girls also followed in my brother's footsteps. Father Peter was crushed and gave my mother many sleepless nights grumbling.

I was doing Grade 5 (Standard Three) at Umsebe Bantu Combined School at Wesselton, and we were renting a room at Mabilisa Street with the Mdlulis. One early Saturday morning, my father woke me up and told me I was going to accompany him to his workplace. He was a miner at Bordeaux Coal Mine. He left me "*eskwereni*", his mine room, and went underground. He returned at midday and his white overall, face and hands were black with coal dust. He looked distressed. Something was on his mind. Something was troubling him.

He called me outside, went down on his knees, and said, "Wanda, Wanda. I want you to listen, and listen carefully. You see my surname, Peter, you must never abandon it. It will work for you. If you use it, white people will think that you are coloured. They will treat you better and pay you better. You understand, Wanda? Don't forsake my last name."

I promised him I would always be a Peter. In fact, I didn't like the encouragement. What other surname did he think I could use? Did he know that Peter was actually such a neutral label for me, not inviting questions about my father which I had no idea about.

That was the first day I heard about the word coloured and coloureds from my distressed father. As he was narrating the benefits of being coloured, something in me on that day said, "Wonderboy, you are not coloured." How could I be? The first thing that went to my mind was my brother Elvis Zulu. He was my point of reference and we were very close to each other. I loved him dearly. It just did not make sense that because of the way I looked and having the right last name, I could earn better than my brother Elvis Zulu, who was of a darker pigmentation. The last name Peter served my own interests and I had no qualms to honour and respect the man who had taken care of me, my mother, my brother and sisters. I had a problem with the unmerited privileges I could access by saying I am coloured and that my brother Elvis could not because he was a Zulu man.

As we travelled back home at the back of a bakkie, I kept saying to myself, I am not a coloured.

BN: Surely your views about coloureds must have changed as you grew and your world expanded.

WP: Indeed they did. In 1990 I went to a multiracial boarding school, St Luke's Senior College, in Midrand. The school called itself non-racial, not multiracial. It was founded by LEAF – the Leadership Education and Advancement Foundation. Our sister school was All Saints, at Bhisho in the Ciskei.

The staff was multiracial and highly qualified. Our principal was an Anglican priest, Mr Richard Hawkins. In Grade 11, my biology teacher was Mr Richards, a coloured teacher. There were a few white students, a few Indians, a handful of coloured students and the majority were African students drawn from all over the country.

I know I did my best in the school's entrance examination, but I doubt it was good enough because I felt during the examination that I was under-prepared to go to such a school. I somehow had a funny feeling that I got a chance to be in because of both the potential I showed and my last name, although the school didn't ask in the examination what race I was. You never know, people say they are non-racial, but when they look at your photograph and potential, they say let's give this lost, poor coloured boy a chance to balance the racial demographics.

I was surprised at St Luke's to meet for the first time African students who spoke English as their first language. I made friends with Kevin Phangalele who was from Soweto. He was articulate and used to top the school in English. Kevin and those in our inner circle of kids who came from impoverished backgrounds used to frown upon the speaking of English by black students through the nose. We scorned them as "*amarwayi rwayi*". Among the few coloureds at the school, it was Edgar Pienaar that I related very well to. Edgar was just a naughty, carefree bastard. He was simple, fun and down to earth. Girls were not allowed in the men's residence, but Edgar and Kevin used to bring them or go to their residence without being found by the school security.

Edgar was just a good friend. I never sensed that I was mingling with a coloured person. After St Luke's, we lost touch and only recently I found him on Facebook. We are still planning to meet and introduce our families to each other.

My years at St Luke's – 1990 and 1991 – were fascinating times in South Africa. The student body was highly politicised and Kevin Phangalele really excelled in this art. We belonged to the Young Christian Movement (YCM), which also had branches at universities, including Wits. The YCM engaged in the national politics of the country.

On 2 February 1990, I was amazed to see St Luke's bursting into revolutionary songs with the announcement by De Klerk of the unbanning of political parties and his decision to release Nelson Mandela. Our English teacher, Mr De Villiers, was singing and dancing with the ANC flag. I had been involved in street and mass protests at Ermelo, but had never seen white people with us in our protests. Here, all our teachers were ululating and celebrating. I realised I had a lot of catching up to do with our history.

Myself, Kevin and Morake, who was from Lesotho, were identified by three senior students at St Luke's as the core of student leaders that were going to provide leadership at the school when they had left. We were informed the three of us were going to constitute what was termed "the core" and we had to identify 20 other leaders that we had to influence, so that the 20 could influence the entire student body. The 20 was not meant to know about the core – about our secret meetings and decisions. Everything had to look spontaneous and real. We had our own unique knock in the evenings for our secret meetings. One of the critical things we had to ensure was to guarantee that St Luke's was not turned into an instrument to isolate black students from their communities. From the teachers, Mr Richards was our contact and he would keep us abreast of boardroom or staff meetings. In 1991, Kevin was president of the Student Representative Council (SRC), and I was his deputy.

At every assembly on Mondays, Mr Richard Todd used to drill it into the students that St Luke's was the cradle of future South African leadership. Our job was to ensure that this was not a leadership divorced from the day-to-day struggles of millions of black South Africans.

I had a friend from the Eastern Cape, Dumisani, I think was his name, who had grown up in a Pan-African Congress home. Kevin used to dismiss him as *izimuzimu*, and he would call us the Charterists. I found him to be robust, though, always promoting the unity of African people. At our school library, I learned about Martin Luther King Junior, and his "I have a dream" speech made a lasting impression. I recall addressing students and quoting the line, "I have a dream that one day my four little children will be judged, not by the colour of their skin, but by the content of their character." Dumisani told me that I must also make time to read Malcom X and Steve Biko.

If there is a lasting legacy of St Luke's to many of us who went there, it was the confidence it inculcated in us. In 1992, I got employed as a teacher at a rural school, Fernie, to teach biology at matriculation level. I only had a matric, but was encouraged to give it my best shot knowing that I had fantastic biology teachers in Mr Richards and Ms Theron. I succeeded in improving the pass rates for the two years I was there.

When I arrived at the school, there were fights between South African teachers and those from Swaziland. The South African teachers, many without qualifications like myself, felt that the Swazi teachers were taking their jobs. A University of Zululand graduate at our high school took a podium and told the learners that the following day, they must not come to school because they are involved in a strike to force the Department of Education to fire what he called the expatriates. As soon as he was done with his tirade, I went forward and told the learners not to listen to the fool. I may have been naïve, but I could not fathom a South African calling teachers from Swaziland expatriates. I started lecturing the kids about our common history and why it was important for them not to be misled by people who already had degrees. The following day, the school was full and teaching went on as normal.

I attended a South African Democratic Teachers' Union (SADTU) Ningizimu Branch meeting at Mayflower. The matter of the expatriate teachers was the main issue on the agenda. I stood up raising my objections and seeking better understanding about the prejudice against Swazi teachers. On the same day, I was elected to be a member of the SADTU Executive Committee for the Ningizimu Branch.

You know, Busani, I miss that rebel spirit in me. I used to be quite vocal and take a principled decision without any fear what others thought of me. I had learned to speak my mind from my friend Kevin Phangalele at St Luke's. I miss him. He is no more. And it is sad that he did not rise that much politically as many of us were confident he would. In his last days, he was a vocal activist in the Treatment Action Campaign.

BN: Later on you went to Wits, and you continued with your studies of isiZulu.

WP: A comrade in SADTU, Tornado Sibande, who had been to the University of Zululand, told me that there was no way I could save enough money to pursue my tertiary studies. He advised that I should just get the registration amount, and that once I am in, I will find my way how to stay there. He told me to visit the SRC office to tell them about my financial difficulties.

When I arrived at Wits, I was surprised that so many students whose circumstances were better than mine had bursaries from the university. When you applied at Wits, the university also included a financial assistance form.

I did not fill in the form. It asked a lot of questions on things I thought would not make sense, like how one could survive on a meagre income. But more than that, the form had a place where you had to disclose the financial situation of your parents, both your mother and father. It was easy with my mother. I could just write deceased and produce the death certificate. I had no answer about my father. How could it make sense to them that, at 21, I had no clue about my biological father and that I had no idea of the whereabouts of my stepfather who had decided to cut himself from our lives when my mother died in 1989. In my mother's death certificate, she was a Mabizela. So how could I begin to explain who Peters was. I just didn't fill in the form, only to learn later that Wits students brought all kinds of affidavits to the university to explain their unique circumstances.

My sister-in-law, Ses Lindi, who had just left my brother for his philandering, gave me R3 000 towards my registration. She stood for me as well, saying she would pay for my accommodation when the SRC assisted me to get into a self-catering residence. I had abandoned my dream of being an engineer. All I wanted to do was become a teacher. The two years at the homeland school had really encouraged me to pursue this career. I wanted to return home or in the rural areas and be just a teacher. I studied education, history, economics, isiZulu and African literature. I passed my Bachelor of Arts degree with a distinction, and isiZulu and African literature also with distinctions. Professor Nhlanhla Maake, head of the African Languages Department, offered me a full-time teaching job in his department. While I was pursuing my Honours degree in African Literature, I was back in the classroom teaching in the department.

BN: So your mother passed away without sharing with you who your biological father was?

WP: Many years after her fight with my aunt, I summoned courage and asked her. I must have been in Grade 6 or 7, and she had just returned from work. Politely, I said, "Mom, can you tell me who my father is?" She said, "My son, I have always known that one day you would ask me this question. But before I answer you, why don't you prepare me a cup of tea." She loved her tea and it was my assigned responsibility at home to serve our visitors with tea. When I returned, she said, "My boy, you are not a McKenzie. I do not know who your father is and you will never know." I was perplexed by how she started by saying I am not a McKenzie. McKenzie was her boss at the time of my birth and nobody had ever suggested to me that I might be related to the McKenzies. Not my grandmother Khwayiza. Not my grandfather Mpiyakhe. No one.

Then she said had she known about *piepirek* (condom), maybe I would not have been born. According to her, she and her friend Kaatjie used to sleep with various white men. She didn't know their names and it could have been anyone of them. She insisted, that is the truth... God's honest truth. She couldn't have known and I would never know, she insisted.

I was crushed, but appreciated her honesty with me. I resolved that I would never bring up the matter with her, which I suspected must have been heavy on her shoulders as well. Until her death far away as a domestic worker in Krugersdorp, we never spoke about this issue again.

BN: So that was the end of it, Mr Peters? No clue. Nothing.

WP: Sometime in 1997 during my first year of teaching at Wits, my uncle Strydom Mavuso just decided to desert his job at what he described as the dangerous and exploitative Spitzkop Mine. He came to where I lived in Parktown. I rented movies and he cooked for me. Just out of nowhere, Uncle Strydom says to me, "Hey, Wonder, do you know who your father is? You do know of course that your father is not that Xhosa man who was married to your mother."

"Yes, I know he was my stepfather, but I also know there is no way I would know who my father is."

My uncle then says he knows that my father was McKenzie. He knew him and used to work for him. He starts speaking about the striking resemblance between me and him. He says my mother also told him so, and they used to joke about this matter. Even more, most of the elder people in the family know that I am McKenzie's son.

My uncle insists my mother was just lying when she said she dated different whites. He left the following day, saying if I don't believe him, I must ask people in the family … they all know.

Confusing, but interesting, I thought. I then recalled that my mother kept old stamps around the time of my birth signed by McKenzie saying her *mlungu* or boss said she must save them and give them to me when I was older. I recall how we used to pass a certain store in town and she would tell me that used to be her *mlungu's* barbershop. She also used to tell me this *mlungu* had pigeons and used to race them in competitions. Oh my God – certainly not an impressive CV if my uncle is correct that my dad is McKenzie.

I suddenly recalled that during school holidays when I was at St Luke's, I once visited gogo Shemeni at the McKenzies. She now lived with the ageing Mrs McKenzie, looking after her. Mrs McKenzie heard I was there and asked gogo Shemeni to make tea for her, her daughter Totjie and myself. I was almost the same age as Totjie, and I recall her looking at me with keen interest and not ceasing to smile. The old woman asked me if I read the Bible and what I thought of Mandela. She said she didn't trust Mandela's eyes. While she was going on and on, she said, "*Jy het mooi tande, mos jy's 'n Mckenzie*" (You have nice teeth [because] you are a McKenzie). I didn't follow this up. I knew I didn't have perfect teeth and my mother had told me many years ago that I was not a McKenzie. Then, I thought old age was catching up with the madam.

After my uncle brought up the McKenzie story, I decided to visit Mrs McKenzie. When I arrived at Ermelo on a Friday afternoon, I learned she had died on Wednesday. She was going to be buried that Sunday next to Mr McKenzie's graveyard.

My next stop was Ses Kaatjie, my mother's friend. Without me asking the question, she just volunteered to tell me McKenzie was my father. She was my mother's friend and confidante. She flatly denied that they were sleeping around with white men, insisting my mother was a decent person. She went on to tell me McKenzie was very possessive of her... He would run after her in the yard and my mother would run laughing saying, "Hey, Kaatjie, can you tell this old man to stop what he's doing."

I attended the funeral, and many people that worked with my mother were there. One I knew very well is McKenzie's driver, Baba Sibanyoni. He pulls me aside laughing a bit: "Hey, Wonder, did you ever discover that your father was McKenzie? He was involved with your mother, and he used to tell me that if it wasn't for apartheid, he would marry a black woman. Your father was a Scottish man, and short just like you. Even Mrs Mckenzie knew that he had a child with your mother."

I go to my sister Delisile's house. She also confirms the story, saying that my mother told her this secret as the eldest child to tell me one day. She says my milk formula came from Mrs McKenzie. My prams and toys from them. I recall I had all these gadgets as a baby and many kids in my family didn't.

Uncle Paulos Mabizela says the same thing, and vows there is no truth whatsoever that his sister slept with many white men. My mother told him my father was McKenzie who died in 1979, aged 69. I must have been six then.

I ask Uncle Mpandlane Mavuso, grandpa Mpiyakhe's first born. "Uncle, do you have any idea who my father is?"

He breaks down in tears: "My sister's child, how can you ask me such a thing! All I know is that you are one of us, a child of my sister. When you were born, my father picked you up, put you at his back. He walked out with you to the kraal, calling his father Maheva and his mother gogo Nkosi. He came back to the house and said, this child is our child. He is my child, a child of the family. No one in this house dare say anything contrary to that or ask any question. He belongs to us."

My uncle was not done: "*Namhlanje mshana, ubuza malume ukuthi ubaba wakho ngubani.* All I know is that you are my sister's child." My uncle wept like a child, and I felt like I had betrayed him about asking about my father.

As I was in a taxi back to Johannesburg, I was angry at my mother for contributing to my nightmare by not disclosing who my father was when it was common knowledge to so many other people. I recalled with a degree of humiliation that, as a kid, I once took a job to sell vegetables for Mrs McKenzie. I wished my mother had advised me against it. How could Mrs McKenzie treat me like a labourer when she knew I was her husband's son?

I had tried to speak to McKenzie's only boy, Ouboet, after the funeral, but he was busy attending family members and I eventually had to leave. I had reminded him that I was Pinky's child, and he knew her extremely well. I suddenly thought that if indeed McKenzie was the one, that maybe my mother was correct to discourage me to associate myself with them. I did not know them and they didn't have a clue who I was.

BN: So you have not interacted with McKenzie's children since the funeral in 1997?

WP: Two years ago, Ses Kaatjie, my mother's friend, encouraged me to reach out to McKenzie's son Ouboet. His real names are Peter and Leslie, McKenzie's own names that he passed on to him. I learned he lives around Pretoria. I got his number from his ex-wife, called him and reminded him I was Pinky's child. He remembered me. After failing to meet for more than a year, we eventually met three months ago at his house in Centurion. He is a pharmacist; pleasant and kind hearted. As I was trying to find words to ask my question, he told me I was his brother. The family, including his mother, was aware of my existence. His elder sister is alive somewhere around Middelburg, and McKenzie's last born, who was almost my age, passed away. He showed me a picture of

McKenzie in his youth, and I was astonished that I was the devil's own spit image. I had thought that I would ask him for the possibility of a DNA test, just to exorcise completely the doubt created by my mother. After seeing the picture and him attesting to this story, I knew I would be asking too much. He told me a bit about McKenzie, and asked me whether my surname Peters was taken from McKenzie's name Peter. I told him no, but that it was good I had not been that much lost from one of his names. We enjoyed coffee and cigarettes together. We agreed I must bring my kids to him so that they can meet him when he is ready.

We haven't spoken again in a few months, and it looks like we are both retreating to our own laagers.

BN: Where are your children in all of this?

WP: Before I married my wife, I had two children with a woman from Soweto. Later on a DNA test excluded me from being their biological father, but I know the children have stuck with Peters as their last name. So their story remains our common story.

My stepdaughter with my wife is a Peters in her ID. So are all the other three children. My last born is a boy and I gave him my stepfather's name. He is Sizo Peters. Even before I met my McKenzie brother, I had told my elder kids that by all indications, my biological father is a Scottish man McKenzie. My daughter Lihle wants to be a designer and loves the idea that some Scottish blood might be running in her veins. She has been researching famous Scottish designers. She is very much at peace that she is of mixed heritage. Lihle and her sister Nobantu instruct me to choose "coloured" when they fill their school registration forms. My wife is always in the background supporting them and telling me that I must not deny that I am coloured. First generation, a 0.5 coloured she insists. She also tells the children with a degree of pride that her father's mother was also like me … so she carries some percentage of white blood. Well, what can I say. I just hope I will live long enough to be there to make my children understand when one day a white, Indian or coloured person makes them feel small because of their skin colour and background, I will be able to tell them why I could never have been at peace to say I am not a grandson of Khwayiza, *intwana ka Elvis, umshana ka malume Mafika.*

My seven-year-old daughter Nobantu insists she is not a black person. She says she is peach. She is happy to be called coloured. It somehow works for them. They grew up speaking English as a first language since

I could not converse in Setswana with their mother who lived in the US for a number of years. When I met her, she couldn't express herself in isiZulu as she does today. She now often says, "You see, honey, it's good I speak isiZulu now. I had to. Remember, I married a Zulu man." Fourteen years ago, English was a language we both understood and, before we knew it, Lihle was born to parents whose language of communication was English.

As a privileged student of African history and African Literature, I identify fully with the continent, its struggles and all its people.

I live and dream this continent, and when it comes to my consciousness and posture, I know it is informed by childhood images of my grandmother Khwayiza Mavuso, running away from an evil racist system trying to protect me. It is informed by my aunts and uncles at the farms and the mines. With all the contradictions in my upbringing, that is the environment I know and call home.

BN: When you apply for a job, which race do you tick?

WP: I have always been consistent on this one. I always tick African. I hope one day we won't have to answer such questions. I hope it will be enough to say I am a South African. It will be a long journey, but I hope one day each one's humanity and dignity will come before any other considerations. I accept the logic of the current status quo, but we must also find ways of communicating elsewhere that some of our experiences are not as simplistic and clear cut as official forms seek to suggest.

BN: Will you consider changing your last name to McKenzie?

WP: I believe I have attained closure on the question of my biological father. I still refuse to accept that if a man does not use his father's name, he may be inviting misfortune upon himself and his children. When people say that, I think about grandpa Mavuso's last born who used to be mocked about his last name. I think about children born from rape who will never know their fathers. I think about myself that had I made this a preoccupation, I might have missed out on so many of the joys of life.

At this point, I have told my children that if they are in love with the name McKenzie, by all means they can use it. They must be free to choose. I made my choices and I am living with them. I am confident, though, that for some time, there will be a hand that will be raised when someone calls the misnomer Peters I crafted in 1989. No matter what,

Peters will remain a big part of my story. The moment you erase it, you may again have to explain so many things. I'm getting old for that nonsense. My kids are young, energetic and have all the time. They live in a different country than the one I grew up in. If anyone of them chooses to be McKenzie, he or she has my blessing. If anyone chooses to be a Mabizela, Mavuso, Zulu – why not!

BN: I have taken a lot of your time. Thanks for your generosity and for sharing your story. Any other thing you may wish to add as we conclude?

WP: Thanks to you for the opportunity. I hope it will enrich research and debates on the notions of the indigenous. I trust it will enhance our understanding of our varied experiences. It must not just be an elitist academic exercise. The insights I hope I have provided must at least teach humanity that, to some, questions around identity and belonging are critical matters of life and death. I mean that literally.

Late in 1999, at the School of Oriental and African Studies, I had a nervous breakdown. I was diagnosed with bipolar mood disorder. I almost lost my life and the only form of positive identity I had was around excelling in academia or education which I had carved for myself. I almost became a vegetable and I had to reach deep, deep down inside myself to recover fully. I know very well what triggered the bipolar.

My country was hurting me and I couldn't make sense of things. I went overseas to look for the space that could afford me a break and possibly the chance to make sense of the chaos around my life. One day at the London house, I locked myself in my room and began to write my story. Patterns began to form and I was amazed how much I had buried in my consciousness as a child. My story was not just about the multitude of voices who always reminded me that I was the other, that I did not belong. That was a small, but important aspect of the bigger story of my family. It was a story about my grandmother Khwayiza, my uncles who ended up brutally killing each, aunts and uncles becoming schizophrenic and the continuing indignity and humiliation around my family. As I wrote, it dawned on me that there was a structure and a system that was actively in place to deprive many black communities of their humanity and dignity.

I hope that one day I will publish the manuscript and share my family story. This interview is a window into the bigger, richer, more complex story. Thank you indeed, Busani, for factoring my voice in this edited volume on 30 years of democracy, in a country that is hard at work towards forging a shared, inclusive national identity.

Zinqunywa amakhanda ziyekwe. Ukwanda kwaliwa umthakathi wena weqhawe!

10

Democratic deliberation and the political functions of the South African news media in the 30 years since liberation

Ylva Rodny-Gumede

The news media and the role it plays in the media-politics nexus has changed dramatically in the last 30 years and in South Africa's transition from autocracy and co-option to liberation and liberalisation. Alongside global debates around the role of the news media amidst competition from social media and declining readership and faltering business models, debates in post-apartheid South Africa have foregrounded ideas of racial and gender equity in the newsroom as well as in the content of the news media. More recently, and emanating specifically from centres in the global South, these debates and concerns have shifted to focus on transformation that addresses colonial histories and legacies that shape the news media and the role that it should play in a changing political landscape.

The news media more than any other sector as the thought fourth estate, no matter how questioned, shines a light on and exemplifies the performance of the democratic state, as well as ongoing struggles for socio-economic transformation, epistemic justice and the restoration of the dignity of the previously oppressed as already cited as the aim of exploration in the introduction to this edition of the *Liberation Diaries*.

As such, this chapter outlines some of the debates around the South African news media and its role in the last 30 years. The role of the news media is highly contested, and arguments about the desired role and functions of the news media have shifted and are bound up in global shifts and technological changes as much as a global as well as national postcolonial discourse around social transformation, equity and the political functions of the news media and journalism in society and in deepening democracy and democratic deliberation.

The contested role of the news media

A free and non-partisan news media is generally thought of as a public good and central to the functioning of a democratic society. South Africa's majority party, the African National Congress (ANC), for example, in its "Ready to Govern" document of 1992, notes that:

> At the core of democracy lies the recognition of the right of all citizens to take part in society's decision-making process. This requires that individuals are armed with the necessary information and have access to the contesting options they require to make informed choices. An ignorant society cannot be democratic.[1]

The news media are considered to play a crucial role in building a new democratic society. An unfettered press, with impartial and accurate coverage, is widely considered to be an essential cornerstone of any democracy, where the quality of democratic decision-making is closely linked to the quality of the information provided by the media.[2]

However, the link between media and democracy is equally contested and debated, no more so than in the context of societies undergoing social and political transitions, with the centrality of the news media to democratic processes, and in facilitating access to public discourse and civic engagement questioned.[3] In particular, questions have been raised about the role of the media, especially the broadcast media, in nation building, and in constructing a common identity, especially in societies where political organisation and state formation have been premised on racial and ethnic divisions as well as exclusionary ethnic politics.[4]

Ultimately, the concept of democracy itself, the ideas and ideals of the role of the news media are highly influenced by the political framework of the nation state. The news media is constantly evolving and operates within specific social, economic, cultural and political frameworks, and contexts that shape the regulatory framework, the structure as well as content of the news.

Importantly, media freedom and freedom of speech were never features of the legal framework nor socio-political make-up of South Africa prior to 1994 and were only entrenched in the Bill of Rights in the Constitution as adopted in 1996. The South African news media, and particularly broadcasting, before the first democratic elections in 1994 was heavily controlled by the Nationalist Party (NP) government and their policy of apartheid and separate development for separate ethnic groups in South Africa. In essence, the South African Broadcasting Corporation existed as a state broadcaster and propaganda instrument for the NP, and the print news media, with certain notable exceptions, closely followed the policies of the NP. This was well set out during the hearings of the Truth and Reconciliation Commission (TRC) into news media during apartheid in 1997.[5] While the hearings did provide insight into the role of the news media during apartheid and its role in upholding the policies of the NP, it did not provide the "reconciliation" needed or a way forward for the news media to play a role in the transition to and building of the new democratic society.[6] This has meant that the news media sector remained largely untransformed as South Africa entered the transition into democracy and held is first democratic elections in 1994.

Thus, some of the most important public, as well as policy, debates in South Africa post-apartheid have concerned transformation in various sectors of society, including the news media.[7] Debates with regards to the news media have foregrounded ideas around transformation and issues have ranged from how to make the journalistic corps and news producers in general more equitable in terms of race and gender to the transformation of news content itself amidst criticism of racism and a narrow focus on issues concerning only a small wealthy urban elite. As this range of priorities suggests, transformation in the media is a contested notion. And whereas equity in the workforce was high on the agenda in the first 10 to 15 years of democracy, diversity in content has emerged as higher on the priority list in later years and this with a strong emphasis on access, in the first instance to mainstream media outlets and, in later years, to new media platforms and social media.

More recently, debates and concerns have shifted to focus on transformation that goes deeper and addresses the colonial histories and legacies that shape the news media and the role they should play in a changing political landscape characterised by renewed and reinforced demands for the decolonisation of all sectors of society.

Debates around equity, skills and standards

Given a constitution that protects gender equality and affirmative action policies targeted at both gender and racial equity, South Africa definitely constitutes the most consistent as well as progressive example of the inroads made to gender equity in the news media on the continent. However, this also reveals weaknesses and fault lines. The fact remains that no matter how progressive the policies of gender equity, hurdles still exist towards the true attainment of gender as well as racial equity in the news media, particularly as this concerns black women.[8] And, despite headways made, women still remain underrepresented in senior positions in the news media and at media company board level.[9]

However, research shows that equity in the workforce has not necessarily translated into a diversification of content.[10] Hence, in later years, more focus has been put on the transformation and diversification of coverage and on reaching a broader audience and, in particular, audiences previously excluded from the mainstream media.[11] Media transformation debates have often highlighted that the broader public discourse shaped through the news media is still dominated by a narrow focus on the interest of a small white wealthy urban elite.[12] This means that the voices of marginalised communities, largely those made up of women and children, seldom come through in media coverage.[13] And, despite the many changes to the news media post-apartheid, much criticism has been levelled against the news media for being too westernised and perpetuating western, eurocentric values that are unfit for local realities and cultural norms.[14]

This has prompted proposals for new media regulation under the auspice of protecting the public amidst accusations of eurocentrism as well as failing professional standards. Such legislation has yet to become a reality as the sector itself has raised concerns that such legislation could have detrimental consequences for media freedom and that it could be seen as a smokescreen created to prevent the media from scrutinising corruption and maladministration emanating from a "logic" that the governing party as liberation movement and a democratically elected party deserves a more sympathetic press.[15] In later years there have also been increased attacks on the news media from various public, as well as private, individuals and the entities they represent. And instead of engaging in public debates around their grievances or taking cases to the Press Ombudsman, political parties and public officials are increasingly attacking journalists and editors through social media. A new threat against women journalists in particular has also emerged through social media[16] and research shows an increase in harassment of women journalists through social media; and so-called cyber bullying is disproportionately directed at women journalists.[17]

A recurring criticism of South African journalists has also been that they do not have the necessary skills to cover the complexities of the South African transition. At the beginning of the 1990s, when reforms were instigated to liberalise the highly state controlled media in South Africa, and after 1994 when such reforms were implemented and also codified in the new constitution, the news media was largely untransformed, with little or no equity in terms of its workforce and a media coverage largely premised on old ideas of the audience, and a decidedly outdated and racist concept of the public interest and who the public is that such a public interest talks to. This relates to how the news media has historically served different segments of the audience and to a certain extent to how they continue to serve audiences in South Africa. Audiences are divided through socio-economic factors that dictate access and ideas around what is considered news in the public interest[18] and importantly "race continues to be a marker of social difference, hierarchy and pain".[19]

Studies of the news media in young democracies as well as transitional societies show that social transformation has often lagged behind political change and, as a result, the news media have also failed to transform, instead, new institutions are formed on the remnants of the old. Added to this are the challenges posed by restructuring a liberation movement into a fully fledged democratic government and counter tendencies of partisanship and co-option of the media. In South Africa, critics argue that the new democracy is being eroded by an all-powerful ANC[20] and, as in many postcolonial societies, the distinction between the state and government has largely been eroded by former liberation movements who once in power have presided over one-party states with little or no opposition.[21] Therefore, contestation over media development is linked to its coverage of the role of the state and political parties; as such, calls for reporting in the national interest are often conflated with the political party interest.[22]

In addition, we have increasingly seen tensions between political control and market-driven changes and the media are caught in the contradiction between controls dictated by the new political establishment, on the one hand, and the market, on the other. And while the media sector has been liberalised and deregulated to a much greater extent than during the years of apartheid. This is a trend that many critics argue has led to increased commercialisation, "infotainment" and ownership concentration, at the expense of media diversity and pluralism.

Of course, in later years, social media has gained importance and the rise of new media platforms and proliferation of social media has without a doubt been the most impactful transformation in the media sector as a whole in the last two decades. And political communication, as observed globally, has become more dependent on social media platforms and a new set of communicators as well as audience. The proliferation of social media platforms have fundamentally changed the way in which the news media interact with their audiences and ultimately the role that the news media play in a democracy – not to mention a nascent democracy and postcolonial society such as South Africa, where audiences are highly fragmented, with large segments of the audience still cut-off from the mainstream news media.

Conclusion

In this chapter, I have looked at how the South African news media have responded to the changes in the political and social environment over the past 30 years and since the country's transition to democracy.

Globally, the media is changing rapidly due to technological advancements and the media has also become much more global in scope and content. In South Africa, these changes are linked to the political, social and cultural revolutions that have taken place in the country since the early 1990s. However, despite the enormous changes that have taken place in the media since the fall of apartheid, much remains to be done in order for the news media to really contribute to the strengthening and deepening of the nascent democracy.

The complex political environment has created a political culture that has defined the formulation of politics in South Africa and has set the framework for the role and conduct of the media and, ultimately, the content of the media. And while the end of apartheid has ushered in an era of new openness and willingness to change the media, it has not automatically stopped the government from trying to impose tighter state control. Nor has the independence of the media brought with it the neutrality and impartiality that many had hoped for. Old ways of doing journalism and relating to the audience do not change so easily.

Race still dominates much of the debates around the news media and there is still some way to go to increase women's participation, especially in the shaping of news agendas and, by extension, broader public discourse. Racial transformation and policies of affirmative race remain important variables to be factored into the discussion around media transformation; there is a need to move away from number games to more constructive debates around how to foster a new ethos for journalism and news coverage in post-apartheid South Africa.

While headways have been made in securing both racial and gender equity in the newsroom, issues of equality in news content and the role that the media can and should play in the new democratic society remain contentious, with critics arguing that the wider public sphere remains the same as during the apartheid years. This is regardless of audiences who have access to traditional news media or newer digital and social media platforms.

References

Chasi, C. and Rodny-Gumede, Y. 2016. 'Smash and grab, truth and dare'. *International Communication Gazette,* 78(7):694–700.

Couldry, N. 2009. 'Does "the media" have a future?' *European Journal of Communication*, 24(4):437–449.

Dahlgren, P. 2005. 'The internet, public spheres, and political communication: Dispersion and deliberation', *Political Communication*, 22:147–162.

Dahlgren, P. and Sparks, C., eds. 1991. *Communication and Citizenship – Journalism and the Public Sphere*. London: Routledge.

Daniels, G. 2022. 'Glass ceilings: Cybermisogyny is a sign of unchecked sexism in the newsroom'. In *Women journalists in South Africa: Democracy in the age of social media*, edited by G. Daniels and K. Skinner. London: Palgrave Macmillan.

Daniels, G. 2021. 'A decolonial analysis of the cyberbullying of South African women journalists'. In *Decolonising journalism education in South Africa: Critical perspectives*, edited by Y. Rodny-Gumede, C. Chasi, Z. Jaffer and M. Ponono. Pretoria: UNISA Press, pp 135–148.

Daniels, G., Nyamweda, T., Nxumalo, C. and Ludman, B. 2018. *Glass Ceilings: Women in South African media houses 2018*. Johannesburg: Gender Links.

Daniels, G. 2012. *Fight for Democracy: The ANC and the media in South Africa*. Johannesburg: Wits University Press.

Duncan, J. 2014. *The Rise of the Securocrats: The case of South Africa*. Johannesburg: Jacana Media.

Frassinelli, P.P. 2018. 'Decolonisation: What it is and what research has to do with it'. In *Making Sense of Research* edited by K.G. Tomaselli. Pretoria: Van Schaik Publishers, pp 3–9.

Gassner, P. 2007. 'The end of the audience: How the nature of audiences changed'. *Global Media Journal–African Edition*, 1(1):120–129.

Gumede, W. 2012. *Restless Nation: Making sense of troubled times*. Cape Town: Tafelberg.

Haffajee, F. 2022. 'The hounding'. In *Women Journalists in South Africa: Democracy in the age of social media*, edited by G. Daniels and K. Skinner. London: Palgrave Macmillan.

Lowe Morna, C. 2018. *Glass Ceiling: Women in South African news media*. Johannesburg: Gender Links.

Reid, J. 2021. *New Concepts in Media Diversity: A view from South Africa*. Pretoria: UNISA Press.

Rodny-Gumede, Y. 2022. 'The triple oppressions: Race, class and gender in South African journalism'. In *Women Journalists in South Africa: Democracy in the age of social media*, edited by G. Daniels and K. Skinner. London: Palgrave Macmillan.

Rodny-Gumede, Y. 2021. 'Transformation, fragmentation and decolonisation: The contested role of the media in postcolonial South Africa'. In *Political Communication as Decolonisation and Performance: Africa and the Diaspora*, edited by Beschara Karam and Bruce Mutsvairo. London: Routledge.

Rodny-Gumede, Y. 2020. 'Expanding comparative media systems analysis from transitional to postcolonial societies'. *International Communication Gazette*. Published online 23 January 2020.

Rodny-Gumede, Y. 2017a. 'Questioning the media-democracy relationship: The case of South Africa'. *Communicatio: South African Journal for Communication Theory and Research*, 43(2):10–20.

Rodny-Gumede, Y. 2017b. 'The centrality of media hearings to transitional justice processes', in *Limits to Transition: A critique of the TRC*, edited by Karen van Merle and Mia Swart. Leiden; Boston: Brill Nijhoff, pp 253–281.

Rodny-Gumede, Y. 2015a. 'An assessment of the public interest and ideas of the public in South Africa and the adoption of "Ubuntu journalism"'. *Journal of Media Ethics,* 30(2):109–124.

Rodny-Gumede, Y. 2015b. 'South African journalists' conceptualisation of professionalism and deviations form normative liberal values'. *Communicare,* 33(2):54–69.

Rodny-Gumede, Y. 2015c. 'Gender and Public Discourse Formation in South Africa: Male and Female Journalists' Influence on News Agendas', *Communicatio: South African Journal for Communication Theory and Research,* 41(2):206–219.

Rodny-Gumede, Y., Milton, V. and Mano, W. 2017. 'Rethinking the link between media and democracy in the post-colony: One size does not fit all'. *Communicatio: South African Journal for Communication Theory and Research*, 43(2):1–9.

Shallom, R. 2018, June 28. 'Women in public-facing journalism jobs are exhausted by harassment'. *Poynter.* https://www.poynter.org/news/cohort-women-public-facing-journalism-jobs-are-exhausted-harassment

TRC. 1998. Final report of the Truth and Reconciliation Commission of

South Africa. Vol. 4, Chapter 6, Institutional hearing on the media. Cape Town: Juta.

Voltmer, K. 2006. 'The mass media and the dynamics of political communication in processes of democratization'. In *Mass Media and Political Communication in New democracies*, edited by K. Voltmer. London: Routledge, pp 1–20.

Wasserman, H. and Garman, A. 2013. 'The meanings of citizenship: Media use and democracy in South Africa'. *Social Dynamics: A Journal of African Studies*, 40(2):392–407.

On Managing Internal and International Motive Forces

11

Bottom-up or top-down continental integration? The unavoidable normative question

David Mohale

There can be no disputing the importance of continental and regional integration as a precondition for Africa's growth and development. There is enough evidence that Europe and (East) Asia have largely succeeded through integration of their economies. It is, therefore, not surprising that Africa would attempt to emulate the success stories from other regions in its effort to catch up and, hopefully, surpass the notable wondrous economic achievements of her counterparts over the centuries. However, the desperation for much-needed growth and development may result in unquestioned adoption of strategies that worked elsewhere without exposing inherent flaws. Although theoretical, this paper is based on an empirical study that focused on the symbiosis of local government and the goal of a developmental state in South Africa. Based on data collected between 2000 and 2014 on the various performance areas of municipalities, the study found that the dream of a developmental state hinges primarily on the performance – its quality and its sustenance – of the entirety of government machinery, which includes the local government sector.

The integration of the continent is not a new phenomenon. It can be traced back to the moment when the postcolonial African leaders formed the Organisation of African Unity (OAU), which would later be renamed the African Union. One of the criticisms attributed to the failure of the mooted integration taking root is the suspected lack of political will from the leaders in the continent. Another criticism could be that several individual African states continue to rely heavily on certain countries outside the continent for aid, thus compromising the integrity of the regional and continental integration. South Africa's solo participation in BRICS is an example of some emergent strategic blocs that may not necessarily aid the efforts of integration. This paper argues that integration efforts will fail unless they are rooted in the localness of the people who must be beneficiaries of development to avoid jobless growth. In other words, discussion on continental and regional integration must involve local leaders as the truest representatives of the people at grassroots level in order to ensure that the fruits of the desired growth are redistributed equitably within national borders.

The necessity for involvement of local governments in Africa

The African Agenda 2063[1] identifies eight critical enablers for Africa's transformation. Four of these enablers – namely, (i) the people's ownership and mobilisation; (ii) accountable leadership and responsive institutions; (iii) capable and democratic developmental states and institutions; and (iv) African approach to development and transformation – require that development plans and strategies must be fashioned with the people on the ground. This is what should be at the heart of the democratic developmental states that Africa aspires to build by 2063. The African Agenda 2063 does not mention local government once in its 22 pages, although inference could be made for the role of local government where the document refers to "all levels" and "all spheres". Further, the document does mention the words "rural" and "urban/urbanisation" three times each, which could imply that there is tacit acknowledgment of the localness of development.

The African Agenda 2063 explicitly commits to the construction of democratic developmental states in the continent. Based on lessons from East Asia, it is sensible why this would be the case. Developmental states are often seen as the cause for development, best captured in Evans' phrase "No developmental state, no development".[2] However, a critical analysis has a duty to expose the blind admiration of both integration and developmental states as causes for growth and development. As Pempel[3] points out, the paradox of growth in East Asia was high levels of social inequality. This was partly because growth in the region was led by central governments, thus removed from the sensitivities at grassroots level. Therefore, centralisation of policy planning and implementation was one of the many blemishes of the twentieth-century developmental state. In the twenty-first century, the state cannot be reified outside the embeddedness in society.

In other words, the important policy question that ought to be asked when discussing integration should be: Integration for whom? If this is for the citizens of the continent, many of whom suffer daily by the debilitating effects of poorly managed urban-rural continuum, the related question ought to be: What spaces are there for citizens to shape their own destinies? The African developmental state in the twenty-first century has to be unapologetically democratic. The only condition for its democratic character is if local governments are included in the discussion on the redistribution of resources that will result from the integration. As Mills, Obasanjo, Herbst and Davis point out, "although the role of municipal actors is frequently overlooked, their direct influence is often greater than that of presidents".[4] This makes sense because municipalities inhabit the space where implementation occurs, and where policymakers come face to face with the real problems of society. Inevitably, the complex yet strategic challenge for local governments will be to build and maintain deliberative spaces within their jurisdictions to ensure that multiple voices bear on the co-authorship, implementation, monitoring and evaluation of policies.

The developmental state paradigm might have emerged as a potential alternative to World Bank-sponsored orthodoxy. Its demonstrable growth of scholarship might be one of the measures of its potency as a theoretical framework. However, there remain some critical issues that the literature has not addressed satisfactorily, including but not limited to gender and environmental affairs, which have become very central in modern-day public policy.[5] Notably, the lacunae on the role and impact of sub-national structures in achieving wondrous economic growth in

East Asia, and therefore the actual role and impact of local government in the present and in future, is the concern this contribution seeks to address. Arguing for the active and prominent role of local government as a sphere of government may help with the amelioration of a number of policy aspects that national governments may not be sensitive to at local level. For instance, the marked climatic changes that result in frequent floods as has been witnessed in KwaZulu-Natal every year since 2020, with wanton destruction of public and economic property, lends credence to the argument for prominence of local government in development planning, including on matters of environmental management as dictated by the Constitution of the Republic of South Africa.

Developmental states were also notably identified by their deliberate political centralisation and subordination of sub-national structures of government and various social classes. Centralisation policy could be justified against the reality that states that ended up being developmental faced a real or potential external threat at some point. It therefore makes security sense. It is also important to point out that colonising countries preferred highly centralised governance systems for the sole purpose of safeguarding their imperial interest of capital flight.[6] It is not surprising therefore that Fine correctly criticises the literature on developmental state for its neglect of central-local relations.[7]

The mainstream literature on developmental state has neglected two important factors over the years, both of which are contributing to the significance of this study. These are central-local relations, or what is alternatively known as intergovernmental relations, and the role of local government as an important institution of delivery. In order to compensate for this gap, there is recently an emergence of the notion of a local developmental state. Bateman notes that:

> The initial narrative of the developmental state in East Asia focused on the contribution of national-level developmental state institutions promoting development "from the top down", such as the Ministry of International Trade and Industry (MITI) in Japan and Economic Planning Board in South Korea. One important initial reason for this emphasis was that only national government institutions had the scale and scope to successfully build large industrial enterprises and industries and endow them

with the most advanced technologies, which was initially seen as the main route to structural transformation and economic growth. However, drilling further down to identify the root causes of many of the most successful development experiences since World War II reveals that much, and in some cases most, of the impetus for development was actually coming not from "top-down" national state institutions, but from "bottom-up" sub-national state institutions. Not least because they were more flexible than central governments with regard to changing markets, technologies, innovations and consumer tastes, it began to become clear that sub-national governments had taken on the responsibility for building their own developmental state institutions, sometimes with and sometimes without the support of central government, and they were achieving major development successes as a result.[8]

The recent re-examination of the development literature by bringing in local government and decentralisation is a welcome gesture. It proves that the concept of the developmental state is not static. It evolves. This type of scholarship is growing at a particularly fast rate on China's developmentalism. For instance, Ahlers[9] argues that urbanisation in China will succeed because it has encouraged "a more comprehensive and sustainable system of localised developmental planning". Schubert and Heberer[10] conclude that local state in contemporary China is developmentalist in nature. According to these authors, developmentalism rests on a "creative mixture that combines the administrative streamlining of local bureaucracies, policy experimentation and innovation, cadre management and, most notably, the economic guidance of the private sector".[11] From this, it is easy to deduce that local state in China is able to carry out similar functions that the central government is undertaking.

The increasing role of local governments both in practice and development literature still falls short of adequately covering the full story. The assessment of success of local government will obviously cover areas such as results, legitimacy and durability. These outcomes are dependent on internal institutional characteristics that are much broader than an assumption of apolitical, insulated bureaucracy. However, local government institutions carry out their mandates and functions within the context of formal and informal systems of intergovernmental relations. By implication, institutional arrangements that give rise to the emergence of a developmental state are no longer reducible to a simplistic corporate bureaucratic coherence within a pilot agency like MITI alone. Within a single institution, there is a need for deliberate facilitation of what Chibber[12] terms "internal cohesiveness", which transcends a functioning bureaucracy. In the context of decentralisation, there must be a deliberate cooperative cohesiveness between the three different spheres of government. The same is expected to be the case between the two tiers of local government (district and local) as they currently exist in South Africa. Similarly, there is a need for cooperative cohesiveness between adjoining municipalities that share boundaries. Smoke[13] notes that:

> National politics can obviously support or undermine specific decentralisation policies. They influence, for example, which functions and revenues are devolved, the degree to which the central government is willing to grant subnational autonomy, and the process and support structures that enable local governments to assume new roles. Reluctance to decentralise may reflect an unwillingness of the centre to relinquish functions and resources, or efforts to pursue reforms superficially may result from clashes between the legislature and the executive or among groups within legislatures (based on party politics).

The challenge with African development strategies is that they are rooted in approaches originated in other countries. The same could be said about the developmental state approach. This may largely explain why Africa continues to be placed on the lowest rung of the development ladder. Africa needs to rise and claim the twenty-second century and make it an African century with regard to rapid development. For this to happen, "the African political leadership and African citizens should pursue a process of unlearning, relearning, unthinking and rethinking dominant thought paradigms".[14] To their credit, the authors of the African Agenda 2063 are committing to "a Pan-African perspective" and an "African approach to development and transformation"[15] which, amongst many other elements, should be people-centred and people-driven. Local government is the best-placed institution to ensure that the regional and continental integration is to the benefit of the citizens of the continent.

Principles of localisation

Local governance is often linked to policy reforms of decentralisation. The main drivers of decentralisation are democratisation of governance processes and expectation that popular participation in public decision-making processes stands a good chance of "increasing efficiency in the provision of goods and services".[16] The reason for this assumption is that local provision of services is more likely to be sensitive to the needs and preferences of communities. Implementation of policy is therefore expected to be met with fewer hurdles as beneficiaries would have participated in the co-production of developmental strategies. For this reason, Kampen[17] argues that municipal space is the rightful unit to construct social capital, or developmental coalitions, which are largely attributable to the outstanding economic performances of East Asian Tigers. Local government therefore does not only serve the purpose of opening up democratic spaces and increasing efficiency of delivery of goods and services. It also salvages the growing loss of trust in governments by expanding the embeddedness of the state in society at the very grassroots level.

The duty of every government is to find strategies to meet the needs of the people. Representative democracy operates on an assumption that individuals freely surrender their sovereignty to the elected public officials with a hope that those elected will use state power, law and resources to meet individual private and public human needs. From this premise, the essence of every government in its entirety is to be responsive to the needs and expectations of the people. That is the basis of political legitimacy, which is an important element of the success of every institution.

Decentralisation has since the early 1980s emerged as one of the key policy innovations by all governments of the world to promote and protect their legitimacy through improved service delivery. Political centralisation has led to "the untenableness of developmental inequality between communities"[18] as national strategies fail to enhance "more context-adapted development programs and projects".[19] As O'Riain[20] argues, only "glocal" states will succeed in the twenty-first century through strategies that promote capital accumulation by linking the local to the global through the deliberate development strategy of decentralisation.

Is there a normative justification for the existence of local government? The world system perspective sees the globe to be consisting of the core, semiperiphery and periphery. It omits the fact that within this tripartite division of the globe, there are constituent geographic spaces or territories that make up the whole national territory of a first, second or third world state. Science teaches that the compound must always be broken into simple elements or least parts of a whole. To assume that the whole of a globe consists only of this tripartite division is superficial. The focus is misplaced in the general without an understanding of the specific. Elements may not make sense on their own if totally removed from the body. By the same measure, a body cannot be defined and understood outside its constituent elements, including those that may be understated because of their share of size or weight of contribution to the sustenance of life. It is rather intellectually curious that development got to be analysed from the lens of compartments of the world system theory despite available evidence that governance originated at the level of city states.

While it may have been sidelined for ages, the staccato continuation of global economic crises from 1930 until the recent one in 2008 has helped to bring back local governance into debate of good governance, economic development and democratisation. It is rare to find any book or journal article on the developmental state since the turn of the twentieth century that does not stress the importance of local government as one of the variables to be considered. Not even the proponents of trivialisation of national borders would ignore the elusiveness of goals of transparency, accountability, pluralism, citizen participation without the involvement of citizens at lower levels of government. It is ahistoric to think of any apolitical development. To achieve any political goal, Fanon[21] argues that there must be decentralisation in the extreme. As part of governance reforms, Edoun[22] observes that "the wind of democratisation and globalisation that blew in the 1980s saw African countries adopting political and administrative decentralisation".

Various spinoffs for localisation of the discussion

The end of the Cold War towards the end of the twentieth century led to the third wave of democratisation under the rubric of decentralisation. In part, decentralisation came as a response to "the flight of faith"[23] from the democratic process as many citizens in the developing world failed to see and taste the returns of investment in democratisation. Although many states had democratised, circumstances of the legacy of their history made national leaders prefer strong central governments, thus inadvertently creating new forms of tyranny as citizens continued to be marginalised and excluded from core governance processes. It was mainly in the economic realm that citizens could not argue the worth of democratisation.

As Smoke[24] points out, analysis of how political economy shapes the initial shape and strength of decentralisation is the priority of decentralisation policy. Essentially, the assessment of transfer of a wide scope of political, economic and administrative functions to local authorities must focus on the "prevailing local economic activity and particular patterns of class forces that arise from it".[25] By implication, decentralisation must not only promote participation and inclusion of citizens. While these are important and seek to promote citizenship, decentralisation equally has an important task of facilitating the integration and insertion of local economy into global processes and world markets and the consequent empowerment or disempowerment of local social groups by that integration. Given this complexity, the task of a local developmental agency (municipality) must, amongst other prerequisites, "entail the capacity of local actors to define jointly problems of development, generate programs that accommodate a diversity of local interests, and jointly mobilise resources for implementation".[26]

Developmental states in the twenty-first century have to be uncompromisingly democratic. Mkandawire[27] labels them "developmental democratic states". Some[28] inversely call them "democratic developmental states". The debate on which adjective should precede another may just be another extension of controversy that seems to be inherently associated with the concept. However, both labels do confirm the compatibility of democracy with development although some commentators argue that this is only possible when democracy is thinly reduced to free and fair elections.[29]

It could be that the difference lies in which goal should be realised first in an event of a need for sequence. Be that as it may, the important element is that the new developmental state needs to abhor the political centralisation of the quintessential developmental states. Political centralisation created insulated bureaucracies that were insensitive to local needs and concerns and failed to tap into local information, initiative and ingenuity.[30] As Planel[31] observes, the programme of agricultural extension in Ethiopia is failing to succeed as intended because the focus on national targets is failing to include influential local specificities in the implementation. Tsukamoto[32] is further illustrating the case for decentralisation as an important twenty-first-century developmental state policy:

> Since the late 1990s, both of Japan's two major political parties, the ruling Democratic Party of Japan (DPJ) and the opposing Liberal Democratic Party of Japan (LDP), have been pressing for state decentralisation reform. Japan's centralised political system might have worked well during the high-growth era of the 1950s and 1960s but its advantages have been long exhausted, they typically argue. It is no longer suitable to deal with today's complex challenges, such as economic globalisation and Japan's demographic changes. Thus, as a solution, both parties prescribe state decentralisation, which would stimulate local initiative and entrepreneurship.

Conclusion

Africa continues to grapple with the perennial challenge of poverty. Integration of regions within the continent and the continent itself has the potential to resolve this stubborn problem. However, for integration to be effective, African leaders need to understand the varied character of poverty within the continent and within cities and rural areas. The poor young person in a rural area experiences poverty differently from a young person who is subjected to living in slum areas on the periphery of a city. Inevitably, integration needs to be sensitive to the context of a growing problem of migration; and how migration perpetuates the pauperisation of the rural poor and excludes the often unskilled or semi-skilled migrants from participating in the mainstream economies in cities. Integration will be useless if it further institutionalises the urban/rural discrimination and inequality in terms of access to opportunities. There is no denying that cities are the engines of economic growth although the opposite is true in Africa. The African cities are nothing but centres of conspicuous consumption and ostentatious display of wealth by the rich.

To correct patterns of skewed development and the normalised exclusion of the rural poor, the African Union and its member states should ensure that the voice of local government is always heard to guarantee that revolutionary interventions are fashioned with the people.

References

African Union. 2013. Agenda 2063 Vision and Priorities. http://www.un.org/en/africa/osaa/pdf/au/agenda2063.pdf

Ahlers, A.L. 2015. 'Weaving the Chinese dream on the ground? Local government approaches to "new-typed" rural urbanisation'. *Journal of Chinese Political Science*, 20:121–142.

Bardhan, P. 2016. 'State and development: The need for a reappraisal of the current literature'. *Journal of Economic Literature*, 56(3):862–892.

Bateman, M. 2016. 'Sustainable, equitable and decent job creation in South Africa: The crucial role of the "local developmental state"'. Paper presented at TIPS Conference on Economic Development for Employment: Sub-national strategies 14–15 November 2016, Pretoria.

Bruszt, L. and Vedres, B. 2013. 'Associating, mobilising, politicizing: Local developmental agency from without'. *Theory and Society*, 42:1–23.

Chibber, V. 2014. 'The developmental state in retrospect and prospect: Lessons from India and South Korea'. In *The End of Developmental State?* edited by M. Williams, pp 30–54. Pietermaritzburg: University of KwaZulu-Natal Press.

Edoun, E.I. 2012. 'Decentralisation and local economic development: Effective tools for Africa's renewal'. *International Journal of African Renaissance Studies*, 7(1):94–108.

Evans, P. 2010. 'Constructing the 21st century developmental state: Potentials and pitfalls'. In *Constructing a Democratic Developmental State in South Africa: Potentials and challenges* edited by O. Edigheji, pp 169–182. Cape Town: Human Sciences Research Council.

Fanon, F. 1963. *The Wretched of the Earth*. New York: Penguin Books.

Fine, B. 2010. 'Can South Africa be a developmental state?' In *Constructing a Democratic Developmental State in South Africa: Potentials and challenges* edited by O. Edigheji, pp 169–182. Cape Town: Human Sciences Research Council.

Gumede, V. 2016. *Post-apartheid South Africa*. New York: Cambria Press.

Kampen, J.K. 2010. 'On the (in)consistency of citizen and municipal level indicators of social capital and local government performance', *Social Indicators Research*, 97:213–228.

Marais, H. 2010. *South Africa Pushed to the Limit: The political economy of change*. Cape Town: University of Cape Town Press.

Mills, G., Obasanjo, O., Herbst, J. and Davis, D. 2017. *Making Africa Work: A handbook for economic success*. Cape Town: Tafelberg Publishers.

Mkandawire, T. 2010. 'From maladjusted states to democratic developmental states in Africa'. In *Constructing a Democratic Developmental State in South Africa: Potentials and challenges* edited by O. Edigheji, pp 59–81. Cape Town: Human Sciences Research Council.

O'Riain, S. 2004. *The Politics of High-tech Growth: Developmental network states in the global economy*. Cambridge: Cambridge University Press.

Pempel, T.J. 1999. 'The developmental regime in a changing world economy'. In *The developmental state*, edited by M. Woo-Cumings, pp 137–181. Ithaca: Cornell University Press.

Planel, S. 2014. 'A view of a bureaucratic developmental state: Local governance and agricultural extension in rural Ethiopia'. *Journal of Eastern African Studies*, 8(3):420–437.

Prado, M.M., Schapiro, M. and Coutinho, D.R. 2016. 'The dilemmas of the developmental state: Democracy and economic development in Brazil'. *Law and Development Review*, 9(2):369–410.

Reddy, P. and Kauzya, J.M. 2015. 'Local government capacity in the Southern African Development Community (SADC) region'. *Public Policy and Administration*, 14(3):200–224.

Routley, L. 2014. 'Developmental states in Africa? A review of on-going debates and buzzwords'. *Development Policy Review*, 32(2):159–177.

Saud, A. and Khan, K.A. 2016. 'Decentralisation and local government structures: Key to strengthening democracy in Pakistan'. *Journal of Political Studies*, 23(2):397–412.

Schubert, G. and Herberer, T. 2015. 'Continuity and change in China's "Local State Developmentalism"'. *Issues and Studies*, 51(2):1–38.

Smoke, P. 2015a. 'Rethinking decentralisation: Assessing challenges to a popular public sector reform'. *Public Administration and Development*, 35:97–112.

Smoke, P. 2015b. 'Managing public sector decentralisation in developing countries: Moving beyond conventional recipes'. *Public Administration and Development*, 35:250–262.

Steiner, S. 2010. 'How important is the capacity of local governments for improvements in welfare? Evidence from decentralised Uganda'. *Journal of Development Studies*, 46(4):644– 661.

Topal, A. 2015. 'Global processes and local consequences of decentralisation: A sub-national comparison in Mexico'. *Regional Studies*, 49(7):1126–1139.

Tsukamoto, T. 2012. 'Why is Japan neoliberalizing? Rescaling of the Japanese developmental state and ideology of state-capital fixing'. *Journal of Urban Affairs*, 34(4):395–418.

12

South Africa's diplomacy to the African continent: A commitment to "leaving no one behind"

Bongani Mayimele

The period between the fifteenth and the nineteenth centuries witnessed the emergence of imperialism and colonialism across the world.[1] In this period, the African continent experienced one of the biggest settler colonisations, which undermined Africans' right to self-determination and disrupted Africa's development path, resulting in widespread poverty and underdevelopment. The ANC since its formation committed to the total liberation of Africa from colonialism and all its associated ills that still afflict Africa today. The ANC has always recognised and maintained that "the struggle against colonialism in South Africa is tied to the defeat of colonialism in Africa and the rest of the colonised world".[2] This commitment is contained in various resolutions of the ANC dating back to the days of the struggle against apartheid and have found concrete expression in democratic South Africa's foreign policy, which is committed to the primacy of the African continent, rejection of colonialism and all forms of oppression; promotion of South–South solidarity in pursuit of inclusive socio-economic development for shared prosperity. The policy also commits to the opposition to structural inequality and the abuse of power in the global system of governance, the abuse of which has contributed to and continues to perpetuate the underdevelopment of most African countries. The apartheid regime led to South Africa being isolated in the international system. Following the democratic takeover from the apartheid regime, which rendered South Africa a pariah state, South Africa, observes authors such as Gomes da Costa, became a significant diplomatic influencer in Africa because of its implementation of a transparent foreign policy[3] with a clear commitment to the African continent.

South Africa's commitment to the African continent transitions from policy to practice and finds expression in various initiatives and interventions of the democratic government led by the ANC. Since being elected to office by an overwhelming majority of South Africans in 1994, the ANC-led government has been involved in various missions on the African continent to contribute towards the restoration of peace and the promotion of development, aiming for the achievement of a united and prosperous Africa free from conflict. This chapter showcases the author's observation of the implementation of South Africa's commitment and role in contributing to improved governance and building of peaceful societies on the African continent, thus contributing to enabling conditions for development and prosperity. The observation is supported by literature from other authors. This is done to indicate that South Africa's foreign policy is not only rhetoric, but a commitment by our political forefathers that has been implemented consistently by the government since 1994 to the current administration whose term is ending in 2024 thus marking 30 years of South Africa's continuous commitment to the total liberation and prosperity of the whole of the African continent. South Africa's foreign policy is therefore a commitment to "leaving no one behind" towards the realisation of a "better life for all". The observation of South Africa's commitment is also drawn from literature.

The nature of South Africa's foreign policy

South Africa's democratic breakthrough heralded optimism for the African continent as the ANC, with its Afrocentric vision, took the reins of government. This breakthrough signalled and saw a radical change in South Africa's foreign policy – from hostility to friendship – and solidarity with the rest of the African continent. The end of apartheid raised expectations on South Africa to take part and play an instrumental role in African affairs.[4] South Africa lived up to these expectations by crafting an inclusive foreign policy deeply rooted in the ANC's historic mission "to build a better Africa and a better world that is humane, just, equitable, democratic and free".[5] The *White Paper on South Africa's Foreign Policy* affirms that since 1994 the international community has looked to South Africa to play a leading diplomatic role in the pursuit of Africa's development and that South Africa has risen to the challenge by playing a leading role in global and continental affairs.[6]

These expectations were in part on the basis of the ANC's consistent historic posture towards the struggle of Africans that underscores the interconnectedness of South Africa's development with that of African countries. This posture was not only in rhetoric. It was demonstrated in action. As early as its inception, true to its commitment to the liberation of the whole of Africa from colonial rule and all forms of oppression and exploitation, the 1918 ANC Special Conference of Amakhosi sent a memo to the British monarch, firmly asserting that the governments of South Africa, Germany and Belgium should refrain from colonial involvement in South West Africa (Namibia), East Africa (Tanzania) and the Congo, respectively, until the aspirations of the native African populations were fulfilled.[7] This was at a time when the ANC was faced with its own domestic struggles in South Africa. However, the ANC has always been outward-looking and consistent in its commitment to the liberation and self-determination of Africa. The second point of selfless and collective struggle of the African people was the ANC's posture to both Woodrow Wilson's 14 Points and US President Franklin D. Roosevelt and British Prime Minister Winston Churchill's Atlantic Charter. The ANC maintained that the vagueness of Woodrow Wilson's 14 Points and the Atlantic Charter were not inclusive of Africans and would further institutionalise the subjugation and exploitation of Africa and its people. As a counter to the Atlantic Charter, the ANC drafted the "African Claims" document in 1943 arguing rights expressed in the Atlantic Charter should be extended also to Africans and all oppressed people in the world.[8] The African Claims also inform present-day South Africa's foreign policy. Therefore, South Africa's present-day foreign policy is born in the ANC's struggle to rid the African continent of the tyranny of colonialism and hegemony, underdevelopment and the indignity and violence of poverty into a peaceful and prosperous Africa. The 48th Conference of the ANC played an instrumental role in weaving together from various ANC resolutions into present-day democratic South Africa's foreign policy. This conference laid the foundation for South Africa's foreign policy by establishing seven principles. The seven principles emphasise, among others, international peace, justice and international law, human rights, democracy and the centrality of Africa. Accordingly, the 48th Conference of the ANC asserted that "South Africa shall strive to maintain world peace and the settlement of all international disputes by negotiation – not war … and will actively promote the objectives of democracy, peace, stability, development and mutually beneficial relations among the people of Africa as a whole … and stand in solidarity with all those whose struggle continue"[9] just like we do with the people of Palestine. These principles are central to South Africa's foreign policy to this day, which the government of South Africa contributes towards through various initiatives. The policy is continuously reviewed considering global developments and consistently commits to the primacy of the African continent guided by the spirit of Pan-Africanism and South–South solidarity. This policy reflects a commitment to the shared development and prosperity of South Africa and the broader African continent with a view of "leaving no one behind". South Africa's foreign policy therefore signals South Africa's intent for a better life for all Africans and peaceful coexistence.[10]

Therefore, none would contest that South Africa's foreign policy was born in the shared struggle of the African people. It is a liberation instrument whose intent is the total liberation of Africa and its elevation to take its rightful place in the family of nations. It infuses Ubuntu and Pan-Africanism, thus is not driven by commercial interests to maximise capital gains but to serve the interests of the people. It is one of solidarity and liberation of the oppressed. For this, Chief Albert Luthuli remarked in 1953, "Our interest in freedom is not confined to ourselves only. We are interested in the liberation of all oppressed people in the whole of Africa and in the world as a whole … Our active interest in the extension of freedom to all people denied it makes us ally ourselves with freedom forces in the world."[11] The policy is development centred and places the development of Africa at its core and thus represents common aspirations and prosperity that the continent yearns for as per the African Union Agenda 2063. It represents common struggles and common aspirations of the African people. The common struggles are the struggle against colonialism, underdevelopment, and abuse of the global system of governance. The common aspirations are the reclaiming of our humanity, dignity, self-determination, human rights and sustainable development with shared prosperity.

Drawing from these historic commitments, South Africa's posture to the African continent is of a non-hegemon and a two-way mutual process. It is this non-hegemonic approach found in the "Diplomacy of Ubuntu" and consistent commitment to its foreign policy in practice that makes South Africa appealing to the African continent. Sharing the same observation in affirmation, Hendricks and Majozi wrote: "Although South Africa dominates SADC economically, it has not been willing to step up to the role of hegemon in the region."[12] In addition to the appeal of South Africa's foreign policy, South Africa's moral authority drawn from the Mandela era also contributed to South Africa's standing in the continent.[13] Not only that is a factor. It can be argued that South Africa's non-hegemonic approach, based on the principle of the Freedom Charter that "there shall be peace and friendship" and "Diplomacy of Ubuntu" infused with Pan-Africanism, gives South Africa a distinctive appeal in Africa and the world. This has given South Africa leverage, allowing the South African government to enjoy an unmatched voice in African affairs[14] and on the global stage where South Africa champions the African Agenda where other African countries are not included given their socio-economic standing. Then South Africa, through its consistent commitment to the African continent in global fora and transparency of its foreign policy, has become an acceptable partner in Africa's development and has lived up to the expectations raised since 1994 and carries forward the liberation struggle to rid Africa of colonialism and underdevelopment. This posture of South Africa's foreign policy to the African continent is in practice a commitment to "leaving no one behind" towards the realisation of a "better life for all".

Implementation of South Africa's foreign policy

Continental renewal: South Africa and the African Union

Central to the foreign policy of South Africa is the African agenda and strengthened multilateralism in a just and equitable world with the consistent commitment to and quest for African unity and shared prosperity. For this commitment to find expression in practice, South Africa contributed to building strong institutions for peace, democracy, governance and human rights, which lay the basis for the development that the African continent yearns for. The role of institutions in promoting peace, and improving governance and development is well known and is at the heart the African Union Agenda 2063, which can be argued mirrors South Africa's foreign policy; and is also at the heart of the United Nations 2030 for Sustainable Development. In fact, also symbolising South Africa's influence and commitment to the "African Renaissance", the AU Agenda 2063 was introduced during South Africa's chairship of the African Union Commission.

Accordingly, given the role and importance of institutions in maintaining peace and promoting development, the notable success of South Africa in terms of implementing this policy commitment could be seen in efforts and contribution to the reform of the Organisation of African Unity (OAU) into the current African Union (AU) as an institution that would then lay the basis for the "African Renaissance" and an instrument towards which an Africa envisioned in South Africa's foreign policy could be realised. South Africa and Nigeria used a Special Session of the OAU held in Libya from 6 to 9 September 1999 to lay proposals for the reform of the OAU. It is reported that this proposal was well received and a legal team from the South African Department of Foreign Affairs led the drafting of the Constitutive Act of the AU during an expert meeting following the meeting in Libya.[15] The Constitutive Act of the AU states among its objectives to "promote peace, security, and stability on the continent; promote democratic principles and institutions, popular participation and good governance; promote and protect human and peoples' rights in accordance with the African Charter on Human and Peoples' Rights and other relevant human rights instruments".[16] These objectives are central to South Africa's foreign policy and lay the foundation for the promotion and achievement of sustainable development.

President Thabo Mbeki became the inaugural chairperson of the AU, thus giving a South African advocate for the re-emergence of the "African Renaissance", which became synonymous with Mbeki's tenure as president of South Africa and chairperson of the AU. In her paper, Kathryn Sturman argued that through South Africa's role in the reform of the OAU into the AU states "the emergence of post-apartheid South Africa as a 'middle power' or 'regional hegemon' in Africa has acted as a catalyst for change of the regional organisation; and how South Africa has influenced the AU's shift from holding sovereignty as sacrosanct, to building mechanisms for intervention".[17] Accordingly, the reform of the OAU led to the establishment of the New Partnerships for Africa's Development (NEPAD), which was the brainchild of South Africa, to take forward the African Renaissance, a Pan-Africanist vision laid by leaders such as Kwame Nkrumah; and South Africa's Pixley Ka Seme through the notable speech "The Regeneration of Africa". South Africa's achievements could therefore be seen in lobbying for the establishment of institutions of development such as the NEPAD; democratic governance such as the Pan-African Parliament; peace such as the Peace and Security Council; and governance through the African Peer Review Mechanism (APRM). The establishment of these institutions is to promote the "African Renaissance" for which states Vale and Maseko, quoted in Kathryn Sturman, was meant "to place Africa at the centre of South African foreign policy, present South Africa's economic power and political success as a shining example of the continent's potential and highlight the country's leading role in promoting Africa's cause to the rest of the world".[18]

Though their effectiveness is a subject of debate, these institutions have been created for a legitimate purpose. Accordingly, the establishment of institutions remains high in the African Union Agenda 2063 and globally in the United Nations 2030 Agenda for Sustainable Development. Recognising the significance of institutions in fostering enduring peace and development, South Africa played a pivotal role in reshaping the peace and security frameworks across Africa. Notably, it contributed significantly to the establishment of key structures such as the Southern African Development Community (SADC) organ, the African Peace and Security Architecture (APSA), and the African Capacity for Immediate Response to Crises, thereby leaving a lasting impact on the continent's security landscape.[19] These are the initiatives championed by South Africa to improve governance, human rights and democracy to create conditions for development and for Africa to take its rightful place in the family of nations, an ideal underpinning South Africa's foreign policy. Institutions, as both laws and organisations, could be instruments of liberation. The Foreign Policy of South Africa (as a law) and the AU (as an organisation) with its agencies are instruments of Africa's liberation from the tyranny of colonialism and subsequent indignity of Africans, which has for many years placed them at the periphery of the "international community" as beggars dependant on western mercy and pity. Today, the AU as an institution enjoys a united and strong voice and has partnerships with various continental bodies outside Africa.

Peace-building: South Africa's consistent commitment to Africa's peace and prosperity

The centrality of peace to development is well documented. Peaceful societies create enabling conditions for development.[20] The centrality of peace to development is at the heart of South Africa's foreign policy and was well captured by Kofi Annan, former Secretary-General of the United Nations, who remarked that "there can be no peace without inclusive development and no development without peace".[21] Sharing the same sentiment, South Africa's Minister of Defence, Thandi Modise, also remarked "an island of peace will never survive a sea of war".[22] With this historic realisation central to South Africa's foreign policy, South Africa has been involved in various peace-keeping missions on the African continent. Seemingly indicating South Africa's readiness for its commitment to peace in Africa, former Chief of the South African National Defence Force (SANDF), General Siphiwe Nyanda, affirmed that the SANDF, unlike its predecessor the South African Defence Force, is ready and "will take a different posture from aggression in foreign policy to be involved in peacebuilding on the African continent for peace, development, and prosperity".[23]

The reform of the OAU into the AU led to the establishment of the Peace and Security Council (PSC) with South Africa being said to have played an influential role in its establishment. The ratification of the PSC was a priority for South Africa and South Africa's diplomats lobbied other member states to ratify the protocol.[24] The successful ratification of the PSC, attributed to South Africa's efforts, is what Clark describes as an unequalled voice that democratic South Africa has on African continental affairs. Accordingly, as an important institution for the achievement of African-led peace operations, the establishment of the PSC saw African states taking on greater responsibility in peace missions[25] thus contributing to the long-held desire of the then OAU for such missions, signalling African solutions to African problems. The PSC paved a way for African-led peace operations. Before that, the United Nations was facing challenges to achieve peace goals in Africa.[26] As a result of the establishment of the PSC as an institution, the AU has since 2003 authorised a number of peace support operations including the AU Missions in Burundi, Sudan and Somalia to resolve conflicts and restore peace. South Africa with its commitment to peace has been taking part in these missions and expectations are still there for it to continue playing a leading role. The establishment of the AU has therefore "heralded (or so it was hoped) a new era in how African conflicts are managed and resolved".[27]

In the beginning, South Africa only sent a few officers to African peace-missions but the number has increased over the years.[28] Today, according to the United Nations, "South Africa is the 14th largest contributor to peace-keeping missions".[29] Whilst South Africa initially sent few officers, it is South Africa's influence in the architecture of the PSC that has created conditions for African-led peace-keeping missions. Building institutions such as the PSC could also be regarded as one of the greatest milestones of South Africa towards building a better Africa. This is in line with building institutions to support governance and development, which is part of the Aspirations of the African Union and could be seen as South Africa's contribution to silencing the guns through strong and capable institutions not only through military presence.

South Africa's involvement in peace keeping remains critical to the achievement of South Africa's foreign policy objectives and of various aspirations of the AU such as "silencing the guns", which is critical for other aspirations such as health, education and ultimately development. South Africa's efforts and contributions to peace missions in an assurance of "leaving no one behind" and a creation of a "better life for all". The pursuit of peace has been consistent and South Africa uses every avenue available to advocate for it. Even before its election to the United Nations Security Council (UNSC), South Africa has been consistent in calls for the reform of the UNSC and used its two terms (2007–2008 and 2011–2012) in the UNSC to elevate the African Agenda calling for greater cooperation between the UNSC and the AU Peace and Security Council in pursuit of peace efforts in Africa. These efforts lay the basis for sustainable development that Africa yearns for. South Africa consistently uses its voice to pursue the African Agenda.

In addition to peace keeping, South Africa prioritises the use of diplomatic solutions to conflicts as its foreign policy prioritises the peaceful resolution of conflicts, which has been proven to be instrumental in getting sustainable solutions. Even before resorting to the armed struggle for the liberation of Africans, the ANC as early as the 1900s, "did not desist from seeking diplomatic solutions to the national question in South Africa".[30] Accordingly, the pursuit of diplomatic solutions is embedded in the DNA of the ANC and has found expression in South Africa's foreign policy. It today continues to pursue peaceful resolution of conflicts and advocates for cooperation over confrontation beyond Africa. It has done so in many conflicts including the Russo-Ukraine conflict and the savage attacks on Palestine by Israel.

Negotiations have been proven to be the most effective tool for restoring peace. The critique of military-led peace-keeping missions is that mostly violence flares up when the troops pull out, especially when conditions for social justice are not laid. Also peace keeping is not an end in itself. It is intended to create a conducive environment for negotiations. Where conditions for negotiations exist, there is no need for military-led peace operations. Negotiations done in good faith by the warring parties lay the basis for peace, redress and social justice. The failure of adhering to negotiated settlements or collapse of negotiations could be attributed to the warring parties not adhering to the conditions set or agreed during negotiations. This cannot be blamed on the mediator, if so, then not entirely.

Given its own successful peaceful political settlement in 1994 and successes elsewhere on the continent and role in the world, South Africa still maintains and advocates for peaceful resolution of conflicts as opposed to war, which leads to the destruction of infrastructure and institutions that take years to rebuild. South Africa has, since 1994, as a proponent of peace, been involved in some mediations in some of the conflicts in Africa albeit with different outcomes and scepticism from certain quarters. South Africa helped negotiate peace agreements based on power-sharing in Cote d'Ivoire, Comoros, Sudan and Zimbabwe.[31]

Efficient power-sharing, according to theory, averts violence by involving key stakeholders in the decision-making process. Dispelling scepticism and cynicism around power-sharing deals, Julian Neal argues that power-sharing deals may not result in full democracies but lay the basis for peace, political development and democratic revival which would be impossible to imagine without such arrangements.[32]

South Africa will always pursue peaceful resolution of conflicts where conditions allow. This approach is aimed at averting the escalation of conflicts into civilian unrest or wars. The goal is to create peaceful conditions before they escalate so as to not disrupt human lives, the economy and infrastructure upon which development and trade rest.

Championing the African Agenda: Leaving no one behind

South Africa's foreign policy rightly holds that the development of South Africa is intertwined with that of African countries and commits to champion the African Agenda with a view of "leaving no one behind". Since 1994, South Africa was accepted back in the international stage and multilateral system, and occupied its rightful place in the family of nations. During this time, South Africa gained readmission to a number of multilateral bodies and has used its voice to advocate for the Africa Agenda. South Africa, whenever invited to the global fora such as the G7 and G20, always carries the African flag.[33] This is done to leave no one behind in the enjoyment of a better life for all. South Africa's advocacy of the African Agenda is the pursuit of its foreign policy for the common development and prosperity of the whole of Africa. As a middle power, South Africa actively uses its voice to pursue a just and equitable world order. It consistently uses it voice to advocate among others the reform of the UNSC; and against the abuse of power in the global governance system whose abuse impedes the development of Africa and the global South.

Recent developments that represent South Africa's commitment to championing the African Agenda include during the outbreak of Covid-19 and South Africa's chairing of the BRICS. These two examples represent South Africa's commitment to a better life for the African continent.

The emergence of Covid-19 put the commitment of "leaving no one behind" under scrutiny as inward-looking, narrow-minded nationalism and signs of vaccine nationalism emerged from certain quarters of the world despite Covid-19 being a global health threat permeating through all sorts of walls. Some resisted to make the vaccine a public good and saw an opportunity to profit.[34] Symbolising the "diplomacy of Ubuntu" and spirit of Pan-Africanism in practice, during that time of uncertainty, increasing inward looking by other countries and despite its domestic brunt, South Africa rose to the challenge and led by example by donating vaccines to the AU and advocating for the Covid-19 vaccine to become a public good. This signalled South Africa's commitment to the African Agenda and "leaving no one behind" for the benefit of African countries whose development gains Covid-19 had the potential to significantly reverse. In the advocacy for the vaccine to become a public good, South Africa put forward that making the vaccine a public good is about reaffirming humanity not only in South Africa but all over the world. That it would be a great injustice amounting to vaccine apartheid if only rich countries are inoculated while watching millions of people die in poor countries.[35]

South Africa was until 2023 the only African country in the BRICS. As per its commitment to South–South solidarity and championing the African Agenda in the multilateral system, South Africa has always advocated for the development of the broader global South. This commitment was even more pronounced during the 15th BRICS Summit under South Africa's Chairship in 2023 whose theme put Africa at the centre. The theme was "BRICS and Africa: Partnership for Mutually Accelerated Growth, Sustainable Development and Inclusive Multilateralism". The theme promotes three concepts of South Africa's foreign policy: inclusive multilateralism, partnerships for development and places Africa in sharp focus. As a promotion of inclusivity, various leaders of African countries attended the summit in Johannesburg, South Africa. This is South Africa's commitment to championing the Africa Agenda and "leaving no one behind" towards a "better life for all". Accordingly, the resolutions of the 15th BRICS Summit also reflect on the aspirations of Africa. The resolutions include the reform of the

UN and its Security Council to support the legitimate aspirations of Africa, Asia and Latin America. The resolutions, arguably reflective of South Africa's foreign policy for the pursuit of peace, also call for the use of dialogue in conflict resolution and emphasise "African Solutions to African Problems". The resolutions, consistent with South Africa's foreign policy of championing the African Agenda, also reiterated support for the African Union Agenda 2063. These resolutions are testament that South Africa's foreign policy is not only in rhetoric. It is a "consistent commitment" of taking forward the vision laid by the founders of the ANC whose vision is the total liberation of Africa from the clutches of the remnants and resurfacing of colonialism.

Conclusion

South Africa's foreign policy, born in struggle, is a tool for liberation. It represents the pursuit of common aspirations of the African continent. Its transparency and emphasis on Pan-Africanism, democracy, human rights, rejection of all forms of oppression and colonisation among its tenants has made the policy appealing in Africa and beyond. Given its economic might, moral authority and non-hegemonic approach drawn from the principles of Ubuntu, which underpins its policy, it has poised South Africa to be a mutual partner in the reconstruction of the African continent. South Africa actively contributed to the reform and establishment of continental institutions that have laid the basis for the pursuit of the African Renaissance as per South Africa's foreign policy.

The centrality of the African Agenda in South Africa's foreign policy is, in practice, a commitment to leaving no one behind. South Africa's foreign policy's commitment to the African Agenda finds expression in practice and is well poised to the achievement of a "better South Africa and a better world", which has, since the days of the struggle against apartheid, been a priority for successive ANC-led South African governments since 1994. The pursuit of the African Agenda is the pursuit for liberation from all forms of colonisation, overt or covert, as well as poverty and underdevelopment. South Africa's foreign policy, founded on the wisdom of the people rallied behind the ANC, is a tool for liberation for Africa to fulfil its aspirations of peace, development and shared prosperity.

References

African Union. 2002. Constitutive Act of the African Union. https:// au.int/sites/default/files/pages/34873-file-constitutiveact_en.pdf

Annan, K. 1998. 'Statement by Mr Kofi Annan, Secretary-General of the United Nations to the opening of the fifty-fourth session of the Commission on Human Rights'. https://www.ohchr.org/en/ statements/2009/10/statement-mr-kofi-annan-secretary-general-united-nations-opening-fifty-fourth

ANC. 1994. 'Foreign policy perspective in a democratic South Africa'. https://www.anc1912.org.za/policy-documents-1994-foreign-policy-perspective-in-a-democratic-south-africa/

ANC. 2012. 'International relations discussion document'. https://www. anc1912.org.za/wp-content/uploads/2021/04/4th-National-Policy-Conference-International-Relations.pdf

ANC. 2015. 'ANC international relations: A better Africa in a better and just world'. https://www.anc1912.org.za/wp-content/ uploads/2021/03/NGC-2015-Discussion-Document-International-Relations.pdf

ANC. 2015. 'ANC international relations: A better Africa in a better and just world'. https://www.anc1912.org.za/wp-content/ uploads/2021/03/NGC-2015-Discussion-Document-International-Relations.pdf

Apuuli, K. 2020. 'The African Union and peacekeeping in Africa: Challenges and opportunities'. *Vestnik RUDN. International Relations*, 20(4):667–677. DOI: 10.22363/2313-0660-2020-20-4-667-677

Clark, J.F. 2016. 'South Africa's reluctant and conflicted regional power'. *ASPJ Africa & Francophonie – 1st Quarter*. https://www.airuniversity. af.edu/Portals/10/ASPJ_French/journals_E/Volume-07_Issue-1/ clark_e.pdf

Department of International Relations and Cooperation. 2011. 'Building a better world: The diplomacy of Ubuntu'. White Paper on South Africa's Foreign Policy. https://www.gov.za/sites/default/files/gcis_ document/201409/final-draft-white-paper-sa-foreign-policy.pdf

Gomes da Costa, M. 2023. 'South Africa as a leading regional power in Africa? An analysis of the implementation of the African Union, AUDA-NEPAD and Agenda 2063'. Revista Brasileira de Política Internacional. DOI: http://dx.doi.org/10.1590/0034-7329202300219

Hendricks, C. and Majozi, N. 2021. 'South Africa's international relations: A new dawn?' *Journal of Asian and African Studies*, 56(1):64–78. DOI: 10.1177/0021909620946851 journals.sagepub.com/home/jas

Mayimele, B. 2022. 'South Africa and China: Pioneers of "leaving no one behind" towards a community with shared future for mankind'. http://www.chinatoday.com.cn/ctenglish/2018/commentaries/202211/t20221104_800312613.html

Ndlovu, S.M. 2013. 'The African agenda and the origins of internationalism within the ANC: 1912–1960'. In *The Future We Chose: Emerging perspectives on the centenary of the ANC* edited by B. Ngcaweni, Africa Institute of South Africa. https://www.researchgate.net/profile/Busani-Ngcaweni/publication/366026314_Emerging_perspectives_on_the_centenary_of_the_ANC_The_Future_We_Chose_Edited_by_Busani_Ngcaweni/links/638ea5a0095a6a777406d908/Emerging-perspectives-on-the-centenary-of-the-ANC-The-Future-We-Chose-Edited-by-Busani-Ngcaweni.pdf#page=62

Neal, J. 2012. 'Power-sharing as a form of democratic development in Zimbabwe and South Sudan'. University of Guelph, Ontario, Canada. https://www.e-ir.info/2012/06/13/power-sharing-as-a-form-of-democratic-development-in-zimbabwe-and-south-sudan/

Neethling, T. 2011. 'The SANDF as an instrument for peacekeeping in Africa: A critical analysis of three main challenges'. *Journal for Contemporary History*, 36(1):134–153. http://hdl.handle.net/11660/3402

Ngcaweni, B. and Mayimele, B. 2023. 'BRICS: A building block towards pluriversality. *Journal of Latin American Studies*, 44(5). https://h5.drcnet.com.cn/docview.aspx?version=g&docid=6705599&leaf-id=16127&chnid=4145

Ramaphosa, C. 10 May 2021. From The Desk of the President. https://www.gov.za/blog/desk-president-66

Rilley-Harris, D. 2013. 'South African peacekeeping, 1994–2012'. *Military History Journal*, 16(1). http://samilitaryhistory.org/vol161dr.html

South African Government. 2022. 'Remarks by Minister of Defence and Military Veterans, Ms Thandi Modise, on the occasion of the 6th United Nations Partnership for Technology in Peacekeeping Symposium'. https://www.gov.za/news/speeches/minister-thandi-modise-sixth-united-nations-partnership-technology-21-jun-2022

Sturman, K. 2004. 'Intervention in Africa? The Mbeki Presidency's role in changing the OAU'. https://afsaap.org.au/assets/sturman.pdf

The Spirit of Bandung. 'Address to the International Conference in Support of the Liberation Movements of Southern Africa and in Support of the Frontline States by O.R. Tambo, Lusaka, 10 April 1979'.

Tschudin, A. and Trithart, A. 2018. 'The role of local governance in sustaining peace'. International Peace Institute. https://www.ipinst.org/wp-content/uploads/2018/02/1802_Local-Governance-and-Sustaining-Peace.pdf

United Nations. 2023. 'Troop and police contributors'. https://peacekeeping.un.org/sites/default/files/02_country_ranking_68_november_2023.pdf

13

The rise and fall of the liberation movement: A leader of society leading itself out of power

Gugu Ndima

With over 350 political parties registered for South Africa's general elections, this article makes reflections on the ANC's ascendancy and decline in the post-liberation era by assessing its presidents. Has the impact of internal battles, allegations of corruption and inability to hold leaders accountable led the leader of society into the graft many national liberation movements of the continent befall into.

Introduction

In South African history, 27 April 1994 marked the beginning of an epoch reconfiguring the South African body politic. The mammoth task of redressing past injustices as a result of apartheid was constitutionally assigned by the people of South Africa to the African National Congress (ANC), through the ballot. This legitimised the ANC in architecting the envisioned National Democratic Society (NDS), through law, policy and a functional bureaucratic machinery – the state.

The ANC's consummate ability to persuade and forge consensus with most social forces towards building its vision of a non-racial and democratic society remains part of its distinct revolutionary ethos. Despite stark contradictions of ideological, economic and cultural caveats, democracy found hegemonic expression in South Africa. Throughout the continent of Africa, the ascendancy of liberation movements usually moulds through two processes of engagement with the oppressor, either through downright victory as a result of a protracted violent military struggle or a negotiated settlement. However, the two processes are never mutually exclusive. Even with negotiated settlements, a preceding violent struggle pushes the oppressor to the negotiation table. This was the experience of the ANC emanating into one of the greatest moments in global political history.

South Africa in 2024 commemorates 30 years of democracy under the constitutional custodianship of the African National Congress. In power for three decades, the ANC has had its once-stellar standing mauled by allegations of corruption and mismanagement, amid a weak economy hampered by power cuts, high unemployment and rampant crime.

Thirty years after former president Nelson Mandela delivered his first State of the Nation address, the ANC faces possible political obliteration.

The glorious movement that once boasted a two-thirds majority vote in April 2004, obtaining 60.7 per cent of the votes,[1] is now facing the possibility of getting less than 50 per cent in the next general elections. In its 112 years of existence, the ANC has produced some of the greatest leadership pedigree, renowned across the globe and the continent. It has in its pedigree humanitarians such as Chief Albert Luthuli, African nationalists such as Pixley ka Isaka Seme, visionaries such as O.R. Tambo, intellectuals such as Sol Plaatje, passionate people-centred fighters such as Mama Winnie Mandela and Chris Hani, and influencers of global agendas such as Thabo Mbeki.

The year 2024 is a determinative year for the ANC and the Republic of South Africa, as both country and leader of government limp towards the country's seventh national elections marred by organisational erosion, policy schizophrenia and precarious political conflagrations from its former and current leaders. What accounts for this Cassandrian atmosphere within the governing party and in the country? Which subjective and objective factors are responsible for the ANC cannibalising itself and the state machinery in full view and to the eternal shame of its unmatched long history in Africa?

It would be disingenuous and an injustice to try to encapsulate the history of the ANC in this chapter, therefore the analysis of its decline post 1994 will be assessed through its presidents and their influence in shaping the organisation. They had not only the privilege of leading the leader of society but the Republic of South Africa.

Genesis

A national liberation movement is born inherently from the shackles of brutality. The birth of the ANC on 8 January 1912 was no pre-empted grand planning. It was a consequence of historical political events impacting the lives of native South Africans. Pixley ka Isaka Seme at the age of 30 congregated representatives of native people from various communities who initially had met on battlefields standing against each other.

Seme's generation, including the first president John Langalibalele Dube, is the generation of founders of the ANC. The ANC under the stewardship of Dube, right to A.B. Xuma, was an organisation of persuasion that did not want to antagonise the crown in Great Britain. The ANC attracted scholars and professionals from law to medicine, distinguished men with accomplishments, such as that of Seme being the second native to be admitted as an attorney and A.B. Xuma being the first medical doctor. Despite the shortcoming of mobilisation during this era, it had clearly distinguished itself as an organisation of astute men with every intention of being taken seriously by the powers that be.

Fire starters emerge

One of the most distinct features of the ANC was its ability to germinate the right seeds at the right time in various epochs of South Africa's political history. Alfred Bathini Xuma had the contentious task of leading a transitional moment in the ANC from its diplomatic posture of petitioning to birthing a radical era led by founders of the ANCYL, who were Nelson Mandela, Walter Sisulu, Oliver Tambo, Anton Lembede, the founding president, Jordan Ngubane, and A.P. Mda. The group of militant young radicals infused a more strategic and defiant approach towards government.

The longevity of the ANC – Tambo's foundations

There is a saying that goes "A society grows great when old men plant trees for shade in which they know they will never sit under". This profound saying summarises the contributions of Oliver Reginald Tambo. Whether by chance or the powers that be, Tambo's death on 24 April 1993 is almost precisely a year before the first democratic elections. O.R. Tambo's vision for South Africa surpassed liberation. His outlook and visionary leadership have sustained the lifespan of the ANC to this end. His adaptation of an internationalist stance towards the recognition of rights and championing non-racialism has avowed his contribution towards building this nation for many generations to come. Justice Albie Sachs in his O.R. Tambo memorial lecture delivered at the University of the Western Cape on 25 April 2017, asked: "If you did a paternity test on the Constitution whose DNA would come up? There can be no doubt; the DNA that would come up would be that of Oliver Tambo. From concept to conception, the trajectory from the ideas of Oliver Tambo in the 1980s in Lusaka to the final text of our Constitution in 1996, is clear and undisputable."

Mandela: The rainbow after the storm

Over the past three decades we have witnessed how strongly the character of the ANC coalesces, warts and all, around the sitting president. During the Mandela era, South Africans were justifiably intoxicated by the Rainbow Nation euphoria. Former president Nelson Mandela's presidency, legitimately collective in its approach, embodied traits of rallying social forces despite stark political contradictions and preserving organisational centrality and discipline. Internally in the ANC no one dared question nor compromise this vision. The former president of the ANCYL Peter Mokaba had to bear the brunt of veering outside this non-compromising vision. The Mandela era yielded a forged peace and freedom dividend as the foundation for a non-racial democracy and Rainbow Nation.

Mbeki: The technocrat

Subsequently, during the Mbeki era, the ANC transitioned towards a technocratic approach to civil administration and revitalising the Pan-

African agenda through the New Partnership for Africa's Development (NEPAD) and regional integration. It was also the era of jagged contradictions in the tripartite alliance as a result of non-consensus on economic growth policies such as the Growth Employment and Redistribution (GEAR) and Accelerated Shared Growth Initiative for South Africa (ASGISA). Critics believed it was an era of elitism and class entrenchment in the ANC. It was during this period that the South African Communist Party (SACP), a strategic member of the tripartite alliance in its 2006 State Power discussion document, came out and criticised the incumbent for "over presidentialising" the ANC. Without labouring the theoretical Marxist literature of its meaning, the crux of the SACP's critique was cautioning against a highly bureaucratised state centred around the presidency. It argued that the "government in fact operated as a 'party'. It set itself over and above parties replacing intellectual and political hierarchy." Mbeki was a fierce bureaucrat in government and reinforced democratic centralism in the African National Congress.

Zuma: The people's man

In turn, the Zuma presidency initially was perceived as the era of "returning the ANC to its character of a mass populist organisation". There were more deployments for the alliance and perceived consultative approaches. However, it was in this era that absolutism in the Presidency became entrenched, with detrimental effects for the country and party. It was sad to witness the ANC sacrifice organisational centrality in defence of the president. With that came institutionalised factionalism, gaping party–society social distance, and voter apathy as was the case in the 2019 national elections. Zuma – the most defended president – became a figure above the ANC. It comes as no shock that today, even outside the ANC, he is seen as a threat within the ANC as he endorses a new party, the MK. It is precisely the cumulative consequences of what the ANC allowed, enabled and affirmed over 15 years. The ANC failed to exercise the disciplinary hand creating a perverse culture of non-accountability.

Ramaphosa: The man of capital

The ANC continues to endorse wanton kleptocracy and policy schizophrenia as President Ramaphosa, ironically a man who preached unity and an end to corruption, has taken not just a page but the whole manuscript from his predecessor. For instance, placing energy and state security portfolios, without tangible positive results, in the Presidency affirms this. Likewise, the ANC NEC has become defunct, and authority and power have been centralised into the machinery of the Presidency. Under Ramaphosa, the ANC is seen – fairly and unfairly so – biased to conglomerates and an organisation that holds no leaders accountable, let alone act against them. Ironically, the fifth policy conference of the ANC converged at a time when the organisation is dealing with the unintended consequences of post-liberation politics and surrogates of reconfigured relations with various sectors of society. One important and influential sector is, irrefutably, capital. Relations with capital post 1994 have evidently changed and its influence inevitably far reaching in the organisation. One of the contentious debates were around the characterisation of monopoly capital. The policy conference reaffirmed the character of white domination as a key descriptive component for the South African economy as the ANC has always stated in its strategy and tactics document. Further to that, monopoly capital is still the enemy of the National Democratic Revolution (NDR). However, the ANC can't ignore the proxies produced by monopoly capital in the form of a parasitic clique of the bureaucratic and comprador bourgeoisie, these equally being enemies of the NDR and anti-development. The strategy and tactics document of 2007 reiterates the existence of this scrounging class and demands vigilance.

The growing parasitic class has inevitably abused its proximity to power and sustains itself within the structures of the ANC, using money as a perverse component for survival. This behaviour largely impacts the functioning of the organisation, undermining organisational centrality and its constitutional values.

Ramaphosa's legacy has also placed scrutiny on the judiciary and compromised impartiality. The inertia in the criminal justice cluster to implement the Zondo Commission's recommendations is an unforgivable indictment on the governing party. The lack of meaningful prosecutions and imprisonment of the kleptocratic mars and compromises the very ethos of democracy.

The above, albeit not entirely, explains why the ANC finds itself in this political rut. The concentration of power in the Office of the President and non-accountability created the narcissistic monstrosity we now witness. It would be disingenuous, however, of any ANC member to assume that the current crisis merely happened overnight. It is this culture of personality elevation that has seen the ANC erode into a cult veering off its "society-centred" character.

Constitutional democracy has created a foundation for a social order that seeks to eliminate injustices of the past. The constitution of the Republic of South Africa is lauded worldwide and undoubtedly reshaped the political image of South Africa from the draconian rule of apartheid to one of a country in line with the global standards of humanity.

South Africans are no longer afraid to move on, with or without the ruling party, whether this means voting for new parties or even using their abstinence from voting as a form of protest. No one disputes the democratic foundation that has been laid by the ANC. Even as it hurdles through its own crisis, the political genealogy of the likes of former president O.R. Tambo and his generation are illustrated by the boisterous nature of South Africa's democracy today.

However, the albatross of "we liberated you" has lost its noose and if the current results and voting patterns are anything to go by, no party should dare say "Do it for Mandela" in their 2024 campaigns. The ANC has a plethora of diagnostic reports of what went wrong in organisational and political reports. The pronouncement of the decade of the cadre in the ANC was supposed to mark an era where a new kind of "political mould" would develop in response to the leadership requirements of society. The ANC remains a product of society, therefore its evolution and existence stem from the people it serves. Ideally, this cadre, wherever stationed or mandated to serve, would take the organisation as well as the Republic of South Africa to greater heights in all sectors; this, of course, ensuring that the ANC remains the trusted leader of society. The current turbulence in South Africa mirrors the turbulence that has characterised the ANC for years now. Instability and cosmetic unity in the ANC have had severe ramifications for organs of the state, the fourth estate and now society at large. No organ of the state has been left untainted by the political chess games of the revolutionary house.

The ANC needs to remould itself from being a political party to lead new forces and other organisations through collaborative efforts.

Its quality of leadership has severely diminished, raising questions of whether it still can lead society. However, its institutional memory, governance literature and vision still remain imperative in the democratic dispensation. Whilst the trust deficit might be low, the majority of South Africans still look up to it. However, its inability to act on its current state will evaporate its existence in the political arena or draw it towards unscrupulous ways of holding on to power. Inclusivity and collaboration are now needed more than ever to lead South Africa out of the current rut. Will the ANC do that? Time will tell.

On Social Transformation

14

Doing life in a free society: An intergenerational conversation on journeying through three decades of democracy

Izimangaliso Malatjie and Ntobeko Magubane

South Africa's 30 years of democracy are filled with many achievements and challenges. The country has certainly come a long way from the dark days of apartheid to the dawn of democracy. A lot has changed in the country and great achievements can be seen all around us. However, despite these achievements, our country is still faced with the triple challenges of poverty, unemployment and inequality. The country has achieved democracy, and the government has moved from the hands of the minority to the majority, however, economic freedom is still a buzzword for the majority of the citizens. To allow citizens to realise their full potential and fully participate in the economic freedom of the country, South Africa needs to transform into a developmental state with competent and capable bureaucracy. It is mainly for this reason that this paper will closely link the authors' experiences of living in democratic South Africa to developmental affairs of the country as a developing state. The lived experiences of the authors bring to the fore the triple challenges of poverty, unemployment and inequality over the past 30 years in democratic South Africa and many other challenges that have mushroomed. These challenges include, amongst others, youth unemployment, limited access to quality education, harassment, patriarchy, colourism and exclusion.

Experiences

Personal Experience of Dr Izimangaliso Malatjie

27 April 1994 was a cool autumn day in Pretoria; it was no ordinary day as South Africans of all races had to go cast votes for the first time in a democratic election. As usual, I woke up at 4am as if I was going to catch my normal 5:30 train from Ga-Rankuwa to Pretoria West, where I was a second-year student at the then Technikon Pretoria. Except that on this morning I was to walk five kilometres to the nearest voting station to be part of the making of history in South Africa. I was very excited and at the same time filled with a bit of apprehension as I did not know what to expect. I quickly bathed and got ready to leave the house with my grandmother "koko" as she had already woken up at 3am for this great occasion. At the last minute I decided to ditch koko and go fetch my friends to walk with to the voting station. I fetched my one friend, then we went to fetch the others and, in no time, there were five of us walking together towards Lesolang Primary School in Zone 5. Along the way we bumped into other youngsters like us and proceeded to walk together. By the time we arrived at the voting station it was around 8am and we were greeted by this long queue that was snaking around the building and out of the school yard. There was a lot of excitement and chattering amongst people of all ages who were there already. However, they did not seem bothered by the long queue. Outside the school gates on the other side of the road there were merchants who were selling anything and everything, from sweets, cooldrinks, food and cigarettes. These merchants were not allowed to be too close to the voting station. Nevertheless, we happily joined the long queue.

All around the voting station there were queue marshalls wearing white Independent Electoral Commission (IEC) T-shirts and keeping everyone and everything in order for the long-anticipated inclusive elections that generations of black people were previously denied. By the time we got to the door of the voting station there were more people wearing the same IEC T-shirts, asking questions, giving instructions and directions. First each of us was requested to produce their green book – identity document (ID) – then we had to proceed into the voting venue where each person was given a ballot paper, then a stamp was put on the ID and thumb was inked. Then individually we had to go into a voting booth and make a cross on the party of choice. I was so nervous and excited that I could not hold the pen still as I put a cross that would determine the lives of many South Africans. Once done with the voting I had to put the ballot paper in a ballot box and exit the voting station. When I got outside my friends were already waiting for me, then we were required to leave the school premises and go and chitchat in the streets. We were so excited that we were screaming and shouting at the top of our voices because we had been part of the making of the history of a new democracy. I don't think we understood the significance of the voting, but all we knew was that we were there when South Africans, black, brown, pink and white, male/female or other, voted for the first time in a democratic election.

Racial divide

Having grown up in Ga-Rankuwa, Bophuthatswana, I was not exposed much to many hardships because in the Bantustan we had everything that we required, from shopping malls in the township to clinics, hospitals, universities, good schools and great infrastructure. As such, going to town where white "makgowas" lived was a seldom if not a rare occasion. However, little did I know that this is how spatial segregation was to be maintained. The racial and economic divide of the past became very clear to me when I joined the then Technikon Pretoria (now Tshwane University of Technology) in 1995. In my class there were only five non-whites and the rest of the hundred-odd were whites and majority male. The lectures were conducted in Afrikaans even though we had English textbooks. The first lecture of the day started at 7:30 on the dot and the lecturer used to lock doors for those who were late. Therefore, I had to leave my home at 5am to be able to make it on time for class. It is to be noted that the only transport system that was available for students coming from the township was a train that dropped us off about a kilometre from campus while "bana ba makgowa" white kids had their own cars. It really bothered me that these kids of my age had their own cars while I did not even have a driver's licence. For me this was a true reflection of the economic divide that we were faced with. I realised later in life that it was not possible for me to have a car if my own parents who were working in the same houses of these white kids could not even afford to buy a bicycle.

Often, I would ask koko about life in the 1950s, '60s and '70s and she would relate stories of how separated they were as black and white. She would tell me about the shops where whites could go in while blacks had to buy through a window, instances where they were arrested for not carrying a "dompas" or being sjamboked by the baas/missis (boss/madam) for not carrying out an instruction correctly. Koko also spoke about times when they had to dig potatoes with their hands on the farms owned by "makgowa", and if someone died they also had to bury them right there on the potato field. She further related how the apartheid government promoted tribalism where black people were divided according to ethnicity, and this was so deep that people from different tribes ended up fighting against each other. Sometimes I would think that koko was making up these stories until I started visiting the library and reading about the injustices of apartheid.

Dawn of democracy

The year 1994 was termed to be the dawn of democracy and there was hope all over the country that things will be brighter and better. Every evening at 19:00 I would watch the news to get an update of what was happening in the country. Suddenly there were people returning to South Africa for the first time after many years in exile. Some of these people were my relatives (aunts and uncles) who had left the country while I was a toddler. Lo and behold, they came back with their families to live with us in the matchbox (four-roomed) houses that we occupied. "Ai, *coming from America/Angola/ Europe and other parts of the world, were they not supposed to come back with loads of money to be able to build their own houses?*" Oh, well, I guess it's a rhetoric question. Other people who were part of the struggle against apartheid were getting higher positions in Parliament and in government. Meanwhile there were those who moved to the white suburbs to live alongside "makgowa" and there were kids who were now going into schools that were previously for "makgowa" only. The country was transforming at a fast pace, and it felt like we were on a roller coaster. Amidst all these changes, I decided to put shoulders to the wheel and focus on my studies. The plan was to finish my studies in record time and go look for a job to support myself and koko! After 1994, there was a lot of transformation happening. For example, in 1995 and 1996 more students of colour were accepted to study at Technikon Pretoria; however the demographics were still very white. Of course, there was change but change was moving at a snail's pace. *Oxymoron*!

Life as a young adult

After completing my studies, I spent the first few months of 1996 going up and down looking for a job. I was posting and dropping off my CV at all the big companies within the streets of Pretoria. In February of that year, there was a huge drive to recruit non-whites to join South African Airways (SAA) as pilots. A move I believe was to contribute to an inclusive racial composition at the airline. The requirement process was quite simple: a pass in English and mathematics at matric level was all that was required. I was confident that I would make it as I had matric and a National Diploma behind my name. I was called up for an interview, which was to be held at Jan Smuts Airport at the time, now O.R. Tambo International Airport. On the day of the interview, it was raining cats and dogs – so as to signify "good luck" in most African cultures – and I had no transport to the airport. I remembered my then white classmates who had cars as students! Determined not to miss the opportunity to get a job and break free, I had to hitchhike from Pretoria to the airport in Kempton Park. Nevertheless, I made it on time for the first round of tests that were set to start at 9am. The first test was English, then mathematics and finally being put in a simulator. All these were conducted by big Afrikaans-speaking "makgowa" who were not sympathetic to us and just treated us like by-the-way kind of objects. I remember when I came out of the simulator the big guy who was in charge told me that I had failed because of the balance in my ears. Then he said because I have a "mooi gesig" – pretty face – I must be on the lookout for an advertisement for airhostesses (cabin attendants) that will be in the newspaper as I stood a better chance there than being a pilot. I felt so humiliated and disgraced as I had set my mind on becoming a pilot and not a cabin attendant.

In my determination to be employed, the very next day I went to the headquarters of the South African Air Force (SAAF) to request job application forms. At the gate I was met by a uniformed official who enquired as to how he could assist me. After explaining myself, he gave me his surname and told me to return on Monday morning. When I arrived on Monday he was not at the gate, and I was told to proceed to the reception area in the building. I was very shy and nervous at the same time because the building was buzzing with men and women in air force uniform, which was a bit intimidating for a 20-year-old. Nevertheless, I summed up courage and proceeded to introduce myself to the lady at reception and told her the name of the person I was looking for. In no time the said gentleman came out with forms in hand and said he would help me complete them. Then we walked out of the building and, as I looked back, I saw some of his colleagues standing by the window looking at us. I really could not understand why there would be such a spectacle. Anyway, we walked between buildings and finally walked through a back door into a building with a long corridor. Then he unlocked one of the rooms, ushered me in and told me to sit at the desk and complete the forms, while he sat on the bed. I could not understand why we had to be in that room, which turned out to be the barracks where they stayed as soldiers, but my naïve self did not ask any questions. Meanwhile, the gentleman was sweating and rocking from side to side, looking at me like a wounded animal. I really felt uncomfortable, but I proceeded to complete the forms at the speed of lightning. Once done with the forms I stood up to make my exit and he quickly rose from the bed to block the door. I could not comprehend what was going on as he tried to put both his hands on my shoulders and said I should just relax. At this point I was panicking, and I started shouting for him to let me out. In the commotion I was rescued by a cleaner who was on the other side of the door and enquired as to what was happening. As soon as he heard the voice of the cleaner, he opened the door, and I made a run for my life! To this day, I have never heard anything from SAAF. I bet you can guess what happened to my application form.

Harsh reality

After the above two incidents I came to realise that life was not easy for a young, black female in the new South Africa. There were so many hurdles that one had to get through. At this point, I was really getting despondent at job hunting and started thinking about going back to study for another qualification. However, the economic situation at home did not make it possible. I guess what university does not teach us is that once you get a qualification behind your name, you are going to join hundreds of other youngsters in search for a job. This really came as a shock to me as I thought qualified people were rewarded with a managerial position, a big salary and a corner office. Five months into my job search, I landed a position at a family-run business in Rosebank. The title of the job was debtors' clerk, but I did everything from manning reception, invoicing, writing letters, answering telephone calls and running errands for the boss and his wife. I was happy to work in Johannesburg as most of "makgowa" there spoke English as compared to in Pretoria where the majority spoke Afrikaans. Another shock came when I received my first pay cheque for R1800. I really expected that the starting salary of a graduate would be much higher, again another fallacy of a student. Once again, I wondered what the purpose was for going to university and studying so hard. I was embarrassed by the kind of work that I was doing and the lousy salary that I got – according to me, it was not befitting for a graduate! If only these things could be taught in universities to prepare students for the harsh reality of the world out there. I hated the fact that the boss wanted to be called sir so-so while his wife was supposed to be addressed as madam so-so. *Madam* was always talking down on me and most especially when she would catch me sharing a joke or laughter with sir (who was friendlier). *Madam* would sometimes even make me re-do my work or work until late in the afternoon as punishment for laughing with uboss! I only worked for five months and soon moved on to work for one of the big banks in Pretoria. It felt like I was finally heading towards the direction of my desires bestowed unto me by my qualifications.

As the saying goes, out of the fire straight into a frying pan. The bank was very conservative, from the way we dressed to how we conducted ourselves. As much as we were in the new South Africa, everything in the bank was still in Afrikaans (systems, forms, supervisors, managers, clients, etc.). It was a serious adjustment having worked in Johannesburg and now being back in Pretoria. There was always that little something or someone who would remind us (non-whites) that we were not good enough. Salaries were not the same, the amount of work that we did was also different. Coloureds and Indians were the ones who held supervisory positions while "makgowa" were at managerial level. Even in the kitchen we had a separate cabinet for keeping teacups; this was disguised as cabinets for juniors, supervisors and for managers. In meetings, only Afrikaans was spoken; often I would miss important announcements and would only know that there was something that concerned us when I heard the words "hulle/julle" as these words were used to refer to black people. The word transformation was used loosely, but looking back there was no transformation at all. As I sing "To be young, gifted and Black", I often wonder if my male counterparts experienced all the difficulties that I as a woman faced daily in my quest for a better life in a democratic country.

Reflection

As I reflect on my journey over the past 30 years since the dawn of democracy, I realise that the challenges that faced us as youth in the early 1990s are still the same as what today's youth are going through. However, these challenges might be on a larger scale than they were before. Issues of youth unemployment, discrimination (gender/colour), inequality, patriarchy, economic divide, sexual harassment, bullying, colourism are still there even today. Now, as a female executive in my late forties, I realise that I came a long way to be where I am today. There were obstacles that I had to overcome, and I was often lucky to be at the right place at the right time in terms of getting opportunities. I was fortunate to meet people who were willing to develop and give me an opportunity to grow and be the best in my field of work. I was quite lucky to have self-appointed mentors in my life and to meet people who propelled me in the right direction. Most of all, I had support from home where I had an opportunity to further my studies and be able to work as hard as my male counterparts. I managed to get employment in the public sector, and I took advantage of the financial assistance/bursaries available to further my studies. This was quite an advantage for me as university education is very expensive in South Africa and without financial support it is hard to make it.

As much as I have been able to move up the corporate ladder, I realise that there are various other challenges that I am still faced with today, both in the working and social environments. These are: pay disparity, sexual harassment, pregnancy discrimination, imposter syndrome, lack of equal opportunities, male privilege, breaking the glass ceiling, work–life balance, lack of child support, ego clashes, exclusion in male-dominated fields, favouritism – I mean, the list is endless depending on where you are on the career ladder. I truly believe that being a woman in the new South Africa is not as easy as we all would like to believe; as much as we are in a democratic country, there is still a long way to go towards the emancipation of women. Now, the big question that we really need to ask is if anything has changed since 1994 or have we only changed the cast and the scene, while the plot has remained the same over the years. In the words of the famous song by Miriam Makeba "A Luta Continua", hopefully in the next 30 years things might change for the better.

Personal Experiences of Mr Ntobeko Magubane

It was January 2011 when I took the inevitable decision of leaving the comfort of my homeland, family and friends to look for greener pastures in Durban. This was a carefully considered decision by the whole family. The quality of education and resources in the rural Izingolweni, on the South Coast of KwaZulu-Natal, were not comparable to that of Durban and her periphery. My family background and circumstances had forced me to relocate at a tender age of 16 to a place where I would be personally responsible for every decision that I made. This premature independence did not come easy as I had to learn and grow very quickly. However, this one decision has been a pillar of strength and support throughout my social, academic and professional life.

My God-fearing parents handed me over to their spiritual elder by means of arranging accommodation for me in the mission house of their church in Durban. This decision made me what I am today because it insulated me from numerous social ills of Mayville township where I was living, and that of Chesterville township where I was studying. Indeed, this move came with a lot of transformation, migrating from a rural to an urban lifestyle, coupled with living under a family umbrella of people whom I had never met before. One thing to underscore, though, is that living with this new very spiritual family provided me with abundant divine support throughout my path. As a nursing theorist, Florence Nightingale writes, "for health, spiritual needs are as important as the physical organs that make up the body. The physical condition we all observe can affect our mind and our soul".[1] Along similar lines, Watson's human care theory puts that creating a calm, pleasant and comfortable environment is one of the critical healing factors[2] and this is what I got from the family I stayed with throughout my schooling years.

The year 2013 brought yet another major transformation in my life as I had matriculated in 2012 and was now moving into varsity life. Scoring a distinction in accounting intensified my inclination to become an accountant. However, the joy of starting my academic journey was coupled with many puzzlements, such as having white lecturers, classmates from all races, mistreatment as a freshman, and a completely new curriculum. Ironically, campus life is a dog-eat-dog lifestyle; there is no time for anyone to babysit another, it is every man for himself. My premature independence paid many dividends in ensuring that I remain focused, disciplined, progressive, and free from social issues and peer pressure. The University of KwaZulu-Natal (UKZN) had the same first-year programme for all B.Com students (B.Com Accounting, B.Com Economics and general B.Com). This is where I got to learn what accounting, as a profession, entails. However, I was more fascinated by economics, and I learnt that it is a study of how all numerous role players and variables are systematically connected in the entire organisation. Therefore, that is how I ended up getting all my academic qualifications in the field of applied economics.

While I was in my first year in 2013 there were developments that would affect me later in life that were happening in the South African developmental agenda. During this time the government was introducing the National Development Plan (NDP) 2030, after it was approved by the cabinet in 2012. The NDP is the country's blueprint for long-term economic development. Its main aim is to eliminate poverty and reduce inequality by 2030.[3] This is by way of "drawing on the energies of its people, growing an inclusive economy, building capabilities, enhancing the capacity of the state, and promoting leadership and partnerships throughout society".[4] As part of our curriculum, we had to follow current affairs and know the developments taking place in our country. To this day, I can still recall the then President Jacob Zuma's 2013 State of the Nation Address (SONA) speech as it touched on the NDP:

On the 15th of August last year, the National Planning Commission handed over the National Development Plan, the vision of the country for the next 20 years, to the President in this house. The NDP contains proposals for tackling the problems of poverty, inequality and unemployment. It is a roadmap to a South Africa where all will have water, electricity, sanitation, jobs, housing, public transport, adequate nutrition, education, social protection, quality healthcare, recreation and a clean environment. The achievement of these goals has proven to be difficult in the recent past, due to the global economic recession. The NDP outlines interventions that can put the economy on a better footing. The target for job creation is set at 11 million by 2030 and the economy needs to grow threefold to create the desired jobs. In my last meeting with the business community, the sector indicated that for the economy to grow threefold, we must remove certain obstacles. We will engage business, labour and other social partners in pursuit of solutions. No single force acting individually can achieve the objectives we have set for ourselves.

Following the SONA, the parliamentary debate by leaders of the opposition reflected a clear support and consensus that the NDP was a good policy framework. However, the critical concerns that were raised were on its implementation,[5] time frames and strategies upon which to hold the then public administration accountable.[6] As an undergraduate economics student, such ramifications in South Africa's grand strategies and policies ignited a desire to further my studies to postgraduate level in anticipation of better employment opportunities with higher returns to education.

Fast forward to 2019, campus days were over, and one had to face the reality of the agonising job-hunting experience in a country with a population of 58.8 million and only 16.4 million people with jobs – 6.7 million unemployed (29.1 per cent), 2.8 million discouraged job seekers, and 12.7 million economically inactive people.[7] Eventually, in 2020, I scored an internship contract in a government department that served as an entrance into the public sector. However, this came with major transitions in my life as I had to relocate from KwaZulu-Natal to the Gauteng Province. The province is the country's economic hub, and therefore attracts people from all corners of the country and around the globe. For me to survive in this fast-moving province, I had to learn other languages, unlearn my previous lifestyle, and kickstart a professional career. I was allocated to work in the executive office of the organisation where I was exposed to high-profile officials, dealing with classified information within the South African public administration. It was a completely new environment and I had to learn to swim or sink. I soon realised that university education does not prepare you for the world of work. As such, continuous training through short courses in public administration, coupled with a formal workplace mentorship programme, assisted me in settling in my new role within the shortest possible time. Now, in 2023, my career is taking off, however its prospects highly depend on the growth and development of the public sector in South Africa and succession planning in my current organisation.

The general experience of young people in a democratic South Africa

The experience of a young black African youth in South Africa when it comes to studying, finding decent work, or starting a self-sustaining business can be influenced by a range of factors, including historical, social, economic and political circumstances. Access to quality education has been a challenge for many young people in South Africa, especially in historically disadvantaged communities.[8] However, efforts have been made to improve access and quality through government policies and programmes. Scholarships and financial aid are available, but disparities in educational opportunities still exist.[9] The South African job market has faced high levels of unemployment, particularly among young people, regardless of their racial background.[10] For young black African individuals, historical inequalities and limited access to networks contribute to additional challenges in finding decent employment.[11] However, affirmative action policies have been implemented to address historical imbalances and promote employment equity.

Starting a self-sustaining business can be a complex endeavour for anyone, including and especially black African youth. Challenges include limited access to capital, lack of business networks, regulatory hurdles and infrastructure constraints.[12] Nonetheless, there has been a growing interest in entrepreneurship in South Africa, and initiatives have been launched to support small businesses and start-ups, through the Land Bank and National Youth Development Agency (NYDA), particularly those owned by historically disadvantaged individuals. As much as there is information available for starting a business, there is lack of support or mentoring for keeping businesses running or for long-term sustainability. Many businesses close down within their first three years of existence. This can be very discouraging for a young person who does not have any other alternatives in life!

South Africa has a history of racial segregation and discrimination under apartheid, which has left a lasting impact on society.[13] While progress has been made since the end of apartheid in 1994, many inequalities persist today. Efforts have been made to address these disparities, including land reform, wealth redistribution and social programmes. Despite this fact, various organisations, both governmental and non-governmental, are working towards empowering young people in South Africa, including those from black African backgrounds. These initiatives aim to provide education and skills training, improve access to opportunities, and foster entrepreneurship. It is important to note that the experiences of youth in South Africa can vary widely based on factors such as location, family background, personal determination, and the broader economic and political environment. While challenges exist, many individuals and organisations are working towards creating a more inclusive and equitable future for all South Africans.

Conclusion

Scoring a successful life as a young South African has proven to be a thorny experience due to both endogenous and exogenous factors. Investing in education is one common characteristic among those who are not struggling to make a living. As a young person, those endogenous factors of success for me include self-discipline, motivation, hard work, focus, divine meditation and respect. They collectively formed a powerful pillar of strength against many turbulences that I encountered in my journey. However, it is critical to underscore the fact that despite having a job, one is still directly affected by the triple challenges (unemployment, poverty and inequality) as one becomes a breadwinner in a household of many economically unstable siblings.

Thirty years into democracy, South Africa is still battling the triple challenges of unemployment, poverty and inequality, while youth are the hardest hit because having an education these days does not automatically translate into employment. Therefore, the youth of the '90s had their own challenges while the youth of today (2000s) are faced with even bigger challenges that are brought about by the current state of the economy. It is to be noted that if the government does not come up with plans of dealing with these challenges as a matter of urgency, our country will not move in the right direction with regards to becoming a developmental state.

References

Asmal, K. and James, W. 2001. 'Education and Democracy in South Africa Today'. *Daedalus*, 130(1):185–204. http://www.jstor.org/stable/20027684

Assouad, L., Chancel, L. and Morgan, M. 2018. 'Extreme Inequality: Evidence from Brazil, India, the Middle East, and South Africa. AEA Papers and Proceedings', pp. 108, 119–123. https://www.jstor.org/stable/26452717

Cross, M. 2018. 'Student Access and Academic Achievement In Higher Education In South Africa: Emerging Discourses'. In *Steering epistemic access in higher education in South Africa: institutional dilemmas* edited by M. Cross. CLACSO. https://doi.org/10.2307/j.ctvn96g5c.5

Cumming, T.L., Shackleton, R.T., Förster, J., Dini, J., Khan, A., Gumula, M. and Kubiszewski, I. 2017. 'Achieving the national development agenda and the Sustainable Development Goals (SDGs) through investment in ecological infrastructure: A case study of South Africa'. *Ecosystem Services*, 27(B):253–260. https://doi.org/10.1016/j.ecoser.2017.05.005.

Gumede, V. 2015. 'Poverty and Inequality'. In *Political Economy of Post-apartheid South Africa,* pp 115–124. CODESRIA. https://doi.org/10.2307/j.ctvh8r1rm.17

Mangaliso, M.P. and Mangaliso, N.A. 2013. 'Transformation to an Equitable Socioeconomic Dispensation: Observations and Reflections on South Africa'. *Journal of Black Studies*, 44(5):529–546. http://www.jstor.org/stable/24573100

Masutha, M. and Rogerson, C.M. 2014. 'Small business incubators: An emerging phenomenon in South Africa's SMME economy'. *Urbani Izziv*, 25, S47–S62. http://www.jstor.org/stable/24920931

National Planning Commission (NPC). 2012. Diagnostic Overview Report. https://www.gov.za/sites/default/files/gcis_document/201409/npcdiagnosticoverview1.pdf

Sehoole, C. and Adeyemo, K.S. 2016. 'Access to, and Success in, Higher Education in Post-apartheid South Africa: Social Justice Analysis'. *Journal of Higher Education in Africa / Revue de l'enseignement.*

Statistics South Africa (Stats SA). 2019. Labour market dynamics in South Africa. https://www.Stats SA.gov.za/?p=12948

Watson, J. (2012). *Human Caring Science: A theory of nursing* (2nd ed.). Sudbury, MA: Jones & Bartlett Learning. https://www.sciencedirect.com/science/article/pii/S0883941718304291#bb0260

Wong, K.F., Lee, L.Y.K. and Lee, J.K.L. 2008. 'Hong Kong Enrolled Nurses Perceptions of Spirituality and Spiritual Care'. *International Nursing Review*, 55(3):333–340. https://onlinelibrary.wiley.com/doi/10.1111/j.1466-7657.2008.00619.x

15

Journeying with freedom: A memoir of a transition-generation child

Mbongiseni Buthelezi

There was a time in the late 1990s and the early 2000s when it felt like not even the sky was the limit for a young person in South Africa. At that time, when I was at university, it seemed like there were opportunities aplenty to try your hand at many things before settling on a career path. It was a heady time: the world was looking upon South Africa as a place of great promise. Money was pouring into the country to help create opportunities to build the skills that were going to be needed to create a better future than the one we had come from in the immediate past under apartheid, especially for black people. There were funding opportunities aplenty to study at local universities or opportunities to go overseas – at least for those of us who had gained university entrance.

I was one of those slightly strange students. I went into an unknown world as only the second person in my family after my elder sister to set foot on a university campus as a student. I was curious about the world, wanting to explore it well beyond the borders of South Africa, but I had no idea how that was going to be possible. I didn't even know what I wanted to study beyond knowing that I liked literature and languages, and had done well in both subjects in high school. I was to end up studying literature and drama, becoming a contemporary dancer and an actor, and then going on to become a lecturer and a researcher. I got to live and study in England in 2000 and 2001, and to live in the United States from 2004 to 2008 and continue studying there until I completed my PhD in 2012. And to this day I continue to travel the world, all on someone else's dime. That is what liberation opened up for me.

At the same time as a coming-of-age youth in newly liberated South Africa was opening up opportunities, it was slowly making me disillusioned and angry. I was interested in politics as a route to contributing to building the country and making better the lives of people who did not have the same opportunities I was getting. That was the thinking of the northern KwaZulu-Natal boarding-school kid who had been sheltered from the world but had been learning throughout high school that something was fundamentally wrong in our society and change was needed. Almost as soon as I arrived at university I became disillusioned with politics. The calibre of leaders in organisations representing students on campus at the time was very disappointing. All they ever seemed to do was spout slogans and jostle for positions with little substance to offer. In hindsight, that was a sign of things to come for the country as a whole. I think I was looking to be blown away by great ideas about how to take the country forward. I was bitterly disappointed and so began to search for other ways to contribute meaningfully to society.

I turned to art – literature and theatre – and to a bit of religion, the latter a bit of an attempt to find community and continuity from Catholic boarding school perhaps. I even became a leader in church, joining the Catholic Students Association and going on to be elected president on my campus. But that didn't last too long either. I soon became disillusioned with religion as well – the more I studied, and after one term as president, I left the organisation, then left church and eventually left religion altogether. At some point I got involved in HIV/AIDS awareness work and joined a student society that was running campaigns on campus. It was a scary time when people were being decimated by that pandemic.

I got angry with President Thabo Mbeki and his government when I heard Nkosi Johnson give his powerful speech at the thirteenth International AIDS Conference held in Durban in 2000 as I was waiting backstage as a performer for our turn to go on. I became an activist of sorts. I was looking for ways to put my skills (while developing further skills) more firmly at the service of people who didn't have the opportunities I did. Maybe I was influenced by being taught by monks and nuns in high school who had spent their lives in the service of others.

I have indeed come to put my skills at the service of others as an activist of sorts because the disillusionments and the anger that liberated South Africa have caused this activism to keep growing in me. Not being content to simply check out, I have tried to do something about things that are going wrong in the country. It no longer feels like the heady early days of democracy any more. The students at universities where I have taught no longer have the same kind of twinkle of optimism in the eye that was everywhere to be discerned in my day as a student. There is what appears to be desperation now. Many are thinking of leaving the country. There is also despair on the faces of many civil servants my colleagues and I encounter in our work about how political interference has rendered their jobs almost impossible. The optimism of the early days is all but gone now.

In this reflection I follow the journey of South Africa's social justice sector with democracy by weaving some of the moments of its evolution with my own journey in and out of the sector. Civil society, in this case social justice organisations, have had a profound effect in helping establish and define the nature of South Africa's democracy. They have done so through involvement in policy processes, protest and court action, research and other means.[1] Some organisations have been filling in gaps left by capacity challenges in the state to bring healthcare services and even food to people in need. Often civil society is given passing recognition for this work.[2] More commonly, much criticism and anger are directed at some non-governmental organisations (NGOs) in moments of crisis.[3]

In my journey so far I haven't been able to bring myself to work for the state or in the corporate world. I always fancied myself a thinker, have always been taken by the work of those who challenge power and fight for justice as a student of colonialism and postcolonial theory. The biggest gift of freedom to me has been that I have been able to combine these things – working for neither the state nor a corporation, being a bit of an academic, and being involved in challenging power and fighting for justice. For that I am grateful for liberation, but it has been disillusionment with the abuse of our freedom by those who hold power in liberated South Africa and anger at how things are not better than they could have been that have precisely brought me to what I do. How did it come to this?

A faltering country that could have been much better

In Chinua Achebe's *A Man of the People*, the narrator Odili Samalu asserts: "From the day a few years before when I had left Parliament depressed and aggrieved, I had felt, like so many other educated citizens of our country, that things were going seriously wrong without being able to say just how".[4] It is the postcolonial transition in the fictive country after a lengthy episode of colonial rule. Odili is a disillusioned teacher in a small village who has chosen to return to his home region after witnessing the corruption and mismanagement of the country in the capital when he was a student there. He goes on to observe: "We complained about our country's lack of dynamism... We listened to whispers of scandalous deals in high places – sometimes involving sums of money that I for one didn't believe existed in the country... But sitting at Chief Nanga's feet I received enlightenment; many things began to crystallize out of the mist – some of the emergent forms were not nearly as ugly as I had suspected but many seemed much worse." Chief Nanga is a corrupt member of the ruling party who was Odili's teacher.

It is striking that what Achebe was observing in 1960 about his fictional country, as a thinly disguised Nigeria, sounds remarkably similar to what South Africa had become by the 2020s. The governing People's Organization Party (POP) which, it is revealed later, takes a 10 per cent cut of state contracts for its coffers.[5] The opposition Progressive Alliance Party (PAP) is just as corrupt whenever it gets access to state power. I find Achebe's observations useful for trying to make sense of South Africa in the 2020s. They are a helpful echo of what we have observed in South Africa's democratic journey. To reflect on that journey, I want to examine four moments of civil society's intervention to try to correct the course of the country when they have been able to name things that were going wrong.

The four moments of civil society intervention that have had a profound influence on the nature and form of our democracy and on me are the following: i) the Treatment Action Campaign's response to then President Thabo Mbeki and his government's AIDS denialism, ii) the 2010 Constitutional Court victory of land activists against the Communal Land Rights Act, iii) #RhodesMustFall (and #FeesMustFall), and iv) #ZumaMustFall.

Moment 1, 2000

I was backstage to perform as part of the opening act of the thirteenth International AIDS Conference when Johnson spoke. He was 11 years old. He had been born HIV-positive and had developed AIDS. I was deeply moved by his appeal to the government to do something when he said: "I hate having AIDS because I get very sick and I get very sad when I think of all the other children and babies that are sick with AIDS. I just wish that the government can start giving AZT to pregnant HIV [positive] mothers to help stop the virus being passed on to their babies. Babies are dying very quickly and I know one little abandoned baby who came to stay with us and his name was Micky. He couldn't breathe, he couldn't eat and he was so sick and Mommy Gail had to phone welfare to have him admitted to a hospital and he died. But he was such a cute little baby and I think the government must start doing it because I don't want babies to die."[6] I went and joined a group raising awareness about HIV/AIDS at the University of Natal. I was soon to have my first opportunity to go and study overseas when in August of that year I went to the London Contemporary Dance School on a scholarship.

The small HIV/AIDS awareness student group I was part of was to find a great deal of inspiration in the work of the Treatment Action Campaign (TAC) when I returned the following year, in 2001. I followed the work of the TAC closely and joined some of their marches when I could between my studies and an early career as a performer that was becoming more demanding. The 2002 Constitutional Court victory that compelled the government to provide antiretroviral treatment to prevent the transmission of HIV from mothers to children was a major moment of inspiration for us.

A couple of years later, in 2004, I would find myself making a play with inmates in a maximum-security prison about how to live with HIV and AIDS as part of my Bachelor of Arts Honours studies. By that point I had had the opportunity to go and study dance and theatre at London Contemporary Dance School for a year. It was one of those opportunities to which I referred above – money being put into skills in dance by an unlikely source: Rio Tinto/Richards Bay Minerals, a mining company, working with the British Council, to send two (black) South Africans to London. A catastrophic knee injury in the last show I was in with the university's Flatfoot Dance Company before going abroad put paid to my career as a contemporary dancer. I couldn't sustain the rigorous training in London and had to give up dance when my knee did not recover. When I came back I explored other opportunities. Being part of the dance company is what had led me to be backstage at the AIDS conference listening to Nkosi Johnson. I had come full circle in a way: theatre, HIV/AIDS work, studying, theatre again. In the prison where a few fellow students and I were working, I was again seeing state power raining misery on people's lives: inmates being arbitrarily denied access to adequate nutrition and healthcare by those in authority. Through plays we managed, in a small way, to create dialogue between prison authorities and inmates. I want to believe we shifted something, however temporary and contingent that win might have been.

Soon afterwards the plentiful opportunities were to take me overseas again – this time to undertake a PhD in literature at Columbia University in New York City from 2004.

Moment 2, 2010

I returned to South Africa to do fieldwork in KwaZulu-Natal, Gauteng, Mpumalanga and perhaps eSwatini and Mozambique. My PhD was exploring the resurgence of pre-Zulu identities in South Africa since the advent of democracy, focusing on Ndwandwe, Nxumalo and related groupings of people. Throughout the fieldwork in 2009, I had begun to listen closely to people relating their experiences of living in traditional authority areas in northern KwaZulu-Natal and Mpumalanga. I was finding it alarming and downright infuriating to hear about the kinds of abuses of power to which people were subjected at the hands of traditional leaders in collusion with private-sector actors in the mining sector in some places. A burning desire to do something to contribute to changing the situation was kindled by the observations and conversations in that year. I also held a memory of being sworn at by an inkosi ("traditional" leader or "chief") in Mahlabathini where my family had a second home when I was a child. Along the way I learned about the whippings my paternal grandfather had been subjected to by white farmers in the Ntabankulu area near Vryheid where he and other members of my extended family had lived as labour tenants on historical Buthelezi land. The abuse eventually led to my grandfather and some of his siblings packing their belongings and leaving in the dead of night to settle in the Nongoma area.

I was working at the University of Cape Town in 2010 when I heard news that the Communal Land Rights Act had been struck down by the Constitutional Court. I had been following the work of the Rural Women's Action Research Programme (RWAR, now the Land and Accountability Research Centre) and the Legal Resources Centre. I found their work to protect the rights of people who were under the heel of unaccountable traditional authorities inspiring. The opportunity to get more closely involved with this line of work came when I joined RWAR as a researcher. I have been able to continue with this work through involvement with the Alliance for Rural Democracy (ARD) and the Council for the Advancement of the South African Constitution (CASAC) to this day.

However, living in Cape Town was difficult. I couldn't settle into what I experienced as the racist ordering of the city and even the university I was working in. And so I jumped at the opportunity to join colleagues who were forming the Black Academic Caucus as far back as 2012 to work to transform the university. Our efforts yielded some forward movement, but it was not nearly enough. Old power was deeply entrenched and was not going to yield without a fight, and so our measured efforts as staff were compelled to give way to something more radical.

Moment 3, 2015

#RhodesMustFall exploded as a surprise to many. Even those of us who were insiders at UCT were caught unawares. The Black Academic Caucus quickly reached a decision to get behind the student movement and offer accompaniment as thought partners and to mobilise public support. Among other things, old activists were invited to offer reflections from the struggles of the United Democratic Front to help think through how to sustain a movement. We collected food for the students' occupations of management buildings. We sat in on debates about actions to take for the movement. Some of our colleagues were even called upon to mediate between the student movement and university management.

When the movement snowballed into #FeesMustFall later in 2015, it was clear there was deep-seated anger and pent-up frustration among young people in the country that needed to be vented. The dream of freedom had turned into a nightmare for many. The open horizons that the future had been for us in our student days appeared to have turned into stormy skies of debt, prospective joblessness after studying and a sense that those in power did not care and/or had no idea how to fix what was going wrong. It was similar frustration to what I was feeling and also sensing growing in the country as someone who watched politics and elections with interest. It felt like things were headed in the wrong direction on many fronts – the running of cities and state-owned companies, education, job creation and others. The high hopes of the late 1990s and early 2000s that things would change for better for everybody in the country were now in tatters. Having returned to the country from my sojourn in the United States at the end of 2008 with perhaps a naïve sense that I was coming back to contribute to a higher goal of building a successful and modern African democracy and state, I was moving from disillusionment with the mirage we seemed to be chasing to despair. My choice to return to South Africa was beginning to seem a poor one.

Moment 4, 2017

There was a renewed energy for change in the country in 2017 when #ZumaMustFall marches calling for an end to corrupt government swept through some of our cities. The Economic Freedom Fighters' march on 2 November 2016 had started that wave. While marches under the #ZumaMustFall name dated back to 2015, by April 2017 the marches had superseded organisation by political parties. Save South Africa, with support from the South African Communist Party among others, rallied the biggest marches against a sitting government that have been witnessed in democratic South Africa. The combination of pressure from people on the streets in their thousands, court cases over many years challenging some of Zuma and his cabinet's decisions on things like appointments to key positions in the state and procurement spending, as well as internal disagreement in the ruling alliance, eventually led to Zuma's resignation on 14 February 2018.

I had relocated to Johannesburg at the end of 2015 to join a research institute working on studying the state. We were engaged in trying to make sense of the structural drivers of state incapacity and forms of corruption that were taking place in state institutions, and the effects of capability on the ability of the state to deliver services to citizens and residents of the country. To this day we continue to try to make sense of how the governance of state institutions has evolved in the democratic era and how we have got to the place the country is in where there are so many points of failure and dysfunction – from the ongoing electricity crisis that necessitates rolling blackouts, through state-owned companies like Transnet that are on their knees, to ineffectual policing as crime rates rise. While all the above has been happening, South Africa has slipped to being the most unequal country in the world in 2023.[7] The dream of 1994 lies is turning into a waking nightmare.

Whither South Africa?

Things could have been a lot worse in the country by now were it not for the role played by civil society organisations in fighting for social justice, i.e. a more equitable distribution of burdens, resources and triumphs, in the country. According to a 2020 Social Justice Sector Review Report, "While it is not possible to conclude exactly where South Africa would have been at this point without an active Social Justice Sector, there is broad recognition of [the] crucial role the Social Justice Sector has played in holding political parties, the different arms of the state and – to a lesser extent – corporate entities, accountable. And in doing so, the sector has pulled South Africa back from the precipice with regards to corruption and state capture."[8] The report recognises that the distance between people who were comrades in the struggle against apartheid (which struggle was supported by many NGOs) who became "state actors" in the transition to democracy and those still fighting for social justice (some of whom were once their comrades) has grown.[9] To those like me who were too young to be in "the Struggle" and came into political and social consciousness in the transition – a kind of the middle generation – being in power has seemingly changed for the worse a large number of those we looked up to and from whom we expected better. The results are plain to see in the arrogance with which the country has been governed and the brazenness with which self-enrichment came to be pursued through corrupt means. The Commission of Enquiry into State Capture (the Zondo Commission) made this abundantly visible.

The bitter disappointment of shattered hopes and expectations that have come to grip many a postcolonial society since the 1960s that authors like Chinua Achebe and Ngũgĩ wa Thiong'o as well theorists such as Jamaica Kincaid and David Scott have chronicled and analysed is where we find ourselves in South Africa today.[10] It is both surprising and not that we find ourselves in such a place – surprising because so many thought South Africa would be different; they and we wanted us to make a success of our freedom. That's why all that money was pouring in to create opportunities for us to develop skills and insights from other parts of the world to succeed as a democracy and a country of prosperity for all who live in it. It is not surprising because we should have foreseen that the need for routes out of the poverty and misery of the more than two centuries of oppression years was far greater than the efforts being put in to change things. Moreover, in hindsight, we should have foreseen that there were people who would do whatever it would take to get ahead at the expense of whichever person or institution needed to be sacrificed, even the country itself. We have seen this over and over again in other countries. So, were we just too naïve, too hopeful to think we would have a well-managed and equitable process of building a new society and economy? Is some of the anger we have seen – of the students who drove #FeesMustFall, of the marchers who called for Zuma's government to fall – therefore arising out of our own disappointment with ourselves for having fallen for the promises of those to whom we gave political power and those they installed to run state institutions like Eskom and Transnet who have brought the country close to ruin?

Yet, despite the growing despair and anger, there remain some glimmers of hope to which we can hold on. Civil society has been able to achieve the victories I have touched on above and many others because of the robustness of our Constitution and of our noisy democracy. Despite the criticism levelled at the Constitution for being a neo-liberal, Eurocentric and even sell-out document, it has so far been the glue that has held our democracy together at moments of high tension. There is something in the Constitution for everyone – from the progressive realisation of socio-economic rights for the marginalised right through protection of property rights (at least for those who have property). Of course, it can be argued that therein lies the problem: the Constitution protects those who have and makes it the responsibility of the state to provide for those who have not. If the state is as incapacitated as it is, there is little hope that those who have not will realise the rights the Constitution promises and protects. So, what then?

As I write, some are looking to the elections in 2024 as a watershed moment when we could turn a corner. It remains to be seen what the electorate will do. What is indisputable is that freedom has given some of us incredible opportunities to study and see the world. The hope that we would bring skills back to contribute to making things better for all of us who live here were not misplaced. It has been possible for me in my journey with, in and through the social justice sector to make a small contribution. Yet I cannot help but wish that the contribution was not to fight for what should have been done routinely by holders of state power since the advent of democracy to realise the promise of 1994.

References

Achebe, Chinua. 1988. *A Man of the People*. London: Heinemann.

Ramaphosa, Cyril. 'Address by President Cyril Ramaphosa at the Presidential Social Sector Summit, Birchwood Hotel, Ekurhuleni', 5 August 2022, https://www.gov.za/speeches/president-cyril-rama-phosa-presidential-social-sector-summit-5-aug-2022-0000

Scott, David. 2004. *Conscripts of Modernity: The Tragedy of Colonial Enlightenment*. Durham, NC: Duke University Press.

Frye, Isobel Sarah, Turton, Jasmin and Hlatshwayo, Mondli. 2020. 'Social Justice Sector Review Report: Critical Reflections on the Social Justice Sector in the Post-apartheid Era'. Johannesburg: Raith Foundation, pp 30–36.

Kincaid, Jamaica. 1988. *A Small Place*. New York: Plume.

Mzangwe, Lunga. 1 September 2023. 'Row sparks over blaze: Officials and NGOs debate JHB fire fallout'. *The Citizen*.

Seeletsa, Molefe. 'Joburg CBD fire: City official slams NGO over hijacked buildings litigation', 31 August 2023, https://www.citizen.co.za/news/city-of-joburg-official-hijacked-buildings-litigation-fire/;

wa Thiong'o, Ngũgĩ. 1980. *Devil on the Cross*. London: Heinemann.

wa Thiong'o, Ngũgĩ. 1982. *Detained: A Writer's Prison Diary*. London: Heinemann.

Johnson, Nkosi. 'Speech given at the Opening ceremony of the 13th International AIDS Conference in Durban, July 2000', http://web.sabc.co.za/digital/stage/trufm/Nkosi_speech.pdf.

World Bank. 2022. 'Inequality in Southern Africa: An Assessment of the Southern African Customs Union'. https://documents1.world-bank.org/curated/en/099125303072236903/pdf/P1649270c02a1f-06b0a3ae02e57eadd7a82.pdf, 2022.

16

The Old-New South Africa: Nostalgia as a political force in the post-apartheid era

Mongi Henda

I n early May of 2018, protesters from the Siqalo informal settlement in Cape Town barricaded several entrance and exit roads, decrying a lack of basic services in their community. Across the road, Mitchells Plain residents responded angrily to the protest from the Siqalo residents.[1] Intercommunal violence then erupted between the Siqalo and Mitchells Plain residents, which led to significant property damage, scores of injuries and arrests, and at least one death. The violence quickly took on broader racial overtones. The fact that Siqalo is an isiXhosa-speaking community whilst Mitchells Plain is among South Africa's largest coloured townships stirred racial tensions. Another notable development was the amount of attention that a certain activist by the name of Fadiel Adams received after making several fiery speeches bemoaning the treatment of the coloured population in Cape Town. To Fadiel, the Siqalo/Mitchells Plain conflict was yet another example of the City administration failing to protect the Western Cape coloured population against the encroachment of what he referred to as migrants from the Eastern Cape. In the months following, Fadiel was able to construct a powerful online presence, and eventually, mainstream news channels would take note of his message. It was a message not just of protest and pain but also a certain nostalgia, a longing for a past that seemed to connect with many, particularly in Cape Town. Through his intense rhetoric, Fadiel was able to awaken a collective nostalgia; it was as though many in Cape Town were asking themselves what happened to the Cape Town they knew and if it could ever be brought back.

Grabbing at the past to help ease the present

The word nostalgia has travelled some distance from its origins as a medical term. Initially, nostalgia described the series of adverse physical and emotional side effects identified in people living and working far from home during the late 1700s. The word was coined by Swiss doctor Johannes Hofer and combined the Greek word *nostos* for return home and *algia* for longing.[2] In later literature, nostalgia was no longer seen as a medical ailment as much as a response to feelings of loss and displacement.[3] It is the condition experienced by both individuals and collectives of not being comfortable with the present environment and longing for something that existed before, whether real or imagined. In the past, many considered nostalgia to be a primarily negative emotion, similar or synonymous with homesickness. More recently, however, research by experts such as Constantine Sedikides refutes this.[4] Sedikides shows that, very often, those experiencing feelings of nostalgia have warm feelings of old times and memories of their childhood.[5] Thus, people experiencing nostalgia feel the pleasure of joyous times and the pain that these times are gone, making the emotion bittersweet.[6] For the purposes of this paper, we need to make a clear distinction between individual and collective nostalgia. Intergroup emotions theory teaches us that individuals can experience emotions based on the group they identify with.[7] Group-based nostalgia describes a longing for a past that is contingent upon thinking of oneself in terms of a particular social identity or as a member of a particular group.[8] It is this collective emotive nostalgia that will be the focus of this paper.

As Jacob Dlamini importantly points out, for all its fixation with the past, nostalgia is about the present. Across the modern world, the rate of technological, political and social change that has been observed has left many feeling disorientated and insecure. Human beings have great propensity for change; nonetheless, people often experience change as stress.[9] In addition to the stress, people are often underwhelmed by the changes that come about. Almost all societal and technological changes that occur either leave some critical problems unresolved or create entirely new challenges. At this point, many begin to grab for the past and its associated stability; they do this regardless of whether this stability ever really existed or not.

Renowned author Svetlana Boym identifies two distinct types of nostalgia – "restorative" nostalgia and "reflective" nostalgia – in her respected study, *The Future of Nostalgia*. Boym explains that restorative nostalgia "puts emphasis on *nostos* (returning home) and proposes to rebuild the lost home and patch up the memory gaps". This form of nostalgia seeks to restore an idealised past. Reflective nostalgia, on the other hand, "dwells in *algia* (aching), in longing and loss, the imperfect process of remembrance". Importantly, reflective nostalgia is based on accepting that the past as it was will not be recreated.[10]

Nostalgia in South Africa

Given what we have discussed about nostalgia, it is in many respects no surprise that South Africans in a post-apartheid society have experienced it as a potent collective emotion. Collective nostalgia is thought to emerge typically in situations of societal transition and uncertainty – this strongly resembles post-apartheid South Africa.[11] South Africans pining for the past reflects other well-researched instances such as the "red nostalgia" of many Eastern European countries. In countries like Bulgaria, capitalism's failure to lift living standards, impose the rule of law and control rampant corruption have given way to fond memories of the times when the jobless rate was zero, food was cheap and social safety was high.[12] In addition, contemporary South Africa is also a site of many unmet expectations. The now defunct slogan "a better life for all" embodied the idea of general improvement in socio-economic standards for the majority. The fact that results have been at best mixed has led to generalised disappointment, which further nudges pockets of society to romanticising the past.

The work of Marcel Paret does well to illuminate broad categories of political nostalgic sentiment in post-apartheid South Africa. Paret expands upon four main categories, which include, first, nostalgia for social protection. This refers to the need for security of employment and other public resources that appeared to be far more prevalent during apartheid, particularly in township areas that were built to house labourers in cities and towns. The lifting of apartheid-era influx-control laws and collapse of the Bantustan governments towards the end of apartheid created a situation in which urbanisation increased significantly. This in turn created higher levels of unemployed people as previously underdeveloped homelands were fully incorporated into South Africa.

Second, Paret elaborates upon migrant exclusion as a form of nostalgia. This refers to the memory of strict population movement controls that apartheid implemented. Indeed, population control was central to the apartheid project and left many with a false sense of security. This imagined sense of safety was disrupted for many during South Africa's transition to democracy. Increasing numbers of migrants moved across different spaces both within and into South Africa.

Another form is bureaucratic nostalgia for the image of the coercive and cohesive apartheid state machinery. This image is often made when criticising the post-apartheid state, which appears disorganised and ineffective. The last instance that Paret refers to in his study is nostalgia for white governance. This is the not so uncommon view that all or most of the inefficiencies observed within the post-apartheid government are due to intrinsic racial differences.[13] This paper adds to the categorisations made by Paret's study by expanding on nostalgia for liberation politics. This form of nostalgia refers to the post-apartheid romanticisation of the anti-apartheid struggle movements.

Nostalgia as a socio-political movement

Nostalgia is not just a psychological phenomenon but also useful for political mobilisation. At its most basic, it can be used as a rhetorical tool to elicit strong emotions and mobilise people. Nostalgia can thus be seen as a key building block to a political narrative seeking to explain the socio-economic conditions of a society and to improve it. It therefore not only provides an explanation to current challenges but also a unifying message that can easily be turned into a programme of action. In addition, nostalgic sentiment can effectively be turned into rallying calls that can attract more people, particularly those in disaffected circles. It is no wonder that many populist parties and movements have depended so heavily on nostalgic messaging over the past decade. Nostalgia can stand as central to narratives of nationhood and social belonging, both through its rhetorical emphasis on an imagined "home", and its practical psychological capacity to strengthen human bonds.[14] From ISIS trying to reinstate a Muslim caliphate, to Donald Trump trying to make America great again, the power of nostalgia as a collective emotion is regularly being harnessed to build political movements.[15]

In post-apartheid South Africa, we see the power of nostalgia through many varying instances, which will be discussed in the section below. What is immediately striking is the diversity of actors who have embraced nostalgia as a method of rhetoric and political mobilisation. It is common in South Africa for political adversaries to accuse one another of being "stuck in the past". What this section demonstrates is that many South Africans engaging in political action regularly draw from and are inspired by the past.

Preserving the Volk

Even before the official conclusion of the apartheid experiment, some were already trying to preserve aspects of it. This was certainly the case for Professor Carel Boshoff, Afrikaner intellectual and son-in-law of former apartheid Prime Minister Dr Hendrik Verwoerd. Together with a small group of Afrikaners, including his wife, Carel Boshoff established Orania in 1991.[16] By the end of the 1980s, it had become increasingly likely to many Afrikaners that minority rule in South Africa was expiring. Some believed that the impending democracy posed an existential threat to the white Afrikaner way of life. A small group led by Professor Boshoff purchased a strip of land on the southern banks of the Orange River, and went about setting up a *volkstaat*, or independent homeland, where Afrikaners would manage their own affairs.[17] Orania would offer its residents a sense of stability during a time of turbulent transition. It would permit time to stand still, regardless of the winds of change sweeping across the rest of the land. With its emphasis on glorifying Afrikaner nationalist history, Orania resembled Afrikaner conquests of the previous century, including the nasty business of expelling the black and coloured residents who lived on the strip of land before the acquisition.[18]

Despite not blatantly barring non-white people from visiting or even living there, Orania has been able to maintain a virtually all-white population since its establishment 33 years ago. Public perception and a raft of stringent qualifications that seek to authenticate a prospective resident's loyalty to Afrikaner-ness have ensured ethnic and racial exclusivity. It is this focus on maintaining a version of the past where separation was key that makes Orania an instance of exclusionary nostalgia. With 2 500 inhabitants at last count, Orania is a growing town, albeit modestly. Nonetheless, their message has found resonance with some. It is an example of how even before the dawn of democracy, nostalgia was harnessed as a political force to mobilise economic and social resources. These resources could then be used to realise and maintain present versions of the past. Orania resembles a form of restorative nostalgia as it emphasises recreating segregated spaces where different groups can develop. There is, however, an acceptance from Orania's leadership that their goal of separateness cannot be achieved through legal mandate. This would contradict core principles of the constitution of the new South Africa, the country of which Orania still forms part.

Nostalgia for a glorious struggle

It is unquestionable that the struggle against apartheid left deep scars on many of those involved. Torture, intimidation, death and exile form part of the countless stories from the period. There is, however, another side to the remembrance. This is a more positive set of memories that glorify the sacrifices that so many were called upon to make. There is a convenient moral simplicity within these narratives that tell the story of those deemed to be on the right side of history. This is extremely potent in a post-apartheid South Africa where so many who were recognised as heroes of the past have had their reputations muddied by the openness of a democratic market society. Corruption is a key term here, not just for its illegality but also for its antipathy to morality and principles. It is this antipathy that brings corruption into sharp contrast with ideas of past struggle, which, as mentioned, are often viewed through morally simplistic lenses. It is to be expected that those who fought against apartheid would look fondly on the past for its moral stability, when faced with a present where it is often difficult to tell heroes from villains.

The desire to idealise the struggle past has become part of the political infrastructure of the post-apartheid African National Congress (ANC) (the ruling political party since 1994). This has tended to be the case particularly at times of increased political infighting. Nostalgia has sometimes been used within the ANC as a means of creating unity in a movement racked with factions. On the other hand, nostalgia has also been used to differentiate between a perceived "genuine" faction and those viewed as imposters and the corrupted. Various leaders have sought to recreate the apparent narrow determination of an organisation that had a single purpose during the struggle. The bruising political contest between former presidents Thabo Mbeki and Jacob Zuma brought this tendency into elucidation. In the aftermath of the political battle, several within the organisation seemed to project a sense that something had been lost in the movement. The cultural norms of political contestation within the organisation seemed to have shifted from those promoting deployment and service to a brasher emphasis on political careerism. This tended to produce more aggressive internal political competition.

The Congress of the People (Cope) was established on 16 December 2007, claiming lineage from the pre-2007 ANC. Cope founders – Mosioua Lekota, Mbhazima Shilowa and Mluleki George – were all senior members of the ANC and therefore had a sense of ownership to the party that they believed had lost its way. Cope leadership felt it was their duty to continue ANC traditions. Explicit in that claim was the assertion that what had become of the ANC after the 2007 National Conference at Polokwane was a perversion of the "real ANC". Cope was therefore in essence styled as the rebirth of the "true" ANC. Cope leadership quickly proceeded to immerse the new party in the symbolism of liberation politics. Bloemfontein for the founding conference, and the date – 16 December – seemed to be aimed at exploiting the town's historical significance with the founding of the national liberation movement. It was there that the ANC was founded in 1912, while its military wing, uMkhonto we Sizwe (MK) was officially formed on 16 December 1960. The date 16 December is thus mythologised in anti-apartheid historiography. The choice of the name for the new party, Congress of the People, was even more blatant in its claim to the legacy of the anti-apartheid struggle. The name derived from a historic mass multiracial gathering in 1955 that adopted the much-revered and popular document, the Freedom Charter. Cope thus located itself within the memory of liberation politics. Although it was a new entity, it presented itself as a continuation of the emancipatory project while also seeking to transcend that tradition.[19]

Cope can therefore be seen, amongst other things, as an attempt to recapture an era that its leaders and supporters perceived to have disappeared from the ANC post-2007. It is no surprise that memory was so central to its formation, including in its name, which it would have to defend in court, as the ANC felt it belonged to its legacy. Cope's establishment can be viewed as an example of reflective nostalgia. The party was primarily focused not on recreation of the past but on the assumption that traditions and practices of the past were applicable to the present. In its birth, Cope seemed to focus on positive memorialisation of the past and celebration of historical symbolism; symbols such as the Freedom Charter and Bloemfontein as a site of anti-apartheid action. The legal battle that ensued between Cope and the ANC in response to its use of historical symbolism presents interesting questions about the role of memory in contemporary political environments. Cope's establishment would not be the last instance of this form of nostalgia. In late 2023, the uMkhonto we Sizwe (MK) party was established. The name, MK, is controversial in that it is named after the ANC's disbanded military wing. Furthermore, former ANC and South African president Jacob Zuma has publicly endorsed MK. The ANC has accused the new MK party of trademark infringement and attempting to steal its heritage. In what appears to be political *déjà vu*, the ANC once again finds itself in court trying to legally prevent another political party from using symbols of the anti-apartheid struggle.

Remembering the Cape of Good Hope

The Cape Independence movement is broadly a collection of social and political organisations that seek to separate the current Western Cape Province from the rest of South Africa. The movement began to gain public prominence around 2007, primarily online. Cape Independence was merely a form of discourse at the time that reflected the dismay that people felt with the direction of national politics. As mentioned in the previous section, national-level politics had become increasingly unstable around 2007. Moreover, Cape Independence was a discourse in response to unmet expectations of life in a post-apartheid South Africa. Crime, corruption and poor economic performance all fed into the narrative that key expectations of life in a democratic South Africa were not coming to fruition. Importantly, Cape Independence was also a means of articulating the sense of insecurity felt by racial minorities. It has always been a fear amongst some that the South African government has majoritarian inclinations, particularly in terms of race.

The Cape Independence Party (CIP) was founded in 2007 as the Cape Party. It was officially registered with the Independent Electoral Commission (IEC) as a political party in 2008.[20] The party and movement in general would maintain a small yet constant presence on the South African political landscape until the stringent Covid-19 lockdowns of 2020.[21] Widespread opposition to the government's lockdown measures rejuvenated calls for the Cape to secede and the movement witnessed an upsurge in attention, particularly online.

Commentators have highlighted the Cape Independence Party's negligible electoral performance thus far as a sign that the movement is losing steam. This view, however, ignores the fact that in most open societies political mobilisation can flourish outside of formal party-political structures. It is therefore not enough to judge the growth of the broader Cape Independence movement by the electoral fortunes of the Cape Independence Party alone. Over the years and particularly since the lockdowns, Cape Independence has been thrust into the mainstream political discourse. Campaigns such as CapeXit (modelled on Britain's Brexit from the European Union) have captured several imaginations, even if others find the ideas laughable. To this point, secession is now actively promoted by a number of other organisations and political parties, such as the Cape Independence Advocacy Group (CIAG), Freedom Front Plus, CapeXit and Cape Coloured Congress.[22] The Independence movement has also been able to engage constructively with other political currents such as the Democratic Alliance's (DA) devolution campaign. The DA seeks a more decentralised South Africa with significant powers devolved down to provincial and local government. On 26 September 2022, the DA (South Africa's official opposition political party) announced a working group for Western Cape devolution, along with several other organisations. The group's first initiative is devolving policing powers from the national government to the provincial level.[23] The working group includes CAIG and the CIP, signalling that secessionists are at least willing to walk some distance of the journey alongside devolutionists such as the DA.

A significant theme across much of the material available from the various Cape Independence movement websites relates to the heritage of an autonomous Western Cape. The CIP's version of the Cape's history starts with a commitment to "return the diverse Cape to her natural independence".[24] This version of South African history places emphasis on the establishment of the Union of South Africa of 1910 under the British Empire. According to this version, the Cape was forced into a unified entity with the Boer Republics and Natal. It is this unification into an entity called South Africa that many within the Cape Independence movement view as an original sin as it ended the short-lived autonomy the Cape had experienced from 1872 to 1910.[25] Cape Independence classifies all the regimes that followed as a continuation of the domination of the Cape. Whether apartheid or the post-1994 democratic project, both are similar in that they have been imposed on the Cape, according to the Cape Independence movement. Therefore, Cape Independence has a particularly restorative mission. Cape Independence is a movement that aspires to a past that was disrupted, in their view; a Cape that was born and then prevented from flourishing.

One of the key currents that flows through much of the Cape Independence narratives are racial demographics. Many who subscribe to Cape Independence narratives view the rest of South Africa's racial demographics as particularly threatening to the Western Cape. The claim is that the Western Cape has unique racial demographics that are part of the province's heritage. Unification with the rest of South Africa has therefore always been considered a potential dilution of the uniqueness of the Western Cape. This assertion has grown particularly towards the end of apartheid and the formal collapse of influx-control laws. Across the Western Cape's towns and cities, the increase of mostly isiXhosa-speaking townships has led to fears of displacement from some. In this sense much of the Cape Independence narrative has taken on particularly racial tones.

Most of the organisations associated with Cape Independence have stressed their non-racial approach. However, it has not been so easy to remove these connotations. Indeed, proponents of Western Cape independence have referred to displeasure at what they feel to be changing demographics within the province. The major cause of these "changing demographics" is thought to be migration from the Eastern Cape in particular. This was certainly the message from Gatvol Capetonian. Gatvol is a civil society group born out of the dissatisfaction scores of coloured people feel from poor governance, marginalisation and a sense that immigration from the Eastern Cape is leaving them vulnerable. Intercommunal competition for employment, housing and other services popularised Cape Independence narratives amongst a larger proportion of the coloured community. One of Gatvol's more controversial calls was for all adults not living in the Western Cape prior to 1994 to leave in preparation for an independent Western Cape.[26] This call is widely understood to be a proposal for cleansing the Western Cape of its black African population who, according to this view, migrated to the Western Cape after influx-control laws were abolished. It is therefore difficult to disentangle Cape Independence from the idea that it is, at least for some, a restorative nostalgia for government policy that was able to maintain certain racial demographics.

Conclusion: Dealing with the past in the present

The examples presented above demonstrate the key role that nostalgia has played in South Africa's post-apartheid political landscape. This is indeed unsurprising given the transitionary nature of contemporary South African life. In addition, the changes associated with transition have left South Africans feeling insecure and unsure. In the face of these feelings of insecurity, fond memories of the past have become ever more appealing. There is thus a certain inevitability to the presence of nostalgia in societies such as South Africa. As a collective emotion, nostalgia creates and reinforces a sense of belonging and assists with mobilisation, particularly during times of instability. As explained, political instability has been increasingly the case in South Africa since 2007. From Afrikaner nationalists, to anti-apartheid veterans, to secessionists, this paper demonstrates how nostalgia has been politically useful to these dissimilar groups. There is therefore a need for the conversation around nostalgia and the past to move beyond petulant accusations of political backwardness. South Africans may have to reclaim their pasts and democratise it as was attempted with the present, given the past's continuing emotional salience to our current identities.

References

Cebulski, Annie. 2018. 'Violent clashes between Mitchells Plain and Siqalo residents', 2 May 2018, https://www.groundup.org.za/article/violent-clashes-between-mitchells-plain-and-siqalo-residents/ (accessed 10 October 2023).

Craig, Phil. 2022. 'Self-determination is the issue of the year in the Western Cape', 4 February 2022, *Mail & Guardian.* https://mg.co.za/thoughtleader/opinion/2022-02-04-self-determination-is-the-issue-of-the-year-in-the-western-cape/ (accessed 15 October 2023).

Day, Julia. 2023. 'CapeXit? The Western Cape Independence Movement', 9 September 2023, https://greydynamics.com/capexit-the-western-cape-independence-movement/ (accessed 15 October 2023).

Dlamini, Jacob. 2009. *Native Nostalgia.* Auckland Park: Jacana Media.

Friedman, Daniel. 2018. 'Gatvol Capetonian still cries for a Western Cape without black people', 23 July 2018, *The Citizen.* https://www.citizen.co.za/news/south-africa/watch-gatvol-capetonian-still-cries-for-a-western-cape-without-black-people/ (accessed 11 October 2023).

Gaston, Sophie and Hilhorst, Sacha. 2018. 'Nostalgia as a cultural and political force in Britain, France and Germany...', Demos. https://demos.co.uk/wp-content/uploads/2018/05/At-Home-in-Ones-Past-Report.pdf

Hamid, Moshin. 2017. 'Moshin Hamid on the dangers of nostalgia: We need to imagine a brighter future'. https://www.theguardian.com/book/2017/feb/25/mohsin-hamid-danger-nostalgia-brighter-future (accessed 10 October 2023).

Henda, Mongi. 2023. 'Milk in the Upington sun', 2 March 2023, Africa is a Country. https://africasacountry.com/2023/02/milk-in-the-upington-sun (accessed 10 October 2023).

McDonald, Hal (PhD). 2016. 'The two faces of nostalgia', 23 June 2016. https://www.psychologytoday.com/intl/blog/time-travelling-apollo/201606/the-two-faces-nostalgia (accessed 12 October 2023)

Mpofu-Walsh, Sizwe. 2022. 'DA flirts dangerously with Western Cape separatists', 24 October 2022, *Mail & Guardian*. https://mg.co.za/thoughtleader/opinion/2022-10-24-da-flirts-dangerously-with-western-cape-separatists/ (accessed 15 October 2023).

Mudeva, Anna. 2009. 'Special report: In Eastern Europe, people pine for socialism', 8 November 2009. https://www.reuters.com/article/us-communism-nostalgia-idUSTRE5A701320091108 (accessed 13 October 2023).

Ndletyana, Mcebisi. 2015. 'Congress of the People: A promise betrayed,' *European Journal of African Elections*, 9(2). https://www.eisa.org/storage/2023/05/2015-journal-of-african-elections-v14n1-eisa.pdf (accessed 8 October 2023).

Paret, Marcel. 2018. 'Critical nostalgias in democratic South Africa', *The Sociological Quarterly*, 59(4):678–696, DOI: 10.1080/00380253.2018.1506689

Sedikides, Constantine, Wildschut, Tim and Routledge, Clay. 2008. 'Nostalgia past, present, and future,' *Current Directions in Psychological Science*, 17(5).

Versteegan, Peter Luca. 2023. 'Those were the what? Contents of nostalgia, relative deprivation and radical right support,' *European Journal of Political Research*, 3.

Webster, Dennis. 2019. '"An indictment of South Africa": Whites-only town Orania is booming', 24 October 2019, *The Guardian*. https://www.theguardian.com/cities/2019/oct/24/an-indictment-of-south-africa-whites-only-town-orania-is-booming (accessed 15 October 2023).

17

The social wage as a springboard to social and economic autonomy

Khaya Sithole

As South Africa reaches the seminal moment marking its first three decades of democracy there will inevitably be a lot of reflections and recollections about the journey that was once lauded for its great sense of promise. The sense of promise was primarily borne out of the extraordinary step taken by the leaders of the time to pursue a different way of reconciling a polarised society. As one of the last countries to emerge from the yoke of colonisation and apartheid, South Africa had the benefit of observing what other nations that had coped with similar transitions had actually done in trying to create a roadmap of a postcolonial state.

South Africa's acute contradictions had naturally been influenced by the intransigence of the apartheid government and its belief that the regime would stand the test of time. In response to international isolation, the apartheid state had manufactured some element of economic autarky whose primary premise was that it simply had to do enough for white citizens to keep them placated for long enough to keep turning a blind eye to the fate of fellow citizens whose colour relegated them to fringe shadows of humanity.

The creation of industrial infrastructure capable of enabling the country to capitalise on its natural endowments simultaneously made South Africa a "gateway" to the continent and a country bedevilled by gross inequities in accessing those resources. Patterns of exclusion meant that existing resources could reach deep into the recesses of white communities whilst being barely accessible to everyone else. In the rollout of accessible infrastructure for non-white citizens, the big idea was that it merely needed to enable them to be "available to serve" the larger economy where the restrictions in participation remained intractable.

It was in the variables of human development where the apartheid regime's practices had the most persistent and fundamental impact. In 1948 – the year that apartheid was formally implemented in South Africa – the United Nations published the Universal Declaration of Human Rights and referred to the right to social security (Article 22) and the right to a "standard of living adequate for the health and well-being of himself and of his family, including food, clothing, housing and medical care and necessary social services, and the right to security in the event of unemployment, sickness, disability, widowhood, old age, or other lack of livelihood in circumstances beyond his control" (Article 25). These ambitious ideals have been a reference point for many states in establishing mechanisms for supporting vulnerable members of their societies.

As one can imagine, the apartheid government's take on this declaration would simply be a question of how far it could go in providing these baseline protections for its primary constituency of white citizens. Consequently, South Africa's commitment to universal social protection remained elusive until 1994 when the new government had to establish mechanisms that catered to the country at large rather than selected classes of citizens. Whilst the UN Declaration espouses the right to social protection for all citizens, it is obvious that citizens would always prefer to reach a state of socio-economic autonomy where the range of variables identified as part of social protection measures are elements they can eventually achieve either on their own or as part of a progressive social support system. A non-discriminatory government-led suite of services must naturally be designed with reference to the floor of the non-negotiable minimum provisions rather than the utopia of self-interested wish list and ambitions. This means that rather than focusing on health infrastructure for elective cosmetic aesthetic treatments, the state's obligation is to build infrastructure that provides baseline universal access defined by clinical necessity rather than personal discretion.

Conceptually, the social protection floor seeks to ensure that all those who are in need of social services are able to access them at a basic level defined with reference to the socio-economic profile of their country. In the South African case, the creation of such a floor did not exactly represent a primary occupation of the apartheid government. The inconsistent rollout of public resources and infrastructure, with arbitrary budget allocations over many years, created a significant backlog and if anyone had defined the social protection floor at any time before 1994, and then compared actual resources against this definition, it would have emerged as a key limitation in the country's capacity for human development.

Naturally, some of the most important elements of the human development continuum are intergenerational in nature and, once compromised at foundational stages, the effects can be almost irreversible. The education of South Africans is a case in point.

Whilst the student protests of 1976 remain a sobering chapter in the history of conflicts between citizens and the apartheid state, they represented the breakout of long-simmering tensions about the model of educating young black South Africans. Some 70 years ago, in the aftermath of the implementation of the Bantu Education Act of 1953, the architect of apartheid, Hendrik Frensch Verwoerd summed up the apartheid government's intention to use education as a tool of intergenerational suppression and oppression. In 1954, Verwoerd stated: "When I have control over native education, I will reform it so that the natives will be taught from childhood that equality with Europeans is not for them." In the execution of that masterplan, the apartheid government embarked on a programme of separation that transcended the pedagogical and infrastructural dimensions of education; and naturally impacted the cultural and human development elements of an entire class of citizens. Given the combination of segregation laws and resource limitations, participation in the system was not exactly high and any efforts to even create an education system for black citizens seemed to be premised on the need to facilitate the creation of cheap labour with at least the bare capacity to understand the type of instructions their jobs – if they ever got any – might require. In essence, the system had sought to ensure that even those black citizens who managed to stay within the education system long enough to transition successfully out of it would only migrate to menial jobs. As Duma Nokwe stated in 1954, "Bantu education was not introduced as a means of raising the cultural level of the Africans, nor of developing the abilities of the African child to the full, but as one of the devices which aim at solving the cheap labour problems of the country". It was a system premised on the singular mission to ensure that black citizens existed on the pathway to eternal servitude.

An illustration of the implementation of this model is that in the period of 1975–76, the per capita spending on each white learner was R591 and the spending on each black learner was just R42, representing a 14-fold difference in spending patterns.[1] Given the volumes of black learners across different communities already suffering from various infrastructural backlogs, one can extrapolate the problems that were developing within the education system whose effects would persist beyond 1994. Poor and suboptimal education outcomes naturally impact the continuum of human development as poorly educated students at school level are unlikely to transition towards higher education and ultimately the world of work. The inevitable domino effect of this underinvestment in education is that those most acutely affected by it are condemned to a lifetime of economic servitude with very few pathways for progress over their lifetimes.

The biggest challenge with addressing the backlog of human development variables is the matter of identifying the spectrum of variables that have the widest reach, the most meaningful impact and the ability to foster a transition towards socio-economic autonomy. The state inherited in 1994 was simply a state of structural inequalities that manifested across every variable of society and every element of the national socio-economic profile. Tackling the multiple issues incrementally and equitably became the guiding mission of the post-1994 government. Over the past 30 years, some of the most critical interventions have been in the dimension of social protection, which have been fundamental in maintaining the social order in the country. As a government that was committed to addressing the most acute impacts of poverty and deep-seated inequalities, the ANC government adopted a pro-poor stance that informed much of the policy orientation of the past three decades. This commitment to development had to address the prism of the historical effects of underinvestment whilst also creating a roadmap for more linear transitions towards socio-economic autonomy.

The sum of intersectional issues that had to be addressed resulted in the implementation of various instruments that collectively make up the national social wage. The National Treasury defines the social wage as an important element of the country's social expenditure that seeks to lower the cost of living for poor and working-class households. The government's commitment to poverty reduction and social development is expressed through its investment in social expenditure across the dimension of the "investment in the social wage which incorporates education, health services, social development, public transport, housing and local amenities". This is in addition to the direct cash transfers through the social grants system and contributory social security programmes.

A point of continuous deliberation relates to the question of whether this investment in the social wage represents the response of a political party that believes this is the only way to address structural issues; or simply the response to the constitutional promise contained in the socio-economic rights chapter in the Constitution. The reality is that the ANC as a political party played a central role in the development of the suite of socio-economic rights embedded in the Constitution and it – like any other party that could have been in government at any point in time over the past 30 years – would have to execute on the obligations inherent in the socio-economic rights promise within the Constitution. Michael Sachs – a former bureaucrat within the National Treasury and now an academic – refers to the spending on elements like the social wage as "constitutionally-mandated spending" to capture the essence of where the social wage lies in our democratic state. This simply means that the debate isn't about whether the social wage would exist but rather the design thereof and the identification of foundational issues that we seek to address through its implementation.

Over the past three decades the evolution of the country's social expenditure has occurred alongside the shifts in the country's economic fortunes that have been more exposed to global developments since the opening up of the economy after 1994. The economic fortunes of the nation are critical in the design of social expenditure frameworks as a more robust economy is a critical condition for the viability of social programmes. A poorly performing economy results in more difficult trade-offs being applied across the board where even social security programmes are not guaranteed to be insulated from the effects of downturns and reduced fiscal capacity. South Africa's spending on the social wage is not insignificant. In the assessment conducted by the World Bank in 2021, it was estimated that South Africa "allocates 3,3% of GDP to social assistance, the fourth-highest share in Sub-Saharan Africa and the tenth-highest share of all countries for which there is data".[2] When one considers the dire trajectory of the country's economic growth over the past decade, coupled with the increase in the population that has resulted in the decline in GDP and GDP growth per capita, it is clear that there are new tension points between the quantum of the spending, the reach and the ultimate impact. Anecdotally, a population growing faster than its economy and simultaneously seeing more citizens onboarded onto the social assistance system will result in less impactful outcomes for recipients and the country at large.

When one looks at the continuum of social services in place today, it is possible to map out the pathway of a citizen from conception until adulthood and identify the various touchpoints where the state's investment in the social wage affects an ordinary citizen's life. The availability of basic healthcare to all citizens enables a pregnant mother to have the guarantee of access to necessary facilities throughout the term of pregnancy. A newborn child can benefit from the child support grant that is designed to facilitate direct cash transfers earmarked for ensuring access to basic necessities through the critical days of early childhood. Access to basic education has been made possible and whilst this is not a direct cash transfer, it represents a significant investment in the life of a child as the absence of free basic education would shift the burden back to the unemployed and underemployed family. As children transition through the basic education system whilst simultaneously benefitting from the direct cash transfers, their pathway towards adulthood is less fragile than it would be in the absence of these interventions.

The questions about the depth of assistance are always contrasted with equally important questions about the coverage of the assistance. The tension point between coverage and depth is analysed through the prism of comparing direct cash grants to the benchmarks of the poverty lines and similar indicators. The answer inevitably shows wide coverage that does not go deep enough and a reality that grants are subject to exogenous factors beyond the control of grant recipients. Recent data provided by the South African Social Security Agency indicates that the number of citizens receiving direct cash transfers has increased in the past decade from 15.9 million to 18.8 million before incorporating the contentious Covid-19 grants.[3] The value of the grants paid out has moved from R109,6 billion to R202 billion in the same period driven primarily by increases to the Old Age Grant and the Childcare Grant.[4]

Less visible in this data is the impact of factors like inflation and how they impact grant recipients, particularly when one considers the low discretion that exists in the spending patterns of grant recipients who are already buying the most "affordable" basic goods and services like transport where the inflation effects may be more acute, but alternatives are not available to grant recipients.

Additionally, data collected by organisations like Black Sash and the Institute for Economic Justice continues to emphasise the importance of grants to many vulnerable citizens. This reality was amplified at the height of the Covid-19 pandemic when it became clear that the current economic structure of the country features too many citizens whose foothold in the economic bandwagon is remarkably fragile. Whilst the current social grant policy filters out some desperate citizens through means testing and age-based qualifying criteria, the Covid-19 grant initially did not apply strict filtering criteria and provided the most acute illustration of the crisis of unemployment and underemployment as evidenced by the large numbers who applied.

Whilst the Covid-19 SRD grant was meant to be a temporary measure that consequently has no policy anchor that ensures its continuity across budget cycles, its importance was highlighted by Black Sash as "a lifeline for caregivers, the majority of whom are black women who are unable to get a job, owing to both the structural unemployment in South Africa and the responsibility of having to care for children and elders in the family".[5]

Contributory social security programmes like UIF also emerged as well-intentioned instruments undermined by low coverage levels at the lower end of the employment and income spectrum. Whilst the number of vulnerable citizens and citizens who qualify for grants continues to increase, the value of the transfers does not always keep up with the general inflation and, in times of inflation spikes that we saw during the onset of the Russian invasion of Ukraine, for example, the adjustments to social grants are not elastic enough to address the cash gap that materialises during such spikes.

In an ideal world, the design of the social assistance programme should be scientific enough to address the social assistance gap of affected citizens. This would mean that a synthesis of needs for citizens of affected groups would result in a costing exercise that establishes the right levels of grants that need to be made available. This is in contrast to the current model, which seeks to establish the resources available for allocation and then distributes them on a basis that seeks to promote equity in light of the intention to assist the most vulnerable citizens.

When one considers the differences in access and proximity to resources that South African citizens of all kinds experience, it is possible that the social grant transfer to a rural citizen has a different reach and utility to the same amount transferred to a citizen based in a more urban environment. The costs of accessing grants for example, whether it is transport or usage fees at transaction points, impacts on the grant's reach and dilutes its impacts. In 2023, Black Sash released a documentary *Broken Promises*, which tracked the challenges faced by grant recipients in accessing grants. These include "exposure to harsh weather conditions, poor customer service at the point of collection, and security risks".[6]

A rather concerning observation relates to the increasing levels of reliance on cash transfers by non-qualifying citizens who are excluded on the basis of age and not having a disability. This represents a phenomenon that the World Bank described as the "blind spot around working-age adults" which has "important implications for other social assistance interventions as benefits received by children and the elderly are shared with working-age adults who have no other means of support".[7] In an instance where a younger member of a family transitions out of the social coverage net due to age whilst also failing to transition into the world of work or higher education where instruments like the National Student Financial Aid Scheme (NSFAS) might offer assistance, their ability to stave off hunger depends on tapping into the grant earmarked for the child or old-age recipient within the family unit. This means that even if one contended that the grants at their current levels are adequate to cater for the social needs of the intended recipient, the recipients are continuously and regularly forced to share the grant through supporting other family members. This simply leads to the well-intentioned social expenditure programmes failing to achieve the type of impact that is envisaged, and this delays the pathway towards poverty alleviation.

As one reflects on the progress and challenges of the first three decades of democracy, it is apparent that the country needs to re-deliberate on the intention of these programmes which have become a deeply embedded element of public governance. In this case, it is important to acknowledge that the investment in the social wage works best if it facilitates the transition towards an economic wage and ultimately, socio-economic autonomy. In 2013, the National Treasury stated that "South Africa's human development challenge and the goals of the NDP are addressed both through public investment in the social wage and expanded participation in employment and economic growth". To facilitate the transition from the reliance on the social wage towards the economic wage associated with "expanded participation in employment and economic growth", one has to regard the social wage as a springboard towards social and economic autonomy.

This simply means that the various elements of the social wage should be capable of facilitating the transition upwards. It is therefore critical to ensure that the access to basic education translates into substantive access to quality education in order for those who participate to exit the basic education system with a fair chance of transitioning into higher education or the world of work. To achieve this, we must explicitly and unequivocally distinguish between the type of system that facilitates a transition to forms of economic servitude like Verwoerd had in mind, versus a system designed to deliver on the constitutional promise across multiple generations. The recent trends of declining participation and success rates in mathematics and science for black learners in particular, undermine the gains associated with universal enrolments and high levels of retention and completion.

To simply laud the investment in basic education without establishing its central role as a springboard into the next phase of an individual's development would miss the point of the investment in the social wage.

The evidence of recent years indicates that the transition has become truncated for some and even broken for others. For most of the past three decades, the deliberations around the entire continuum of human development have failed to tackle the obvious challenge that has emerged since 1994 where the currency of the matric certificate has diminished.

In a country with high unemployment levels, the matric certificate on its own no longer offers strong prospects of accessing the job market. In the data provided by Statistics SA regarding unemployment trends, the unemployment crisis is most acute amongst those whose educational pathway did not progress beyond matric. In the 2024 Quarterly Labour Force Survey, unemployment amongst graduates was 9.6 per cent whilst those with less than matric recorded a 38.6 per cent unemployment rate. The more alarming data relates to citizens aged 15 to 24 who have a 59 per cent unemployment rate and 25- to 34-year-olds who have a 39 per cent unemployment rate. Access to higher education therefore emerges as one of the instruments for addressing the social crisis due to the fact that achieving graduate status significantly enhances the prospects of economic participation. The #FeesMustFall crisis addressed some of the bottlenecks relating to financial access and resulted in a reduction in the patterns of financial exclusion for a large number of students. Yet the access dimension must be paired with the success dimension in order for the investment in higher education to address the foundational challenges. The evidence in front of us 30 years into the journey is that as we have progressed, we have found new challenges that required new responses that, regrettably, did not always materialise rapidly enough to avoid a series of outcomes that indicate regress rather than progress.

The social wage–education continuum story is just one illustration of the problem that emerges when the best-laid plans and intentions find themselves floundering against more difficult resultant challenges. More threateningly for the stability of the social order is the reality that a stagnant economy with high levels of reliance on debt results in higher debt service costs, which crowds out other forms of spending and eventually creeps into the territory of even the constitutionally mandated spending. The evidence of this possibility is already being acknowledged by policymakers and noted through the various squeezes on public spending that are austerity in everything but definition – so far.

Whilst education is just one component of the social wage where the intentions are not commensurate with the outcomes, all elements of the investment in society should be regarded as potential springboards for better and more sustainable livelihoods. The feedback loop is just one reason this actually matters.

Citizens who achieve socio-economic autonomy and access to the economic wage become the taxpayers whose contributions to the fiscus is critical for the viability of the social wage. This is the positive loop that South Africa's policy orientation needs to tackle with urgency if we are to see another 30 years of a stable democracy. In the absence of that, the great promise that was supplemented by well-conceptualised initiatives is increasingly at risk of creating a society whose reliance on the social wage represents an illustration of secondary policy failures that poses a great threat to the very pillars of our social fabric.

References

Black Sash. 2024. Response to 2024 Budget Speech. https://www.blacksash.org.za/black-sash-response-to-2024-budget-speech/#:~:text=The%20SRD%20Grant%20has%20been,or%20elders%20in%20the%20family

Legodi, M.P. 2001. 'The transformation of education in South Africa since 1994: A historical-educational survey and evaluation', thesis, University of South Africa.

Mohlamme, J.S. 1990. *The Early Development of Education in Soweto as Seen in the Pimille School.* Johannesburg: Skotavile Publishers.

South African Social Security Agency (SASSA). Annual Report 2022/23.

Steyn, D. 2023. 'Black Sash film challenges SASSA's closure of cash pay points in rural areas', *Ground Up.* https://groundup.org.za/article/black-sack-documentary-highlights-challenges-for-rural-beneficiaries-over-cash-point-closures/

World Bank. 2021. *South Africa: Social Assistance Programs and Systems Review.* Washington: The World Bank.

18

The Rainbow Nation: Exploring the loss of indigenous languages among the "Born Free" in the New South Africa – Reflections of Gen X

Tebogo Gumede, Nompumelelo Zungu, Karabo Mohapanele, Nomthandazo Mbandazayo, Nkululeko Shabalala, Tawanda Makusha

> *"Everyone has the right to use the language and to participate in the cultural life of their choice, but no one exercising these rights may do so in a manner inconsistent with any provision of the Bill of Rights."*[1]

The 1990s brought forth a series of remarkable and expansive transformations in South Africa. Key among these were the legislative deconstruction of apartheid (racial segregation), the establishment of a democratic system, the introduction of a globally recognised progressive constitution, and the birth of a black middle class.[2] The less tangible changes involved efforts aimed at realising the values enshrined in the new Constitution of the Republic of South Africa.

They include values such as "human dignity, the achievement of equality and advancement of human rights and freedoms; non-racialism and non-sexism; and supremacy of the Constitution and the rule of law", and its ensuing policies. Nonetheless, some have argued that achievements thus far seem to have realised a more symbolic significance than a substantive impact. A number of scholars have written about the persistent challenges in uplifting the previously marginalised, the undereducated,[3] eradicating poverty, enhancing healthcare,[4] safeguarding the rights of children and women, and reforming the education system.

According to Amnesty International, the education system, in particular, continues to grapple with the lasting effects of past segregation and inequalities. A consequence of segregation was that it maintained cultural cohesiveness and language dominance of marginalised groups. However, the promotion of diversity and integration that was brought about by South Africa's new democratic dispensation introduced, or perhaps embedded, the use of the English language as the primary language of communication in formal and informal diverse settings around the country. Arguably, it may even have established itself as the "new dispensation's language identity". The use of English and its preference by second-language English speakers inside and outside the home, however, is not without consequence on the cultural identities of black and other persons of colour.

Article 13 of the United Nations Declaration on the Rights of Indigenous Peoples states in part that indigenous peoples have the right to revitalise, use, develop, and transmit to future generations their histories, languages, oral traditions, philosophies, writing systems and literature, and to designate and retain their own names for communities, places and persons[5] and that this should be backed by national and international policies. The Ethnologue[6] estimates that worldwide there are 7 168 languages. Some of these languages (42 per cent) are categorised as being endangered, meaning that they are not being "transmitted from one generation to the next and there are no new speakers, adults or children".[7]

Language plays a pivotal role in shaping identity, preserving one's cultural heritage, serving as a conduit for group emotions, indicating belonging (i.e., social distinctions) to a particular group and delineating boundaries that exclude those outside the group. In his description of the social identity theory,[8] illustrates how language, culture and identity are intertwined. Seethal[9] points to how language became "enmeshed with hegemony and power on the one hand and powerlessness on the other in South Africa". When one studies language use and dominance, one observes "the politics of inclusion and exclusion; racism, culture, and ethnicity; colonialism and postcolonialism; and access and denial to employment and socio-spatial opportunities" playing out in South Africa.

Linguistic diversity is common in South Africa, with many black people speaking three or more languages, while white people and other groups tend to be bilingual, i.e., only speaking Afrikaans and English. Alexander[10] states that "[t]here was never any serious or systematic attempt on the part of the colonists to acquire a knowledge of the local languages which, to them, sounded like the clucking of turkeys". When the British and the Dutch colonised South Africa, they took the land, resources (both the riches from the earth and its people), and also its culture, and by extension languages, which is the main instrument of communication, consequently, the specific language(s) in which the production processes take place become(s) the language(s) of power.[11] There are, however, some exceptions to bilingualism that are observed mostly in industries such as mining, farming, missionaries, and to some extent rural healthcare settings, where English is not widely spoken in the community. Some white, Indian, and coloured people in these communities, in addition to speaking English or Afrikaans, may speak the dominant African language fluently.

Post-1994, the South African government developed various multilingual language policies to ensure equity of access.[12] Multilingualism that is encouraged through the education system can have positive implications for cultural identity and social cohesion, education, economic development and political representation if it is fostered together with one's home language. While language diversity is ideal and is encouraged, at a social level there has been an observed loss of African languages (i.e., the ability to speak, read and write) among children born post-1994. This is mostly due to the use of English in schools and social settings where diverse groups are found.

This chapter explores factors that have led many African children born post-1994, living in urban areas, to lose the use of their mother tongue. Drawing from literature, personal experiences and research, we reflect on the cost of diversity and use of English on African languages by asking a series of questions in an attempt to map how we got here. We attempt to paint a picture of the cost African languages have paid to achieve this socially constructed Rainbow Nation that is embedded in multiracialism in social and educational settings that have continued to privilege English as a "preferred or unifying" language for communicating, especially by those who do not speak any South African indigenous language (both white and black) and in most cases are not prepared to learn any one of these languages. We conclude the chapter by exploring what needs to be done to preserve African languages and identity while encouraging diversity, inclusion and social cohesion.

The transition

Apartheid was a racial segregation system that inferiorised indigenous languages and promoted Afrikaans and English as the two official languages that aided oppression.[13] English was introduced to South Africa by the British in the sixteenth century and, to date, some indigenous South Africans still consider it superior. Colonisers across Africa used language as a tool to transmit their cultures and impose their reality.[14] The dominance of English is not unique to South Africa; it is used globally in domains such as education, media, government departments, finance, sports, health, science and technology.[15] Speaking, reading and writing English is synonymous with achieving an elevated social status.[16] Today in most South African communities, speaking English well is not only used as a proxy for being educated, but also for being "intelligent" and this is not unique to South Africa.

A UNESCO 2010 report noted that "Africa is the only continent where the majority of children start schooling using a foreign language"; something that seems to have been encouraged widely post-1994 in South Africa too. Pre-1994, children started schooling using their mother tongue and this changed as the schools became diversified, with English and Afrikaans privileged in these new multiracial schools. At a social level, the same was observed, where one found individuals who did not speak any of the African languages. English and, to a limited extent, Afrikaans became the common language that is used in certain settings to communicate. The dominance of these two languages used in South Africa continues to be reinforced in education and in the workplace.

This dominance has often served the purpose of excluding non-English and -Afrikaans speakers also from certain economic opportunities. Parmegiani[17] argues that mastering English and, to some extent, Afrikaans is often a precondition for employment. When applying for jobs that require good English skills and most professional jobs in South Africa and other parts of the world, native speakers are likely to have an unfair advantage.[18]

Consequently, the culture of indigenous South Africans was not left unscathed. South Africa finds itself in a situation where in certain settings indigenous languages are rarely spoken, nor used as languages of instruction and, as such, the traditions and the history of black persons in South Africa are slowly disappearing, even though one may not see this erosion and loss of mother tongue when looking at national statistics from the recent census as published by Stats SA in 2023.

Language and politics in South Africa

The 1976 youth uprising in South Africa was a protest against the racist language policies of the National Party government and the use of Afrikaans as the primary language of instruction in black South African schools. It remains a vivid and enduring memory in the country's history as the last language battle of the pre-democratic era. It serves as a poignant reminder that language has always played a significant role in our politics and indoctrination. As stated previously, language and its significance was a crucial aspect on the colonisers' agenda, leading to their endeavours to enforce their languages on the subjugated population through policies such as British Anglicisation and the apartheid government's imposition of Afrikaans.[19]

The underlying resistance to Afrikaans by students supported by their parents came from a recognition that the question of language could not be separated from the fundamental problem of social inequality, national oppression and democratic rights. Black African students were always at a disadvantage educationally because, unlike white students, they were not instructed in their home languages. In addition, many came from economically deprived families and community backgrounds.[20] It is for this reason that language and politics have always been central to South African liberation politics. Hence, in post-apartheid South Africa, the issue of language is still central as witnessed by the democratic government's development of a language policy with many facets that are core to the Constitution of South Africa[21] and articulated in the second chapter of the Constitution – see the Bill of Rights.

Subsequently, the Use of Official Languages Act (Act No.12 of 2012) was passed in order to help fast-track and correct decades of injustice in relation to the use and perception of indigenous languages. However, the lack of language transformation and the continued dominance of English raises questions about the effectiveness of the new language policy in maintaining language diversity in the country.[22] Bamgbose[23] suggests that South Africa's language diversity is supported by arguably the most progressive constitutional language provisions on the African continent, which allows the inclusivity of indigenous languages. However, the major concern has been the government's will to properly implement the policies that are already in place.

The role of the home in the loss of mother tongue

In South Africa, even though only 8.7 per cent of the population reported speaking English at home in 2022, English is continuing to be commonly used for business and for learning. This globalised minority language use has however been at the expense of indigenous languages. Afrikaans mother-tongue speakers on the other hand have continued to fight and protect their language and by extension their culture and identity,[24] in many cases even using the South African courts to enforce their rights to use Afrikaans as a language of teaching and learning.[25] In the recent census, Afrikaans was found to be the third most spoken language by South African households, after IsiZulu and isiXhosa, ahead of English, which is the fifth dominant language at home. However, these statistics mask a lot of nuances and the reality on the ground and in the homes.

One of the authors shared how she grew up in a rural village where they learned everything in isiZulu and the only time they had contact with English and non-African persons was in the local town. For her, trips to town were an excursion to practise English learned in the classroom. It was not until she moved to tertiary level that she was forced to communicate daily in English. This has changed her vocabulary and, subsequently, the language she speaks with her children. However, her friends and family members who remained in KwaZulu-Natal still speak isiZulu fluently with their children. This story shows how the move from rural to urban areas had an impact on her and the household's language story.

The shift in language use is far more marked in middle-class and upwardly mobile black and mixed-race families in South Africa. Various factors facilitate this shift, including education.[26] The authors' observations have been that the pressure to fit in and the upward mobility status has forced black African family members to speak English with their children in an attempt to help them learn English before they are enrolled at previously "white schools". This is often done in order to secure access to "better or good" schools and opportunities. At a personal level, the authors observed that their parents, the baby boomers, and that generation of extended family tend to insist on speaking English with their grandchildren because the grandchildren are studying in former Model-C or private schools.[27]. In many black families it has been observed that even where parents and grandparents do not speak the English language fluently, they still attempt to converse in it. In many cases young grandchildren who speak English fluently (with an English accent) are a source of pride. They often represent the transition for the family and are symbols of an upward mobility economically and socially. However, the use of English within Black family homes often results in Generation Z not hearing African languages being spoken to them, and therefore they do not learn and may not understand their own home languages.

One of the authors in this chapter shared how her choice to live in the suburbs,[28] because of proximity to her workplace, resulted in her, and therefore her children, assimilating into the culture and by default the languages of the area, which were English and Afrikaans. This resulted in her children being schooled in former Model-C schools where teaching, learning and socialisation are in English or Afrikaans. The pressures of fitting in resulted in a situation where, as an isiZulu-speaking parent, she could not adequately communicate her values and culture to her children. The nuances of isiZulu practices and expressions may be lost and remain with her and her generation (X).

The history of apartheid had an additional impact on family dynamics in that some freedom fighters were forced into exile in foreign countries, both within Africa and abroad. Madoda's[29] parents,[30] for example, sent him to the United Kingdom to study because of the scourge of civil violence in the country in the late 1980s. His parents considered the advantages of educating him in stable political climates overseas. On his return to South Africa, he could not speak any of the South African indigenous languages, including his mother tongue. The loss of language was transferred to the couple's children. These family dynamics expand to school (including higher education) and social environments.

Language and education in South Africa

Following the promulgation of the Language Policy for Higher Education, a number of initiatives were introduced by the then Ministry of Education (later, Higher Education and Training (DHET)) to assess the status of indigenous languages at public higher education institutions, and map out the interventions required to strengthen the development and use of these languages.[31] The Ministerial Advisory Panel on African Languages in Higher Education's report published in 2015 recommended a review of the 2002 Language Policy and addressing of identified gaps in the policy, language and concepts that were now obsolete, and not in line with new developments in the Post-School Education and Training (PSET) system introduced in 2009. It was also noted that the split of the former Department of Education into the Department of Basic Education (DBE) and the Department of Higher Education and Training (DHET) had contributed to misalignment with the curriculum and language policy of the DBE, which was cited as a major hurdle for the development and use of indigenous languages at the university level. Greater partnership and collaboration between the DHET and DBE to ensure systemic development of indigenous languages, from school to tertiary levels, was recommended. Partnerships between universities (as custodians of scholarship) in the development of languages were also underscored, and support for African language departments at universities was highlighted as critical.[32]

Contrary to what was intended by the language policies, in the last 30 years, there has been a large-scale shift towards using English, especially in former Model-C and private schools.[33] Consequently, numerous scholars such as Munyai and Phooko, De Klerk, Sibanda and Dyers have explored this phenomenon. Language is a terrain that is used to resist transformation by some former Model-C and private schools.[34] Imposing English among indigenous learners serves to silence the voices of learners who are not proficient in English in both the classroom context and on the school premises.[35] "English is for most South Africans ... a divisive and excluding linguistic barrier".[36] Black African children are often forced into environments that do not want them and language is used to exclude them. At times, African learners in these schools have reported that they are not allowed to speak their home languages during school hours.[37]

Where schools have been forced to teach the dominant African language, some have responded, for example, by hiring white teachers to teach isiXhosa in the Western Cape and isiZulu in Gauteng.[38] Where issues of white teachers teaching African languages with an English diction, accent and low levels of mastery of language have been raised by black parents, most of these schools have sometimes responded by hiring foreign nationals, mainly Zimbabwean teachers, to teach isiZulu in these previously white-only schools.[39] These Zimbabwean teachers' mother tongue is isiNdebele from Zimbabwe (very different from isiZulu or isiNdebele, which is spoken in South Africa). This has not only frustrated the progress toward transformation but has also not assisted in promoting all South African languages. Instead, it has contributed to the undermining of indigenous South African languages and contributed to their suppression. Children who attend these former Model-C and private schools are often not afforded an opportunity to be taught by teachers who are not only trained to teach African languages but are also native speakers of the language.

Non-mother tongue languages that are privileged as languages of teaching and learning have negative implications on the epistemological access and academic performance of indigenous learners[40] and contribute to the continued marginalisation of indigenous languages leading to the confusion of our culture.

> We have to understand that unless the vast majority of the South African population are organically motivated to learn and use English for the conduct of their affairs, English will become or remain, as in so many African and Asian countries, the language of the privileged neo-colonialist middle class.[41]

In a piece written for the *Daily Maverick*,[42] Professor Ditsele argues that we should let go of romanticising indigenous languages. He concludes by saying:

> Change is inevitable and always happens to humankind. It is change that makes humankind adapt to life in his current circumstances. Long after our time, a day will rise in this country and region when communication will take place in a "melted pot language".

While we agree that change is inevitable and technology is able to facilitate learning, its use should not disadvantage other languages. Instead, technology and social media platforms should be used to preserve African languages.

Language and education in South Africa: A focus on higher education

Within the higher education sector, similar trends of dominance of English have been observed. A study conducted in KwaZulu-Natal seeking to comprehend and interrogate the integration of indigenous knowledge systems (IKS) in the schooling curriculum concluded that most pupils felt that they might perform much better academically if the language of teaching and learning was their home language.[43] Mphasha, Nkuna and Sebata[44] found that students at the University of Venda (UV) struggled to comprehend subject matters because they were taught in English. The adoption of a single use of an African language in a multilingual classroom has been met with diverse views and opinions. In a study by Shabalala, two Generation Z learners had different views regarding this, one advocating for the adoption of the single use of the African language:

> In the past, Afrikaans was forcefully imposed on the Africans and the major implications of it are still much prevalent in modern-day South Africa. Therefore, we can adopt a single African language, depending on the environment and the community in which that school is located. We need to start and embrace our own customs.

Contrary to the above statement, another Generation Z learner thought that:

The adoption of this idea will create some sort of a hierarchy within the African communities because the adopted language will have a sense of superiority and dominance over others because it is the language of teaching and learning of the day.

Education in particular has been identified as the facilitator of language shift in South Africa. In multilingual classrooms and where the language of teaching and learning is different from the home language, learners operate in linguistic and cultural backgrounds different from their own.[45] However, the importance of using local languages in various aspects of life is equally paramount. Makhubele[46] argues that the utilisation of local languages in life skills education could render the learning to be educationally and culturally relevant and sustainable. This is vividly demonstrated by rural African communities in their enhanced understanding, experience and knowledge of African values, norms, traditions and customs in addressing health and other social pathologies.

The key objective of language policy is to maintain home-language teaching and learning for as long as possible so that learners achieve sufficiently strong reading and writing skills in this language while they simultaneously learn a second language. However, the education system in South Africa has not allowed this process to take its course, allowing the opposite, where the second language is preferable to the home language of communication as the language of teaching and learning in classrooms. Shava and Manyike[47] argue that, in this regard, schooling serves as a colonial process of dispossessing indigenous learners of their indigenous language, culture, values, practices and knowledge, erasing any reference to the indigenous context. The policies were based on non-discriminatory language use. However, the biggest challenge is that there is very limited consultation with the citizens in the formulation of policies like the Language in Education Policy, yet they are the recipients.[48] One Generation Z raised his frustrations and argued:

The Department of Basic Education has failed us. We cannot be major recipients, yet we are not included in the decision-making of our future. The future is dependent on our hands; therefore, we cannot allow the government to impose what it thinks is best suitable for us.

The introduction of IKS within the school curriculum is long overdue. This can include the utilisation of African languages in teaching and learning, although not mandatory. Phakeng[49] rightfully concurs that the policy (Language in Education Policy) promotes but does not mandate the use of African languages alongside English in classrooms. This is despite science showing that language is a critical resource in the multilingual approach to teaching and learning. On the other hand, Mkhize and Ndimande Hlongwa[50] argue that IKS was systematically undermined to erase African contributions to history and knowledge production. This intentional neglect of indigenous knowledge sought to invalidate speakers of indigenous language and erase their associated bodies of knowledge from formal education processes.[51]

A recent study conducted in Limpopo by Kretzer and Kaschula[52] showed that the real daily language policy within classrooms differs significantly from the official language policy document of the school. Teachers used code-switching as well as a translanguaging processes, alternating and blending languages to help pupils understand concepts. This is consistent with other studies that proved that pupils learn best in their own mother tongues.[53] This is not unique to South Africa as it happens in all multilingual societies to a certain degree.[54] The documentary *Sink or Swim*[55] by Project for the Study of Alternative Education in South Africa (PRAESA) explicitly reveals the challenges faced by learners who are taught in languages that are not spoken at home.

At the higher education level, the Language Policy for Higher Education was adopted in November 2002 to facilitate the equitable use and development of all official languages in academia.[56] This policy was meant to be applied by all higher education institutions in South Africa, including private higher education institutions. Besides the use of English as a language of teaching and learning, there are further complex dynamics that underpin the use of English at higher education institutions. This may include the accents and the manner in which English is spoken. In a study conducted at the University of Cape Town exploring the social psychology of self-segregation among university student friendship groups, Zuma[57] found that there is a view that a good command of the English language is linked to social class, such that being fluent in English indicated a middle-class status and a poor command of English indicated a working-class status.

Furthermore, Zuma[58] also brought to the fore the symbolism of language loss in the new South Africa within the context of institutions of higher learning. He provides a dichotomous view of how students tend to speak their mother tongue at home and English at these institutions. Zuma's work suggests that these students are not only dealing with language and identity, but also different worlds that are partly instituted through language and accent. He argues that some "university students, particularly those who are at the previously White only institutions, [choose to not speak indigenous languages and neglect their ethnic identity] by taking up an accent and language that is not spoken at home".

The above observation should be understood within a broader context of contested identities, language and race relations, especially the rejection and undermining of black people. In this context, speaking English with a white South African English accent is a social currency. It opens doors and opportunities that are often closed to the majority because of the colour of their skin. Taking up an English accent that is not of the indigenous language is widely celebrated and complimented. The modification of one's accent itself is a social manifestation of navigating systematic exclusions that have orchestrated a reward-based system that is associated with black exceptionalism. It is designed to elevate a few so-called "brilliant blacks" by socially constructing them as "different or better black people", who are worthy of access to selected, but limited, spaces, opportunities and resources that are necessary for one's success but are locked in a system that has largely remain unchanged, discriminatory and exclusionary.

Clearly, language shift is an education barrier. Mkhize and Ndimande-Hlongwa[59] have argued that for many African learners, European languages constitute a significant barrier to education; in some cases, this also applies to educators. Evidence suggest that the DHET's recommendations around the importance of developing and strengthening indigenous languages as languages of meaningful academic discourse, as well as sources of knowledge in the different disciplines of higher education, remains largely a pipe dream that is complicated by the fact that some students themselves are not fluent in their mother-tongue languages,[60] as demonstrated in the sections above.

Language and economics in South Africa

Language is not only a medium of communication but also the leading economic ingredient of a wide range of language commodities or language products and services marketed by a number of sectors.[61] Language contributes to several industries in South Africa, including the creative and copyright industries. Joffe and Newton[62] argue that the Accelerated and Shared Growth Initiative of South Africa (ASGISA) identified the creative industries, and particularly the craft and film sectors, as drivers of sustainable economic opportunities and livelihoods for local communities whilst expanding business opportunities for small, medium and micro enterprise (SMME). However, the creative industry and its role in developing and reserving African languages remains neglected in mainstream trade and industry policy in South Africa, even though it is recognised as a significant contributor to the economies of developed economies such as Canada, the UK and Australia.[63]

The role of technology in the dominance of English

The era of the Fourth Industrial Revolution (4IR) has meant that information is increasingly shared via technologies that use various social media platforms, which young people particularly use and consume. Research on communication technologies and language emphasises linguistic and social differences between online and offline interactions and the impact of global English on the non-English-speaking world.[64] Furthermore, advances in modern technology are seen as a contributing factor to language loss; however, technology has been embraced by many developers, philanthropists and linguists to preserve endangered languages across the globe. As a result of this shift, there are technology initiatives established to preserve languages, including Google Translate. Google Translate claims to help people "communicate in over 100 languages", roughly 1–2 per cent of the world's living languages.[65]

In South Africa, a number of universities and research organisations, such as the Council for Scientific and Industrial Research (CSIR), have in the years since democracy invested in language technologies research in an effort to assist the government in teaching, learning and sharing information in indigenous languages. The CSIR partnered with the Department of Arts and Culture in developing language technologies for government departments to communicate with citizens in rural areas.[66] These technologies, however, were not promoted or widely shared because of a lack of funds and human resources competent enough in South African indigenous languages.[67]

The role of media in encouraging multilingualism

Despite the language shift facilitated through the education system in South Africa, since the dawn of democracy the media, to some extent, have maintained the use of all official languages – even though many will argue that coverage is not equitable and adequate.[68] The state broadcaster, South African Broadcasting Corporation (SABC), unlike other commercial broadcasters, is tasked with following a pragmatic multilingual approach in an endeavour to find a general language platform without ignoring language diversity. Pre-1994, the SABC used to screen dramas in selected African languages such as *Inkintsela yase Mgungundlovu, Mopheme, Ityala lama Wele, Bophelo Ke Semphekgo* and *Lesilo Rula,* etc. where actors spoke African languages without code-switching. These stories were designed to celebrate different languages but also increase one's vocabulary and ability to learn other African languages. It should be noted that the promotion and coverage of African languages were not at the same level – isiSwati, isiNdebele, Tshivenda and Xitsonga have not enjoyed the same status.

Content flighted by SABC such as dramas, educational shows, news and soapies have changed over time to accommodate diverse language users or groups. In many cases, television shows that marked the transition to democracy, such as *Generations, Egoli,* etc. also reflected this change by favouring English. These were prominent TV shows targeting youth, mixed audiences, the new middle class and the growing foreign national population. Pre-1994 radio and TV content tended to target specific ethnic groups and the language used was in line with that target, with little or no multilingualism accommodated in the delivery. This reinforced language use, preserved it and also promoted culture using drama, documentaries and educational shows. In such cases, English subtitling was generally used to benefit those who do not understand the African language. Changes at SABC have been driven by the changing market and the demand for newer content by youth – a demographic group that is young and prefers using English to communicate. Other factors include audiences who wanted new and international content, often rejecting old repeats and archived materials; this modern audience, the emergence and dominance of paid TV platforms such as DStv and other streaming platforms has slowly eroded the income streams at the public broadcaster.

The movement of the bulk of paying audiences and the refusal by citizens to pay their SABC TV licences as a protest for outdated content have meant that the SABC cannot compete with the likes of DStv and, in turn, cannot fund locally driven content in all the languages that are spoken in South Africa equally. This weakening of platforms that offer content using African languages is seen also in print media. Posel et al.[69] argue that while the popularity of print media has also decreased, the isiZulu and isiXhosa *Isolezwe* newspaper's demand seems to be on the increase. Social media platforms like X and Facebook are also slowly replacing print media. However, radio continues to be popular, with stations that cater for African-language speakers continuing to have high numbers of audiences. Bosch[70] elaborated that many radio stations struggled to continue operating because funders pulled out after the fall of apartheid.

Conclusion

In conclusion, the exploration of the loss of indigenous languages among the "Born Free" generation in the New South Africa sheds light on a complex and multifaceted issue. While the concept of the "Rainbow Nation" celebrates unity and diversity, it is clear that the erosion of indigenous languages poses a significant challenge to preserving the rich cultural tapestry of the nation. The "Born Free" generation, born after the end of apartheid, has grown up in a rapidly changing society where the dominance of English and Afrikaans has taken precedence. This trend not only threatens linguistic diversity but also carries implications for the preservation of cultural heritage and the transmission of traditional knowledge.

Efforts to address this issue must be multifaceted, encompassing educational reform, community engagement and the promotion of indigenous languages in various aspects of South African life. These languages are not just a means of communication; they are repositories of history, culture and identity. As South Africa continues its journey towards a more inclusive and equitable society, it is imperative that the preservation and revitalisation of indigenous languages be recognised as an essential component of this transformative process. The Rainbow Nation's true strength lies in the vibrant and diverse mosaic of its people, their languages and their shared commitment to a more inclusive and culturally rich future.

References

Akena., F.A. 2012. 'Critical analysis of the production of western knowledge and its implications for indigenous knowledge and decolonization'. *Journal of Black Studies*, 43(6):559–619.

Alexander, N. 2012. 'The centrality of the language question in post-apartheid South Africa: Revisiting a perennial issue'. *South African Journal of Science*, 108(9):1–7.

Alexander, N. 2013. *Language Policy and National Unity in South Africa/ Azania*. The Estate of Neville Edward Alexander. South Africa.

Bamgbose, A. 2011. 'African languages today: The challenge of and prospects for empowerrment under globalization'. In *Selected proceedings of the 40th annual conference on African linguistics*, pp 1–14. Somerville: Cascadilla Proceedings Project.

Bamgbose, A. 2003. 'Intellectualization of African languages: The Nigerian Experience'. In *Workshop on Intellectuaization of African languages*, PRAESA, University of Cape Town.

Bornman, E., Álvarez-Mosquera, P and Seti, V. 2018. 'Language, urbanisation and identity: Young black residents from Pretoria in South Africa'. *Language Matters*, 49(1):25–44, DOI: 10.1080/10228195.2018.1440318

Bosch, T. 2022. 'Radio is thriving in South Africa: 80% are tuning in'. *The Conversation*. https://theconversation.com/radio-is-thriving-in-south-africa-80-are-tuning-in-176846 (accessed on 31 October 2023)

Bostock, W.W. 2018. 'South Africa's evolving language policy: Educational implications'. *Journal of Curriculum and Teaching*, 7(2):27–32.

Brenzinger, M. 2017. 'Eleven official languages and more: Legislation and language policies in South Africa'. *Revista de Llengua i Dret*, 67.

Cakata, Z. and Segalo, P. 2017. 'Obstacles to post-apartheid language policy implementation: Insights from language policy experts'. *Southern African Linguistics and Applied Language Studies*, 35(4):321–329.

Cele, N. 2021. 'Understanding language policy as a tool for access and social inclusion in South African Higher Education: A critical policy analysis perspective'. *South African Journal of Higher Education*, 35(6):25–46.

Chang-Castillo and Associates. 2019. 'Language preservation: How countries preserve their language(s)'. https://ccalanguagesolutions. com/language-preservation-how-countries-preserve-their-languages/

Calteaux, K. 1996. *Standard and Non-Standard African Language Varieties in the Urban Areas of South Africa. Main Report for the STANON Research Programme.* Pretoria: HSRC Publishers.

Calteaux, K., De Wet, F., Moors, C., Van Niekerk, D., McAlister, B., Grover A.S., Reid, T., Davel, M., Barnard, E. and Van Heerden, C. 2013. 'Lwazi II Final Report: Increasing the impact of speech technologies in South Africa'. Technical report. Pretoria: CSIR, p 280.

Chimbga, W.W.M. and Meier, C. 2014. 'The language issue in South Africa: The way forward'. *Mediterranean Journal of Social Sciences*, 5(20):1424–1433.

Cook, S.E. 2004. 'New technologies and language change: Toward an anthropology of linguistic frontiers'. *Annual Review of Anthropology*, 33:103–115.

Cummins, J., 2009. 'Literacy and English-language learners: A shifting landscape for students, teachers, researchers, and policy makers'. *Educational Researcher*, 38(5):382–384.

Department of Higher Education and Training. 2001. 'Language policy framework for public higher education institutions'. *Government Gazette.*

Ditsele, T. 2023. 'Language may be fragile, but it is very stubborn to die – a future potjiekos taal awaits Mznsi'. *Daily Maverick.* https:// www.dailymaverick.co.za/opinionista/2023-10-10-languages-are-stubborn-to-die-future-potjiekos-taal-awaits-mzansi/ (accessed 13 October 2023).

Du Plesis T. 2006. 'The development of a multi-lingual language policy at the SABC since 1994'. *Acta Academica Supplementum*, 2006(2):45–75.

Dyers, C. 2008. 'Language shift or maintenance? Factors determining the use of Afrikaans among some township youth in South Africa'. *Stellenbosch Papers in Linguistics*, 38, 49–72. DOI: 10.5774/38-0-22. University of the Western Cape, South Africa.

Ferreira-Meyers, K.A.F. and Horne, F. 2017. 'Multilingualism and the language curriculum in South Africa: Contextualising French within the local language ecology'. *Stellenbosch Papers in Linguistics Plus* (SPiL Plus). http://www.scielo.org.za/scielo.php?script=sci_arttext&pid=S2224-33802017000100003

Gumede, T. 2020. 'Perceptual evaluations and attitudes of the visually impaired toward synthesised speech: A study of isiXhosa and Northern Sotho voices'. Unpublished doctoral dissertation, Tshwane University of Technology, Pretoria, South Africa.

Heugh, K. 2017. 'The case against bilingual and multilingual education in South Africa'. https://www.praesa.org.za/wp-content/uploads/2017/01/Paper6.pdf

Joffe A. and Newton, M. 2017. Creative Industries Sector Report, prepared for the HSRC, 15 December 2007. The Creative Industries in South Africa.

Kaiper, A. 2018. '"If you don't have English, you're just as good as a dead person": A narrative of adult English language literacy within post-apartheid South Africa'. *International Review of Education*, 64:737–757.

Kamwendo, G.H. 2006. 'No easy walk to linguistic freedom: A critique of language planning during south Africa's first decade of democracy'. *Nordic Journal of African Studies*, 15(1):53–70.

Kim, Young Yun. 2007. 'Ideology, identity and intercultural communication: An analysis of differing academic conceptions of cultural identity'. *Journal of Intercultural Communication Research*, 36(3):237–253. https://doi.org/10.1080/17475750701737181.

Kretzer, M.M. and Kaschula, R.H. 2019. 'South African teachers switch languages in class: Why policy should follow'. *The Conversation*, 8.

Lin, E. 2021. 'The role of technology in preserving linguistic diversity'. *Columbia Undergraduate Science Journal*. https://journals.library.columbia.edu/index.php/cusj/blog/view/378

Madiba, M. 2013. 'Multilingual education in South African universities: Policies, pedagogy and practicality'. *Linguistics and Education*,

24(4):385–395. https://doi.org/10.1016/j.linged.2013.09.002

Madiba, M. 2004. 'Treading where angels fear most: The South African government's new language policy for higher education and its implications'. *Alternation*, 11(2):26–43.

Madonsela, S. 2013. 'Using language in the media: A vehicle for indigenous cultural practices in selected SABC drama series'. *Southern African Journal for Folklore Studies*, 23(2):301–320.

Makhubele, J.C. and Qalinge, L.I. 2009. 'The relevance of language in the process of indigenising life skills education in South Africa: A social work perspective – IKS community development and resilience'. *Indilinga African Journal of Indigenous Knowledge Systems*, 8(2):199–208.

Phakeng, M. 2018. 'One country, many languages: Exploring a multilingual approach to mathematics teaching and learning in South Africa'. Proceedings of the IV ERME Topic Conference 'Classroom-based research on mathematics and language', pp 8–16, March 2018, Dresden, Germany. hal-01849650v2

Meighan, P.J. 2021. 'Decolonising the digital landscape: The role of technology in Indigenous language revitalization'. *AlterNative: An International Journal of Indigenous Peoples*. https://doi.org/10.1177/11771801211037672

Mekoa, I. 2020. 'The politics and nuances of language in South Africa: A critical appraisal'. *Journal of African Languages and Literary Studies*, 1(1):55–69.

Mkhize, N. and Ndimande-Hlongwa, N.P. 2014. 'African languages, indigenous knowledge systems (IKS), and the transformation of the humanities and social sciences in higher education'. *Alternation* 21(2):10–37. https://www.researchgate.net/publication/274006185_ African_Languages_Indigenous_Knowledge_Systems_IKS_and_ the_Transformation_of_the_Humanities_and_Social_Sciences_in_ Higher_Education

Mncwango, E.M. 2012. 'The stuttering implementation of language policies in the South African education system'. *Inkanyiso: Journal of Humanities and Social Sciences*, 4(1):58–62.

Mohamed. S. 2020. 'South Africa: Broken and unequal education perpetuating poverty and inequality'. Amnesty International. https://www.amnesty.org/en/latest/news/2020/02/south-africa-broken-and-unequal-education-perpetuating-poverty-and-inequality/

Mphasha, L.E., Nkuna, K.J. and Sebata, M.B. 2022. 'The impact of English language as medium of instruction versus South African indigenous languages offered as modules on academic progress of first year higher education students: A case study of the University of Venda, Limpopo Province, South Africa'. *Gender and Behaviour*, 20(1):19251–19265.

Munyai, A. and Phooko, M.R. 2021. 'Is English becoming a threat to the existence of indigenous languages in institutions of higher learning in South Africa?' *De Jure Law Journal*, 54(1):298–327.

Nguse, S. 2023. 'Intersectionality in South African health care – What is to be done?' *South African Journal of Psychology*, 53(3):305–315.

Nugraha, S.I. June 2019. 'The language-in-education policy in South Africa: A gap between policy and efficacy'. In *Eleventh Conference on Applied Linguistics (CONAPLIN 2018)*, pp 568–572. Atlantis Press.

Parmegiani, A. 2008. 'Language ownership in multilingual settings: Exploring attitudes among students entering the University of KwaZulu-Natal through the Access Program'. *Stellenbosch Papers in Linguistics*, 38:107–124.

Phindane, P. 2015. 'Learning in mother tongue: Language preferences in South Africa'. *International Journal of Educational Sciences*, 11(1):106–111.

Rao, S.P. 2019. 'The importance of speaking skills in the English classromm'. *Alford Council of Interntional English & Literature Journal*, 2:6–18.

Republic of South Africa. Use of Official Languages Act 12 of 2012. https://www.gov.za/documents/use-official-languages-act (accessed 31 October 2023)

Seethal, C. 2023. 'The state of languages in South Africa'. In *Language, Society and the State in a Changing World* edited by S.D. Brunn and R. Kehrein. Springer, Cham. https://doi.org/10.1007/978-3-031-18146-7_7

Shabalala, N. 2018. 'Interrogating the relevance of the Language Policy and the measures taken by Department of Basic Education to integrate Indigenous Knowledge Systems in the schooling curriculum: A case study of KwaZulu-Natal'. Durban: University of KwaZulu-Natal.

Sharma, A., Gumede, T., Kuun, C. et al. 2010. 'Lwazi community communication service: Design and piloting of a telephone-based Information Service for South Africa'. CSIR 3rd Biennial Conference 2010: Science Real and Relevant. CSIR International Convention Centre, Pretoria, South Africa, 30 August – 01 September 2010, p 14.

Shava, S. and Manyike, T.V. 2018. 'Decolonial role of African indigenous language'. *Indilinga: African Journal of Indigenous Knowledge Systems*, 17(1):36–52.

Sookrajh, R. and Joshua, J. 2009. 'Language matters in rural schools in South Africa: Are educators making the implementation of the Language in Education Policy (1997) work?' *Language Learning Journal*, 37(3):323–338.

Tajfel, H. 1981. *Human Groups and Social Categories*. Cambridge: Cambridge University Press

Tyler, R., Ramadiro, B., McKinney, C. and Guzula, X. 2022. 'Bilingual education can work in schools: Here's how'. *Sowetan Live*. https://www.sowetanlive.co.za/news/south-africa/2022-08-03-bilingual-education-can-work-in-schools-heres-how/ (accessed 31 October 2023)

The University of Melbourne. n.d. International Decade of Indigenous Languages 2022–2032. https://about.unimelb.edu.au/reconciliation/resources/international-decade-of-indigenous-languages

UNESCO. 2023. 'Best practices and lessons learned to preserve, revitalize and promote Indigenous Languages'. https://www.unesco.org/en/articles/best-practices-and-lessons-learned-preserve-revitalize-and-promote-indigenous-languages

USAF. 2022. 'The complexities surrounding multilingualism in South African universities'. https://www.usaf.ac.za/the-complexities-surrounding-multilingualism-in-south-african-universities/#:~:text=She%20said%20other%20challenges%20include,as%20a%20social%20justice%20issue

Van der Walt, C. 2004. 'The challenge of multingualism in response to the language policy for higher education: Perspectives on Higher Education'. *South African Journal of Higher Education*, 18(1). https://journals.co.za/doi/epdf/10.10520/EJC37048

Van Rheede, C. 2014. 'Using indigenous languages for job and wealth creation'. https://www.news24.com/news24/xarchive/voices/using-indigenous-languages-for-job-and-wealth-creation-20180719

Varthana. 2023. 'Multilingual Education: Benefits and Challenges'. https://varthana.com/school/multilingual-education-benefits-and-challenges/

wa Thiong'o N. 1986. *Decolonizing the Mind*. London: Heinemann.

Toth, K. 2022. 'The death and revival of indigenous languages'. *Harvard International Review*. https://hir.harvard.edu/the-death-and-revival-of-indigenous-languages/

Weda, Z. and De Villiers, R. 2019. 'Migrant Zimbabwean teachers in South Africa: Challenging and rewarding issues'. *Journal of International Migration and Integration*, 20:1013–1028.

Zuma, B. 2013. 'The social psychology of self-segregation'. Unpublished doctoral dissertation, University of Cape Town, Cape Town, South Africa. https://www.ethnologue.com/insights/how-many-languages/

19

Evaluating South Africa's agricultural progress 30 years into democracy

Wandile Sihlobo

We are now 30 years into democracy, which is an appropriate time for us to reflect on the progress of South African society in addressing many social ills of the past. From an economic perspective, we are now, as a society, generally better off than we were in 1994. Our economy is almost twice as big in size when compared to the dawn of democracy.

The growth of the economy is underpinned by progress in various sectors. However, I want to limit my short contribution to the agriculture sector for the purpose of bringing a diverse voice to this book. If one talks to South Africans, the first thing to realise is that there are divergent views about the effectiveness and extent to which South Africa's agricultural policies have been implemented.

Regardless of how experts feel about the capacity of the state and the policy stance of the South African government since the dawn of democracy, the one undeniable fact is that the sector has grown tremendously – as illustrated in the figure below. Data from the Department of Agriculture, Land Reform and Rural Development (DALRRD) show that domestic agricultural output in 2022/23 was twice as much as in 1993/94.

Whether this growth has been inclusive and transformative is a question I will return to later. For now, it's important to emphasise the growth of the industry and the drivers of its expansion. Significantly, this expansion was not driven by a few sectors but has been widespread -- livestock, horticulture and field crops have all seen strong growth over this period.

Of course, the production of some crops, most notably wheat and sorghum, has declined over time. This, however, had a lot to do with changes in agroecological conditions and falling demand in the case of sorghum, not policies.

Figure 19.1: South Africa's agriculture's journey from 1994 (volumes of production of all agricultural subsectors)

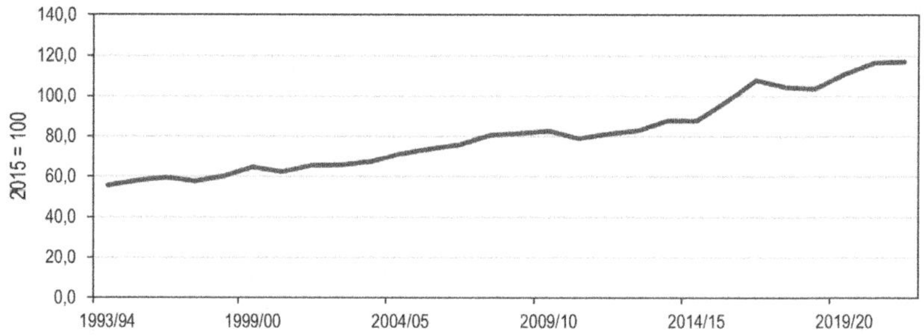

Source: DALRRD and Agbiz Research

These higher production levels have been underpinned mainly by adopting new production technologies, better farming skills, growing demand (locally and globally) and progressive trade policy. The private sector has played a major role in this progress.

I use the words "progressive trade policy" solely to highlight South Africa's standing in global agriculture. South Africa was the world's 32nd largest agricultural exporter in 2022 – the only African country within the top 40 world's largest agricultural exporters in value terms. This is according to data from Trade Map.[1]

This was made possible by a range of trading agreements the South African government secured over the past decades, with the most important ones being with the African continent, Europe, the Americas and some Asian countries. The African continent and Europe now account for about two-thirds of South Africa's agricultural exports. Asia is also an important market for South Africa's agricultural exports.

The agricultural subsectors that have primarily enjoyed these signs of progress in exports are horticulture (and wine) and grains. Broadly, South Africa now exports roughly half its agricultural products in value terms. In 2023, South Africa's agricultural exports reached a record US$13.2 billion.

Aside from the exports

The increase in agricultural output is why South Africa is now ranked 59th out of 113 countries in the Global Food Security Index,[2] making it the most food secure in Sub-Saharan Africa. I recognise that boasting about this ranking when millions of South Africans go to bed hungry every day may ring hollow, as I pointed out after a few presentations where I cited these statistics. However, it is essential to note that the lack of access to food that most South Africans face is due to the income poverty challenge rather than lack of availability due to low agricultural output, as is the case elsewhere in other parts of Africa. In essence, we need to ensure that there is employment and that households have a sufficient income.

We must remember that the Global Food Security Index balances the four elements (affordability and availability, as well as quality and safety) to arrive at a rating and covers matters at a broad national level. In this regard, South Africa produces enough food to fill the shelves of supermarkets with high-quality products but still has a long way to go in addressing household food insecurity, as many households cannot afford the food that is available in a way that meets their nutritional demands. This is a topic for another day!

Transformation

Earlier on, I noted that the consensus on agricultural growth is at variance with the diversity and sometimes polarising views around the extent to which this growth is sustainable, inclusive and transformative. To my admission, the gains we've seen in agricultural production over the past two decades have not been equitably distributed across the agricultural industry. Specifically, the growth in the agricultural sector has been mainly restricted to organised commercial agriculture, sometimes at the expense of a distinct but heterogeneous cohort of farmers in South Africa.

As I argued in my recent book, *A Country of Two Agricultures*,[3] "Nearly three decades after the dawn of democracy, South Africa has remained a country of 'two agricultures'. On the one hand, we have a subsistence, primarily non-commercial and black farming segment; on the other, we have predominantly commercial and white farmers."

The book adds that:

> The democratic government's corrective policies and programmes to unify the sector and build an inclusive agricultural economy have suffered failures since 1994. The private sector has also not provided many successful partnership programmes to foster the inclusion of black farmers in commercial production at scale. It is no surprise that institutions such as the National Agricultural Marketing Council estimate that black farmers account for less than 10%, on average, of commercial agricultural production in South Africa. This lacklustre performance by black farmers in commercial agriculture cannot be blamed solely on historical legacies.

While this paints a bleak picture of transformation in the agricultural sector, what we can also not ignore is the anecdotal evidence pointing to a rise of black farmers in some corners of South Africa. We see this in field crops, horticulture and livestock in provinces such as Free State, Western Cape, Eastern Cape and other regions.

Employment

Even with the adoption of technology that catalyses agricultural productivity improvements, employment in South Africa's agriculture industry has remained robust. For example, there were about 922 000 people employed in South Africa's agriculture industry in 1994, according to data from Statistics South Africa.[4] This is both seasonal and permanent labour. While the share of seasonal and regular labour changed over time, the broad employment conditions remained vibrant. In the third quarter of 2023, there were about 956 000 people working in primary agriculture, up 4 per cent from 1994.

The path ahead and the Master Plan's role

As South Africa moves forward, we should always be mindful of the progress that has been made in boosting our agricultural fortunes (see Figure 1). And in the quest to grow and be more inclusive, be forever vigilant of the unintended consequences of the policies we seek to implement. Equally, we must never be complacent with the dualism we continue seeing in South Africa's agricultural sector.

The task, then, is how to grow South Africa's agricultural sector more inclusively and transformatively.

I think this will need both the private sector (organised agriculture groups and agribusinesses, etc.) and the government to craft a common vision for the sector with clear rules of engagement and monitoring systems. This can build on the work of the National Development Plan (Chapter 6 to be specific), Agriculture and Agro-processing Master Plan, Land Reform Agency (yet to be launched by the government), and other progressive programmes and policies available to the nation.

Why has implementing the Master Plan been so painfully slow?

As we are fast approaching the two-year anniversary of South Africa's Agriculture and Agro-processing Master Plan (AAMP), there is very little to show for in terms of implementation on the ground.

A series of compounding crises has seized the attention of government and inadvertently led to a minimal implementation of various critical plans and policies. Public and private sector attention has entirely shifted to resolving persistent load-shedding, logistical constraints at ports, protectionism in export markets and animal diseases.

These events meant that the government and various industry stakeholders moved into 'crisis' mode, and the attention shifted from the AAMP and its promise for growth in the sector to addressing serious structural challenges that are hampering growth. The political economy tensions that often arise between industry role-players and government while resolving these urgent and near-term issues have further strained trust and the collaborative vision.

Add all these problems to the age-long reasons for lack of

implementation – namely, corruption, lack of focus and lack of capacity – and you have a perfect storm of stagnation and stalled progress in actioning the AAMP.

It doesn't help that, at the time of writing, the 2024 general elections were just around the corner, and peak election season sees the political leadership devoting more time to campaigns geared towards winning another election bid. None of the above aspects has much to do with the AAMP and, if at all, the action plan is nothing more than a footnote in any serious policy or political discussion. We will see if after the elections the path forward will change.

Why is the AAMP essential?

The AAMP should be implemented as it offers the government and the private sector a framework to grow the sector, build competitiveness, attract more investment, improve inclusion and create jobs.

These bold prospects directly address South Africa's social challenges, such as rising poverty, low economic growth and high unemployment. Each party involved in the AAMP has a bigger mission of resolving these broad societal challenges through relentless work in their businesses.

The AAMP is rooted in evidence-based research that outlines the possibilities for growth and the current growth-inhibiting factors. For example, growth constraints such as biosecurity, infrastructure, widening of export markets, registration of new crop protection chemicals, and various commodity-specific and regionalised plans are some of the aspects that the AAMP aimed to address.

These were to be tackled simultaneously with managing the financial needs in the sector, specifically for new entrant farmers through the blended finance instrument, and the land needs for expansion through the yet-to-be-launched Land Reform and Agricultural Development Agency that was mentioned several times in the State of the Nation Address (SONA) by President Cyril Ramaphosa.

The promise of these bold reforms in South Africa's agricultural economy led to estimates that the gross value added to the sector could expand by over 15 per cent in the following decade.

What should the government and private sector leadership do?

Still, given the importance of this developmental and progressive plan for the sector, leadership is needed across all stakeholders to realign and rekindle the AAMP's vision and outline steps for implementation. Therefore, implementation and operational planning are critical across various levels of government, mainly provincial and municipal governments, to ensure alignment and coherence in policy implementation.

Failure to operationalise the AAMP will be tragic for the agricultural sector and create a precedent of premature abandonment of yet another well-conceived plan that was never fully implemented.

Further negative implications will emerge – a damaging loss of confidence in the government and questions regarding the state's credibility, competence and capability to implement government mandates. The loss of trust will imply that any other plan in the future will not receive the seriousness and commitment it deserves.

What must be done?

The first step should be geared towards designing implementation and operational modalities where each role-player has a sense of ownership, responsibility and clarity about the steps they must take to see the AAMP through. The DALRRD will be at the centre of this process to lead the way, with the support of the private sector.

Notably, the DALRRD should have a dedicated desk that is fully staffed and focused mainly on AAMP implementation matters and stakeholder engagements. These personnel should not be dragged into "crisis" issues or other programmes that the government views as urgent but spend their time mainly on AAMP matters.

I live and dream agriculture. We cannot talk about livelihoods and food security without being drawn into the health of the agriculture sector in the country. Neither can we talk about economic growth without asking the question: What is agriculture's share of the GDP and how can export earnings be increased from this sector? If water is life, sanitation is dignity, agriculture is the white blood cells of society. When that collapses, so will a country slide into chaos. No government can claim to be the leader of society until it creates conditions for a thriving agriculture sector that guarantees livelihoods and food security.

References

Economist Impact, Global Food Security Index 2022: 'Exploring challenges and developing solutions for food security across 113 countries'. https://impact.economist.com/sustainability/project/food-security-index/

Sihlobo, Wandile. 2023. *A Country of Two Agricultures: The disparities, the challenges, the solutions.* Johannesburg: Tracey McDonald Publishers.

Statistics South Africa. 2000. 'Employment trends in agriculture'.

Trade Map, 2024. Trade statistics for international business development. https://www.trademap.org/Index.aspx?nvpm=1%7c%7c%7c%7c%7c%7c%7c%7c%7c%7c%7c%7c%7c%7c%7c%7c%7c%7c

20

Scuba diving into the future: Forecasting South Africa's political economy beyond apartheid

Siyabonga Hadebe

This chapter employs the metaphor of an "Olympic-size swimming pool" as a conceptual framework to explore South Africa's political future post-apartheid. By analysing the depth and shallowness levels of this metaphorical pool, the chapter aims to shed light on the transitions, both in terms of opportunities and challenges, within the political economy of the South African state over the past three decades and anticipates future developments. Therefore, as South Africa emerged from apartheid 30 years ago, there was a prevailing optimism, or perhaps an illusion, that overcoming the lingering effects of apartheid would be a straightforward endeavour. In response, the democratic South African state embarked on a dual approach to addressing historical injustices through legal means and economic policy. Concurrently, the nation began to shape its unique character, influenced by a combination of state-driven initiatives and actions independent of the state.

The rights-based Constitution guided transformation within the state, while voluntary actions and initiatives took place in parallel, often operating without direct political guidance. This external influence resulted in significantly hollowing out or privatising the state's *raison d'être*. The convergence of these two trajectories set the country on an unpredictable journey, leading to the perception that the realisation of freedom had been deferred. Thus, the analogy organises the last 30 years and beyond into five distinct eras, each characterised by a different depth in the swimming pool: the euphoria era (Nelson Mandela, shallow); existential reflection era (Thabo Mbeki, to-the-hip shallow); a reckoning with squandered potential era (Jacob Zuma, to-the-chest deep); a tangled web of uncertainty era (Cyril Ramaphosa, to-the-neck deep); and scuba diving below water era (beyond 30 years, submerged deep).

Euphoria era (*shallow*)

South Africa transitioned into a new era under Mandela's leadership, marked by euphoria and optimism. Despite the desire to move beyond apartheid injustices, two significant realities emerged. Firstly, the end of apartheid coincided with the collapse of the Soviet Union, ushering in the unquestioned global dominance of neoliberal economics. Secondly, Mandela navigated a delicate compromise between entrenched economic and political interests and the inexperienced liberation movement. Confronted with a profoundly divided society, Mandela aimed for inclusivity, seeking to "repair the irreparable". While the initial euphoria subsided, Mandela's presidency laid the groundwork for transformative achievements, turning South Africa from apartheid to democracy. His leadership spearheaded legislative reforms on restitution, land tenure, fair workplaces and affirmative action, epitomising Mandela's enduring legacy and paving the way for a future of peace and stability.

Now, the substantive challenges regarding the economy, encompassing the triple burden of high levels of unemployment, poverty and inequality, along with various other obstacles, squarely faced the new government. At this juncture, the consequential political compromise and the emergence of a neoliberal economic order were poised to exert their influence, potentially undermining the democratic project and hard-won freedoms for many South Africans. The political compromise yielded a constitution often lauded as the best in the world, albeit with significant flaws that are challenging to reconcile. For instance, section 25 guarantees private property rights, a provision that would forever tip the scales in favour of the victors – predominantly white, powerful economic and political groups – against the downtrodden black majority. Scholar Mogobe Ramose contends that despite its progressive ideals, the Constitution failed to address the lingering injustices and consequences of the country's history of conquest. Thus, the post-conquest constitution ignored the historical reality of land dispossessions, forced removals, exploitation and economic exclusion.

Mandela implemented two economic policies: the short-lived Reconstruction and Development Programme (RDP) and Growth, Employment and Redistribution (GEAR). GEAR shifted the government's economic strategy to an orthodox neoliberal framework, highlighted by market fundamentalism. Naomi Klein highlights the irony of South Africa's economic situation, noting that the country serves "as a living testament to what happens when economic reform is severed from [meaningful] political transformation". Despite achieving political freedom and enshrining voting rights, civil liberties and majority rule, South Africa paradoxically emerged as the world's most economically unequal society. All these difficulties unfolded against the backdrop of a determined economic class inherited from apartheid, chiefly comprising mining corporations and banks. This influential group not only shepherded the ANC's rise to power but also exerted its influence to steer the government away from its ambitious economic reforms.

Despite economic challenges, Mandela's presidency instituted a robust welfare state. While the social grant system played a crucial role in preventing destitution among the poorest South Africans, participation in the economy for the black majority was shoved aside. The state became the primary employer, diverting attention from creating a new vibrant and viable economy. Additionally, strides in education and health outcomes remained stagnant, reflecting a broader societal challenge that persisted beyond the euphoria era. Mandela's five-year presidency exemplified leadership measured by impact, not tenure. While Mandela quietly departed, subsequent presidents left office dramatically, contributing to the ongoing definition of ANC misrule and confusion.

Existential reflection era (*to-the-hip shallow*)

Mbeki's two-term presidency left an indelible mark on South Africa, showcasing both remarkable achievements and significant challenges. Focused on running an efficient state, building international influence and forging a working economy, Mbeki elevated South Africa's global standing. Mbeki showcased how a middle-power state could punch above its weight to influence the global agenda. South Africa became a key player in influential forums like BRICS (formerly IBSA), demonstrating its growing influence on the world stage. South Africa's opposition to the Iraq War and its participation in discussions with the G20 and G8 further solidified its position as a global power. The rights to host the FIFA World Cup in 2010 and other major events, including the WSSD in 2001, were secured under Mbeki. On the economic front, Mbeki's presidency witnessed a period of sustained growth, with the economy expanding at an average rate of 4.5 per cent over a decade. This remarkable economic performance positioned South Africa as a rapidly developing nation on the global stage.

The Mbeki era, initially marked by hope for accelerated redistribution, revealed new challenges that would shape South Africa's economic trajectory. As a self-confessed adherent of neoliberal economic policy dogma ("just call me a Thatcherite"), Mbeki focused on attracting foreign investment and stimulating growth. His economic reforms led to increased corporate dominance and exacerbated existing socio-economic disparities, highlighted by "jobless growth" and growing inequalities. This was partly due to the prevailing notion that the market was the only viable path to social change. As a result, corporations gained considerable influence in political and economic decision-making, leading to a paradoxical situation where the same entities that had been accused of human rights abuses over time were now seen as saviours of the economy. In turn, the companies extended "corporate gifts" such as the Broad-Based Black Economic Empowerment (B-BBEE) and affirmative action.

Companies also enjoyed a growing aura of invincibility, as the government shielded them from criticism and overseas litigation. Mbeki's staunch defence of these companies, even in the face of overwhelming evidence of their complicity in apartheid crimes, underscored the paradoxical nature of his economic philosophy. Additionally, the mass exodus of companies troubled Mbeki. Sampie Terblanche claims that

Mbeki was frustrated by "the dismal way the corporate sector [had] lived up to its promises ... in spite of all the privileges granted to it by the ANC government". This mass exodus highlighted the shortcomings of Mbeki's economic policies and cast doubt on his ability to address South Africa's economic challenges. In 2004, for example, a surge in service delivery protests nationwide set a precedent for future protests.

Nonetheless, Mbeki still led the ANC to its most resounding victory in 2004, securing a massive majority in the national elections. This remarkable electoral success marked a high point in the ANC's history and cemented his position as a dominant figure in South African politics. Despite these accomplishments, Mbeki's presidency was not without its shortcomings. The period of AIDS denialism stands as a dark stain on his legacy. South Africa's struggle with the HIV/AIDS pandemic led to a decline in life expectancy, and Mbeki's controversial stance on the issue prolonged the debate and delayed the implementation of life-saving antiretroviral treatment. Moreover, criticism of the country's quiet diplomacy towards the Zimbabwean government's human rights abuses during the Mugabe era cast a shadow over Mbeki's foreign policy record. While he played a role in brokering a peace accord in 2008, concerns persisted regarding the ANC's outdated approach to regional issues, rooted in outdated liberation movement solidarities.

Corruption allegations, particularly linked to the arms deal, also emerged during Mbeki's presidency. While these allegations did not yet reach the pervasiveness of later years, they raised concerns about the ANC's integrity and its ability to combat corruption. The Mbeki era concluded with a contested ANC conference, driven by his desire to extend his presidency beyond two terms, launching the enduring "battle for the soul of the ANC". This decision not only paved the way for Zuma's rise to power but also ended relative stability within the ANC and government. Mbeki's presidency stands as a testament to the complexities of leadership and the challenges of navigating a nation through a period of transition and transformation. His recall as the country's president sent South Africa on a downward spiral and unending contestation of power, both inside and outside the ANC.

The bridge between the Mbeki and Zuma administrations was Kgalema Motlanthe. Motlanthe's brief tenure as South Africa's leader, spanning just nine months, took place amidst internal ANC turmoil and the global financial crisis. Following a court ruling, he made significant changes to the HIV/AIDS policy, marking a turning point in the country's fight against the pandemic. However, Motlanthe's presidency was also overshadowed by the disbandment of the Scorpions, an anti-corruption unit established during Mbeki's administration. This decision was seen as a setback in the fight against corruption and raised concerns about the ANC's commitment to transparency and accountability. In fairness, Motlanthe's brief presidency was primarily focused on managing the ANC's internal divisions, which led to the formation of Cope, the first breakaway party from the ANC.

A reckoning with squandered potential era (*to-the-chest deep*)

Upon assuming the presidency following the 2009 elections, Zuma pledged to restore the promise of the democratic era – namely, *A Better Life for All!* However, his presidency proved to be a period of mixed outcomes, characterised by both significant achievements and concerning failures. Discussing the Zuma era does not merely evoke charged emotions; it serves as a quick reminder of how far the post-apartheid order had advanced but without making any substantial progress. It was a time of reckoning, revealing that the country's potential was being squandered under the ANC, which had promised much but delivered little. Initially, Zuma's administration had a promising start. His administration played a pivotal role in expanding access to HIV/AIDS treatment, significantly curbing infection and mortality rates. Furthermore, the successful hosting of the 2010 FIFA World Cup stood out as a major national triumph, underscoring South Africa's elevated global standing.

Zuma's presidency was also marred by economic stagnation, policy incoherence and rampant corruption. Members of corporate South Africa no longer felt the need to support the ANC, leading them to withhold their gifts from its leaders and associates, who consistently prioritised their own interests. This, coupled with an over-reliance on the state for jobs and economic opportunities through the now notorious procurement system known as *tenderpreneurship*, resulted in a decline in corporate contributions, causing internal battles within the ANC to spill into the government. The state proposed a mining charter requiring mining companies to hold 26 per cent of their shares in perpetuity and to purchase 70 per cent of goods and 80 per cent of services from black-owned companies. The mining industry expressed concerns about the charter, arguing that it would stifle investment and dilute shareholders. The charter was also criticised for giving the mining minister too much power to revise and review the obligations imposed under it. In response, companies argued, "once empowered always empowered" and turned to the courts.

On the economic front, growth remained sluggish, unemployment levels rose and inequality persisted, falling short of the promises of *A Better Life for All*. It became increasingly evident that the state was evolving into a battleground for different political and economic groups. The concept of "state capture", wherein private interests infiltrated and manipulated government decisions for personal gain, came to the forefront. While often portrayed as being centred on Zuma's relationship with the Gupta family, it became evident that the state had been plundered for the benefit of a select few for many years. This corruption extended to state-owned enterprises, leading to financial mismanagement and a decline in service delivery. Evergreen contracts held by corporations and how these powerful players spread their wings to cover every aspect of state administration were exposed.

It appeared that Zuma, with all his faults, was put as collateral to conceal the depth of South Africa's problems. Zuma's personal integrity was also questioned, as he faced numerous corruption allegations, including his alleged relationship with the Gupta family, who exerted undue influence over government affairs. However, the Zondo Commission, while exposing some wrongdoing, failed to fully address the underlying systemic failures that allowed such corruption to flourish. The extent of the deep state in South Africa still remains unknown because the system is designed to protect itself and uses the state to expand its influence and power. The Marikana massacre, where police killed striking mineworkers, stands as a dark stain on the Zuma presidency, highlighting the government's siding with corporate interests over the welfare of its citizens. Finally, the Zuma era saw the highest rise in service delivery protests, which was a sign that South African society was growing impatient under a dispensation that was emitting less and less democratic dividends. Like Mbeki, the ANC removed Zuma from office before the end of the term.

A tangled web of uncertainty era (to-the-neck deep)

The end of Ramaphosa's first term will mark exactly three decades since the first democratic elections in 1994. The much-hyped hope and optimism that accompanied his inauguration, also called the New Dawn, were astounding: anticipations of a new era marked by a stern stance against corruption, streamlined governance and economic revitalisation. However, as the tenure unfolded, these lofty expectations clashed with the harsh reality of economic stagnation, policy setbacks and unfulfilled promises. Ramaphosa positioned himself as someone who was committed to constitutional principles and who was going to champion a shift away from the state repression experienced during previous administrations. His handling of the Phalaphala matter, with the assistance of the state apparatus, left a bitter taste and eroded whatever little political capital he had. Similar to the disbandment of the Scorpions, Ramaphosa engineered the sacking of the head of the Office of the Public Protector.

Under Ramaphosa, the public expected swift actions, including dismissals and structural changes, but the reality has been a lacklustre effort, marked by delays and rhetoric rather than tangible results. The persistence of issues like load-shedding, water crises and service delivery challenges has further eroded public confidence. While Ramaphosa strives to be a unifying figure, leveraging events like the Rugby World Cup for national cohesion, the overall sentiment remains one of bewilderment and frustration. One of the critical disappointments lies in the economic sphere. Despite facing challenges like the Covid-19 pandemic, the economy under Ramaphosa's leadership has generally performed worse than during the Zuma presidency. Unemployment soared, poverty deepened and inequality persisted, painting a bleak picture of economic prospects. The anticipated growth, especially leveraging promised investments, has fallen short, leaving many disillusioned. South Africa recorded more than 900 service delivery protests in six months, from 1 August 2020 to 31 January 2021. The much-touted anti-corruption drive, a cornerstone of Ramaphosa's promises, has also faltered.

Scuba diving below water era (*beyond 30 years, submerged deep*)

The evolution of the South African state has been marked by the ascendance of capitalism, a force that has gained strength at the expense of the general population. Cloaked beneath the guise of apparent failures of the ANC government, the growing complexities lie in the old magic wand of capitalism: the system engineers endless crises to create manufactured consent. This deliberate process has led to the systematic hollowing out of the state, a calculated manoeuvre that involves strategic failures, including the collapse of critical institutions such as municipalities, Eskom, Transnet, education and health. The citizens, unwittingly caught in this intricate web, find themselves voluntarily surrendering to the influence of capital, perceiving its market mechanisms as saviours amid the chaos. The free-market lobby employs skewed arguments to advocate for the minimisation of the state's role, creating an environment fraught with panic, fear and continuous gaslighting of society.

As South Africa looks beyond the three-decade mark, it stands on the precipice of confronting formidable challenges, primarily attributed to the relentless fragmentation and pillaging of state power. Despite the uncertainties that loom on the horizon, South Africa possesses immense potential. Anchored by a youthful and expanding population, abundant natural resources and a robust cultural heritage, the country can chart a course towards prosperity and equity. Realising this potential, however, hinges on the imperative of effective leadership and well-crafted policies. A critical aspect of this journey involves taming the metaphorical raging bull within the free-market system, not only within South Africa but on a global scale. The interests of powerful white economic and political classes must be reined in for democratic South Africa to transcend its lingering apartheid character.

The looming spectre of "mexicanisation" serves as a stark warning, illustrating the potential outcome if the entrenched powers continue to shape the trajectory of South African society. It underscores the urgency for a recalibration of economic and political structures, fostering inclusivity, dismantling systemic inequalities and ensuring that the shadows of its tumultuous past do not mar South Africa's promising future. The "scuba diving below water era" beckons for a collective effort to navigate the depths, steering South Africa towards a future where prosperity and equity stand as beacons guiding the nation beyond the challenges that lie submerged deep beneath the surface.

Conclusion

South Africa's political economy has undergone profound transformations since the end of apartheid, marked by periods of hope, disillusionment and uncertainty. This analysis exposes a strategic hollowing out of the state influenced by global neoliberal forces and internal dynamics. Despite facing economic disparities, corruption and a looming threat of "mexicanisation", South Africa possesses immense potential anchored in its youth, resources and cultural heritage. However, unlocking this potential necessitates recalibrating power structures, addressing inequalities and navigating the depths collectively. The metaphorical "scuba diving below water era" calls for concerted efforts to guide the nation towards a future marked by prosperity and equity, transcending historical challenges submerged beneath the surface.

21

What of the #TotalShutdown?

Matshepo Seedat

On 1 August 2018, 24 years after democracy, South African women, "non-gender conforming womxn, cisgender womxn, and transgender womxn" declared a #TotalShutdown on gender-based violence and femicide (GBVF). The mass action was accompanied by a memorandum of demands to the government of South Africa, addressed to President Cyril Ramaphosa. In the memorandum, the women acknowledged that it will take all sectors of society coming together to end the scourge of GBVF and called for political will to change the state of things. The memorandum also clearly articulated what the challenges are and what government needs to do to address these, accompanied by 24 tabulated demands of the government with specific timelines.

This mass protest was not the first march that ever took place with similar demands to the Union Buildings; however, this particular march attracted international attention. UN Women, the organisation mandated to uphold women's human rights, called on all of its staff to "play an active role in ending violence against women in South Africa". The agency further called for "zero tolerance for sexual harassment in the United Nations offices".

Ninety-two days after the #TotalShutdown and in response to the issues raised by the women of South Africa and the world, President

Ramaphosa convened the first Presidential Gender Summit at the St George Hotel.

When announcing the first Presidential Gender Summit since the dawn of democracy, the president correctly observed that there is "a war that was being waged against women's bodies, their dignity and their right to freedom and equality, which necessitated a collective response". The summit was harrowing, as women related their experiences and expressed to the president and the government collective that was present at the summit. They discussed what is wrong in South African society that made women hunted and targeted by men. The historic summit gave birth to the first ever National Strategic Plan (NSP) on Gender-Based Violence and Femicide – true to a couple of the demands of the #TotalShutdown. The NSP is not only comprehensive in articulating what our society faces, but also in setting out clearly what must be done. What was needed was a collective response to end this scourge and the plan was accepted and embraced by all the non-conforming, cis gender and transgender womxn. The plan envisions "a South Africa that is free of gender-based violence".

The situation analysis of the NSP on Gender-Based Violence and Femicide starts with:

> During the course of 2018 and 2019, South Africa has increasingly acknowledged the crisis of GBVF and its profound impact on the lives and well-being of survivors, children, families, communities and society as a whole. Gender-Based Violence can be described as a range of harmful behaviours, such as physical, sexual, psychological, and economic abuse, all of which are directed at someone based on their gender.

This was a welcome acknowledgement as this is the first step that gears us into action. Over the years since South Africa joined the many nations who have chosen the path of democracy, the crisis of gender-based violence was something that was not confronted. South Africa experienced the serious crisis of gender-based violence and women were practically on their own as other "pressing" matters of reconciliation, economic development and racism were addressed. The denial of the crisis prevented solutions from being sought and coerced the nation to focus on arguing about what is and what is not. The NSP was a refreshing lens to finally coming to terms with the repercussions of turning a blind eye to the social wound that the country would have if we left the issues of GBVF unaddressed.

A sharp example of this denial was demonstrated by the banning of the advertisement by Charlize Theron, 20 years ago, decrying the abnormally high rape statistics in South Africa. At the time, it was a fact we were not yet willing to accept, as our young democracy was still trying to develop, grow and shed its violent past, while transforming itself as a new player on the global stage, worthy of respect from other nations. It is such denials that entrenched the stigma that victims experienced, and prevented many from reporting incidents of gender-based violence. Speaking out and reporting cases were taboo and the perpetrators were free to roam and repeat their crimes.

With acknowledgment, we are able to find ways to address the crisis that confronts us. This is the first step that was needed to tackle, head on, what women have always believed was a deliberate denial of their rights. What is also significant to recognise is that between 1999 and 2023, the law changed and improved to support women who had fallen victim to gender-based violence. During this time activism improved, men joined the causes to oppose gender-based violence and have become instrumental in fighting GBVF, and the media played a significant role in reporting cases of gender-based violence, therefore conscientising the nation.

However, numbers have not decreased, at least not considerably, in such a way that GBVF is not considered endemic. In fact, during the early years of democracy, South Africa was named the rape capital of the world. Gender-based violence thrives due to the widespread existence of gender disparities and is deeply entrenched in outdated traditional norms rooted in patriarchy that are still widely practised, and favour men to the detriment of women. In order to make an impact in our programmes, this is the root cause that we must confront, without fear or favour.

This is particularly the reason the "Real Men Don't Rape" ad by Charlize Theron, without any editing, can make its way back into the media decades later. Any individual who was born in the year 2000, after the banning of the ad, would be forgiven for thinking that it was created in present-day South Africa. Thus, despite our utmost endeavours and the implementation of all relevant policies, we have yet to even begin to scratch the surface of adequately addressing GBVF. Perhaps then, rather than focusing on laws and policies as preventative measures of GBVF, we should first and foremost strive for a shift in mind-set, change perceptions and behaviour, especially of would-be perpetrators.

The challenge faced by our nation is a socialisation, mind-set and behavioural challenge. For as long as women are not valued as human beings, worthy of dignity and respect, GBVF will remain rampant for the next 30 years of democracy.

What is needed is to acknowledge that there is something that we are not confronting, that does not include acting when the crime has already been committed.

What we need to ask ourselves is WHY? Why do all our sincerest actions at the highest level not change and make an impact on the lives of those who are most affected by GBVF? The answer is that we are not focusing on preventative measures. As the old saying goes, "prevention is better than cure". So is the case in curbing GBVF. Focusing on preventative measures means that there are less women and children affected by the psychological, physical and emotional trauma that is left by GBVF. IT means we have families that can focus on building communities, rather than trying to heal from the trauma that is visited on them by gender-based violence. We have a legal system that is not burdened by many cases that could have been prevented by just spending some of our resources on information and education about GBVF, when we just teach boys and girls about the simple concepts of consent, dignity and respect.

Government successes

Notwithstanding the many policies that the government has put in place since the beginning of a democratic government in 1994, the South African Constitution recognises the need for women's equal participation and equality for all before the law. As such, Act 39 of 1996 establishes the Commission for Gender Equality. Chapter 2 of the Constitution establishes the prohibition of discrimination on the basis of gender, race, sex, religion, marital status, etc.

Under the democratic government, an Office on the Status of Women was established in the Presidency. This office was later incorporated into the Ministry of Women, established in the fourth administration under

President Zuma. Additionally, there have been policies outside of the Ministry of Women that were approved by the cabinet to ensure that issues of GBV were addressed and found expression in the governance system prior to the #TotalShutdown. These include a Policy Framework to address Gender-Based Violence in the Post-School Education and Training System. The Department of Higher Education recognised that institutions of higher learning are a microcosm of society and are therefore not immune from what is taking place in the broader society.

However, after the #TotalShutdown, there was a need to ensure that government speaks with one voice and has a multi-sectoral, all-encompassing plan to tackle GBVF head on. As expected, the president provided leadership on this and brought all involved under one roof. The convening of the Presidential Summit on Gender-Based Violence and Femicide, after a lot of consultation with gender groups, was the beginning of this journey – the womxn were heard. 1 183 days after the first GBVF Summit was held, President Ramaphosa assented a trio of bills, namely:

- The Criminal Law (Sexual Offences and Related Matters) Amendment Act. The amendment aimed to expand the scope of the offenders, the list of people to be offended as well as the time the offenders stay on the register.
- The Criminal and Related Matters Amendment Bill to prevent the secondary victimisation of vulnerable persons in court proceedings.
- The Domestic Violence Amendment Bill to address gaps in definitions of abusive behaviours and impose on government departments to provide services to victims of domestic abuse.

This announcement was made by his spokesperson on 28 January 2021. The amendments would go a long way in ensuring that those who commit gender-based crimes are not protected due to gaps in the law and that real protection would be afforded to victims of the crime. When an act that violates a woman occurs and is reported, the law must take its course and reach its natural conclusion. That is the only way that victims and survivors naturally receive justice and are able to rebuild.

The cornerstone of solace for those impacted by GBVF, be it survivors or victims' families, lies in the perpetrator's full accountability and comprehensive rehabilitation. While the role of the president encompasses these crucial aspects post-crime, true progress demands a relentless pursuit of prevention. This entails an unwavering focus on dismantling root causes and implementing proactive strategies to eradicate GBVF before it takes root in our communities.

Shifting the focus

The president must provide leadership in the process of addressing the problem of GBVF, but it is not something the Presidency alone can eradicate, as has been evinced through the road towards the NSP on GBVF. The relevant departments have put the policies in place and Parliament continues to play its legislative and oversite role on the GBVF front. I would argue, however, that political will does not change entrenched patriarchal beliefs, political will does not compel society to see the importance of women as human beings in society, political will does not transform the way boys and girls are differently socialised and political will certainly does not transform the normalisation of violence in any society.

What political will can do is ensure formulation of the right policies, embarking on various campaigns, prioritising of the relevant legislation, ensuring collaboration with all sectors to society and imposing stringent laws on perpetrators. While political will is pivotal in enacting laws and policies on GBVF in South Africa, its total eradication, as envisaged by the National Strategic Plan, necessitates a transformative change in individual mind-sets. From redefining gender roles within families to reforming media representations and challenging societal norms, every individual working and operating in societal structures like the family and the community plays an integral role in fostering a culture of respect, equality and empowerment. Only through collective efforts aimed at reshaping attitudes and behaviours can we visualise a future free from the scourge of GBVF.

Two Presidential GBVF Summits later, change in legislation and prioritisation of issues raised by womxn, but not much has changed in statistics. We can all agree that over-emphasising solutions to come from the Union Buildings is not the solution. Rather, the change we seek lies in each and every one of us. As I pen this chapter, focusing on what we have achieved in 30 years of our democracy, we cannot pat ourselves on the back in what we have done to save the lives of South African womxn. We still have a crisis and we need to look at what we have done, what works, what makes the most impact, and then reprioritise our efforts so that we can make a difference, and end violence visited on womxn's bodies. We are not losing the battle because the president is not providing leadership – he is! We are losing because we are not confronting the perpetrators and looking at what motivates the crimes and studying the mind of an abuser and what enables him. Surely this is the genesis of the GBVF problem and the solution thereof.

Why has nothing changed?

Patriarchy: The situation analysis of the NSP alludes to the causes of GBVF as a result of cultural beliefs, patriarchy and religious practices. GBVF has been linked to patriarchy by a number of scholars. For example, Javed and Chattu[1] posit that there is a direct link between power structures and inequalities, and abuse of power. These unequal structures are a breeding ground for the vulnerable to be abused.

These unequal societal structures begin in the family, where male figures are not to be questioned and everything they do and say is never questioned. So when a patriarch decides to have intercourse with underage girls in the family, this anomaly is enabled by those who are at the bottom of the hierarchy and they may face adverse consequences if they disagree with the one who holds all the power.

In a patriarchal society, women are objects with no agency. Girl children are currencies to be bargained with and women there to provide for any needs that powerful men have. When women are not seen as human beings, they are vulnerable to abuse. Perceiving women as human, deserving of respect and dignity, is key to ending gender-based violence.

Socialisation: How children are raised and socialised is a direct cause of structural patterns, so patriarchy has a lot to do with socialisation. The fact that girls are taught to "keep their legs closed", while the boys are told to have as many sexual partners as they wish is a gross contradiction. Which girls must the boys have sexual relations with when the girls are closing their legs?

On 23 November, former Deputy President David Mabuza made off-the-cuff remarks at the Men's Parliament that was focused on men's role in ending GBVF. Although he had a prepared speech, he elected to put it aside and spoke from the heart. The deputy president, who was the Chairperson of the South African National AIDS Council, a position held by every deputy president since the establishment of the Council, said:

> The way the boy and girl child are socialised must be equal in order to dismantle patriarchy.

To mould a South African future free of gender-based violence begins in the family, and affects the community and builds a society. In this instance, it is the parent, the guardian and the role model who will ensure that, in the future, boys and girls have equal roles in society and both are entitled to equal respect; that neither are the hunter or the hunted, but equal players with different roles in leading families and communities.

The path to eradicating GBVF starts with raising boys who will stand up against harassment of women, shun sexism and sexualisation of women and who will not be shy to tell their male counterparts that it is not okay to treat women badly.

Public servants who do not walk the talk: In 2020, the amapiano group Mapara a Jazz released the song "John Vuli Gate". The lyrics of the song were interpreted in many different ways, and the part that says "nantsi stocko" was very clear to the objectification of women. Calling women "istocko" is the ultimate objectification of the female body. I am still in awe of the silence from the feminist corners in terms of the effects of objectification.

That year, I happened to be working on a project that required different parts of state institutions to bring it all together. Among the team members was a young twenty-something-year-old woman who was interning at a government department. What I remember about her is that she was pretty, light-skinned and had a curvy body. These are things I wouldn't have otherwise noticed, until one of the males on the project, upon seeing, her loudly remarked, "Yhaaaa, we have stocko here." This was rather unpalatable; that this male who was senior to the intern but was also a Presidency employee looked at a colleague and saw *stocko*. I later wrote an article for an internal publication about the incident. I was asked questions and when I refused to disclose who the individuals were my story was not published.

This may seem small given the proportions of GBVF we face in this country; however, if the people at the apex of government are not activists for change, and unlearning disempowering behaviours, what then do we expect of the rest of society? Even more, the silencing of my voice for bringing an issue like this to the right platform is exactly the problem, and if this does not change, we will still be hearing of sexual harassment that leads to violence in government, where it should not be.

Ultimately, it is important for public servants (elected and appointed) to do what they should in their duties, familiarising themselves and adhering to the prescripts of the Public Service Act. They can ensure that their actions are in line with the law and ethical standards of the public service. At the very basic level, that is what public servants are supposed to do. If even the people who write the documents do not look within and change their attitudes and mind-sets, what hope do we have?

Economic situation: Pillar five of the NSP on GBVF is dedicated to economic empowerment. An important consideration in ensuring that women are able to access financial resources that are key to removing dependency.

In 2022, post the two Presidential Gender Summits, South African women still faced higher unemployment rates and subsequently higher poverty levels. Women who depend on men for their bread and butter are more susceptible to abuse because of their dependency.

While the world is facing economic struggles, and South Africa is not immune to the economic downturn, this is a breeding ground for GBVF.

Confronting myths about GBVF

In her book *Rape: A South African Nightmare*, feminist and author Pumla Gqola lists some rape myths that, in my opinion, have prevented us from having a significant impact on GBVF in South Africa. In reaction to GBVF, we tap dance around these simple but essential issues. If we do confront them, I believe we will have a different story to tell in the next 30 years.

One harmful myth, stated by Gqola, is that sex workers cannot be raped and, in the same way, a husband cannot rape his wife – because marriage is supposed to be 24/7/365 consent. A woman who trades in sex is a sex commodity, free and available to anyone who so desires to consume the commodity. When *lobola* has been paid for women, "the cow has been bought", therefore the cow must produce the milk on demand. This particular myth also feeds into the notion that women who are sexually active are promiscuous and owe any men sex.

Similarly, men have a perception that consent is eternal, and that when there was a sexual relationship previously, it can be ignited again at any time in the future. This perception prevents men from recognising a woman's right to say no, despite a previous sexual relationship. Equally, when a woman smiles at a man or even displays friendliness, this is misconstrued as an invitation for sexual solicitation.

What will it take to change?

Part of what contributes to low impact is our over-reliance on political leadership, especially at a national level. This tends to blur the direct responsibility of the family and upbringing, the impact of the community, civil organisations, community involvement, and bottom-up approaches in effecting behavioural change.

This tells us that as we work towards eradicating GBVF, we have to dig deeper to reach the root causes embedded within societal structures and attitudes and shed the violence that our society has become accustomed and polarised to. The journey towards ending GBVF demands a fundamental shift from what we have been socialised into – one where we individually learn, unlearn and relearn what it means to value and respect every individual, irrespective of their gender. unearth

This underscores the importance of delving deeper into the fabric of society to uncover the entrenched root causes of GBVF. We must confront the normalised violence and polarisation ingrained within our societal structures and attitudes. The mission against the GBVF scourge necessitates a departure from the status quo, compelling us to collectively dismantle ingrained social norms. This journey requires a transformative process of individual introspection, unlearning deeply rooted biases, and relearning the essence of valuing and respecting every individual, regardless of gender.

It begins with a national educational campaign, similar to the

Khomanani campaign that we had in the 1990s, which taught the nation about HIV and AIDS. This includes awareness efforts through schools, places of business and communities, with children, the elderly, men and women. Education is the basis for transformation, not just in academic settings but as a lifelong process. The end goal is to make sure that everybody understands that women are not objects to be possessed, and children have agency and require protection, and they have needs, interests and aspirations.

We need to challenge these patriarchal attitudes and present alternatives, in ways that can be accepted by the majority.

We need to confront and reshape cultural norms, particularly those that are harmful to women and children and seek to cause extensive wounds physically, emotionally and psychologically. We require a media that is transformed and reports using the correct language. Language that recognises that a child cannot give consent, that a 13-year-old cannot have a boyfriend, according to the law, and that any sexual intercourse that takes place between a minor and an adult is purely and simply rape. The portrayal of diverse and non-stereotypical gender roles in media is also a powerful tool in changing harmful perceptions and fostering empathy and ending GBVF. Ultimately, it is about instilling values of equality, empathy and mutual respect in every member of our society.

The consequences of gender-based violence – whether, physical, psychological or sexual – are profound, not only for the immediate survivors but also for their families and the communities they reside in as well as society in its entirety. In order to address this societal wound effectively, we need to be decisive and adopt practical solutions that can help eliminate this scourge.

While putting laws and support programmes in place for survivors is key to the healing, we would not like to live in a society with wounded women and girls who cannot live their best lives because they are busy healing from the trauma of gender-based violence.

If we are not able to change things, then we are still playing *diketo* on the issue of GBVF. This is my challenge to the next 30 years of our liberation – it is the liberation of the mind, the ability to take every South African, rich and poor, young and old, black and white, male and female along the journey of a new dawn; one that does not excuse anyone from accountability, but empathises with them, while also expecting them to play by the rules of society and live harmoniously together without seeing others as anything less than what they are – human.

Educating citizens about their rights and obligations can be a significant and effective way to combat gender-based violence. Equipping children with information from an early age to recognise disturbing behaviour, and knowing that keeping secrets is not okay, is how we will beat GBVF; ensuring that there are trusted institutions within communities where skilled and caring people are available to listen and advise anyone who encounters gender-based violence; having people who will believe anyone when they say "I have been raped, I have been touched inappropriately, I have been told to keep a secret" and having a system that supports such individuals rather than looking the other way.

We CAN create a society where all individuals, regardless of their gender, can live free from violence and fear, and where true gender equality is a reality.

References

Gcola, Pumla Dineo. 2005. *Rape: A South African Nightmare.* (Johannesburg: MF Books Joburg).

Javed, S. and Chattu, V.K. 2021. 'Patriarchy at the helm of gender-based violence during COVID-19', *AIMS Public Health*, 8(1):32–35.

MGreal, Chris. 1999. 'Anti-Rape Ad Banned for Offending Men'. https://www.theguardian.com/world/1999/oct/04/chrismcgreal1

National Strategic Plan on Gender-Based Violence and Femicide. 2020. 'Human dignity and healing, safety, freedom & equality in our lifetime'. https://www.justice.gov.za/vg/gbv/nsp-gbvf-final-doc-04-05.pdf

President Cyril Ramaphosa assents to laws that strengthen fight against Gender-Based Violence, 28 June 2022. https://www.gov.za/news/media-statements/president-cyril-ramaphosa-assents-laws-strengthen-fight-against-gender-based

UN Women. 2018. 'In South Africa, women call for #TotalShutDown of Gender-based violence'. www.unwomen.org

22

Transforming the mining sector in democratic South Africa: A practitioner's perspective

Sandile Nogxina

The essence and centrality of history in the understanding of the constituent elements of contemporary social realities is aptly captured by one of the most prolific of nineteenth-century thinkers, Karl Marx, in one of his most intelligent and epic monographs, *The Eighteenth Brumaire of Louis Bonaparte* first published in 1852. Marx describes the salience of history in shaping the present in the following terms:

> Men make their own history, but they do not make it just as they please; they do not make it under self-selected circumstances, but under circumstances existing already, given, and transmitted from the past. The tradition of all dead generations weighs like a nightmare on the brains of the living.[1]

It is in the context of this axiom that Colin Bundy proffers that for a comprehensive understanding of the present conjuncture in South Africa, it is critical to predicate such an understanding on the historical trajectory as well as the constraints and opportunities spawned by such history.[2]

Similarly, the contemporary mineral regulatory dispensation in South Africa can only be understood in the context of the specificity of the evolution of the global system of political and economic relations. This system of political and economic relations resulted in the ultimate subordination of South Africa's political and economic interests to neo-liberalism as the prevailing ideology at the time of South Africa's political transition. It is in this context that this paper seeks to situate the recent trajectory of South Africa's mining industry.

In 2002, the South African government passed the Mineral and Petroleum Resources Development Act (MPRDA), which changed the regulation of mining by placing mineral resources under the custodianship of the state. The MPRDA does not recognise the common law mineral rights as they existed prior to the promulgation of the MPRDA. The defining feature of the common law-based mineral rights system was the inexorable link between land ownership and mineral rights ownership informed by the Roman law principle of *ad coelum*. Whereas anyone is now free to apply for mining rights from the state and, once granted, the holder of the mining right is entitled to access the land upon which the mining right is granted, the surface rights landowner, on the other hand, is required by law to sacrifice some of his/ her rights to facilitate mining activities. The surface rights landowners are, however, not entitled to compensation for the loss of minerals that are part of their ownership of the land.[3]

While there have been limited successes in terms of the empowerment of blacks through mining transactions under the provisions of the MPRDA, there is growing consensus that there have been few beneficiaries. Further, such transactions have been restricted to political elites and those with the right connections to political and economic power. It is, however, not inevitable that mining transformation and empowerment would have by default seen failures; there are inherent deficiencies within the policy and the administrative system that have and continue to paralyse meaningful realisation of state objectives.

Shaping access to "cheap labour": A whiplash of history

In South Africa, the violent conquest and subjugation of Africans by Europeans has been characterised as the "White Settler" phenomenon, the essence of which is its role as a historic instrument created by capitalism to function as a beachhead in certain parts of the world that were being incorporated.[4] Specifically, the discovery of diamonds and gold in South Africa in the latter part of the nineteenth century fundamentally transformed South Africa, with mining as the fulcrum of the country's political economy.[5] It is in this context that Feinstein has characterised the symbiotic relationship between the discovery of minerals and the subjugation of Black South Africans in the following terms:

> From that point forward the economic history of South Africa becomes, in essence, the story of how this unique combination of the indigenous population, European settlers, and mineral resources was brought together in a process of conquest, dispossession, discrimination, and development to promote rapid economic progress.[6]

In this regard, successive colonial and apartheid governments consistently developed and adopted favourable policies and legislative responses to the demands of the mining industry since the turn of the last century. These policies and legislation effectively reconfigured the patterns of landholding and property rights, including mineral rights.

While the colonial and apartheid land policies and legislation served to divest black South Africans of most of their land, the mining laws specifically excluded them from meaningful participation in mining activities except as purveyors of cheap labour. The Glen Grey Act (1894), passed by the colonial regime in the Cape Colony, only set the stage for further statutes that sought to abolish communal land tenure. Primarily, the Act was designed to coerce Africans from their agricultural economy into labour market in the mines and farms owned by whites. This was justified based on the "backwardness and inferiority" of Africans in the constructs of race and civilisation created in the late nineteenth century. Overall, this reality was characterised by hostility towards communal land tenures as they were believed to retard economic development.

The effect of this was the creation of what came to be known as a dual economy in South Africa, that is, the contrast between "modern" and "traditional" economies. The essence of this economic dualism has been described as the juxtaposition of the structural features of the relatively developed modern economy that produces the bulk of the country's wealth on the one hand, and the underdeveloped and marginalised economy that comprises most of the population and yet contributes minimally to the country's Gross Domestic Product.[7] Mbeki observes that the marginalised economy incorporates the poorest members of the South African society whose circumstances render them structurally disconnected from the developed and world economies. The consequence of this is the race-based socio-economic inequalities currently besetting South African society. This has earned the country the unenviable title of being the most unequal society in the world.

For well over a century, the mining industry had been the main contributor to aggregate economic output, a key foreign-exchange earner, a significant employer, employing well over a million mineworkers by the late 1980s. However, prior to 1990, South Africa's mining laws contained discriminatory provisions that included systematic exclusion of blacks from obtaining mining licenses or participating meaningfully beyond providing cheap labour. The language of the laws themselves documents the discriminatory intent of the legislation. For instance, section 133 of the Gold Law of the South African Republic (Law 15 of 1898) stated that:

> No coloured person defined to mean African, Asiatic, Native or coloured American, Coolie, or Chinaman may be a license holder or in any way be connected with the working of diggings but shall be allowed only in the service of Whites.

Consequently, the history of the South African mining industry is inextricably linked to the power dynamics that have and continue to characterise the country's political and socio-economic landscape. Central to South Africa's democratisation process has been the legal abolition of racial capitalism and the conservative features that made up the social, cultural and economic structures and the implementation of more egalitarian socio-economic system.[8]

Transformative justice as the bedrock of the SA mining law

With the advent of democracy and the need to reconstruct South Africa's political, social and economic structures, the mining industry became one of the critical industries for the post-apartheid state's transformative and redistributive agenda. Scholarship in the recent past has alluded to the pressing need for societies emerging from conflict to implement policies and laws framed by transitional justice as a means of achieving a society anchored on a greater concern for social justice and human rights.[9] In particular, Mutua predicates his argument on the reasoning that:

> There is no future without a past, and the future is a result of the past. Unless we construct a future based upon the lessons of the past, we are bound to repeat our own mistakes and retard the development of our society.[10]

Thus the concept of transitional justice emerged – whose foundation is the notion that the successful construction of any future political system must acknowledge and address injustice of the past. It is noteworthy, however, that a sizeable number of scholars have identified some weaknesses in the concept of transitional justice as a vehicle to address broader human rights issues and socio-economic inequalities engendered by structural violence.[11]

For example, Teitel[12] decries the fact that the current literature and scholarship on transitional justice are steeped in the same liberalism that provided the ideological underpinnings of nineteenth-century imperialism. It is in this context that the concept of transformative justice has emerged as an alternative conception of justice that goes beyond the traditional remit of transitional justice to incorporate issues of social justice and redistributive justice. In contradistinction to transitional justice, transformative justice implies radical and far-reaching societal changes. In South Africa transformative justice constitutes the foundation of the country's transition from apartheid to democracy and seeks to reverse, among others, the economic patterns resulting from a system designed to supply labour to the farms, mines and factories. It encompasses broader issues of redress of socio-economic imbalances engendered by history ranging from political to economic marginalisation of black South Africans.

It was the realisation of this truism that the ANC in its Constitutional Guidelines of 1989 called for the state and all social institutions in the democratic South Africa to be under a constitutional mandate to take active steps to eradicate the social and economic inequalities engendered by racial discrimination. It is instructive that the preambular paragraph to this document provided for the need to convert the Freedom Charter adopted in 1955 from a vision for the future into a constitutional reality. With regard to mineral resources, the Freedom Charter provides that "the mineral wealth beneath the soil shall be transferred to the people as a whole".

Subsequent to the Constitutional Guidelines, the ANC published a document titled "A Bill of Rights for a New South Africa". Article 11 of this document deals with the economy, land and property. With reference to mineral resources, section 3 of Article 11 provides that all natural resources above and below the surface area of the land shall be owned by the state provided that they were not owned by any person at the time of coming into force of the new constitution. The formulation of this clause was clearly at odds with the Freedom Charter as it served to exclude privately owned mineral rights from being transferred to the people as whole. This was one of the manifestations of the compromises the ANC made on its historical egalitarian rhetoric in response to neo-liberal hegemony following the fall of the Berlin Wall and the collapse of the Soviet Union. Section 5 of this Article enjoined the state to legislatively take steps to overcome the effects of the past statutory discrimination.

Echoing the position articulated in the previous policy documents, the ANC adopted at its Conference in 1992 a policy document titled "Ready to Govern". Among the four basic objectives the document identified was "to overcome the legacy of inequality and injustice created by colonialism and apartheid in a swift, progressive and principled way". These are the policy documents that informed the ANC positions during negotiations for a democratic South Africa – which ultimately found expression in the transformative clauses of the South Africa's Constitution, thus shaping its transformative character and the paradox that inheres to its idiom.

However, it is noteworthy that the notion of transformative constitutionalism has as its defining feature juxtaposition of contradicting imperatives. The idea of transformation embodies within itself radical change while on the other hand constitutionalism implies the maintenance of stability, security, predictability, and certainty.[13] It is for this reason that scholars have seen times of constitutional transition as throwing into sharp relief the inescapable tension inherent between radical change occasioned by transformative politics on the one hand and stability associated with the status quo that finds expression in the constraints to such change.[14] This is the paradox that is discernible in the letter of South Africa's Constitution and the legislation flowing from it. It appears to constrain change in its protection of the historically acquired property rights while it simultaneously enjoins the state to redress injustices of the past.

With regards to the minerals and mining industry, the democratic government, using the transformative clauses of the Constitution as a lodestar, embarked on a wide consultative process to formulate policy that would underpin the legislation and administrative decisions in the management of the country's mineral resources. This culminated in the adoption of the White paper on Minerals and Mining in 1998. Among other things, the White Paper had to specifically deal with the pre-1994 restrictions on blacks and landownership, and the concomitant mineral rights ownership. Towards this end, the government exercised its regulatory power by defining mineral rights as a national patrimony and therefore the heritage of all South Africans.

The Mineral and Petroleum Resources Development Act 28 of 2002 (MPRDA), informed as it was by the new mining policy, was the first step towards addressing the race- and gender-based historical imbalance in mineral rights ownership. After having proclaimed that mineral resources belong to the nation, the state vested the custodianship of same to itself. Accordingly, the state has the authority to administer and manage all mineral rights in line with its policy objectives at the epicentre of which is the attainment of social justice.

While access to the country's mineral resources was, since the imposition of common law in South Africa, intrinsically bound to landownership prior to 1994, a critical consequence of the new regulatory dispensation was the abrogation of this arrangement. In this regard, the state assumed the common law privileges of landowners to decide where, when, and by whom the country's minerals can be mined. In effect, the MPRDA reversed almost a century of black dispossession by declaring mineral resources a national patrimony and vested its custodianship in the state. In his articulation of the essence of the change brought about by the promulgation of the MPRDA, Nogxina argues that:

> At the heart of the idea of the social function of property lies the notion that property goes beyond a mere relationship between the owner and the subject matter of ownership to encompass societal concerns. It is for that reason that legislation began to eschew the notion of sacredness of property as an individual right by recognizing its social function… This not only applied to individuals but to the state. Essentially, the state assumed custodial powers rather than proprietary powers over natural resources. The nation remained the owner of natural resources.[15]

This is in line with the notion of egalitarian redistributionalism, which establishes that the conceptualisation of property must take on board the historic injustice concomitant with the acquisition of such property. In this way, the legal character of property must not insulate it from state intervention to redefine its content for the purpose of redistribution in the interest of social justice.[16]

As the common law-based concept of mineral rights did not lend itself to more equitable distribution of wealth, it had to be abrogated to realise the idea of the social function of property. Thus, the MPRDA defines mineral resources as "the common heritage of all the people of South Africa and the state is the custodian thereof for the benefit of all South Africans". Indeed, South Africa as a newly independent state did not only use its regulatory authority over the mining industry to assert its national sovereignty, but also as a mechanism to redress historical injustices engendered by colonialism and apartheid. The rationale for this course of action is an incontrovertible fact that land is a finite resource and there is an accepted nexus between land ownership and wealth as well as landlessness and poverty.

Miranda[17] sees the international law principle of permanent sovereignty over natural resources, which gained its apogee during the decolonisation era of the 1960s, as an internal distributive mechanism. This is in contradistinction to the historical role of the notion of permanent sovereignty over natural resources that has been the theoretical foundation for newly independent states to assert their political and economic sovereignty against other states and international organisations. It is in this context that the MPRDA has specifically invoked this doctrine in section 2(a) when it enjoins "the state to exercise sovereignty over all mineral and petroleum resources in the Republic".

Furthermore, the Act states that among its objectives is to give effect to the principle of the state custodianship of the nation's mineral and petroleum resources in order to promote equitable access to same. This is a good example of the application of the international doctrine of permanent sovereignty over natural resources to predicate intrastate resource redistribution both as an exercise of sovereignty by the democratic state and the extension of human rights to the majority of South Africans.

Indeed, mining law scholars have argued that natural resources are a national patrimony and, as such, there is societal pressure on policymakers to leverage national resources for strategic objectives through state-interventionist policies.[18] This is what is known as resource nationalism. Building on the notion of resource nationalism, Nogxina[19] avers that natural resource-endowed countries tend to utilise their legal jurisdiction over natural resources to advance and achieve certain national strategic objectives, including objectives framed by the goals of transformative justice or national interest. The paradox inherent in the South African Constitution has, however, cascaded to the language of the MPRDA. In its objectives, the Act calls for the equitable and meaningful participation of the historically disadvantaged South Africans in the mining and petroleum industry while simultaneously guaranteeing security of tenure for the historically acquired mineral rights.

In the meantime, the MPRDA contains several provisions that serve to give effect to resource nationalism. These were designed to rupture the historical path embodied in the policies and laws that created and buttressed race- and gender-based power imbalances in the mining industry. Given the role that was played by the common law concept of mineral rights, based as it was on the private law notion of private property, in the marginalisation of the majority of South Africans the new constitutional dispensation had to expand the notion of property to accommodate the transformative agenda.

According to Van der Schyff,[20] the promulgation of the post-apartheid constitution made it imperative that the property concept should not remain stagnant but must change to accommodate the new constitutional values. In this regard:

the exclusive private law character has changed due to the applicability of the concept within the public law sphere.[21]

In the same vein, Mostert and Pope allude to the essence of change introduced by the MPRDA in the South African mineral rights dispensation as:

> the replacement of the apartheid system of mineral law which was rooted in the principles of private law, with a system of public law rights to achieve the regulatory control that is necessary to manage the process of ensuring socially and environmentally approaches to the extraction of minerals.[22]

In the same vein, Katzarov maintains that, through regulation, the substance of property has been expanded in what he refers to as the invasion of private law by public law to bring within its purview the social concept of function. He explains the provenance of the inordinate influence of public law on the institution of property as follows:

> But, perhaps because of this extreme refinement, private law has long time past begun to show itself vulnerable to the assimilatory tendencies of its rival, public law, having a range of more powerful legal weapons, including such weapons as public policy, public interest … often succeeds to oust private law from the foremost position. We must also recognise that, purely theoretic research, the evolution of private law, founded on the absolute property on liberalism, had arrived at results too extreme.[23]

Nogxina characterises the encroachment of public law in the historical absolute private law realm of mineral rights through the prism of the paradox that inheres in South Africa's transformative Constitution. According to him:

> The legal and proprietary character of mineral rights, based as it was on common law private law principles, did not lend itself to social function. It was indeed the product of history, the mature crop of colonialism and had to be separated from its iniquitous

historical bedrock. In its new incarnation, the institution of property in mineral rights had to assume a form that would functionally serve the proprietary entitlements of the holder on the one hand, and social function on the other. This is emblematic of the paradox that is inherent in our transformative constitution which protects historically acquired mineral rights while it simultaneously enjoins the state to redress the historical injustices.[24]

Between Scylla of economic nationalism and Charybdis of neo-liberalism

As part of its objective to give effect to the constitutionally prescribed transformative agenda, the democratic government adopted the Black Economic Empowerment (BEE) programme. This followed a report commissioned by the Black Business Council in May 1998. In its assessment of the progress made in deracialising the South African economy, the Report painted a gloomy picture. It identified the provenance of what was described as crisis in the South African economy as the continued exclusion of the Black South Africans from meaningful participation in the economic activities since the advent of democracy.

The BEE Commission accordingly recommended that the notion of BEE must incorporate comprehensive strategies designed to enhance access to productive assets without compromising the concomitant productivity and growth of those assets. The Commission further recommended that increased levels of black participation should be promoted in ownership, management, and control of assets and economic activities. Towards this end, the Commission called for the promulgation of a legislative instrument that provides that the private sector should agree on targets, not less than 25 per cent in each sector, and mechanisms to deracialise business ownership.

It was in this context that the Department of Minerals and Energy (DME) – inspired by the Freedom Charter as a consensus-building mechanism and invoking the spirit of the negotiated settlement that had just ushered in constitutional democracy in South Africa – proposed the South African Charter for the Petroleum and Liquid Fuels industry signed in November 2000. It is noteworthy that although this Charter dealt with some of the problems and implemented some of the BEE Commission recommendations, its effectiveness was compromised by its lack of a regulatory foundation.

Section 100 of the MPRDA enjoins the minister to develop a broad-based Charter that assumes the language of its constitutive Act in the definition of its beneficiaries. It defines its beneficiaries as historically disadvantaged South Africans, being black people, women and disabled. Its adoption was preceded by a protracted and sometimes acrimonious process of negotiations between the Department and the private sector represented by the Chamber of Mines. According to Nogxina, South Africa, at this point, was confronted by what normally is faced by countries in transition, which is the imperative to maintain a healthy balance between the legitimate need for the state to have policy space to legislatively respond to the changing values and new societal demands, on the one hand, and the expectations of investors to preserve their investments and profits on the other.

This situation was further compounded by the global investment context. According to Tienhaara,[25] mining laws are a rational reflection of the prevailing world view. In the post-Cold War period, the prevailing world view was emblematic of the global balance of power in favour of neo-liberalism. Accordingly, the government had to tread carefully in the articulation of its transformative agenda as international investors were quick to invoke the provisions of the international trade agreements. Thus:

> ... transformative agenda recognises the confluence of geopolitical factors, particularly the dominance of the neo-liberal ideology... Neo-liberal hegemony served to constrain the policy space for the ANC government to adopt and implement policies freely that would decisively deal with the structural realities of historical colonial and apartheid dispossession.[26]

It was this context that necessitated a nuanced approach to policy and legislative changes. Upon assumption of power on the back of a negotiated settlement, the ANC found itself ensconced between the Scylla of economic nationalism and Charybdis of neo-liberalism. The ANC had to moderate its egalitarian transformative agenda in the face of limitations imposed by the post-Cold War global neo-liberal political and economic hegemony. Tshitereke puts the ANC's economic dilemma actuated by the global ideological landscape in perspective when he argues that:

> Notwithstanding its ideology and rhetoric while in exile and opposition, once in power the ANC government implemented orthodox macro-economic policy that coalesced with trade liberalism … while the challenge for redistribution to address apartheid imbalances remained daunting, the ANC had to tread carefully to maintain optimal equilibrium between the need for social justice and the interests of corporate South Africa.[27]

As part of this nuanced approach to change, the MPRDA contained transitional arrangements in terms of which mineral rights holders were required to convert their old-order rights acquired under the previous iniquitous legislation into new-order rights. The paradox inherent in South Africa's transformative Constitution cascades to the MPRDA. This becomes more pronounced in its objectives. On the one hand the Act seeks to promote security of tenure for the historically acquired mineral rights. On the other hand, the Act has as its objective the opening up of access to historically disadvantaged South Africans.

In order to surmount this paradox, the MPRDA had a built-in mechanism, known as transitional arrangements, which was designed to operate as a bridge between the old common law-based rights and the new regime of mineral rights undergirded by new constitutional values. In this way, these two apparent contradictory objectives would be reconciled. Accordingly, old-order mineral rights holders were required to submit such rights for conversion within a period of one year for prospecting rights and five years for mining rights. Failure to comply would result in the lapse of those whereupon they would revert to the state. Importantly, although the conversion process did not create new rights, it brought old-order rights within the purview of the new dispensation, they were required to bring their rights within the ambit of the new dispensation.

The process of conversion created in the regulatory space a mechanism by which the government was able to link the licensing process to compliance with the Charter. In order to achieve a substantial change in the disparities prevalent in the ownership of mining assets, stakeholders committed to "achieve a minimum target of 26 per cent ownership to enable meaningful economic participation of HDSA by 2014". This became an effective strategy between the Department of Minerals and Energy and the mining industry for the latter to aggressively drive the transformation agenda. On the back of this, BEE transactions were concluded in the mining industry. By introducing the conversion of old-order rights into new-order rights the government ensured that it could monitor the compliance with the new law. In as much as the transitional arrangements facilitated the seamless continuation of existing operations, they also served to force the converted rights to be in line with the new dispensation.

According to a report by the Department of Mineral Resources, BEE transactions worth R1 billion were concluded in 2000. The value of these transactions exponentially increased after the promulgation of the MPRDA, reaching R18 billion in the year 2006 and peaking at R43 billion in 2007. This trajectory was disrupted by the 2008 global financial crisis and its knock-on effect on commodity prices. Since then, there has been a sharp decrease in the value of BEE transactions, which fluctuated from a high of R13 billion in 2011 to a low of R1 billion in 2013. The costs of mining operations exacerbated by other challenges associated with BEE transactions discouraged the transformation process in the mining industry. Chief among these were lack of access to financial resources and requisite skills necessary for mining operations.

In line with the provisions of the Charter, the Department of Minerals and Energy conducted a comprehensive assessment of transformation in the mining industry against the Charter objectives. The findings of the assessment exposed several shortcomings in the way the industry had implemented and achieved various elements and targets of the Charter. In particular, the ambiguity residing in the then construct of the Charter made it amenable to interpretation by industry in ways that frustrate the transformation agenda. The result was malicious compliance.

The case in point is the element of ownership that all stakeholders recognised as key to the substantial and meaningful participation of the designated groups in the mining industry. The Department of Mineral Resources construed this element as entailing voting rights, economic interest and net value. On its part, industry interpreted this element as only limited to economic interest excluding the rest. As a result of this misalignment, a dispute arose between the Department and the Chamber of Mines on the extent to which the mining industry had met the ownership target. Thus, whilst the mining industry presented a glowing picture of their members' compliance with this element of the Charter, the Department placed them only at 9 per cent of the set target. Today, no element of the Mining Charter has attracted more controversy and disagreement between government and industry than ownership. Equity ownership is perceived as the measure of wealth and epitome of change.

Another source of difference between the Department and the industry was the notion of the continuing consequences of past empowerment deals. In assessing compliance with the equity ownership element of the Charter, the government believed that compliance with the prescribed target of 26 per cent must endure indefinitely and the consequences of past deals must not be included. The net effect of this interpretation was that mining companies must maintain the historical empowerment credentials, notwithstanding the fact that there has been change in the ownership composition or structure. Where the BEE share had decreased below 26 per cent, the right holder must supplement it to sustain required thresholds.

On the contrary, the mining industry relied on the notion of "once empowered always empowered" and argued that the consequences of past deals must form part of the equation in the assessment of the ownership element. This matter was ultimately resolved by a court decision in 2015 in the case of *The Minerals Council of South Africa vs Minister of Mineral Resources and Energy et al.*

Following the publication of a 2009 Mining Impact Assessment Report, the mining industry stakeholders negotiated and adopted amendments to the 2002 Mining Charter to incorporate changes in response to the shortcomings identified by the Assessment Report. This came in the form of the 2010 Mining Charter. The critical amendments pertained to the meaning and calculation of the Historically Disadvantaged South Africans (HDSA) ownership element of the Charter.

According to these amendments, stakeholders in the mining industry recognised that effective ownership is a requisite instrument to effect integration of HDSA into the mainstream economy. Towards this end, the stakeholders committed to:

- Achieve a minimum target of 26 per cent ownership to enable meaningful participation of HDSA by 2014.

- The only offsetting permissible under the ownership element is against the value of beneficiation, as provided for by section 26 of the MPRDA and elaborated in mineral beneficiation framework.
- The continuing consequences of all previous deals concluded prior to the promulgation of the Mineral and Petroleum Resources Development Act 28 of 2002, would be included in calculating such credits\offset in terms of market share as measured by attributable units of production.

Regarding beneficiation offset, the 2010 Charter required companies to offset the value level of beneficiation achieved by the company against its HDSA ownership requirements not exceeding 11 per cent. In addition, the amended Charter requires that BEE transaction should have beneficiaries, communities, employees and black entrepreneurs. This is the regulatory framework within which the transformation agenda in the mining industry has been driven.

Undoubtedly, change has been incremental and compounded by various contestations both between the mining industry and the government and between government and communities. As such, an objective assessment of the extent to which government has achieved its transformational objectives through regulation has produced mixed results. Litigation against government by both the mining industry and communities is evidence of the complexities of the regulatory space and its transformation imperatives.

There have been various reports that seek to analyse the successes or failures of South Africa's transformation agenda in the mining industry. In its assessment of the socio-economic impact of the Mining Charter in 2015, the Department of Mineral Resources found that only 6 per cent (not weighted) and 20 per cent (weighted) had fulfilled the requirements of meaningful economic participation as prescribed in the Mining Charter.

Madinginye, in his analysis of the correlation between the DMR and the Chamber of Mines's transformation assessments, concludes that the two disagree on all of the results presented except employment equity. In his words:

They either have differing measurement approaches or they simple report different results even when using similar measurement approaches. While the DMR makes the case that the mining Charter has largely not been complied with, the Chamber of mines contends there is broad compliance by mining companies.[28]

In September 2017, PricewaterhouseCoopers released its report on the status of South Africa's mining industry. According to this report, black ownership as per the 2017 Mining Charter was set at 30 per cent. Having analysed shareholder information supplied by the listed holding companies in their financial statements, only 5 per cent of the 29 analysed equal to or greater than 30 per cent.

Conclusion

Nogxina established that the transformative objectives of the MPRDA have, in the main, been thwarted by the creation of sophisticated and complex empowerment transactions. Such empowerment transactions appear to advance the objectives of the transformational agenda while they do not result in any real benefit to the HDSA partners. Nogxina identifies this practice as malicious compliance, which became the subject of contention between government and the mining industry.

Effective implementation of the MPRDA is further compounded by the dearth of specialist skills and expertise within the Department of Minerals and Energy to analyse and evaluate complex commercial and financial transactions. Importantly, the historical mandate of the Department of Mineral Resources, which is ensuring orderly and optimal exploitation of the country's mineral resources, has expanded to incorporate the transformation agenda. This includes economic empowerment of historically disadvantaged South Africans and social upliftment of communities, thus fusing commercial and social issues into the regulatory framework.

This has implications for both the organisational architecture and the requisite skill base of the department. Its officials are now required to analyse and assess complicated and complex commercial transactions as well as social and labour plan projects, which have become standard requirements for the granting of mining licenses. Yet, the organisational structure of the department remains informed by its historical mandate. The inevitable outcome of the departmental skills deficit is the prevalence of fronting and malicious compliance by the mining companies.

Another contributing factor to the limits of transformation in the mining industry is the efficiency and effectiveness of the instruments for assessing progress. The Department of Mineral Resources uses the Mining Charter Scorecard as an instrument for measuring progress against set targets. Its architecture is based on a binary approach, with targets informed by time frames. According to the Scorecard, progress in achieving the aims of the Charter can be measured in two ways: first are the specific targets in the Charter, and second are the targets set by the Companies.

The way the Scorecard has been formulated has attracted criticism that it resembles a checklist and some of its questions lend themselves to vagueness.[29] Nogxina argues that there is a fetish for measurement without assessing the extent to which there has been meaningful transformation.

> In essence the Scorecard-based transformation assessment has distorted and impoverished the value of transformation by reducing it to numbers that are meaningless if beneficiaries of BEE in the mining industry have essentially been impoverished.[30]

The effectiveness of the MPRDA and the Mining Charter should not only be assessed through lenses of compliance with defined targets, but also through the extent to which it achieved its primary objectives as current law in South Africa's statutes.

References

Booysens, S.A. 2011. *The South African Mining Charter: A Performance Measuring Instrument: Scorecard for the Broad-Based Socio-Economic Empowerment Charter for the Industry*. Riga: VDM Verlag, Muller.

Bundy, C. 1979. *The Rise and Fall of the South African Peasantry*. London: James Currey.

Daly, K. 2002. 'Restorative justice: The real story', *Punishment and Society*, 4(1):55–79.

Feinstein, C.H. 2005. *An Economic History of South Africa: Conquest, discrimination and development*. Cambridge: Cambridge University Press.

Glen Grey Act, Act 25 of 1894, Parliament of the Cape Colony, South Africa.

Gready, P., Boesten J., Crawford, G. and Wilding, P. 2010. *Transformative Justice: A concept note*. Unpublished manuscript, retrieved from https://wun.ac.uk/files/transformative_justice_-_concept_note_web_version.pdf

Katzarov, K. 1964. *Theory of Nationalisation*. The Hague: Martinus Nijhoff.

Leubolt, B. 2014. 'Social policies and redistribution in South Africa'. Global Labour University Working Paper 25. Berlin: The Global Labour University.

Madinginye, T.D.S. 2016. Compliance with the Mining Charter: 10 Years on what has been achieved? Implications for South Africa's industrial development. http://forum.tips.org.za/images/forum%20 papers/2016/58c2c3_2bcba7a1faee4aa4ad69862a265d7b33.pdf

Magubane, B. 1986. 'The political economy of the South African revolution'. *African Journal of Political Economy*, 1(1):1–28.

Mani, R. 2008. 'Dilemmas of expanding transitional justice, or forging the nexus between transitional justice and development'. *International Journal of Transitional Justice*, 2(3):253–265.

Marx, K. 1852. *The Eighteenth Brumaire of Louis Bonaparte, Die Revolution*, New York City: Joseph Weydemeyer.

Mbeki, T. 2004. 'Meeting the challenge for the second economy'. *New Agenda: South African Journal of Social and Economic Policy*, Second Quarter (14).

Merrill, T.W. 2009. 'Accession and original ownership'. *Journal of Legal Analysis*, 1(2):459–510.

Mineral and Petroleum Resources Development Act, Act 28 of 2002, Republic of South Africa.

Miranda, L.A. 2012. 'The role of international law in intrastate natural resource allocations: Sovereignty, human rights, and peoples-based development'. *Vanderbilt Journal of Transnational Law*, 45:784–840.

Mostert, H. and Pope, A. 2010. *The Principles of the Law of Property in South Africa*. Cape Town: Oxford University Press.

Mutua, M.W. 2011. 'A critique of rights in transitional justice: The African experience'. In *Rethinking Transitions: Equality and social justice in societies emerging from conflict* edited by Agui, G.O. and Isa, F.G. Cambridge: Intersentia, pp 31–45.

Nogxina, S. 2019. 'The Paradox of Transformative Constitutionalism, and the Regulation of Minerals Rights in South Africa: 1994–2014'. Unpublished Ph.D. Thesis, School of Governance and Development Management, University of the Witwatersrand.

PricewaterhouseCoopers. 2017. *Annual Review of Global Mining Trends*. Johannesburg: PricewaterhouseCoopers.

Ratsheko, T. 2018. 'A critical analysis of the extent to which SA law protects the surface rights of landowners over whose property mining rights have been granted'. Unpublished Master of Laws mini dissertation, University of Pretoria.

Tienhaara, K.S. 2009. *The Expropriation of Environmental Governance: Protecting foreign investors at the expense of public policy*. Cambridge, MA: Cambridge University Press.

Teitel, R.G. 2020. *Transitional Justice*. Oxford: Oxford University Press.

Tshitereke, C. 2006. *The Experience of Economic Redistribution: The Growth, Employment and Redistribution Strategy in South Africa*. Abington-on-Thames, UK: Routledge.

Van der Schyff, E. 2012. 'South African mineral law: A historical overview of the State's regulatory power regarding the exploitation of minerals'. *New Contree*, 64:131–153.

Van der Walt, A.J. 2006. 'Legal history, legal culture and transformation in a constitutional democracy'. *Fundamina*, 12(1).

Wilson, J.D. 2011. 'Resource nationalism or resource liberalism? Explaining Australia's approach to Chinese investment in its minerals sector'. *Australian Journal of International Affairs*, 65(3):283–304.

Windholz, E.L. 2018. *Governing through Regulation Public Policy, Regulation and Law*. New York: Routledge.

23

A thematic reflection of the inclusion of individuals with impairments in a democratic South Africa

Zukiswa Nzo

The Constitution of 1994 enshrines the rights of all people in South Africa, emphasising democratic values like human dignity, equality and freedom.[1] Section 9 ensures equality before the law and prohibits discrimination against those with disabilities.[2] International agreements like the UN Convention on the Rights of Persons with Disabilities and domestic policies such as the White Paper on the Rights of Persons with Disabilities (WPRPD) further reinforce these principles,[3] aiming to overcome barriers to participation faced by individuals with impairments. Over the past 30 years of democracy, the South African Human Rights Commission has noted significant challenges in achieving equality for persons with disabilities, including systemic issues highlighted by numerous complaints.[4] However, progress has been made through initiatives such as establishing the Disability Advisory Committee and the Independent Monitoring Mechanism.[5] Despite efforts, the recent annual report indicates that targets still need to be fully met.[6] This reflects ongoing struggles in areas like access to justice, empowerment and accessibility compared to constitutional and policy frameworks. The situation regarding access to justice, empowerment and accessibility for individuals with disabilities in South Africa is complex and multifaceted. A reflection of this is unpacked below, based on reports from grey literature, scholarly material and tracking of issues that caught the attention of the media in this period.

Access to justice

Freedom from torture, exploitation, violence and abuse

Despite constitutional protections and the WPRPD, significant challenges persist, particularly concerning freedom from violence and abuse. The UN Committee has highlighted extreme forms of violence against persons with disabilities, including kidnapping and killings of persons with albinism, with inadequate measures for prevention and prosecution. The Life Esidimeni tragedy exemplifies this, where 144 individuals died due to neglect and starvation after being relocated to unfitting residential facilities. Despite formal inquest hearings, no criminal charges have been filed to date.

Stigma also plays a central role in the exploitation of women with disabilities, shaping their experiences of sexual violence and relationships. Studies have highlighted encroachments on the sexual and reproductive rights of individuals with disabilities stemming from assumptions and prejudices about their sexuality. Gender-based violence towards persons with disabilities remains prevalent, encompassing various forms of abuse. These findings emphasise the urgent need for comprehensive interventions addressing structural inequalities and stigma to ensure the protection and empowerment of individuals with disabilities in South Africa.[7]

Equal recognition before the law

Section 43 of the Bill of Rights guarantees equal recognition before the law, ensuring fair public hearings for all disputes, and provisions for reasonable accommodations are mandated to accommodate diverse needs.[8] However, persons with disabilities face increased risks of violence, with communication disabilities exacerbating their vulnerability.[9] Challenges persist in accessing the criminal justice system due to insufficient support for those with communication challenges.[10] Furthermore, inadequate accessibility of legal information and support services hampers the effective participation of persons with disabilities in legal proceedings.[11] Article 12 of the Convention calls for support in legal decision-making for persons with disabilities, which has sparked a debate over supported versus substituted decision-making.[12]

Strengthening monitoring systems is imperative to track access to justice and empower persons with disabilities.[13] However, a limited understanding of reasonable accommodation and the absence of specific anti-discrimination legislation perpetuates intersecting discriminating forms against persons with disabilities in South Africa.[14] Notably, the lack of legal mechanisms for redress and compensation further marginalises victims, particularly women and girls.[15]

Empowerment

While there has yet to be a consensus about the definition of empowerment, broadly defined empowerment involves enhancing individuals' capacity to make choices that lead to desired outcomes.[16] It addresses the challenges faced by marginalised individuals, who have fewer opportunities due to discrimination. Empowered individuals are envisaged to have the freedom to influence their lives and decisions, leading to improved social well-being and inclusion, mainly through increased participation in economic activity.[17]

Education

The right to education, as outlined in section 29 of the Bill of Rights, emphasises access to basic education, considering equity and redress for past discrimination.[18] Aligned with international standards, the White Paper aims to ensure inclusive education, yet legal action and reports highlight significant challenges. Pather[19] and Fish Hodgson[20] underline scepticism and systemic failures in inclusive education, with many children with disabilities still out of school or segregated. Studies by Mukwevho and Gadisi[21] and McKinney and Swartz[22] reveal persistent challenges and underrepresentation of disabled students in higher education, emphasising the need for further data disaggregation and analysis. Additionally, researchers such as Makuyana,[23] Mutanga[24] and Ndlovu[25] highlight gaps in inclusive education support systems and curricula development, suggesting a need for comprehensive reforms to enhance educational success among learners with disabilities in South Africa.

Employment

Article 27 of the Convention mandates states to ensure equal employment opportunities for persons with disabilities.[26] However, concerns arise regarding low employment rates, inadequate provision of reasonable accommodation, and the lack of statistical data on employed persons with disabilities.[27] The 23rd Commission for Employment Equity Report of 2022–2023 reveals that designated employers have employed only 1.3 per cent of persons with disabilities.[28]

Pillay, Raga and Taylor[29] investigated the practice of democratisation in South Africa's development, highlighting a slowed pace of transformation despite the country's diversity, which has historically been regarded as a strength. They emphasised the continued exclusion of persons with disabilities, undermining their contributions to effective organisational practices. Similarly, Ebrahim, Lorenzo and Kathard[30] examined employers' perspectives on disability-inclusive employment, revealing that the social capital of individuals with impairments is often overlooked during the hiring process. Organisational attitudes appear to prioritise compliance rather than recognising inclusivity's potential benefits and goals.[31] These challenges include difficulties in vagueness on reasonable accommodation provisions; societal and self-stigma; and thus, limitations in the Employment Equity Act of 1998.

Entrepreneurship

The United Nations General Assembly acknowledges entrepreneurship as crucial for job creation, economic growth, innovation, inequality reduction and social cohesion.[32] While many member states lack policies fulfilling obligations under Article 27 of the Convention,[33] South Africa has implemented a 7 per cent procurement quota for small and medium enterprises (SMEs) owned by persons with disabilities. However, limited research makes its precise effectiveness uncertain.[34] Maziriri and Madinga[35] conducted a qualitative study revealing challenges faced by entrepreneurs with disabilities in South Africa, including education and training gaps, limited access to finance and inadequate government support.[36] They recommended integrating need-based entrepreneurship support into South Africa's policies and practices.

On the other hand, the effectiveness of the Preferential Procurement Policy Framework Act of 2000 in supporting entrepreneurs with disabilities lacks clarity, and no studies have been found to confirm its impact. While government departments, districts and local municipalities have dedicated disability desks, there is limited support for developmental initiatives such as protective workshops, which the Department of Social Development funds through a subsidy system.[37] Brynard emphasises that successful disability programmes hinge on adequate funding, which is lacking from both the government and the private sector. Despite a commendable policy framework, South Africa's implementation plan needs to be revised.[38]

Social protection

Section 27 of the South African Bill of Rights guarantees access to social security and assistance, mandating the state to enact appropriate measures to fulfil these rights.[39] Since 2013, South African youths with albinism have urged the Department of Social Development (DSD) to establish eligibility criteria for a childcare dependency grant aimed at providing support for children with albinism up to age 18. This grant would assist impoverished families in obtaining essential items like sunscreen and adequate eye care. However, existing literature lacks evidence to confirm whether this initiative has been implemented.[40]

Article 28 of the Convention on Adequate Standard of Living and Social Protection[41] advocates aligning social assistance with disability costs for persons with disabilities and their families. However, persons with disabilities face challenges accessing social grants, leading to financial strain in meeting daily expenses.[42] Studies commissioned by the Department of Women, Youth and Persons with Disabilities in 2015 and 2021 highlight the financial burden on households with a family member with a disability, demonstrating potential savings if support systems covered disability-related costs. While social grants may mitigate indirect costs, such as loss of household income, additional expenses persist for parents or caregivers of children with disabilities and adults with disabilities themselves. Hence, social grants alone cannot fully address disability-related costs, necessitating comprehensive support systems to achieve household and national cost savings.

Accessibility

South Africa's commitment to ensuring equal access for persons with disabilities aligns with the principles of the Convention. The White Paper emphasises access to physical environments, transportation, information and other facilities for individuals with disabilities in urban and rural areas.[43] To enforce these standards, the South African Bureau of Standards was tasked with developing universal design access standards applicable to all public- and private-sector institutions, with ongoing monitoring and compliance.[44] Despite these efforts, there is a lack of accessibility laws and strategies, and meaningful participation of persons with disabilities in developing and monitoring accessibility solutions remains deficient.[45] However, in 2021, progress was seen when South Africa introduced the national strategic framework on universal design, marking a significant step forward in addressing accessibility issues.[46]

Built environment

Article 9 of the Convention on Accessibility mandates that states ensure equal access to the physical environment for people with disabilities.[47] However, Mckinney and Amosun[48] contend that despite this, the built environment still inadequately caters to the accessibility needs of individuals with disabilities, leading to feelings of dependence and disempowerment. Jackson[49] adds that practitioners often lack an understanding of accessibility and fail to consider diverse needs. Article 19 of the Convention emphasises independent living and community participation,[50] yet Fransolet[51] highlights a correlation between poor planning and inaccessibility, especially in low-cost housing where universal design principles are overlooked. Part S of the National Building Regulations and Building Standards Act, 1977, has historically been the most effective regulatory measure for enhancing facility accessibility in the country.[52] Part S of 2011 thus addresses physical access but needs to be more widely enforced, leading to a lack of awareness and implementation.[53] Consequently, built environment practitioners need to engage in dialogue with disabled individuals to co-create and improve awareness of accessibility needs. Fransolet[54] suggests incorporating universal design requirements into local tender processes to improve their application in public low-cost housing. Monama[55] also stresses the importance of state-owned buildings complying with accessibility mandates to uphold the rights of individuals with disabilities.

Transport

South African disability policy mandates integrating universal design and access into all transport licences and permits, alongside conducting transport access audits.[56] This requirement aligns with the 2022 White Paper on National Transport Policy, which aims to prioritise the needs of persons with disabilities in the planning and design of new transport infrastructure and operations.[57]

Chakwizira, Bikam and Adeboyejo[58] investigated transportation access and challenges faced by individuals with disabilities, particularly concerning public transport. They found that despite efforts, persons with disabilities still encounter difficulties in being included in transportation systems. These findings align with the conclusions of Duri and Luke,[59] who emphasise the systemic challenges faced by people with disabilities in commuting, spanning strategic, policy and operational realms. Additionally, Vanderschuren and Nnene[60] attribute the isolation experienced by persons with disabilities to a lack of understanding of their needs, leading to reduced trip-making. Comparatively, individuals with disabilities travel significantly less per week, ranging from 27.2 per cent to 65.8 per cent, compared to non-disabled individuals. This study stresses the importance of disability-inclusive planning and actions to address the isolation challenges. Municipalities are urged to play a pivotal role to enhance the quality of life for persons with disabilities by conducting and reporting transport accessibility audits for continuous improvement.

In May 2023, the South African Human Rights Commission received a complaint from the Johannesburg High Court, forwarded by the Transport User's Group of Persons with Disabilities South Africa (TUGSA), regarding the accessibility of buses, trains and taxis for individuals with disabilities. They alleged that the current conditions at transportation hubs pose safety risks to disabled commuters, constituting unfair discrimination based on disability. No outcomes were reached on this matter when drafting this article.

Access to information and communication

In line with Article 9 of the Convention, South Africa must take appropriate steps to enable accessible information and communications, including related systems, technologies and other services open or provided to the public in urban and rural areas.[61] Activities include sign language, provision of captioning on television programmes, development and regulation of Braille standards, and provision of access to print mediums for persons with print disabilities.[62]

Ayaya, Makoelle and Van der Merwe[63] investigated the implementation of inclusion in schools, advocating for a comprehensive framework extending from Early Childhood Development (ECD) through tertiary education. They highlighted concerns regarding the adequacy of teacher training and accessibility of information, as outlined by the United Nations Committee observations.[64] However, noteworthy is that in response to activism by disability organisations, the National Assembly (NA) subsequently approved an amendment of section 6 of the Constitution, and enacted South African Sign Language (SASL) as an official language in July 2023.[65]

Furthermore, challenges persist, as emphasised by section 32 of the South African Constitution, which underscores the right to access information. This is exemplified by the call for ratification of the Marrakesh Treaty by section 27 in 2023, which aims to address the "book famine" for visually impaired individuals. Despite constitutional rulings, progress remains stagnant, with less than 0.5 per cent of books accessible in South Africa.

South Africans witnessed other advocacy activities, including when the National Council of and for Persons with Disabilities (NCPD) challenged the validity of the Independent Communications Authority South Africa (ICASA) Code for Persons with Disabilities Regulations of 2021 in the High Court, Pretoria, arguing for mandatory open captioning and subtitles on television broadcasts in South Africa. ICASA's regulations require closed captioning and subtitles but do not mandate open captioning. NCPD contends that the absence of open captioning limits accessibility for individuals with hearing loss, particularly those who do not use sign language. They advocate for universal principles, highlighting the broader population benefitting from subtitles. The case against ICASA was heard on 9 November 2023.[66] These advocacy activities that result in protests and legal steps are an indication of the level of frustration experienced by South Africans with disabilities on various inclusion matters despite the examples identified above.

Independent living

In collaboration with Japanese development agency funding, the Department of Social Development (DsD) established an Independent Living Centre (ILC) in 2013.[67] South African activists received training in Japan, visited Japanese ILCs, and engaged with movement pioneers.[68] Subsequently, a South African study on the economic costs of disability by the Department of Women, Youth, and Persons with Disabilities revealed that the leaders of the ILC reported they had succeeded in arranging financial support from the DsD to employ personal assistants, aligning with Pillar Three of the White Paper.[69] Despite progress, individuals with disabilities still face additional costs hindering independent living.[70]

Informal care by family members, though cost-effective, imposes burdens on caregivers, leading to various issues, including post-traumatic stress disorder and emotional distress.[71] Recommendations highlight the role of social workers in addressing caregiver burdens and concerns.[72]

Concerns persist regarding the need to revise legislation such as the Older Persons Act (2006) and address issues in mental healthcare, institutionalisation and staff training.[73] Challenges to independent living include inaccessible transport and spaces, which can potentially lead to social isolation and depression.[74]

Concerns through media tracking within the disability custodian department

After extensive advocacy from the disability rights movements, the then president of the country announced the relocation of the disability unit from DsD to the Presidency, signalling that he heard their cries, and subsequently inaugurated the Presidential Working Group on Disability, as experts from the disability rights commission who, through the newly formed department, would work together and provide policy advice to the president on the fast-tracking of implementation of the policy directives. With concerns raised in the literature above on progress towards inclusion of persons with impairment, one cannot help but consider probing into the affairs of the custodian department. Within the department,[75] matters on disability are located within programme five (in some documents referred to as programme four), known as the Rights of Persons with Disabilities. Through media articles and the Portfolio Committee (PC) of Parliament's discussions, the following cases came to light:

Case one: Human resource optimisation and capacity of the disability unit

In December 2019, the position of the Deputy Director-General: Rights of Persons with Disabilities was advertised, aiming "to provide strategic leadership, coordination, and oversight for the effective implementation of the White Paper, inclusive of international treaties which advocate for the rights of persons with disabilities". One can deduce that the position was planned and budgeted for informed by need; however, according to the PC meeting recordings, there had been an internal Deputy Director-General (DDG) who was then introduced to the Rights of Persons with Disabilities programme. However, shortly after that, that was not the case; thus, this DDG is still on the payroll with no specific portfolio. The committee shared concerns about the lack of optimisation of available human resources.[76]

Case two: Economic empowerment of persons with disabilities

According to the *City Press*,[77] the position of the Chief Director was advertised and awarded to the then-wife of the Director, who was already working for the department. Allegations of irregularities led to an investigation by the Public Service Committee (PSC), which was said to have found no irregularities in the appointment.[78] However, at a later date, the PC requested findings of the internal audit to be presented, and they revealed that the said candidate should have been disqualified at the pre-screening phase and that a more qualified candidate who is a person with a disability should have been considered. In light of that presentation, the PC requested further investigations which, at the date of writing this article, the author had not found any new information on despite the latest one highlighted in the figure below as an excerpt of the concluding remarks of the audit report stating that it was not clear why affirmative action was not applied in this scenario as one candidate with a disability possessed the qualifications and relevant experience as opposed to the appointed candidate. The report presents a former case where affirmative action was applied to substantiate this point.[79]

Case three: Questionable reporting

The department's Annual Performance Plans (APPs) have historically lacked input from the disability rights movement, potentially leading to recurring issues. The Annual Reports of 2019/20, 2020/21 and 2021/22 highlight the development of various frameworks without any apparent deviations.[80] These frameworks, such as reasonable accommodation and self-representation, have been consistently reported as achievements. However, suspicions arise regarding the repetition of these accomplishments, as the frameworks were initially drafted when the disability programme was under the Department of Social Development before 2019. This concern was raised in parliamentary committee meetings in February 2021 and May 2012,[81] where it was noted that frameworks reported on were awaiting approval despite being developed.[82] This raises questions about whether the department continuously presents the exact deliverables as achieved without actual progress or deviations.[83]

Conclusion

South Africa shows advancements in disability inclusion through policy development yet faces challenges in implementation, leading to the perpetuating exclusion of persons with disabilities. Obstacles include inadequate socio-economic evidence and statistics, unclear recognition of poverty-disability connections, government and private sector accountability deficits, and ineffective policy enforcement. While the slogan "nothing about us without us" communicates that no decisions regarding individuals with impairments should be made on their behalf without their involvement, this notion is yet to be realised.

This paper concludes that there are observable milestones. However, both the UN Committee on the Rights of Persons with Disabilities and scholars' evaluations raised concerns of poor disability-inclusive planning in government, their agencies and private sectors for effective implementation of disability policy.

Through its policy, the department values evidence-based policy, informed by rigorous research, reliable data and analytical skills, rather than ideology, anecdotes and intuitions. This is aligned with the call of the Convention's Article 31 on data collection, which requires member states to collect appropriate information and research data to ensure the effective implementation of policies. This can be achieved through collaborations with disability organisations and their affiliates as the go-to organisations with a vast network of rights holders. Because of that, they have access to up-to-date data, which positions them well to support the implementation of this article for accuracy and evidence-based policy and programme development. The department must comprehend the capacity of non-profit organisations (NPOs) to manage substantial data effectively, given their reliance on funding, often with specific focus areas for disbursement.[84] While data may be available, lacking resources for synthesis and analysis hinders operationalisation. To address this, the department's Monitoring and Research budget could support NPOs in processing data for usability and informing policymaking. Presently, data collection methods rely on templates from various departments, neglecting input from persons with disabilities, as emphasised by the Convention. Inadequate resource mobilisation and budget allocation pose significant barriers to disability inclusion in humanitarian efforts, necessitating deliberate resource allocation.

This chapter emphasises the importance of addressing persistent issues faced by individuals with disabilities in South Africa, not to undermine progress made through advocacy efforts of persons with disabilities and related organisations, but as a plea for action and urgent intervention to ensure inclusive policies are effectively implemented. They highlight the need to uphold the Constitution's principles of eliminating discrimination, which remains prevalent among people with impairments. Furthermore, the passage underscores the compounded challenges faced by youth, women and black individuals with impairments, calling for duty-bearers to acknowledge and address these intersecting barriers.

References

Ayaya, G., Makoelle, T.M. and Van der Merwe, M. 2021. 'Developing a framework for inclusion: A case of a full-service school in South Africa'. *International Journal of Qualitative Studies in Education*, pp 1–19.

Brynard, P.A. 2010. 'Challenges of implementing a disability policy'. University of Pretoria.

Chakwizira, J., Bikam, P. and Adeboyejo, T.A. 2021. 'Access and constraints to commuting for persons with disabilities in Gauteng Province, South Africa'. In *Urban Inclusivity in Southern Africa* edited by H.H. Magidimish-Chipungu and L. Chipungu, pp 347–394. Springer, Cham.

City Press. 2020. 'Directors wife gets a top job meant for the disabled'. https://www.news24.com/citypress/news/directors-wife-gets-top-job-meant-forthe-disabled-20201108

Constitution of the Republic of South Africa 1996.

Darry, K., Walter, A. and Knupp, H. 2010. 'Attitudes and perceptions towards disability and sexuality'. *Disability and Rehabilitation*, 32(14):1148–1155.

Department of Labour. 2023. *23rd Commission for Employment Equity (CEE) Annual Report 2022/2023*. Pretoria: Department of Labour.

Department of Social Development. 2016. *White Paper on the Rights of Persons with Disabilities*. Pretoria: Department of Social Development.

Department of Transport. 2022. *White Paper on National Transport Policy*. Pretoria: Department of Transport.

Duri, B. and Luke, R. 2022. 'The structural barriers to universally accessible transport: the Tshwane (ZAF) metropolitan area study case'. *International Journal of Transport Development and Integration*, 6(4):428–442.

DWYPD. 2021. *Annual Report*. Pretoria: Department of Women Youth and Persons with Disabilities.

DWYPD. 2020. *Annual Report*. Pretoria: Department of Women Youth and Persons with Disabilities.

DWYPD. 2021. *Study on the Elements and Economic Costs of Disability for Children with Disabilities and Persons with Physical Disabilities in South Africa, Part 2*. Commissioned by the and the Department of Women, Children and People with Disabilities.

DWYPD. 2023. www.dwypd.gov.za. Department of Women Youth and Persons with Disabilities.

DWYPD. 2015. *Elements of the Financial and Economic Costs of Disability to Households in South Africa: A pilot study – Part one.* Commissioned by UNICEF and the Department of Women, Children and People with Disabilities.

DWYPD and UNDP. 2022. *The Elements And Economic Costs Of Disability For Children With Disabilities And Persons With Physical Disabilities In South Africa.* Commissioned by UNDP and the Department of Women, Youth and Persons with Disabilities.

Ebrahim, A., Lorenzo, T. and Kathard, H. 2022. 'Traversing disability: Employers' perspectives of disability inclusion. *Disabilities,* 2(2):317–329.

Fish Hodgson, T. 2018. 'The right to inclusive education in South Africa: Recreating disability apartheid through failed inclusion policies'. *South African Law Journal,* 135(3):461–501.

Fransolet, C. 2016. 'Mobile app to assess universal access compliance'. In *Universal Design 2016: Learning from the Past, Designing for the Future.* Amsterdam: IOS Press, pp 642–651.

Fransolet, C.G.C. 2015. *Universal design for low-cost housing in South Africa: An exploratory study of emerging socio-technical issues.* Cape Peninsula University of Technology.

Gov.za. 2013. News/Media Statements. https://www.gov.za/news/media-statements/youth-albinism-make-passionate-plea-equal-opportunity-13-may-2013 (accessed 2023).

Grobbelaar-du Plessis, I. and Njau, J.J. 2019. 'Payday: Business as usual or a new dawn rising for persons with disabilities in the workplace'. *De Jure Law Journal,* 52(1):267–294.

Jackson, M. 2018. 'Models of disability and human rights: Informing the improvement of built environment accessibility for people with disability at neighbourhood scale?', *Laws,* 7(1):10.

Japan International Corporation Agency. 2013. 'Japanese NGO has started three-year project with two South African NGOs in Johannesburg'. https://www.jica.go.jp/southafrica/english/activities/c8h0vm00005zn0hv-att/activities01_07.pdf.

Koon, L.M., Remillard, T.E., Mitzner, L.T. and Rogers, A.W. 2020. 'Ageing concerns, challenges, and everyday solution strategies (ACCESS) for adults ageing with a long-term mobility disability'. *Disability and Health*, 13(4):100936.

Makuyana, T. 2022. 'Towards interventions on school dropouts for disabled learners amidst and post-COVID-19 pandemic'. *African Journal of Disability,* 11, 1009.

Maphosa, N. and Chiwanza, V. 2021. 'Caregiver experiences and the perceived role of social workers in caring for people with disabilities in South Africa'. *African Journal of Social Work,* 11(3):155–163.

Marsay, G. 2014. 'Success in the workplace: From the voice of (dis)abled to the voice of enabled'. *African Journal of Disability,* 3(1):1–10.

Maziriri, E.T. and Madinga, N.W. 2016. 'A qualitative study on the challenges faced by entrepreneurs living with physical disabilities within the Sebokeng Township of South Africa'. *International Journal of Research,* 1.

McKinney, E.L. and Swartz, L. 2022. 'Integration into higher education: Experiences of disabled students in South Africa'. *Studies in Higher Education,* 47(2):367–377.

McKinney, V. and Amosun, S.L. 2020. 'Impact of lived experiences of people with disabilities in the built environment in South Africa'. *African Journal of Disability,* 9(1):1–11.

Monama, N. 2017. *Department of Public Works compliance with measures for disabled access in public buildings.* Johannesburg: Wits University Press.

Mukwevho, M.H. and Gadisi, A. 2021. 'Perceptions of students with disabilities on reasonable accommodation at a tertiary education: A case of a rural university in Limpopo Province, South Africa. *Journal of Intellectual Disability-Diagnosis and Treatment,* 9(6):592–600.

Muller-Kluits, N. and Slabbert, I. 2020. 'The role of social workers in addressing caregiver burden in families of persons with disabilities'. *South African Health Review,* 2020(1):137–145.

Muruzi, Y.L. and Gutura, P. 2022. 'The Vulnerability to Violence among Women with Physical Disabilities in the City of Tshwane Pretoria, South Africa'. *African Journal of Gender, Society & Development,* 11(3):85.

Mutanga, O. 2019. 'Disability models or approaches'. In *Students with Disabilities and the Transition to Work,* London: Routledge, pp 41–50.

Ndlovu, S. 2019. 'Access into professional degrees by students with disabilities in South African higher learning: A decolonial perspective'. *African Journal of Disability,* 8(1):1–12.

Ndlovu, S. 2021. 'Provision of assistive technology for students with disabilities in South African higher education'. *International Journal of Environmental Research and Public Health*, 18(8):3892.

Neille, J. and Penn, C. 2017. 'The interface between violence, disability, and poverty: stories from a developing country'. *Journal of Interpersonal Violence*, 32(18):2837–2861.

Nzo, Z., Makuyana, T., Yabunaga, C. and Pretorius, L. 2023. 'Disability and aging: A literature review on advocacy and activism for sustainable and resilient community living'. *Handbook of Disability: Critical Thought and Social Change in a Globalizing World*, pp 1–24.

Parliament. 2023. https://www.parliament.gov.za/press-releases/na-approves-south-african-sign-language-12th-official-nguage

Pather, S. 2011 'Evidence on inclusion and support for learners with disabilities in mainstream schools in South Africa: Off the policy radar?' *International Journal of Inclusive Education*, 15(10):1103–1117, DOI: 10.1080/13603116.2011.555075.

Pather, S. 2019. 'Confronting inclusive education in Africa since Salamanca'. *International Journal of Inclusive Education*, 23(7–8):782–795.

Pillay, S., Raga, K. and Taylor, D. 2015. *Towards an inclusive South African state: The role of equality and human rights in promoting equal opportunities for persons with disabilities in the workplace.* Department of Public Management and Leadership Nelson Mandela Metropolitan University Port Elizabeth.

PMG. 2023a. *Portfolio Committee Meeting.* https://pmg.org.za/committeemeeting/34383.

PMG. 2023b. *Portfolio Committee Meeting Video Recording.* https://www.youtube.com/watch?v=NezDVKirSC0

Richardson, G. 2012. 'Mental disabilities and the law: From substitute to supported decision-making?' *Current Legal Problems*, 65(1), pp 333–354. https://doi.org/10.1093/clp/cus010

SAHRC. 2017. *Disability Toolkit: A quick reference guide and monitoring framework.* SAHRC.

SAHRC. 30 September 2022. Media Statement: *SAHRC seminal*

establishment of the Disability Advisory Committee. SAHRC.

SAHRC. 2022. *Annual Report*. SAHRC. https://www.sahrc.org.za/home/21/files/SAHRC%20Annual%20Report%202023%20-%2004March2024.pdf (accessed 2023).

SAHRC. 17 November 2023. 'Media Advisory: SAHRC Gauteng Provincial Office to conduct an Investigation Inquiry into the Accessibility of Public Transport in Gauteng for People with Disabilities'. https://www.sahrc.org.za/index.php/sahrc-media/news-2/item/3792-media-advisory-sahrc-gauteng-provincial-office-to-conduct-an-investigation-inquiry-into-the-accessibility-of-public-transport-in-gauteng-for-people-with-disabilities (accessed 2023).

SAHRC. 2023. *Focus Area: Disability*. sahrc.org.za:https://www.sahrc.org.za/index.php/focus-areas/disability-older-persons/disability (accessed 2023).

Section 27. 20 June 2023. 'Blind SA and section 27 marched to urge the South African government to ratify the Marrakesh Treaty'. https://section27.org.za/2023/06/blind-sa-and-section27-march-to-urge-the-south-african-government-to-ratify-the-marrakesh-treaty/

The Citizen. 9 November 2023. The case against Icasa on behalf of the disability sector is to be heard in Pretoria today'.

The Conversation. 16 March 2021. 'South African study gives insights into the sexual health needs of people with disabilities'. https://theconversation.com/south-african-study-gives-insights-into-sexual-health-needs-of-people-with-disabilities-156324

The Presidency. 2016. *President Zuma convenes the first meeting*. https://www.thepresidency.gov.za/pressstatements/president-zuma-convenes-first-meeting-presidential-working-groupdisability?_escaped_fragment_=slider&page=37

Trialogue. 2023. *The Trialogue Business in Society Handbook 2023*.

Truter, L. 2016. 'All talk, talk, talk…: Transforming disabilities'. *TFM Magazine*, 2(7):50–53.

United Nations. 2006. *Convention on the Rights of Persons with Disabilities and Optional Protocol*. Geneva: United Nations.

United Nations. 2018. *Concluding observations on the initial report of South Africa*. Geneva: United Nations.

United Nations. 2022. *Conference of State Parties to the Convention on the Rights of Persons with Disabilities*. New York: United Nations.

Van der Heijden, I., Abrahams, N. and Harries, J. 2019. 'Additional layers of violence: The intersections of gender and disability in the violence experiences of women with physical disabilities in South Africa'. *Journal of Interpersonal Violence,* 34(4): 826–847. https://doi.org/10.1177/0886260516645818

Vanderschuren, M.J. and Nnene, O.A. 2021. 'Inclusive planning: African policy inventory and South African mobility case study on the exclusion of persons with disabilities'. *Health Research Policy And Systems,* 19(1):1–12.

White, R.M., Bornman, J., Johnson, E., Tewson, K. and Van Niekerk, J. 2020. 'Transformative equality: Court accommodations for South African citizens with severe communication disabilities'. *African Journal of Disability* (Online), 9:1–12.

White, R. and Msipa, D. 2018. 'Implementing Article 13 of the Convention on the Rights of Persons with Disabilities in South Africa: Reasonable accommodations for persons with communication disabilities'. *African Disability Rights Yearbook*, 6:99–120.

Wiesel, I., Smith, E., Bigby, C., Then, S.N., Douglas, J. and Carney, T. 2022. 'The temporalities of supported decision-making by people with cognitive disability'. *Social & Cultural Geography*, 23(7). https://openknowledge.worldbank.org/handle/10986/27711 License: CC BY 3.0 IGO

World Health Organization (WHO) and World Bank. 2011. *World Report on Disability*. Geneva: WHO. http://whqlibdoc.who.int/publications/2011/9789240685215_eng.pdf (accessed 20 December 2022).

Notes

Chapter 2

1   S. Dubow, *The African National Congress* (Johannesburg: Jonathan Ball Publishers, 2000), p 51.

2   Dubow, *The African National Congress*, p 51.

3   African National Congress African National Congress, 'Ready to govern: ANC policy guideline for a democratic South Africa', 1992.

4   African National Congress, 'Ready to Govern'.

5   H. Marais, *South Africa: Limits to Change: The Political Economy of Transition* (Cape Town: University of Cape Town Press, 1998), p 91.

6   See Interim Constitution, Schedule 4: Constitutional Principles of the 1993 Interim Constitution, pp 244–249.

7   Marais, *South Africa*, p 92.

8   Marais, *South Africa*, p 94.

9   Ibid.

10   A. Adelzadeh, 'Why is the South African economy stuck in chronic crises?', 2022. Applied Development Research Solutions Working Paper, May.

11   Adelzadeh, 'Why is the South African economy stuck in chronic crisis?', p 148.

12   SA Reserve Bank figures (June 1995), calculated in 1990 constant prices.

13   Marais, *South Africa*.

14   Marais, *South Africa*, p 149.

15   Marais, *South Africa*, p 192.

16   Ibid.

17   Ibid.

18   Ibid.

19   S. Gelb, 'The RDP, GEAR and all that: Reflections ten years later', *Transformation*, 62(2006).

20   Gelb, 'The RDP'.

21   T. Mbeki, 'Statement at opening of debate in National Assembly on

"Reconciliation and Nation-Building"', 1998, Republic of South Africa.

22   S. Akojee and S. McGrath, 'Post-basic education and training and poverty reduction in South Africa: Progress to 2004 and Vision to 2014', Post-basic Education and Training Working Paper Series, No. 2, October 2005, Centre for African Studies, University of Edinburgh.

23   R.M. Mthethwa, 'New growth path and the transformations of the ANC government policy', *New Agenda, South African Journal of Social and Economic Policy*, 43.Third Quarter(2011), p 32.

24   Mthethwa, 'New growth path', p 32.

25   Ibid.

26   A. Jeffery, *Chasing the Rainbow: South Africa's Move from Mandela to Zuma* (Johannesburg: South African Institute of Race Relations, 2010), p 248.

27   D. Monyae, 'The liberation movement's conception of the pre-1994 South African state', 2011, Paper presented at Mapungubwe Institute for Strategic Reflection (MISTRA), Woodmead, Johannesburg.

28   Akojee and McGrath, 'Post-basic education and training and poverty reduction in South Africa', p 5.

29   Ibid.

30   The Presidency, Green Paper: National Strategic Planning, 2009, Pretoria, South Africa, p 2.

31   The Presidency, Green Paper, p 4.

32   Mthethwa, 'New growth path', p 34.

33   N. Nattrass, 'The new growth path: Game changing vision or cop-out?' 2011, School of Economics, University of Cape Town, p 1.

34   National Planning Commission, National Development Plan, 2012, launch speech by Trevor Manuel, 15 August.

35   National Planning Commission, National Development Plan.

36   Ibid.

37   Adelzadeh, 'Why is the South African economy stuck in chronic crises?'

38   Ibid.

39   Ibid.

40   Ibid.

41   Ibid.

42   Ibid.

43   Ibid.

44   Ibid.

45   Statistics South Africa 2022, in Adelzadeh, 'Why is the South African economy stuck in chronic crises?'

46   Adelzadeh, 'Why is the South African economy stuck in chronic crises?'

Chapter 3

1   Charmaine L. Wijeyesinghe, Pat Griffin and Barbara Love, 'Racism-Curriculum Design', in *Teaching for Diversity and Social Justice* edited by Maurianne Adams, Lee Anne Bell and Pat Griffin (New York and London: Routledge, 1997).

2   F. Bou Zeineddine and C.W. Leach, 'Feeling and thought in collective action on social issues: Toward a systems perspective'. *Social and Personality Psychology Compass*, 15.7(2021), Article e12622. https://doi.org/10.1111/spc3.12622

3   Bou Zeineddine and Leach, 'Feeling and thought in collective action on social issues'.

4   A. Toivonen and T. Seremani, 'The enemy within: The legitimating role of local managerial elites in the global managerial colonization of the Global South', *Organization*, 28.5(2021):798–816.

5   Toivonen and Seremani, 'The enemy within'.

6   P. Wolfe, 'Settler Colonialism and the Elimination of the Native', *Journal of Genocide Research*, 8.4(2006).

7   T. Nkosi and N. Mahlako, 'Are courts going out of their way to accommodate racists? A critique of *South African Revenue Service v Commission for Conciliation, Mediation and Arbitration and Others*', *Law, Democracy and Development*, 24(2020).

8   Nkosi and Mahlako, 'Are the courts going out of their way to accommodate racists?'.

9   Ibid.

10   Rianna Oelofsen, 'Decolonisation of the African mind and intellectual landscape', *Phronimon*, 16.2(2015).

11   Oelefsen, 'Decolonisation of the African mind', p 134.

12   Wijeyesinghe, Griffin and Love, 'Racism-Curriculum Design'.

13   C. Jeske, 'Why work? Do we understand what motivates work-related decisions in South Africa?' *Journal of Southern African Studies*, 44.1(2018): 31.

14   Statistics South Africa, 'Inequality trends in South Africa: A multidimensional diagnostic of inequality, 2019', p 26. http://www.StatsSA.gov.za/publications/Report-03-10-19/Report-03-10-192017.pdf

15   Statistics South Africa, 'Inequality trends in South Africa', p 27.

16   Human Rights Watch, 'South Africa: Submission to the UN Committee on the elimination of all forms of discrimination', 111th Session, 2023, p 18.

17   A. Chatterjee, L Czajka, and A. Gethin, 'Estimating the distribution of household wealth in South Africa', 2020, Wits University, p 1.

18   Vanessa Barolsky, '"A better life for all", social cohesion and the governance of life in post-apartheid South Africa', *Social Dynamics*, 38:1(2012):134–151.

19   A. Lemon and J. Battersby-Lennard, 'Overcoming the apartheid legacy in Cape Town schools', *Geographical Review*, 9.4(2009):520–521.

20   Socio-Economic Rights Institute of South Africa (SERI). 'Informal settlements and human rights in South Africa submission to the United Nations Special Rapporteur on adequate housing as a component of the right to an adequate standard of living', 2018, OHCHR.

21   SERI, 'Informal settlements and human rights'.

22   Department of Human Settlements, Annual Report 2019/2020.

23   Abahlali baseMjondolo/the Shack Dwellers Movement of South Africa,

Mourn Unfreedom Day Rally, 2014.

24   B. Mdlalose, 'Marikana shows that we are living in a democratic prison,' 22 September 2012. http://abahlali.org/node/9061/

25   'South Africa: UN experts condemn xenophobic violence and racial discrimination against foreign nationals', OHCHR, 2022.

26   Michael Neocosmos, 'From "foreign natives" to "native foreigners": Explaining xenophobia in post-apartheid South Africa' 2006, CODESRIA: Senegal, p vi.

27   D. Addae and K.P. Quan-Baffour, 'Afrophobia, "black on black" violence and the new racism in South Africa: The nexus between adult education and mutual co-existence', *Cogent Social Sciences*, 8.1(2022):1–13.

28   Institute for Justice and Reconciliation, South African Reconciliation Barometer Survey: 2021 Report, p 12.

29   M. Mamdani, 'Amnesty or impunity? A preliminary critique of the report of the Truth and Reconciliation Commission of South Africa (TRC)', *Diacritics* 32.3/4(2002); T. Madlingozi, 'Good victims, bad victims: Apartheid beneficiaries, victims and the struggle for social justice', in *Law, Memory & Apartheid: Ten Years after Azapo v President of South Africa*, edited by Wessel Le Roux and Karin van Marle (Pretoria: PULP, 2007).

30   C. Cathrine Byrne, *All that was lost: Apartheid violence: Thirty TRC participants speak* (Benoni: Sheron Printers, 2010).

31   K. Gillespie and L. Naidoo, 'Between the Cold War and the fire: The student movement, anti-assimilation, and the question of the future in South Africa', *South Atlantic Quarterly*, 118.1(2019):233.

32   S. Stuurman, 'Student activism in a time of a crisis in South Africa: The quest for "black power"', *South African Journal of Education*, 38.4(2018):2.

Chapter 4

1   Jacob Zuma, Statement of the National Executive Committee of the African National Congress read on the occasion of the 98th Anniversary of the ANC, 8 January 2008.

2   T. Mkandawire, 'Thinking about developmental states in Africa', *Cambridge Journal of Economics*, 25.3(2001):290.

3   Mkandawire, 'Thinking about developmental states in Africa', p 290.

4   P. Bond, 'South Africa's "developmental state" distraction', *Mediations*, 24.1(2008).

5   D. Ukwandu, 'South Africa as a developmental state: Is it a viable idea?' *African Journal of Public Affairs*, 11.2(2019).

6   R. Hendrickse, 'Towards a South African developmental state: The Electricity Supply Commission (Eskom) – victor or villain in this endeavour?' *International Journal of Research in Business and Social Science (2147–4478)*, 11.9(2022):289–299.

7   G. Mhone, *Organizational and Institutional Implications of a Developmental State*. Human Social Research Council paper (Pretoria: HSRC, 2004).

8   T. Mkandawire, 'Thinking about developmental states in Africa', *Cambridge*

Journal of Economics, 25.3(2001).

9   Education Training Unit, Community Organisers Toolbox, 2014, p 1.

10   Jacob Zuma, Address by His Excellency President Jacob Zuma on the occasion of the 5th anniversary of the adoption of the National Development Plan, Cape Town, 12 September 2017.

11   Education Training Unit, Community Organisers Toolbox.

12   S. McCorriston and D. MacLaren, 'Parastatals as instruments of government policy: The Food Corporation of India'. *Food Policy*, 65(2016):53–62.

13   Auditor-General's 2021 report cited in the Presidency Annual Report 2020–2021.

14   See Mhone, *Organizational and Institutional Implications of a Developmental State*; G. Motsaathebe, 'Journalism education and practice in South Africa and the discourse of the African Renaissance', *Communicatio: Journal of Communication Theory and Research*, 37.3(2011); V. Gumede, 'Policy making in South Africa'. In *South African Government and Politics*, 4th Edition, edited by C. Landsberg and A. Venter (Pretoria: Van Schaik, 2011).

15   Mhone, *Organizational and Institutional Implications of a Developmental State*.

16   Motsaathebe, 'Journalism education and practice in South Africa'.

17   D.J. Teece, 'Business Models, Business Strategy and Innovation', *Long Range Planning*, 43(2010):174.

18   B. Flyvbjerg, 'Five misunderstandings about case-study research', *Qualitative Inquiry*, 12.2(2006).

19   D. McLeod, 'SABC CEO Mokhobo resigns', 3 February 2014, *Mail & Guardian*.

20   H. Wasserman, 'EXPLAINER: How SAA landed in such a mess', 2020, News24.

21   Wasserman, 'How SAA landed in such a mess'.

22   L. Omarjee, 'Eskom's revolving door: 10 CEOs in 10 years', 2019, Fin24.

23   See eNCA, 'Eskom's CEO André de Ruyter resigns', 2023.

24   Omarjee, 'Eskom's revolving door'.

25   SA Government News Agency, 'Dr Kgosientsho Ramokgopa appointed Minister of Electricity in the Presidency', 6 March 2023.

26   Education Training Unit, Community Organisers Toolbox.

27   G. Motsaathebe and R. Rena, 'Towards an aggressive economic growth: Promoting entrepreneurship as a catalyst for development in the Global South with special reference to South Africa', a conference paper presented at a BRICS-SA conference held in Durban, South Africa, 3–6 April 2022.

28   R. May, 'Implementing a leadership development program for your business', *Journal of the Knowledge Economy*, IX(2014).

29   Ukwandu, 'South Africa as a Developmental State'.

Chapter 5

1   ANC, 'Adopted Strategy and Tactics of the ANC', 2007.

2   DPME, 'The Developmental State – An exploration of South Africa's National Development Plan, 2nd Draft'. Department of Planning, Monitoring and Evaluation: Research Unit, 2017.

3   National Planning Commission, 'National Development Plan 2030: Our future – make it work', 2012. Pretoria.

4   Johnson, Chalmers, *MITI and the Japanese Miracle: The growth of industrial policy. 1925–1975* (Stanford: Standford University Press, 1982).

5   G. White, ed., *Developmental States in East Asia* (Johannesburg: MacMillan, 1988).

6   R. Wade, *Governing the Market: Economic theory and the role of government in East Asian industrialisation* (Princeton, New Jersey: Princeton University Press, 1990); G. Rice Jones, 'A Beginner's Guide to the Developmental State', 2013.

7   G. Mhone, 'Organisational and Institutional Implications of a developmental state', 2004, Human Social Research Council paper. Pretoria: HSRC.

8   S.J. Mosala and J.C.M. Venter, 'South Africa's economic transformation since 1994: What influence has the National Democratic Revolution (NDR) had?' *The Review of the Black Political Economy*, 44(2017).

9   A. Habib, *South Africa's Suspended Revolution: Hopes and prospects* (Johannesburg: Wits University Press, 2013).

10 M. Gevisser, *Thabo Mbeki: The dream deferred* (Cape Town: Jonathan Ball Publishers, 2009).

11 Mosala and Venter, 'South African's economic transformation since 1994'.

12 Mosala and Venter, 'South African's economic transformation since 1994'; A. Jeffery, *Chasing the Rainbow: South Africa's move from Mandela to Zuma* (Johannesburg: South African Institute of Race Relations, 2010).

13 A. Hirsh, 'Global economic crisis hinders AsgiSA efforts', 2009.

14 V. Gumede, 'Policy making in South Africa', in *South African Government and Politics*, edited by C. Landsberg and A. Venter, 4th ed (Pretoria: Van Schaik, 2011); A. Habib, *South Africa's Suspended Revolution: Hopes and prospects* (Johannesburg: Wits University Press, 2013).

15 National Planning Commission, National Development Plan 2030: Our future – make it work, 2012, Pretoria.

16 Gumede, 'Policy making in South Africa',

17 V. Gumede, 'Public policy making in a post-apartheid South Africa: A preliminary perspective', *Africanus: Journal of Development Studies*, 38.2(2008).

18 Gumede, 'Public policy making in a post-apartheid South Africa'.

19 Gumede, 'Policy making in South Africa'.

20 Ibid.

21 Ibid.

22 Ibid.

23 Ibid.

24 Trade Economics, Singapore unemployment rate, 2023; Statista, Gini coefficient after taxes in Singapore from 2013 to 2022, 2023.

25 S. Sanith and A.J.R. Saravanakumar, 'The economic development of Singapore: A historical perspective'. *Aut Aut Research Journal*, XI.VII(2020):441–459; W. Gumede, 'What can the ANC learn from Singapore's People Action Party in remaking itself into an effective Developmental Party?' 2022, Occasional Paper – Inclusive Society Institute, Cape Town.

26 Sanith and Saravanakumar, 'The economic development of Singapore'; Gumede, 'What can the ANC learn from Singapore's People Action Party in remaking itself into an effective Developmental Party?'

27 Gumede, 'What can the ANC learn from Singapore's People Action Party in remaking itself into an effective Developmental Party?'

28 Ibid.

29 Sanith and Saravanakumar, 'The economic development of Singapore'; Gumede, 'What can the ANC learn from Singapore's People Action Party in remaking itself into an effective Developmental Party?'

30 K. Bercuson, 'Singapore. A Case Study in Rapid Development', 1995, International Monetary Fund.

31 Bercuson, 'Singapore. A Case Study in Rapid Development'; Gumede, 'What can the ANC learn from Singapore's People Action Party in remaking itself into an effective Developmental Party?'

32 Ibid.

33 Ibid.

34 Ibid.

35 Gumede, 'What can the ANC learn from Singapore's People Action Party in remaking itself into an effective Developmental Party?'

Chapter 6

1 NDP 2030, pp 392–393.

2 A. Faull and R. Rose, 'Professionalism and the South African Police Service: What is it and how can it help build safer communities?', 2012, ISS Africa.

3 S. Ndlovu, 'State Fragility as State Incapacity: The Case of Post-apartheid South Africa'. In D. Olowu and P. Chanies (eds) *State Fragility and State Building in Africa: Cases from Eastern and Southern Africa* (Germany: Springer, 2016) pp:61–87. https://www.researchgate.net/publication/300334510_State_Fragility_as_State_Incapacity_The_Case_of_Post-apartheid_South_Africa (accessed 20 February 2024).

4 G. Newham, T. Masuku and J. Dlamini, 'Diversity and transformation in the South African Police Service: A study of police perspectives on race, gender and the community in the Johannesburg policing area'. Criminal Justice Programme March 2006.

5 I. van Kessel, 'Transforming the South African Police Service (SAPS): The changing meaning of change'. Paper delivered at the South African Sociological Association congress, 1–4 July 2001.

6 Van Kessel, 'Transforming the South African Police Service'.

7 J.D. Brewer. *Black and Blue: Policing in South Africa* (Oxford: Clarendon Press, 1994).

8   Bouckaert et al. cited in P.O. Bello, 'Do people still repose confidence in the police? Assessing the effects of public experience of police corruption in South Africa', *African Identities*, 19.2(2021).

9   F.D. Boateng, 'Trust in the police: An analysis of urban cities in Ghana', 2015, doctoral dissertation. USA: Washington State University.

10   F.D. Boateng, 'Trust in the police: An analysis of urban cities in Ghana', 2015, doctoral dissertation, USA: Washington State University.

11   Boateng, 'Trust in the police'.

12   Public Service Commission, 'Building a capable, career-oriented and professional public service to underpin a capable and developmental sate in South Africa', 2016, discussion document.

13   *Staatskoerant*, 'A National Implementation Framework towards the Professionalisation of the Public Service', 2020, *Government Gazette*, p 42.

14   T. Mgweba, Framework Towards Professionalisation of the Public Sector, 2023, NSG, PSC & DPSA briefing.

Chapter 8

1   Ginger Thompson, 'THE SATURDAY PROFILE: In Grip of AIDS, South African Cries for Equity,' 10 May 2003, *The New York Times*, https://www.nytimes.com/2003/05/10/world/the-saturday-profile-in-grip-of-aids-south-african-cries-for-equity.html (accessed 23 August 2023).

2   Alexander Parker, *50 People Who Stuffed Up South Africa* (Kenilworth: Burnet Media, 2012), p 208.

3   Frantz Fanon, *The Wretched of the Earth* (New York: Grove Press, 2021), p 97.

4   Roshila Nair, 'Fanon's land', in *Nobody Ever Said AIDS: Poems and Stories from Southern Africa*, ed. Nobantu Rasebotsa et al. (Plumstead: Kwela Books, 2004), p 179.

5   Sayyed Mirenayat and Elaheh Soofastaei, 'Gérard Genette and the categorisation of textual transcendence,' *Mediterranean Journal of Social Sciences*, 6.5(2015):533.

6   Mirenayat and Soofastaei, 'Gérard Genette', p 534.

7   Ibid.

8   Gérard Genette and Marie Maclean, 'Introduction to the paratext', *New Literary History*, 22.2(1991):261.

9   Genette and Maclean, 'Introduction to the paratext', pp 261–262.

10   Genette and Maclean, 'Introduction to the paratext', p 267.

11   Genette and Maclean, 'Introduction to the paratext', p 269.

12   Elliot Ross, '"Fanon's no man's land": The difficult inheritance of anti-apartheid struggle in South Africa's HIV/AIDS literature', *Scrutiny2: Issues in English Studies in Southern Africa*, 18.2(2013):37.

13   Donald G. McNeil Jnr, 'Neighbors kill an H.I.V.-positive AIDS activist in South Africa,' 2 December 1998, *The New York Times*. https://www.nytimes.com/1998/12/28/world/neighbors-kill-an-hiv-positive-aids-activist-in-south-africa.html (accessed 18 August 2023).

14   Ross, '"Fanon's no man's land"', p 37.

15   Roshila Nair, 'Fanon's land', p 179.

16   Ibid.

17   Ibid.

18   Ibid.

19   Fanon, 'Medicine and Colonialism', in *A Dying Colonialism*, trans. Haakon Chevalier (New York City: Grove Press, 1967), p 139.

20   Fanon, *The Wretched of the Earth*, p x, xii.

21   Fanon, 'Medicine and Colonialism', p 121.

22   Ibid, p 126.

23   Ross, '"Fanon's no man's land"', 2013, p 39.

24   Ross, '"Fanon's no man's land"', p 41.

25   Roshila Nair, 'Fanon's land', p 179.

26   Fanon, *The Wretched of the Earth*, p 98.

27   Fanon, *The Wretched of the Earth*, p 112.

28   Fanon, *The Wretched of the Earth*, pp 105, 117.

29   Fanon, *The Wretched of the Earth*, p 113.

30   Roshila Nair, 'Fanon's land', p 179.

31   Fanon, *The Wretched of the Earth*, p 114.

32   Fanon, *The Wretched of the Earth*, p 1.

33   Fanon, *The Wretched of the Earth*, p 239.

34   Roshila Nair, 'Fanon's land', p 179.

35   Frantz Fanon, *Black Skin, White Masks* (London: Penguin Books, 2021), p 136.

36   Achille Mbembe, 'Frantz Fanon's *Ouvres*: A Metamorphic Thought', *Nka: Journal of Contemporary African Art*, 32(2013):15.

Chapter 10

1   Y. Rodny-Gumede, V. Milton and W. Mano, 'Rethinking the link between media and democracy in the post-colony: One size does not fit all', *Communicatio: South African Journal for Communication Theory and Research*, 43.2(2017).

2   K. Voltmer, 'The mass media and the dynamics of political communication in processes of democratization'. In *Mass Media and Political Communication in New Democracies*, edited by K. Voltmer (London: Routledge, 2006).

3   See Y. Rodny-Gumede, 'Questioning the media-democracy relationship: The case of South Africa', *Communicatio: South African Journal for Communication Theory and Research*, 43.2(2017a); Y. Rodny-Gumede, V. Milton and W. Mano, 'Rethinking the link between media and democracy in the post-colony: One size does not fit all'; H. Wasserman and A. Garman, 'The meanings of citizenship: Media use and democracy in South Africa', *Social Dynamics: A Journal of African Studies*, 40.2(2013); N. Couldry, 'Does "the media" have a future?', *European Journal of Communication*, 24.4(2009); P. Dahlgren and C. Sparks, eds. *Communication and Citizenship – Journalism and the Public Sphere* (London: Routledge, 1991).

4   Y. Rodny-Gumede, 'Expanding comparative media systems analysis from transitional to postcolonial societies', 2020, *International Communication Gazette*.

5   See TRC, Final report of the Truth and Reconciliation Commission of South Africa, Vol. 4, Chapter 6, Institutional Hearing on the Media (Cape Town: Juta, 1998).

6   Y. Rodny-Gumede, 'The centrality of media hearings to transitional justice processes', in *Limits to Transition: A critique of the TRC*, edited by Karen van Merle and Mia Swart (Leiden; Boston: Brill Nijhoff, 2017b).

7   Y. Rodny-Gumede, 'Transformation, fragmentation and decolonisation: The contested role of the media in postcolonial South Africa'. In *Political Communication as Decolonisation and Performance: Africa and the Diaspora*, edited by Beschara Karam and Bruce Mutsvairo (London: Routledge, 2021).

8   See G. Daniels, 'Glass ceilings: Cybermisogyny is a sign of unchecked sexism in the newsroom', in *Women Journalists in South Africa: Democracy in the age of social media*, edited by G. Daniels and K. Skinner (London: Palgrave Macmillan, 2022); Y. Rodny-Gumede, 'The triple oppressions: Race, class and gender in South African journalism', in *Women Journalists in South Africa: Democracy in the age of social media*, edited by G. Daniels and K. Skinner (London: Palgrave Macmillan, 2022); J. Reid, *New Concepts in Media Diversity: A view from South Africa* (Pretoria: UNISA Press, 2021).

9   See Daniels, 'Glass ceilings'; G. Daniels, T. Nyamweda, C. Nxumalo and B. Ludman, *Glass Ceilings: Women in South African media houses* (Johannesburg: Gender Links, 2018); C. Lowe Morna, *Glass Ceiling: Women in South African news media* (Johannesburg: Gender Links, 2018).

10   Rodny-Gumede, 'The triple oppressions'.

11   Rodny-Gumede, 'Transformation, fragmentation and decolonisation'.

12   Rodny-Gumede, 'Transformation, fragmentation and decolonisation'; H. Wasserman and A. Garman, 'The meanings of citizenship: Media use and democracy in South Africa', *Social Dynamics: A Journal of African Studies*, 40.2(2013).

13   T. Rodny-Gumede, 'Gender and public discourse formation in South Africa: Male and female journalists' influence on news agendas', *Communicatio: South African Journal for Communication Theory and Research*, 41.2(2015c):206–219.

14   C. Chasi and Y. Rodny-Gumede, 'Smash and grab, truth and dare', *International Communication Gazette*, 78.7(2016).

15   G. Daniels, *Fight for Democracy: The ANC and the media in South Africa* (Johannesburg: Wits University Press, 2012), p 1.

16   Daniels, 'Glass ceilings'; F. Haffajee, 'The hounding', in *Women Journalists in South Africa: Democracy in the age of social media*, edited by G. Daniels and K. Skinner (London: Palgrave Macmillan, 2022).

17   Daniels et al., *Glass Ceilings*; R. Shallom, 'Women in public-facing journalism jobs are exhausted by harassment', *Poynter* (2018, June 28).

18 Rodny-Gumede, 'Transformation, fragmentation and decolonisation'.

19 P.P. Frassinelli, 'Decolonisation: What it is and what research has to do with it', in *Making Sense of Research*, edited by K.G. Tomaselli (Pretoria: Van Schaik Publishers, 2018), p 4.

20 J. Duncan, *The Rise of the Securocrats: The case of South Africa* (Johannesburg: Jacana Media, 2014).

21 W. Gumede, *Restless Nation: Making sense of troubled times* (Cape Town: Tafelberg, 2012).

22 Daniels, 'Glass ceilings'.

Chapter 11

1 African Union, Agenda 2063 Vision and Priorities, 2013.

2 P. Evans, 'Constructing the 21st century developmental state: Potentials and pitfalls', in *Constructing a Democratic Developmental State in South Africa: Potentials and challenges*, edited by O. Edigheji (Cape Town: Human Sciences Research Council, 2010), pp 169–182.

3 T.J. Pempel, 'The developmental regime in a changing world economy, in *The Developmental State*, edited by M. Woo-Cumings (Ithaca: Cornell University Press, 1999), p 156.

4 G. Mills, O. Obasanjo, J. Herbst and D. Davis, *Making Africa Work: A handbook for economic success* (Cape Town: Tafelberg Publishers, 2017), p 31.

5 Evans, 'Constructing the 21st century development state', p 52; H. Marais, *South Africa Pushed to the Limit: The political economy of change* (Cape Town: Cape Town University Press, 2010), p 343.

6 E.I. Edoun, 'Decenralisation and local economic development: Effective tools for Africa's renewal'. *International Journal of African Renaissance Studies*, 7(2012):100.

7 B. Fine, 'Can South Africa be a developmental state?' in *Constructing a Democratic Developmental State in South Africa: Potentials and challenges*, edited by O. Edigheji (Cape Town: Human Sciences Research Council, 1963), p 173.

8 M. Bateman, 'Sustainable, equitable and decent job creation in South Africa: The crucial role of the "local developmental state"' (paper presented at the TIPS Conference on Economic Development for Employment: Sub-national strategies, Pretoria, 14–15 November 2016), p 6.

9 A.L Ahlers, 'Weaving the Chinese dream on the ground? Local government approaches to "new-typed" rural urbanisation', *Journal of Chinese Political Sciences*, 20(2015):121.

10 G. Schubert and T. Herberer, 'Continuity and change in China's "Local State Developmentalism"', *Issues and Studies*, 51(2015).

11 Schubert and Herberer, 'Continuity and change', p 3.

12 V. Chibber, 'The developmental states in retrospect and prospect: Lessons from India and South Korea', in *The End of Development*, edited by M. Williams (Pietermaritzburg: University of KwaZulu-Natal Press, 2014), p

34.

13 P. Smoke, 'Rethinking decentralisation: Assessing challenges to a popular public sector reform', *Public Administration and Development*, 35(2015):102.

14 V. Gumede, *Post-apartheid South Africa* (New York: Cambria Press, 2016).

15 African Union, Agenda 2063 Vision and Priorities, 2013. http://www.un.org/en/africa/osaa/pdf/au/agenda2063.pdf.

16 S. Steiner, 'How important is the capacity of local governments for improvements in welfare? Evidence from decentralised Uganda', *Journal of Development Studies*, 46(2010):644.

17 J.K. Kampen, 'On the (in)consistency of citizen and municipal level indicators of social capital and local government performance', *Social Indicators Research*, 97(2010).

18 T. Tsukamoto, 'Why is Japan neoliberalizing? Rescaling of the Japanese development state and ideology of state-capital fixing', *Journal of Urban Affairs*, 34(2012):396.

19 P. Reddy and J.M. Kauzya, 'Local government capacity in the Southern African Development Community (SADC) region', *Public Policy and Administration*, 14(2015):206.

20 S. Ó Riain, *The Politics of High-tech Growth: Developmental network states in the global economy* (Cambridge: Cambridge University Press, 2004), p 4.

21 F. Fanon, *The Wretched of the Earth* (New York: Penguin Books, 1963), p 159.

22 Edoun, 'Decenralisation and local economic development', 2012, p 100.

23 A. Saud and K.A. Khan, 'Decentralisation and local government structures: Key to strengthening democracy in Pakistan', *Journal of Political Studies*, 51(2016):397.

24 P. Smoke, 'Managing public sector decentralization in developing countries: Moving beyond conventional recipes', *Public Administration and Development*, 35(2015b):253.

25 A. Topal, 'Global processes and local consequences of decentralization: A sub-national comparison in Mexico', *Regional Studies*, 49(2015):1127.

26 L. Bruszt and B. Vedres, 'Associating, mobilizing, politicizing: Local developmental agency from without, *Theory and Society*, 42(2013):5.

27 T. Mkandawire, 'From maladjusted states to democratic developmental states in Africa', in *Constructing a Democratic Developmental State in South Africa: Potentials and challenges*, edited by O. Edigheji (Cape Town: Human Sciences Research Council, 2010).

28 See L. Routley, 'Developmental states in Africa? A review of on-going debates and buzzwords', *Development Policy Review*, 32(2014).

29 M.M. Prado, M. Schapiro and D.R. Coutinho, 'The dilemmas of the developmental state: Democracy and economic development in Brazil', *Law and Development Review*, 9(2016).

30 P. Bardhan, 'State and development: The need for a reappraisal of the

current literature', *Journal of Economic Literature*, 56(2016):874.

31 S. Plane, 'A view of a bureaucratic developmental state: Local governance and agricultural extension in rural Ethiopia', *Journal of Eastern African Studies*, 8(2014).

32 T. Tsukamoto, 'Why is Japan neoliberalizing? Rescaling of the Japanese developmental state and ideology of state-capital fixing', *Journal of Urban Affairs*, 34(2012):395.

Chapter 12

1   ANC, 'ANC international relations: A better Africa in a better and just world', 2015.

2   ANC, 'International relations discussion document', 2012.

3   M. Gomes da Costa, 'South Africa as a leading regional power in Africa? An analysis of the implementation of the African Union, AUDA-NEPAD and Agenda 2063'. Revista Brasileira de Política Internacional, 2023.

4   J.F. Clark, 'South Africa's reluctant and conflicted regional power'. *ASPJ Africa & Francophonie – 1st Quarter*, 2016.

5   ANC, 'ANC international relations: A better Africa in a better and just world', 2015.

6   Department of International Relations and Cooperation, 'Building a better world: The diplomacy of Ubuntu'. White Paper on South Africa's Foreign Policy, 2011.

7   S.M. Ndlovu, 'The African agenda and the origins of internationalism within the ANC: 1912–1960'. In *The Future We Chose: Emerging perspectives on the centenary of the ANC* edited by B. Ngcaweni (Africa Institute of South Africa, 2013).

8   Ndlovu, 'The African agenda and the origins of internationalism within the ANC', 2013.

9   ANC, 'Foreign policy perspective in a democratic South Africa', 1994.

10 Ibid.

11 The Spirit of Bandung. 'Address to the International Conference in Support of the Liberation Movements of Southern Africa and in Support of the Frontline States by O.R. Tambo, Lusaka, 10 April 1979'.

12 C. Hendricks and N. Majozi, 'South Africa's international relations: A new dawn?' *Journal of Asian and African Studies*, 56.1(2021):64–78.

13 Clark, 'South Africa's reluctant and conflicted regional power', 2016.

14 Ibid.

15 K. Sturman, 'Intervention in Africa? The Mbeki Presidency's role in changing the OAU', 2004.

16 African Union, Constitutive Act of the African Union.

17 Sturman, 'Intervention in Africa?', 2004.

18 Ibid.

19 Hendricks and Majozi, 'South Africa's international relations', 2021.

20 A. Tschudin and A. Trithart, 'The role of local governance in sustaining peace', 2018. International Peace Institute.

21 K. Annan, 'Address by Mr. Kofi Annan, Secretary-General of the United Nations to the opening of the fifty-fourth session of the Commission on Human Rights, 1998'.

22 South African Government, 'Remarks by Minister of Defence and Military Veterans, Ms Thandi Modise, on the occasion of the 6th United Nations Partnership for Technology in Peacekeeping Symposium', 2022.

23 T. Neethling, 'The SANDF as an instrument for peacekeeping in Africa: A critical analysis of three main challenges', *Journal for Contemporary History*, 36.1(2011):134–153.

24 Sturman, 'Intervention in Africa?', 2004.

25 D. Rilley-Harris, 'South African peacekeeping, 1994–2012', *Military History Journal*, 16(2013).

26 Rilley-Harris, 'South African peacekeeping', 2013.

27 K. Apuuli, 'The African Union and peacekeeping in Africa: Challenges and opportunities'. *Vestnik RUDN. International Relations*, 20.4(2020):667–677. DOI: 10.22363/2313-0660-2020-20-4-667-677

28 Rilley-Harris, 'South African peacekeeping'.

29 United Nations. 'Troop and police contributors', 2023.

30 Ndlovu, 'The African agenda and the origins of internationalism within the ANC'.

31 Clark, 'South Africa's reluctant and conflicted regional power', 2016.

32 J. Neal, 'Power-sharing as a form of democratic development in Zimbabwe and South Sudan', 2012. University of Guelph, Ontario, Canada.

33 B. Ngcaweni and B. Mayimele, 'BRICS: A building block towards pluriversality, *Journal of Latin American Studies*, 44(2023).

34 B. Mayimele, 'South Africa and China: Pioneers of "leaving no one behind" towards a community with shared future for mankind', 2022.

35 C. Ramaphosa, From the Desk of the President, 10 May 2021.

Chapter 13

1 Electoral Commission of South Africa. Accessed January 2024, https://www.elections.org.za/pw/.

Chapter 14

1 K.F. Wong, L.Y.K. Lee and J.K.L Lee, 'Hong Kong enrolled nurses perceptions of spirituality and spiritual care', *International Nursing Review*, 55.3(2008):333–340. https://onlinelibrary.wiley.vom/doi/10.1111/j.1466-7657.2008.00619.x.

2 J. Watson, *Human Caring Science: A theory of nursing* (2nd edition) (Sudbury, MA: Jones & Bartlett Learning, 2012). https://www.sciencedirect.com/science/article/pii/S0883941718304291#bb0260.

3 T.L. Cumming, R.T. Shackleton, J. Förster, J. Dini, A. Khan, M. Gumula and I. Kubiszewski, 'Achieving the national development agenda and the Sustainable Development Goals (SDGs) through investment in ecological infrastructure: A case study of South Africa', *Ecosystem Services*, 27.B(2017).

4 National Planning Commission, Diagnostic Overview Report, 2012.

5   Parliament of the Republic of South Africa, SONA 2013 Debate: 02 Leader of the Opposition – DA, 2013.

6   Parliament of the Republic of South Africa, SONA 2013 Debate: 04 M G Buthelezi – IFP, 2013.

7   StatsSA, Labour market dynamics in South Africa, 2019.

8   M. Cross, 'Student access and academic achievement in higher education in South Africa: Emerging discourses'. In *Steering Epistemic Access in Higher Education in South Africa: Institutional dilemmas*, edited by M. Cross (CLACSO, 2018).

9   K. Asmal and W. James, 'Education and democracy in South Africa today'. *Daedalus*, 130.1(2001); C. Sehoole and K.S. Adeyemo, 'Access to, and success in, higher education in post-apartheid South Africa: Social justice analysis', 2016, *Journal of Higher Education in Africa / Revue de l'enseignement*.

10   V. Gumede, 'Poverty and inequality'. In *Political Economy of Post-apartheid South Africa* edited by V. Gumede (CODESRIA, 2015).

11   L. Assouad, L. Chancel and M. Morgan, 'Extreme inequality: Evidence from Brazil, India, the Middle East, and South Africa' 2018, AEA Papers and Proceedings.

12   M. Masutha and C.M. Rogerson, 'Small business incubators: An emerging phenomenon in South Africa's SMME economy'. *Urbani Izziv*, 25(2014).

13   M.P. Mangaliso and N.A. Mangaliso, 'Transformation to an equitable socioeconomic dispensation: Observations and reflections on South Africa', *Journal of Black Studies*, 44.5(2013).

Chapter 15

1   See Isobel Sarah Frye, Jasmin Turton and Mondli Makhanya, 'Social Justice Sector Review Report: Critical Reflections on the Social Justice Sector in the Post-apartheid Era' (Johannesburg: Raith Foundation, 2020), pp 30–36.

2   For example, President Cyril Ramaphosa's speech at the Presidential Social Sector Summit on 5 August 2022: https://www.gov.za/speeches/president-cyril-ramaphosa-presidential-social-sector-summit-5-aug-2022-0000.

3   The Socio-Economic Rights Institute, for example, was heavily criticised in the aftermath of the fire in a hijacked building in Marshalltown, Johannesburg in August 2023 by city officials and political office bearers for taking government to court when it has attempted to evict people from unsafe buildings. See Molefe Seeletsa, 'Joburg CBD fire: City official slams NGO over hijacked buildings litigation'. Much of the criticism misrepresented the work of SERI according to their own response: https://www.702.co.za/articles/482991/jhb-fire-city-must-stop-blaming-ngos-for-something-that-s-their-own-fault.

4   Chinua Achebe, *A Man of the People* (London: Heinemann, 1966), p 35.

5   Achebe, *A Man of the People*, pp 106–107.

6   http://web.sabc.co.za/digital/stage/trufm/Nkosi_speech.pdf.

7   See World Bank, 'Inequality in Southern Africa: An Assessment of the

Southern African Customs Union', 2022.

8   Page 11 of the 2020 Social Justice Sector Review Report.

9   Page 24 of the 2020 Social Justice Sector Review Report.

10   See Ngũgĩwa Thiong'o, *Devil on the Cross* (London: Heinemann, 1980) and *Detained: A Writer's Prison Diary* (London: Heinemann, 1982); Jamaica Kincaid, *A Small Place* (New York: Plume, 1988), and David Scott, *Conscripts of Modernity: The Tragedy of Colonial Enlightenment* (Durham, NC: Duke University Press, 2004).

Chapter 16

1   Annie Cebulski, 'Violent clashes between Mitchells Plain and Siqalo residents', 2 May 2018, GroundUp.

2   Jacob Dlamini, *Native Nostalgia* (Auckland Park: Jacana Media, 2009), pp 15–16.

3   Dlamini, *Native Nostalgia*, pp 16.

4   Peter Luca Versteegan, 'Those were the what? Contents of nostalgia, relative deprivation and radical right support', *European Journal of Political Research* (2023):3.

5   Constantine Sedikides, Tim Wildschut and Clay Routledge, 'Nostalgia past, present, and future', *Current Directions in Psychological Science* (October 2008).

6   Versteegan, 'Those were the what?'

7   Ibid.

8   Ibid.

9   Moshin Hamid, 'Moshin Hamid on the dangers of nostalgia: We need to imagine a brighter future', *The Guardian*, 25 February 2017.

10   Hal McDonald PhD, 'The two faces of nostalgia', 23 June 2016.

11   Marcel Paret, 'Critical nostalgias in democratic South Africa', *The Sociological Quarterly*, 59.4(2018):678–696.

12   Anna Mudeva, 'Special report: In Eastern Europe, people pine for socialism', 8 November 2009, Reuters.

13   Paret, 'Critical Nostalgias in Democratic South Africa'.

14   Sophie Gaston and Sacha Hilhorst, 'Nostalgia as a cultural and political force in Britain, France and Germany…', *Demos*, 2018, p 33.

15   Mongi Henda, 'Milk in the Upington sun', 2 March 2023, *Africa is a Country*.

16   Dennis Webster, '"An indictment of South Africa": Whites-only town Orania is booming', 24 October 2019, *The Guardian*.

17   Webster, 'An indictment of South Africa'.

18   Ibid.

19   Mcebisi Ndletyana, 'CONGRESS OF THE PEOPLE: A promise betrayed,' *European Journal of African Elections*, 9.2(2015).

20   Cape Party, www.capexitparty.com/about.html.

21   Julia Day, 'CapeXit? The Western Cape Independence Movement', 9 September 2023.

22 Phil Craig, 'Self-determination is the issue of the year in the Western Cape', 4 February 2022, *Mail & Guardian*.

23 Sizwe Mpofu-Walsh, 'DA flirts dangerously with Western Cape separatists', 24 October 2022, *Mail & Guardian*.

24 Cape Party, www.capexitparty.com/about.html.

25 Cape Party, www.capexitparty.com/about.html.

26 Daniel Friedman, 'Gatvol Capetonian still cries for a Western Cape without black people', 23 July 2018, *The Citizen*.

Chapter 17

1 J.S. Mohlamme, *The Early Development of Education in Soweto as Seen in the Pimville School,* Johannesburg: Skotaville Publishers, 1990); M.P. Legodi, 'The transformation of education in South Africa since 1994: A historical-educational survey and evaluation', thesis (Pretoria: University of South Africa, 2001).

2 World Bank, *South Africa: Social Assistance Programs and Systems Review* (Washington: The World Bank, 2021), p 27.

3 SASSA, Annual Report 2022/23, p 26.

4 SASSA, Annual Report 2022/23, p 27.

5 Black Sash, Response to 2024 Budget Speech.

6 Daniel Steyn, 'Black Sash film challenges SASSA's closure of cash pay points in rural areas' 2023, GroundUp.

7 World Bank, *South Africa: Social Assistance Programs and Systems Review*, p ix.

Chapter 18

1 Government of South Africa, 1996.

2 https://www.sahistory.org.za/article/convention-democratic-south-africa-codesa-codesa-1 (accessed 13 September 2023).

3 S. Mohamed, 'South Africa: Broken and unequal education perpetuating poverty and inequality', 2020, Amnesty International.

4 S. Nguse, 'Intersectionality in South African health care – what is to be done?' *South African Journal of Psychology*, 53.3(2023):305–315.

5 UNESCO, 'Best practices and lessons learned to preserve, revitalize and promote Indigenous Languages', 2023.

6 https://www.ethnologue.com/insights/how-many-languages-endangered/ (accessed 13 September 2023)

7 UNESCO, 'Best practices and lessons learned to preserve, revitalize and promote Indigenous Languages', 7.

8 H. Tajfel, *Human Groups and Social Categories* (Cambridge: Cambridge University Press, 1981).

9 C. Seethal, 'The state of languages in South Africa', in *Language, Society and the State in a Changing World* edited by S.D. Brunn and R. Kehrein (Cham: Springer, 2023), p 169.

10 N. Alexander, *Language Policy and National Unity in South Africa/Azania* (South Africa: The Estate of Neville Edward Alexander, 2013), pp 9–10.

11   N. Alexander, 'The centrality of the language question in post-apartheid South Africa: Revisiting a perennial issue'. *South African Journal of Science*, 108.9(2012), p 2.

12   M. Madiba, 'Multilingual education in South African universities: Policies, pedagogy and practicality' *Linguistics and Education*, 24.4(2013).

13   W.W.M. Chimbga and C. Meier, 'The language issue in South Africa: The way forward', *Mediterranean Journal of Social Sciences*, 5.20(2014).

14   N. wa Thiong'o, *Decolonizing the Mind* (London: Heinemann, 1986)

15   See S.P. Rao, 'The importance of speaking skills in the English classroom', *Alford Council of Interntional English & Literature Journal*, 2(2019).

16   A. Kaiper, '"If you don't have English, you're just as good as a dead person": A narrative of adult English language literacy within post-apartheid South Africa'. *International Review of Education*, 64(2018).

17   A. Parmegiani, 'Language ownership in multilingual settings: Exploring attitudes among students entering the University of KwaZulu-Natal through the Access Program', *Stellenbosch Papers in Linguistics*, 38(2008).

18   Parmegiani, 'Language ownership in multilingual settings'.

19   Z. Cakata and P. Segalo, 'Obstacles to post-apartheid language policy implementation: Insights from language policy experts'. *Southern African Linguistics and Applied Language Studies*, 35.4(2017).

20   I. Mekoa, 'The politics and nuances of language in South Africa: A critical appraisal', *Journal of African Languages and Literary Studies*, 1.1(2020).

21   Mekoa, 'The politics and nuances of language in South Africa'.

22   D. Posel and J. Zeller, 'Language Use and Language Shift in Post-Apartheid South Africa', in *English in Multilingual South Africa: The Linguistics of Contact and Change*, edited by R. Hickey (Cambridge: Studies in English Language. Cambridge University Press), pp 288–309.

23   A. Bamgbose, 'Intellectualization of African languages: The Nigerian Experience. In Workshop on Intellectualization of African languages' Cape Town: PRAESA, University of Cape Town, 2003).

24   As illustrated in these articles: https://www.bbc.com/news/world-africa-47001468 (accessed 10 October 2023); https://theconversation.com/more-than-an-oppressors-language-reclaiming-the-hidden-history-of-afrikaans-71838 (accessed 10 October 2023); https://www.dailymaverick.co.za/opinionista/2022-11-22-where-did-this-story-that-afrikaans-is-a-white-persons-language-come-from/ (accessed 10 October 2023).

25   https://www.timeslive.co.za/news/south-africa/2021-09-22-concourt-rules-for-afriforum-in-five-year-battle-over-afrikaans-at-unisa/ (accessed 10 October 2023).

26   C. Dyers, 'Language shift or maintenance? Factors determining the use of Afrikaans among some township youth in South Africa', *Stellenbosch Papers in Linguistics*, 38(2008).

27   Model-C schools were schools in which the state only paid the salaries of permanent teachers and the school governing body ran the finances of the school, setting their own fees and admission requirements. Even

though Model-C schools were allowed to decide on their own admission requirements, they were required to keep the majority of learners white (Radebe, 2015). "Model C schools are previously only white schools that integrated after apartheid, they had their systems. Teaching in English or Afrikaans as the medium of instruction, these schools are some of the best in the country because they have spent up to centuries perfecting their infrastructure, teaching models and extracurricular support to provide students with a holistic learning experience. Black parents wanted this for their children too – so post-apartheid, the working and growing middle class took their children to these schools and their children got the kind of education that their parents couldn't have." https://www.bettertospeak. org/stories/racism-in-former-model-c-schools by Naledi Sikhakhane. Site updated in 2023.

28   Previously white-only urban areas

29   Pseudonym

30   A husband to one of the authors

31   Department of Higher Education and Training, 'Language policy framework for public higher education institutions', 2001, *Government Gazette*.

32   T. Ditsele. 'Language may be fragile, but it is very stubborn to die – a future potjiekos taal awaits Mzansi', 2023, *Daily Maverick*. https://www. dailymaverick.co.za/opinionista/2023-10-10-languages-are-stubborn-to-die-future-potjiekos-taal-awaits-mzansi/.

33   Dyers, 'Language shift or maintenance?'

34   https://www.dailymaverick.co.za/article/2020-02-19-the-status-of-african-languages-in-previously-white-schools/ (accessed 08 February 2024).

35   S. Shava and T.V. Manyike, 'Decolonial role of African indigenous language'. *Indilinga* (2018).

36   M. Brenzinger, 'Eleven official languages and more: Legislation and language policies in South Africa', *Revista de Llengua I Dret*, 67(2017).

37   https://mg.co.za/article/2016-08-29-pretoria-girls-high-school-pupil-i-was-instructed-to-fix-myself-as-if-i-was-broken/ (accessed 08 February 2024).

38   https://www.news24.com/news24/not-just-quite-a-white-ou-20150429 (accessed 31 October 2023).

39   Z. Weda and R. de Villiers, 'Migrant Zimbabwean teachers in South Africa: Challenging and rewarding issues', *Journal of International Migration and Integration*, 20(2019).

40   Shava and Manyike, 'Decolonial role of African indigenous language'.

41   Alexander, 'The centrality of the language question in post-apartheid South Africa', p 59.

42   Ditsele, 'Language may be fragile'.

43   N. Shabalala, 'Interrogating the relevance of the Language Policy and the measures taken by Department of Basic Education to integrate Indigenous Knowledge Systems in the schooling curriculum: A case study of KwaZulu-Natal', 2018, Durban: University of KwaZulu-Natal.

44   L.E. Mphasha, K.J. Nkuna and M.B. Sebata, 'The impact of English language

as medium of instruction versus South African indigenous languages offered as modules on academic progress of first year higher education students: A case study of the University of Venda, Limpopo Province, South Africa, *Gender and Behaviour*, 20.1(2022).

45   Shava and Manyike, 'Decolonial role of African indigenous language'.

46   J.C. Makhubele and L.I. Qalinge, 'The relevance of language in the process of indigenising life skills education in South Africa: a social work perspective: IKS community development and resilience', *Indilinga African Journal of Indigenous Knowledge Systems*, 8.2(2009).

47   Shava and Manyike, 'Decolonial role of African indigenous language'.

48   Shabalala, 'Interrogating the relevance of the Language Policy and the measures taken by Department of Basic Education to integrate Indigenous Knowledge Systems in the schooling curriculum'.

49   M. Phakeng, 'One country, many languages: Exploring a multilingual approach to mathematics teaching and learning in South Africa', Proceedings of the IV ERME Topic Conference 'Classroom-based research on mathematics and language', Dresden, Germany, 2018.

50   N. Mkhize and N.P. Hlongwa, 'African Languages, Indigenous Knowledge Systems (IKS), and the Transformation of the Humanities and Social Sciences in Higher Education Alternation', 21.2(2014).

51   Shava and Manyike, 'Decolonial role of African indigenous language'.

52   M.M. Kretzer and R.H. Kaschula, 'South African teachers switch languages in class: Why policy should follow', 2019, *The Conversation*.

53   R. Tyler et al., 'Bilingual education can work in schools: Here's how', 2022, *Sowetan Live*.

54   Kretzer and Kaschula, 'South African teachers switch languages in class'.

55   https://www.youtube.com/watch?v=1bJt5FVJYis (accessed 31 October 2023)

56   M. Madiba, '"Treading where angels fear most": The South African government›s new language policy for higher education and its implications'. *Alternation*, 11.2(2004).

57   B. Zuma, 'The social psychology of self-segregation. Unpublished doctoral dissertation', 2013, University of Cape Town.

58   Zuma, 'The social psychology of self-segregation'.

59   Mkhize and Ndimande-Hlongwa, 'African Languages'.

60   P. Phindane, 'Learning in mother tongue: Language preferences in South Africa', *International Journal of Educational Sciences*, 11.1

61   C. van Rheede, 'Using indigenous languages for job and wealth creation', 2014, News24.

62   A. Joffe and M. Newton, Creative Industries Sector Report, prepared for the HSRC, 15 December 2007. The Creative Industries in South Africa.

63   Joffe and Newton, Creative Industries Sector Report.

64   S.E. Cook, 'New technologies and language change: Toward an anthropology of linguistic frontiers'. *Annual Review of Anthropology*, 33(2004):103–115.

65   E. Lin, 'The role of technology in preserving linguistic Columbia', *Undergraduate Science Journal* (2021).

66   A. Sharma, T. Gumede, C. Kuun et al. 2010. 'Lwazi community communication service: Design and piloting of a telephone-based Information Service for South Africa'. CSIR 3rd Biennial Conference 2010: Science Real and Relevant. CSIR International Convention Centre, Pretoria, South Africa, 30 August – 1 September 2010, p 14; K. Calteaux, F. de Wet, C. Moors, D. van Niekerk, B. McAlister, A.S. Grover, T. Reid, M. Davel, E. Barnard and C. van Heerden, 'Lwazi II Final Report: Increasing the impact of speech technologies in South Africa', 2013. Technical report. Pretoria: CSIR, pp 280.

67   T. Gumede, 'Perceptual evaluations and attitudes of the visually impaired toward synthesised speech: a study of isiXhosa and Northern Sotho voices', 2020. Unpublished doctoral dissertation, Tshwane University of Technology, Pretoria, South Africa.

68   S. Madonsela, 'Using language in the media: A vehicle for indigenous cultural practices in selected SABC drama series'. *Southern African Journal for Folklore Studies*, 23.2(2013).

69   D. Posel, M. Hunter and S. Rudwick, 'Revisiting the prevalence of English: Language use outside the home in South Africa'. *Journal of Multilingual and Multicultural Development*, 43.8(2022):774–786.

70   T. Bosch, 'Radio is thriving in South Africa: 80% are tuning in', 2022, *The Conversation*.

Chapter 19

1   Trade Map. Trade statistics for international business development, 2024.

2   Economist Impact, 'Global Food Security Index 2022: Exploring challenges and Developing solutions for food security across 113 countries'. https://impact.economist.com/sustainability/project/food-security-index/

3   Wandile Sihlobo, *A Country of Two Agricultures: The disparities, the challenges, the solutions* (Johannesburg: Tracey McDonald Publishers, 2023).

4   Statistics South Africa, 'Employment trends in agriculture', 2000.

Chapter 21

1   Sumbal Javed and Vijay Kumar Chattu, 'Patriarchy at the helm of gender-based violence during COVID-19', *AIMS Public Health*, 8.1(2021):32–35.

Chapter 22

1   Karl Marx, *The Eighteenth Brumaire of Louis Bonaparte, Die Revolution*, (New York: Joseph Weydemeyer).

2   Colin Bundy, *The Rise and Fall of the South African Peasantry* (London: James Currey, 1979).

3   T. Ratsheko, 'A critical analysis of the extent to which SA law protects the surface rights of landowners over whose property mining rights have been granted', 2018, unpublished Master of Laws mini dissertation, University of Pretoria.

4   B. Magubane, 'The political economy of the South African revolution',

African Journal of Political Economy, 1.1(1986), pp 1–28.

5   Magubane, 'The political economy of the South African revolution'; C.H. Feinstein, *An Economic History of South Africa: Conquest, discrimination and* development (Cambridge: Cambridge University Press, 2005).

6   Feinstein, *An Economic History of South Africa,* p 3.

7   T. Mbeki, 'Meeting the Challenge for the Second Economy', *New Agenda: South African Journal of Social and Economic Policy*, Second Quarter.14(2004).

8   B. Leubolt, 'Social policies and redistribution in South Africa', 2014, Global Labour University Working Paper 25. Berlin: The Global Labour University.

9   P. Gready, J. Boesten, G. Crawford and P. Wilding, 'Transformative justice: A concept note', 2010. Unpublished manuscript, https://wun.ac.uk/files/ transformative_justice_-_concept_note_web_version.pdf; M.W. Mutua, 'A critique of rights in transitional justice: The African experience'. In *Rethinking Transitions: Equality and social justice in societies emerging from conflict* edited by G.O. Agui and F.G. Isa (Cambridge: Intersentia, 2011), pp 31–45; R.G. Teitel, *Transitional Justice* (Oxford: Oxford University Press, 2020).

10 Mutua, 'A critique of rights in transitional justice', p 91.

11 K. Daly, 'Restorative justice: The real story', *Punishment and Society*, 4.1(2002); R. Mani, 'Dilemmas of expanding transitional justice, or forging the nexus between transitional justice and development', *International Journal of Transitional Justice*, 2.3(2008); Gready, 'Transformative justice'.

12 Teitel, *Transitional Justice.*

13 E.L. Windholz, *Governing through Regulation Public Policy, Regulation and Law* (New York: Routledge, 2018).

14 A.J. van der Walt, 'Legal history, legal culture and transformation in a constitutional democracy', *Fundamina*, 12.1(2006); Teitel, *Transitional Justice.*

15 S. Nogxina, 'The paradox of transformative constitutionalism, and the regulation of minerals rights in South Africa: 1994–2014', 2019, Unpublished PhD thesis, School of Governance and Development Management, University of the Witwatersrand, p 53.

16 T.W. Merrill, 'Accession and original ownership'. *Journal of Legal Analysis*, 1.2(2009), pp 459–510.

17 L.A. Miranda, 'The role of international law in intrastate natural resource allocations: Sovereignty, human rights, and peoples-based development'. *Vanderbilt Journal of Transnational Law*, 45(2012), pp 784–840.

18 J.D. Wilson, 'Resource nationalism or resource liberalism? Explaining Australia›s approach to Chinese investment in its minerals sector'. *Australian Journal of International Affairs*, 65.3(2011), pp 283–304.

19 Nogxina, 'The paradox of transformative constitutionalism'.

20 E. van der Schyff, 'South African mineral law: A historical overview of the State's regulatory oiler regarding the exploitation of minerals'. *New Contra*, 64(2012):131–153.

21   Van der Schyff, 'South African mineral law', p 64.

22   H. Mostert and S. Pope, *The Principles of the Law of Property in South Africa* (Cape Town: Oxford University Press, 2010), p 281.

23   K. Katzarov, *Theory of Nationalisation* (The Hague: Martinus Nijhoff, 1964), p 97.

24   Nogxina, 'The paradox of transformative constitutionalism', p 55.

25   K.S. Tienhaara, *The Expropriation of Environmental Governance: Protecting foreign investors at the expense of public policy* (Cambridge, MA: Cambridge University Press, 2009).

26   Nogxina, 'The paradox of transformative constitutionalism', p 237.

27   C. Tshitereke, *The Experience of Economic Redistribution: The Growth, Employment and Redistribution Strategy in South Africa* (Abington-on-Thames, UK: Routledge, 2006).

28   T.D.S. Madinginye, 'Compliance with the Mining Charter: 10 Years on what has been achieved? Implications for South Africa's industrial development', 2016. http://forum.tips.org.za/images/forum%20papers/2016/58c2c3_2bcb a7a1faee4aa4ad69862a265d7b33.pdf, p 18.

29   S.A. Booysens, *The South African Mining Charter: A Performance Measuring Instrument: Scorecard for the Broad-Based Socio-Economic Empowerment Charter for the Industry* (Riga: VDM Verlag, Muller, 2011).

30   Nogxina, 'The paradox of transformative constitutionalism'.

Chapter 23

1   Constitution of the Republic of South Africa, 1994.

2   Ibid.

3   United Nations, *Convention on the Rights of Persons with Disabilities and Optional Protocol* (Geneva: United Nations, 2006); Department of Social Development, *White Paper on the Rights of Persons with Disabilities* (Pretoria: Department of Social Development, 2016).

4   South African Human Rights Commission, 'Media Advisory: SAHRC Gauteng Provincial Office to conduct an Investigation Inquiry into the Accessibility of Public Transport in Gauteng for People with Disabilities', 17 November 2023.

5   SAHRC, *Disability Toolkit: A quick reference guide and monitoring framework*, 2017.

6   SAHRC, *Annual Report*, 2022.

7   J. Neille and C. Penn, The interface between violence, disability, and poverty: stories from a developing country'. *Journal of Interpersonal Violence*, 32.18(2017):2837–2861; I. van der Heijden, N. Abrahams and J. Harries, 'Additional layers of violence: The intersections of gender and disability in the violence experiences of women with physical disabilities in South Africa', *Journal of Interpersonal Violence*, 34.4(2019):826–847, https:// doi.org/10.1177/0886260516645818; K. Darry, A. Walter and H. Knupp, 'Attitudes and perceptions towards disability and sexuality'. *Disability and Rehabilitation*, 32.14(2010):1148–1155. *The Conversation*, 'South African

study gives insights into the sexual health needs of people with disabilities', 16 March 2021, https://theconversation.com/south-african-study-gives-insights-into-sexual-health-needs-of-people-with-disabilities-156324; Y.L. Muruzi and P. Gutura, 'The Vulnerability to Violence among Women with Physical Disabilities in the City of Tshwane Pretoria, South Africa'. *African Journal of Gender, Society & Development*, 11.3(2022):85.

8   United Nations, *Convention on the Rights of Persons with Disabilities and Optional Protocol*; Department of Social Development, *White Paper on the Rights of Persons with Disabilities.*

9   R. White and D. Msipa, 2018. 'Implementing Article 13 of the Convention on the Rights of Persons with Disabilities in South Africa: Reasonable accommodations for persons with communication disabilities', *African Disability Rights Yearbook*, 6(2018), pp 99–120; White et al., 'Transformative equality: Court accommodations for South African citizens with severe communication disabilities', *African Journal of Disability* (Online), 9(2020):1–12.

10   White and Msipa, 'Implementing Article 13'.

11   United Nations, *Concluding observations on the initial report of South Africa* (Geneva: United Nations, 2018); White and Msipa, 'Implementing Article 13'.

12   G. Richardson, 'Mental disabilities and the law: From substitute to supported decision-making?' *Current Legal Problems*, 65.1(2012):333–354; Wiesel et al., 'The temporalities of supported decision-making by people with cognitive disability', *Social & Cultural Geography*, 23.7(2022).

13   Department of Social Development, *White Paper on the Rights of Persons with Disabilities* (Pretoria: Department of Social Development, 2016).

14   UN, *Concluding observations on the initial report of South Africa.*

15   Ibid.

16   World Health Organization (WHO) and World Bank. 2011. *World Report on Disability*. Geneva: WHO.

17   WHO and World Bank, *World Report on Disability.*

18   Constitution of the Republic of South Africa, 1994.

19   S. Pather, 'Evidence on inclusion and support for learners with disabilities in mainstream schools in South Africa: Off the policy radar?' *International Journal of Inclusive Education*, 15.10(2011):1103–1117; S. Pather, 'Confronting inclusive education in Africa since Salamanca', *International Journal of Inclusive Education*, 23.7–8(2019):782–795.

20   T. Fish Hodgson, 'The right to inclusive education in South Africa: Recreating disability apartheid through failed inclusion policies', *South African Law Journal*, 15.3(2015):461–501.

21   M.H. Mukwevho and A. Gadisi, 'Perceptions of students with disabilities on reasonable accommodation at a tertiary education: A case of a rural university in Limpopo Province, South Africa', *Journal of Intellectual Disability-Diagnosis and Treatment*, 9.6(2021):592–600.

22   E.L. McKinney and L. Swartz, 'Integration into higher education:

Experiences of disabled students in South Africa', *Studies in Higher Education*, 47.2(2022):367–377.

23 T. Makuyana, 'Towards interventions on school dropouts for disabled learners amidst and post-COVID-19 pandemic', *African Journal of Disability*, 11(2022):1009.

24 O. Mutanga, 2019. 'Disability models or approaches'. In *Students with Disabilities and the Transition to Work* (London: Routledge, 2019):41–50.

25 S. Ndlovu, 'Access into professional degrees by students with disabilities in South African higher learning: A decolonial perspective', *African Journal of Disability*, 8.1(2019):1–12; S. Ndlovu, 'Provision of assistive technology for students with disabilities in South African higher education', *International Journal of Environmental Research and Public Health*, 18.8(2021):3892.

26 United Nations, *Convention on the Rights of Persons with Disabilities and Optional Protocol*; Department of Social Development, *White Paper on the Rights of Persons with Disabilities*.

27 United Nations, *Concluding observations on the initial report of South Africa*.

28 Department of Labour, *23rd Commission for Employment Equity (CEE) Annual Report 2022/2023*.

29 S. Pillay, K. Raga and D. Taylor, *Towards an inclusive South African state: The role of equality and human rights in promoting equal opportunities for persons with disabilities in the workplace* (Department of Public Management and Leadership Nelson Mandela Metropolitan University, Port Elizabeth, 2015).

30 A. Ebrahim, T. Lorenzo and H. Kathard, 'Traversing disability: Employers' perspectives of disability inclusion'. *Disabilities*, 2.2(2022):317–329.

31 I. Grobbelaar-du Plessis and J.J. Njau, 'Payday: Business as usual or a new dawn rising for persons with disabilities in the workplace', *De Jure Law Journal*, 52.1(2019):267–294.

32 United Nations, *Conference of State Parties to the Convention on the Rights of Persons with Disabilities* (New York: United Nations, 2022).

33 United Nations, *Convention on the Rights of Persons with Disabilities and Optional Protocol*.

34 United Nations, *Conference of State Parties to the Convention on the Rights of Persons with Disabilities*.

35 E.T. Maziriri and N.W. Madinga, 'A qualitative study on the challenges faced by entrepreneurs living with physical disabilities within the Sebokeng Township of South Africa', *International Journal of Research*, 1(2016).

36 Maziriri and Madinga, 'A qualitative study on the challenges faced by entrepreneurs living with physical disabilities'.

37 P.A. Brynard, 'Challenges of implementing a disability policy' (Pretoria: University of Pretoria, 2010).

38 G. Marsay, 2014. 'Success in the workplace: From the voice of (dis) abled to the voice of enabled'. *African Journal of Disability*, 3.1(2014):1–10.

39 United Nations, *Convention on the Rights of Persons with Disabilities and Optional Protocol*; Department of Social Development, *White Paper on the*

Rights of Persons with Disabilities.

40   Gov.za, News/Media Statements, 2013.

41   *White Paper on the Rights of Persons with Disabilities*, 2016.

42   United Nations, *Concluding observations on the initial report of South Africa.*

43   Department of Social Development, *White Paper on the Rights of Persons with Disabilities.*

44   Ibid.

45   United Nations, *Concluding observations on the initial report of South Africa.*

46   DWYPD, *Annual Report* 2021. Department of Women Youth and Persons with Disabilities.

47   United Nations, *Convention on the Rights of Persons with Disabilities.*

48   V. McKinney and S.L. Amosun, 2020. 'Impact of lived experiences of people with disabilities in the built environment in South Africa', *African Journal of Disability*, 9.1(2020):1–11.

49   M. Jackson, 'Models of disability and human rights: Informing the improvement of built environment accessibility for people with disability at neighbourhood scale?', *Laws*, 7.1(2018):10.

50   United Nations, *Convention on the Rights of Persons with Disabilities.*

51   C.G.C. Fransolet, *Universal design for low-cost housing in South Africa: An exploratory study of emerging socio-technical issues* (Cape Town: Cape Peninsula University of Technology, 2015).

52   Fransolet, C. 2016. 'Mobile app to assess universal access compliance'. In *Universal Design 2016: Learning from the Past, Designing for the Future* (Amsterdam: IOS Press, 2016) pp 642–651.

53   Fransolet, *Universal design for low-cost housing in South Africa.*

54   Ibid.

55   N. Monama, *Department of Public Works compliance with measures for disabled access in public buildings* (Johannesburg: Wits University Press, 2017).

56   United Nations, *Convention on the Rights of Persons with Disabilities*; Department of Social Development, *White Paper on the Rights of Persons with Disabilities.*

57   Department of Transport, *White Paper on National Transport Policy.*

58   J. Chakwizira, P. Bikam and T.A. Adeboyejo, 'Access and constraints to commuting for persons with disabilities in Gauteng Province, South Africa'. In *Urban Inclusivity in Southern Africa* edited by H.H. Magidimish-Chipungu and L. Chipungu (Springer, Cham, 2021):347–394.

59   B. Duri and R. Luke, 'The structural barriers to universally accessible transport: The Tshwane (ZAF) metropolitan area study case'. *International Journal of Transport Development and Integration*, 6.4(2022):428–442.

60   M.J. Vanderschuren and O.A. Nnene, 2021. 'Inclusive planning: African policy inventory and South African mobility case study on the exclusion of persons with disabilities', *Health Research Policy And Systems*, 19.1(2021):1–12.

61 United Nations, *Convention on the Rights of Persons with Disabilities.*

62 Department of Social Development, *White Paper on the Rights of Persons with Disabilities.*

63 G. Ayaya, T.M. Makoelle and M. van der Merwe, 'Developing a framework for inclusion: a case of a full-service school in South Africa'. *International Journal of Qualitative Studies in Education* (2021):1–19.

64 United Nations, *Concluding observations on the initial report of South Africa.*

65 Parliament, 2023.

66 *The Citizen. 'The case against Icasa on behalf of the disability sector is to be heard in Pretoria today'*, 9 November 2023.

67 Japan International Corporation Agency, 'Japanese NGO has started three-year project with two South African NGOs in Johannesburg', 2013, https://www.jica.go.jp/southafrica/english/activities/c8h0vm00005zn0hv-att/activities01_07.pdf.

68 Z. Nzo et al., 'Disability and aging: A literature review on advocacy and activism for sustainable and resilient community living'. *Handbook of Disability: Critical Thought and Social Change in a Globalizing World* (2023), pp 1–24.

69 DWYPD and UNDP, *The Elements and Economic Costs of Disability for Children with Disabilities and Persons with Physical Disabilities in South Africa*, 2022.

70 Muller-Kluits, N. and Slabbert, I. 2020. 'The role of social workers in addressing caregiver burden in families of persons with disabilities'. *South African Health Review*, 2020(1):137–145; N. Maphosa and V. Chiwanza, 'Caregiver experiences and the perceived role of social workers in caring for people with disabilities in South Africa', *African Journal of Social Work,*11.3(2021):155–163.

71 Muller-Kluits and Slabbert, 'The role of social workers in addressing caregiver burden in families of persons with disabilities'; Maphosa and Chiwanza, 'Caregiver experiences and the perceived role of social workers'.

72 Ibid.

73 United Nations, *Concluding observations on the initial report of South Africa.*

74 L.M. Koon et al., 'Ageing concerns, challenges, and everyday solution strategies (ACCESS) for adults ageing with a long-term mobility disability'. *Disability and Health*, 13.4(2020):100936.

75 DWYPD, 2023.

76 PMG, *Portfolio Committee Meeting*, 2023a; PMG, *Portfolio Committee Meeting Video Recording*, 2023b.

77 *City Press,* 'Director's wife gets a top job meant for the disabled', 2020.

78 PMG, *Portfolio Committee Meeting.*

79 PMG, *Portfolio Committee Meeting Video Recording.*

80 DWYPD, 2022.

81 PMG. 'Disabilities rights framework and disability bill: SALRC and

department briefing', 2021.

82   PMG, 'DYWD 2021/22 annual performance plan; with Ministry', 2021.

83   DWYPD, 2023.

84   Trialogue, *The Trialogue Business in Society Handbook 2023.*